FINAL FANTASY TYPE-0 SIDE STORY

THE I PER

Takatoshi Shi tsuya Nomura

03

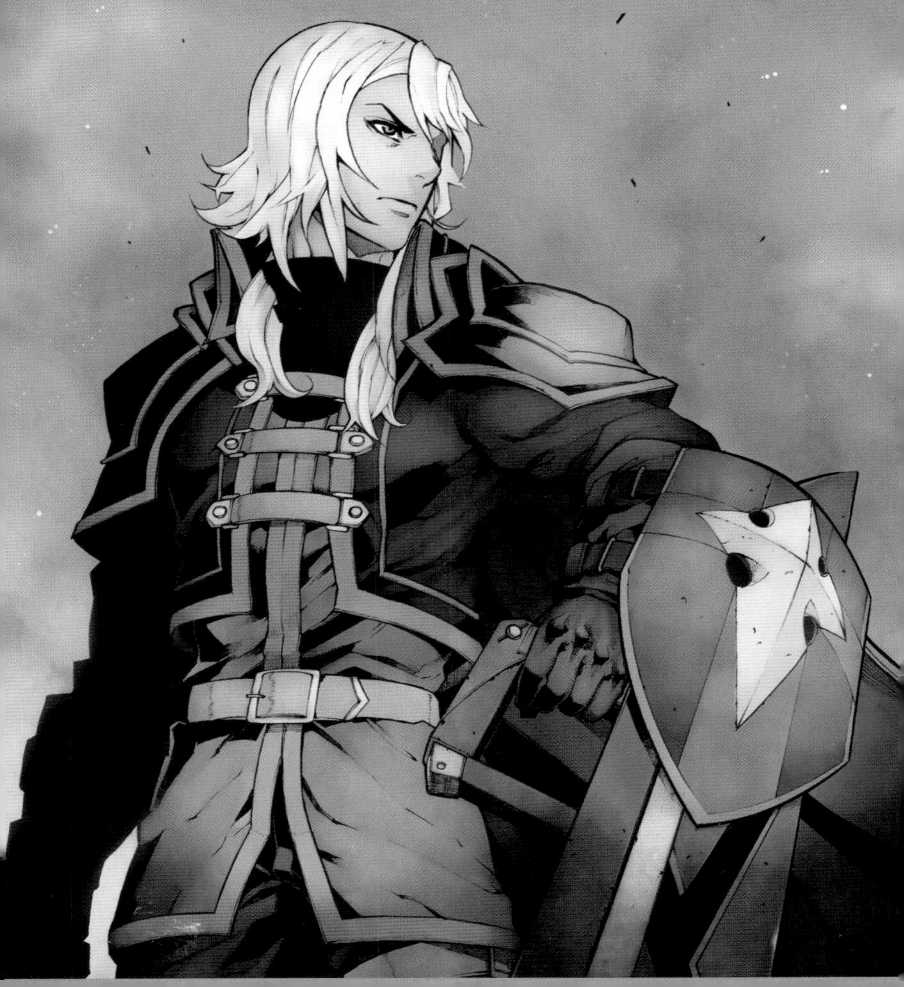

CONTENTS

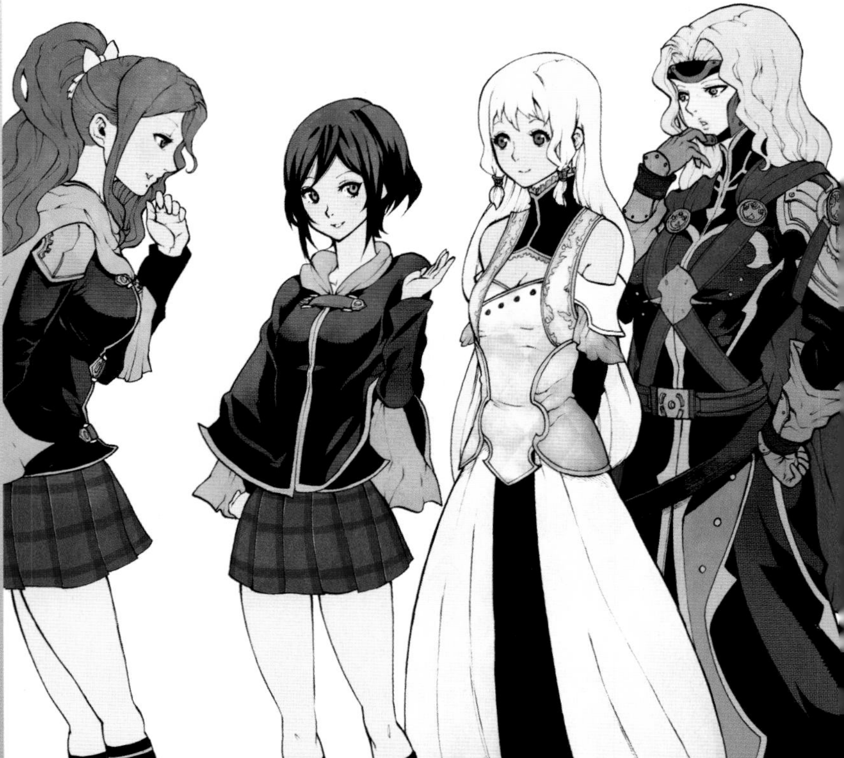

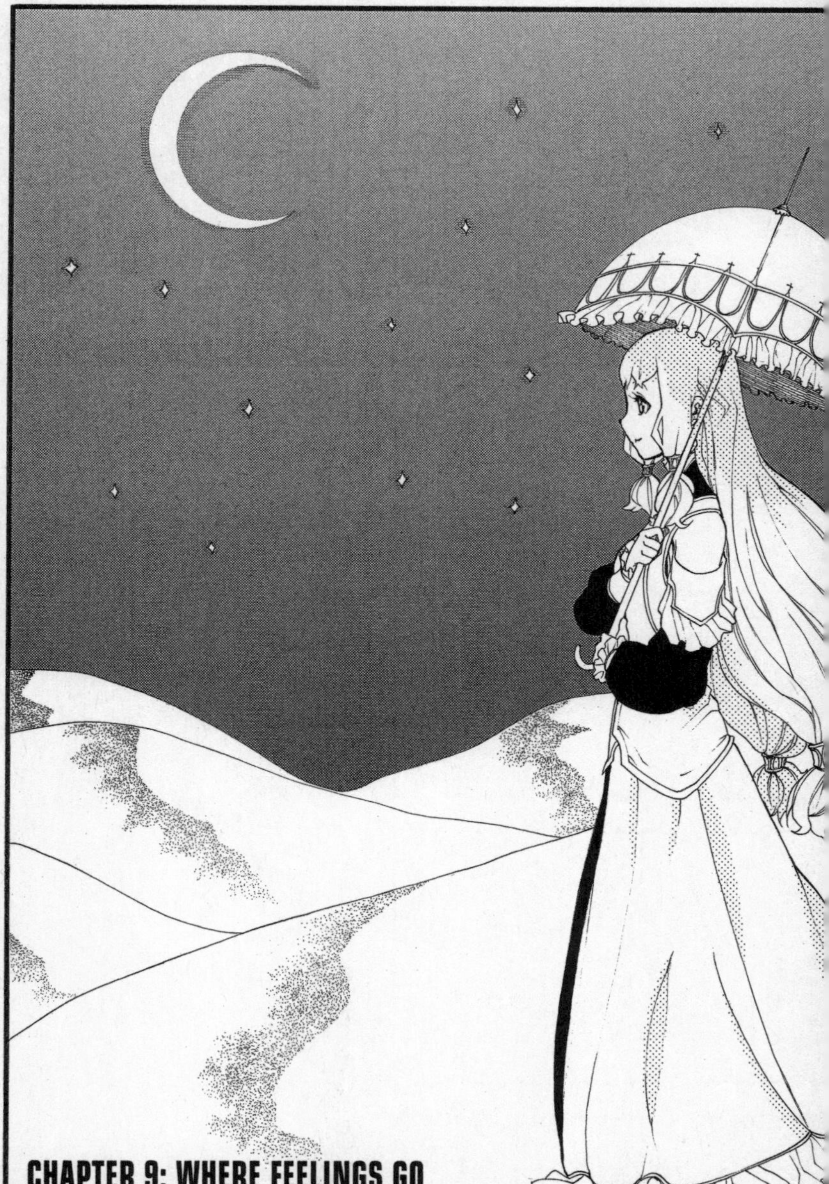
CHAPTER 9: WHERE FEELINGS GO

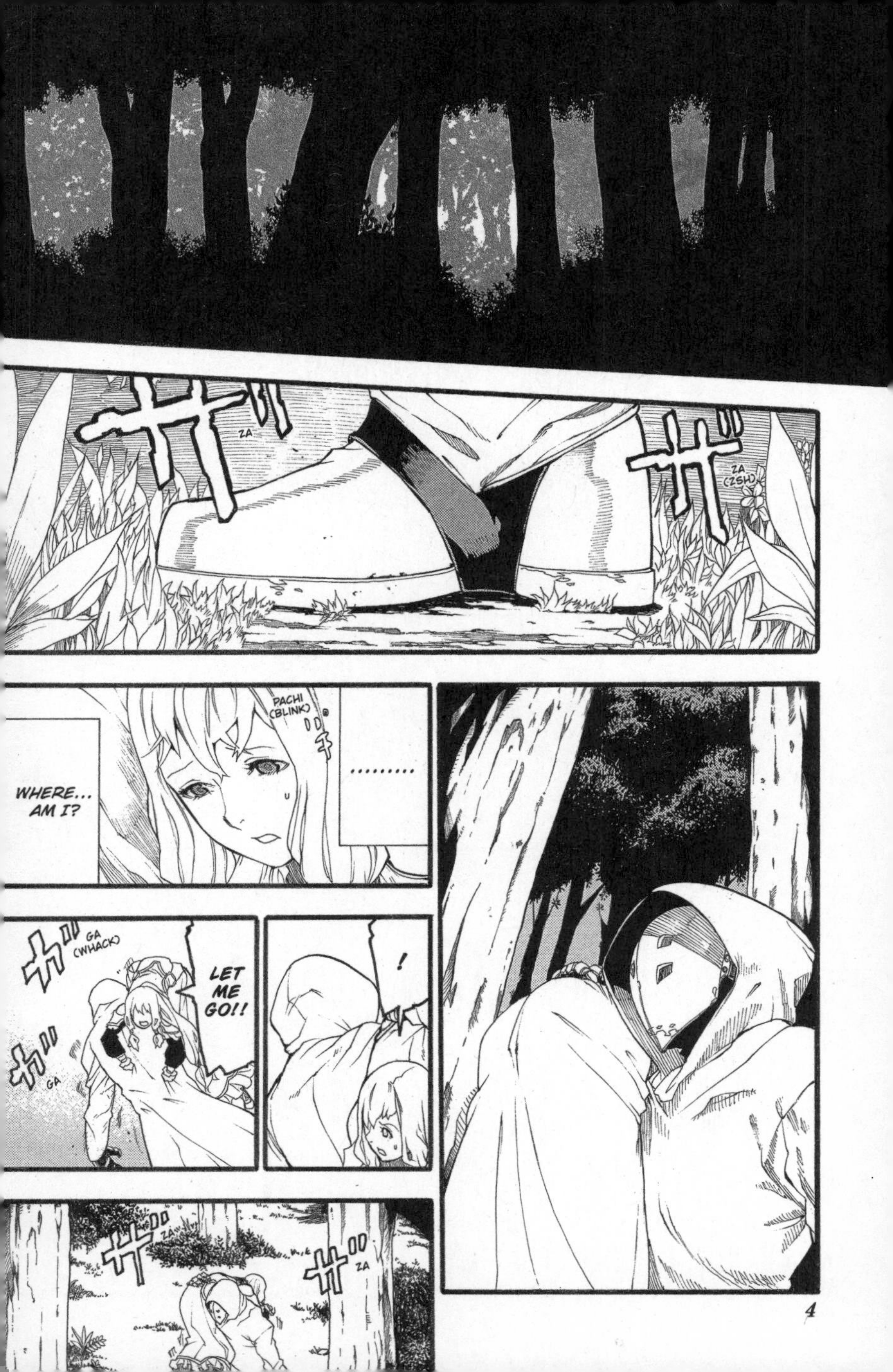
ZA (ZSH)
ZA
PACHI (BLINK)
....
WHERE... AM I?
!
GA (WHACK)
LET ME GO!!
GA
ZA
ZA

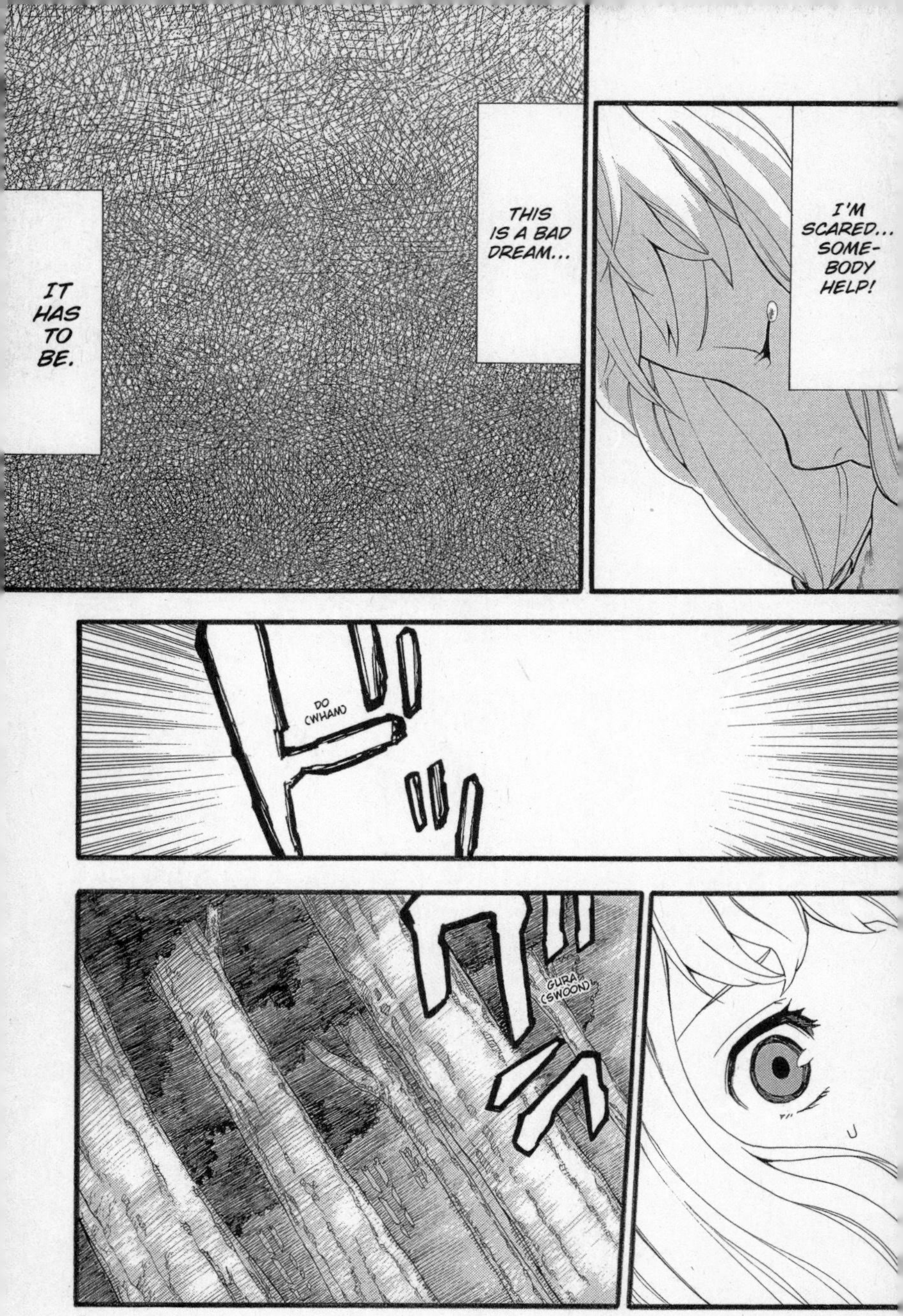
I'M SCARED... SOME-BODY HELP!
THIS IS A BAD DREAM...
IT HAS TO BE.
DO (WHAM)
GURA (SWOON)

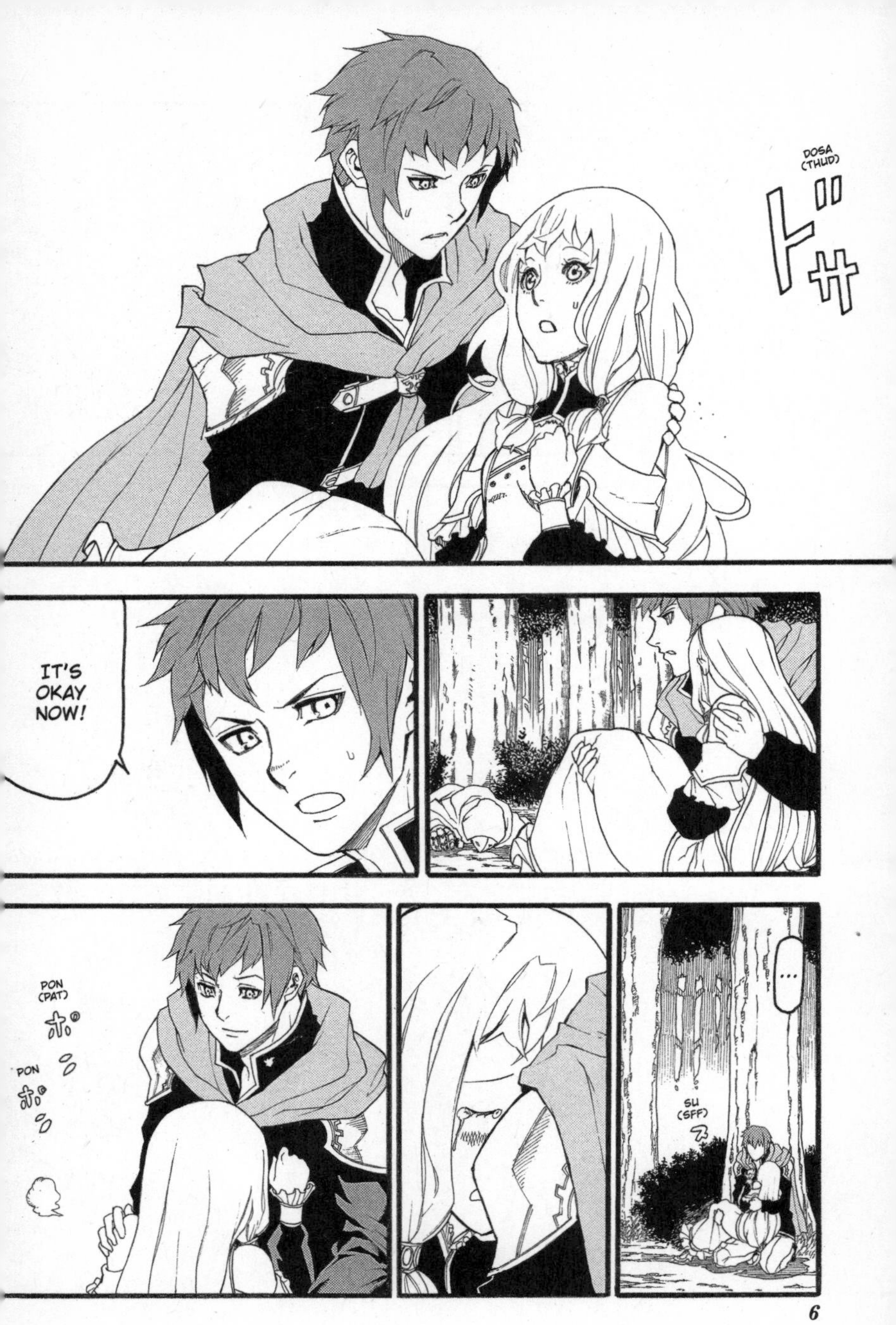
DOSA (THUD)
ドサ
IT'S OKAY NOW!
...
SU (SFF)
ス
PON (PAT)
PON

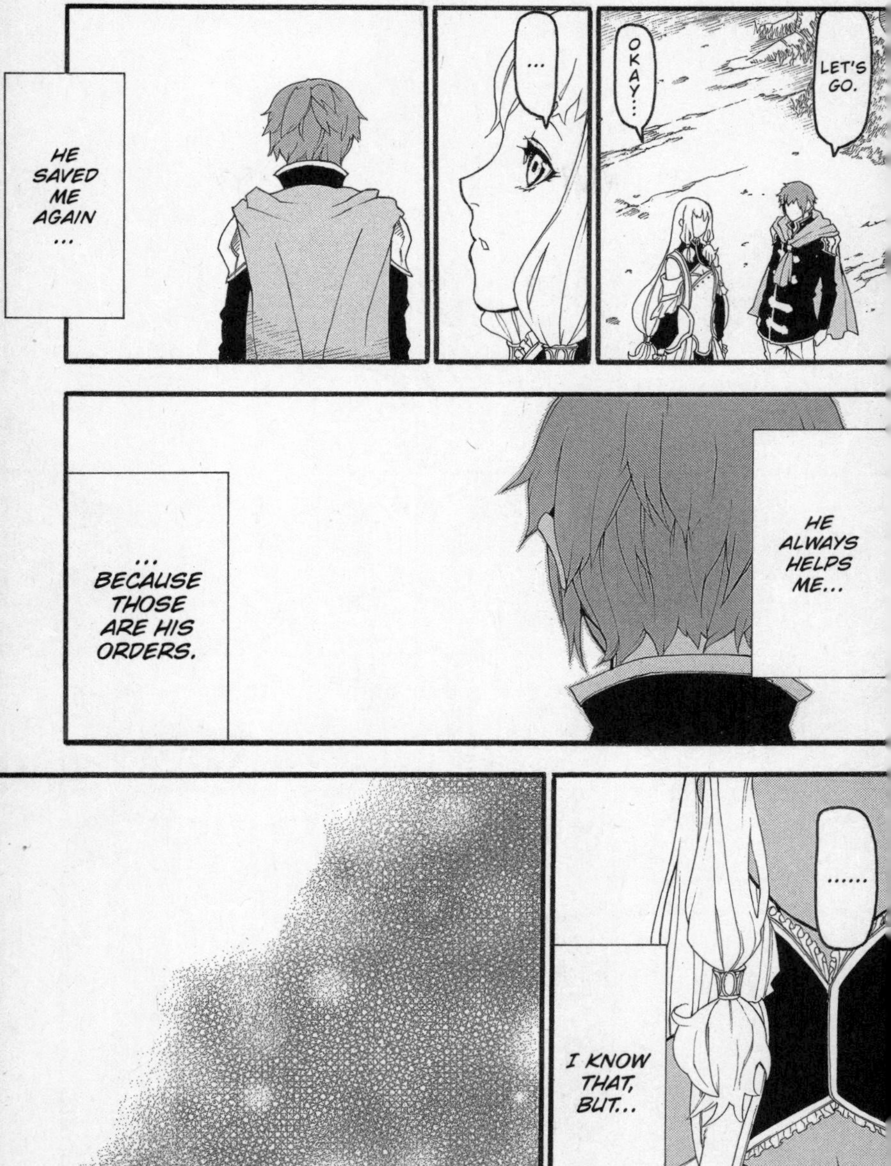
LET'S GO.
OKAY...
...
HE SAVED ME AGAIN...
HE ALWAYS HELPS ME...
...BECAUSE THOSE ARE HIS ORDERS.
......
I KNOW THAT, BUT...

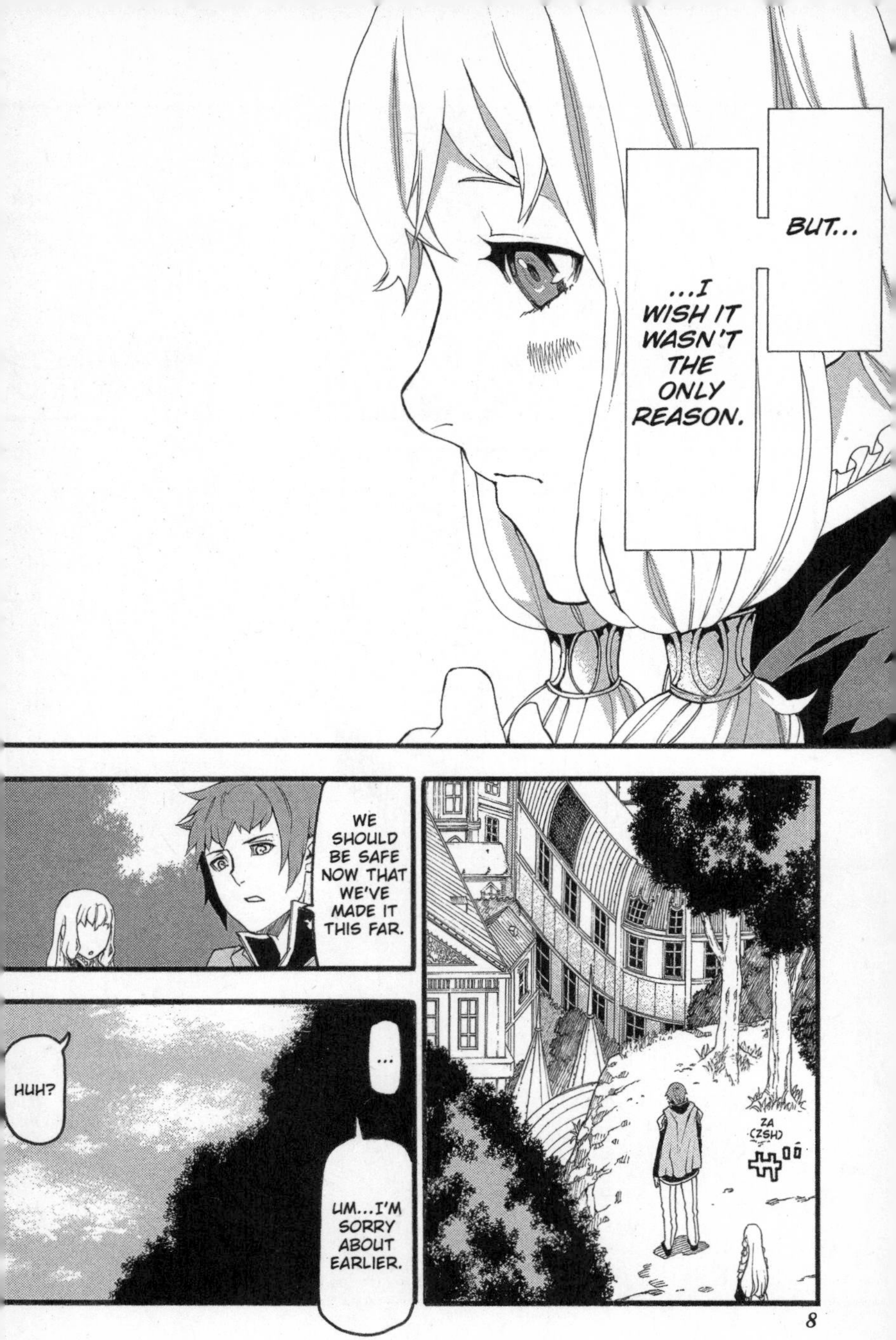
BUT...
...I WISH IT WASN'T THE ONLY REASON.
ZA (ZSH)
WE SHOULD BE SAFE NOW THAT WE'VE MADE IT THIS FAR.
...
UM...I'M SORRY ABOUT EARLIER.
HUH?

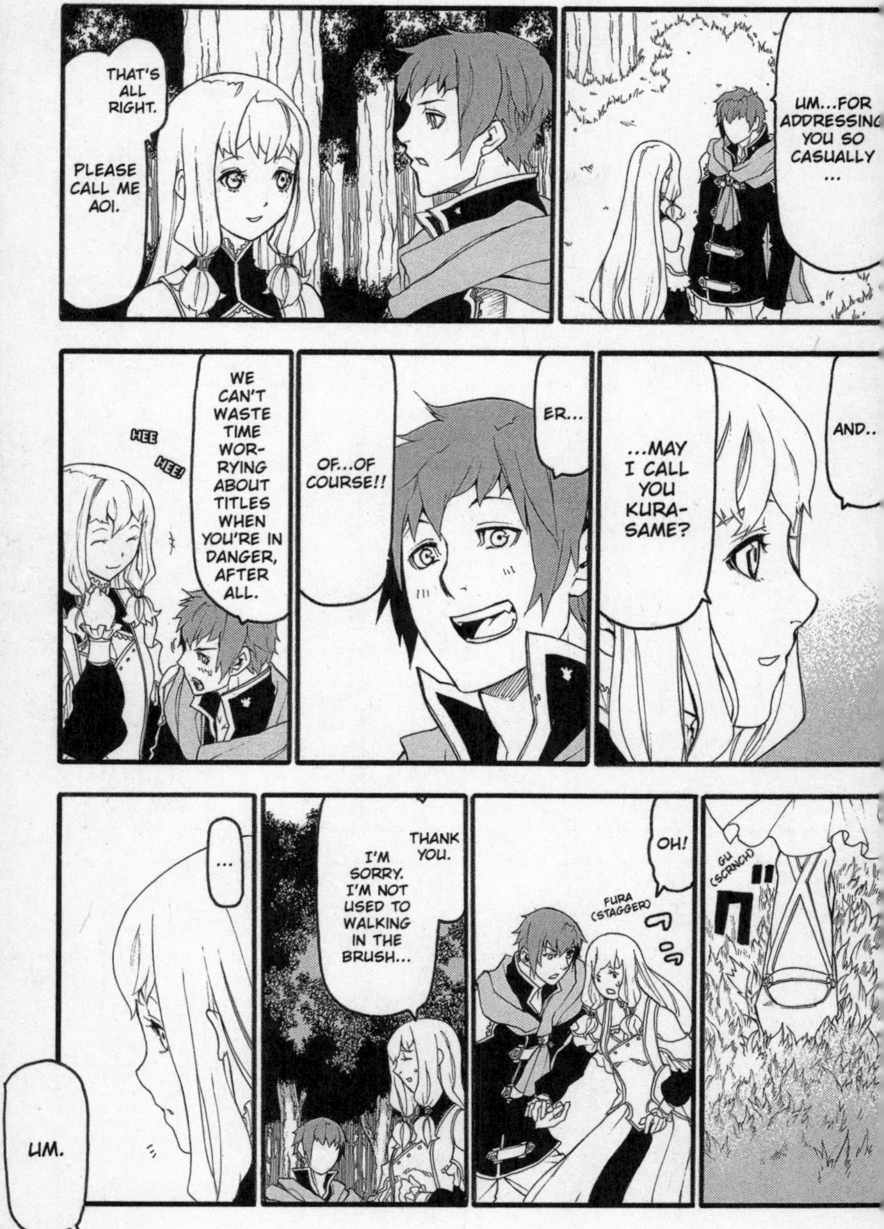
UM...FOR ADDRESSING YOU SO CASUALLY ...
THAT'S ALL RIGHT.
PLEASE CALL ME AOI.
AND..
...MAY I CALL YOU KURA-SAME?
ER...
OF...OF COURSE!!
WE CAN'T WASTE TIME WOR-RYING ABOUT TITLES WHEN YOU'RE IN DANGER, AFTER ALL.
HEE HEE!
GU (SCRNCH)
OH!
FURA (STAGGER)
THANK YOU.
I'M SORRY. I'M NOT USED TO WALKING IN THE BRUSH...
...
UM.

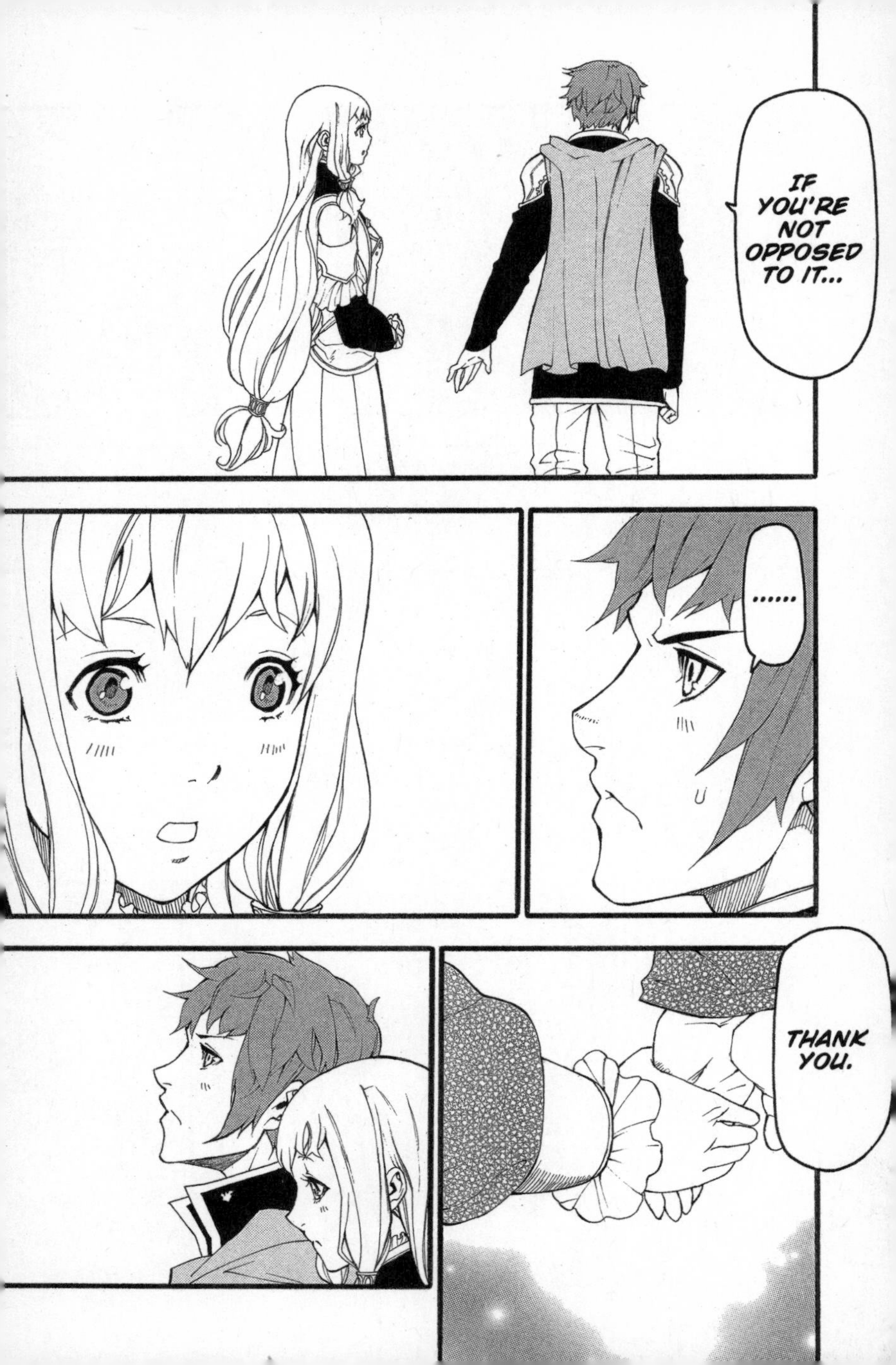
IF YOU'RE NOT OPPOSED TO IT...
......
THANK YOU.

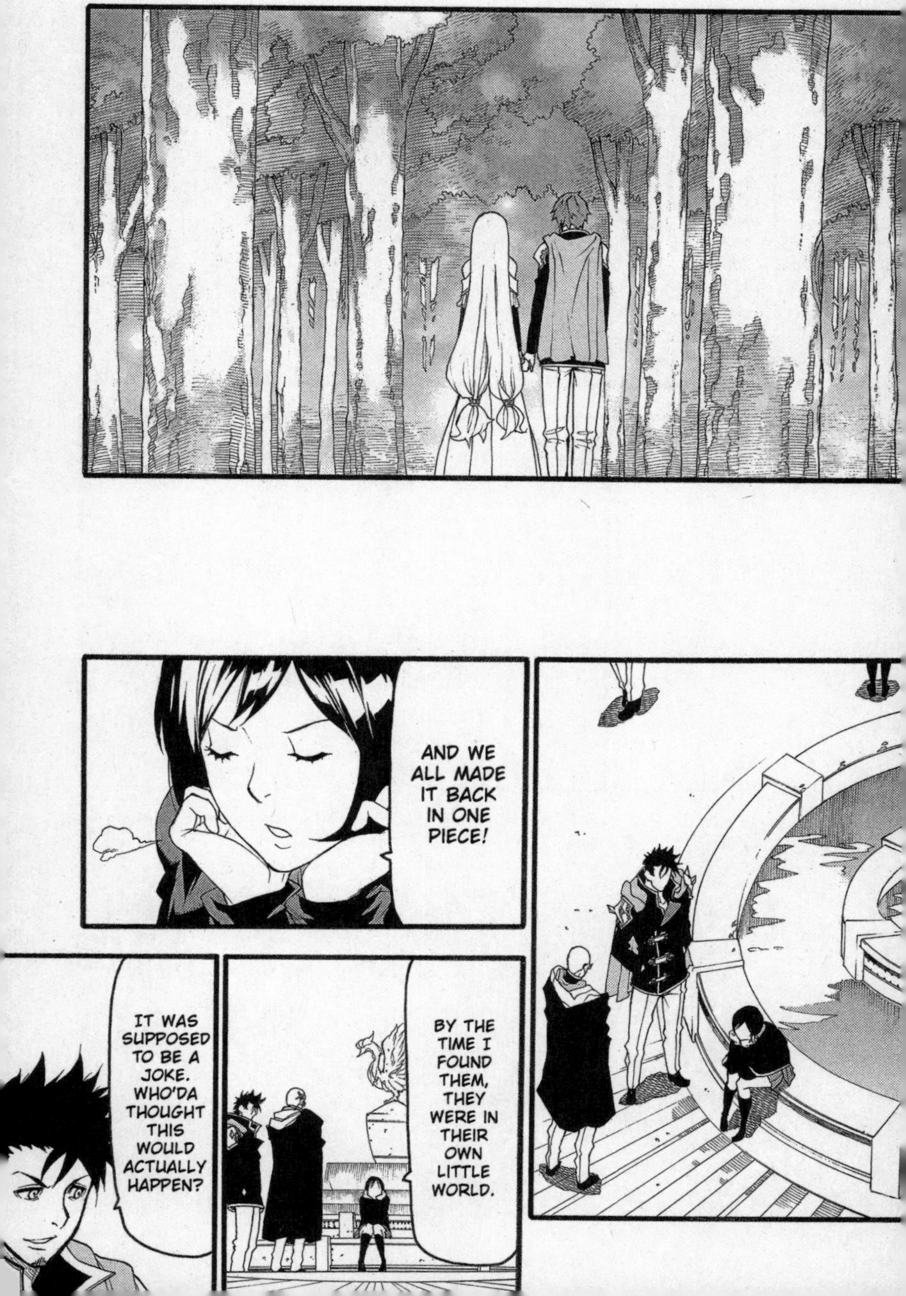
AND WE ALL MADE IT BACK IN ONE PIECE!
BY THE TIME I FOUND THEM, THEY WERE IN THEIR OWN LITTLE WORLD.
IT WAS SUPPOSED TO BE A JOKE. WHO'DA THOUGHT THIS WOULD ACTUALLY HAPPEN?

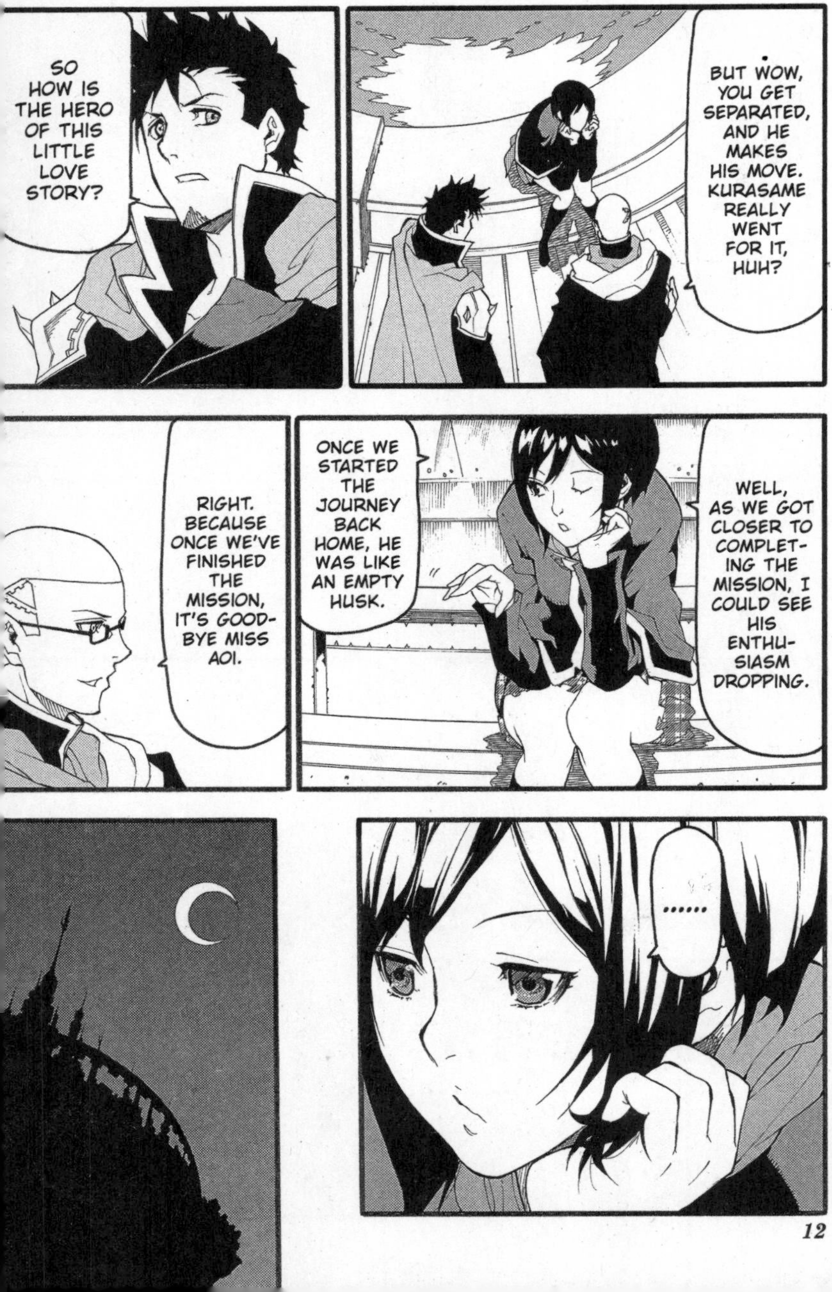

BUT WOW, YOU GET SEPARATED, AND HE MAKES HIS MOVE. KURASAME REALLY WENT FOR IT, HUH?
SO HOW IS THE HERO OF THIS LITTLE LOVE STORY?
WELL, AS WE GOT CLOSER TO COMPLETING THE MISSION, I COULD SEE HIS ENTHUSIASM DROPPING.
ONCE WE STARTED THE JOURNEY BACK HOME, HE WAS LIKE AN EMPTY HUSK.
RIGHT. BECAUSE ONCE WE'VE FINISHED THE MISSION, IT'S GOOD-BYE MISS AOI.
......

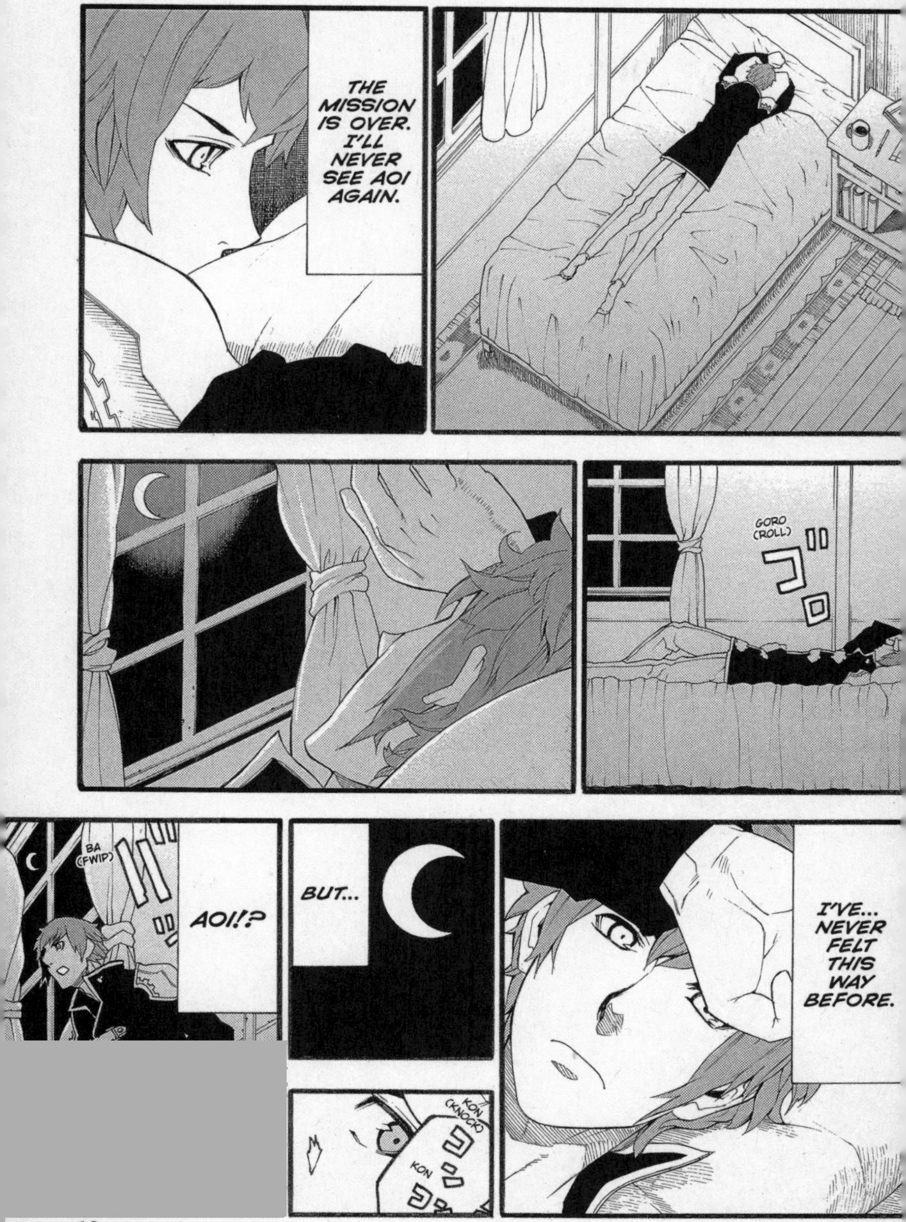
THE MISSION IS OVER. I'LL NEVER SEE AOI AGAIN.
GORO (ROLL)
I'VE... NEVER FELT THIS WAY BEFORE.
BUT...
KON (KNOCK)
KON
BA (FWIP)
AOI!?

......

OH.
IT'S
YOU.

WHAT'S
UP?

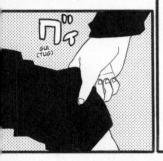

GUI
(TUG)

GACHA
(KACHAK)

HUH?

LET'S
GO.

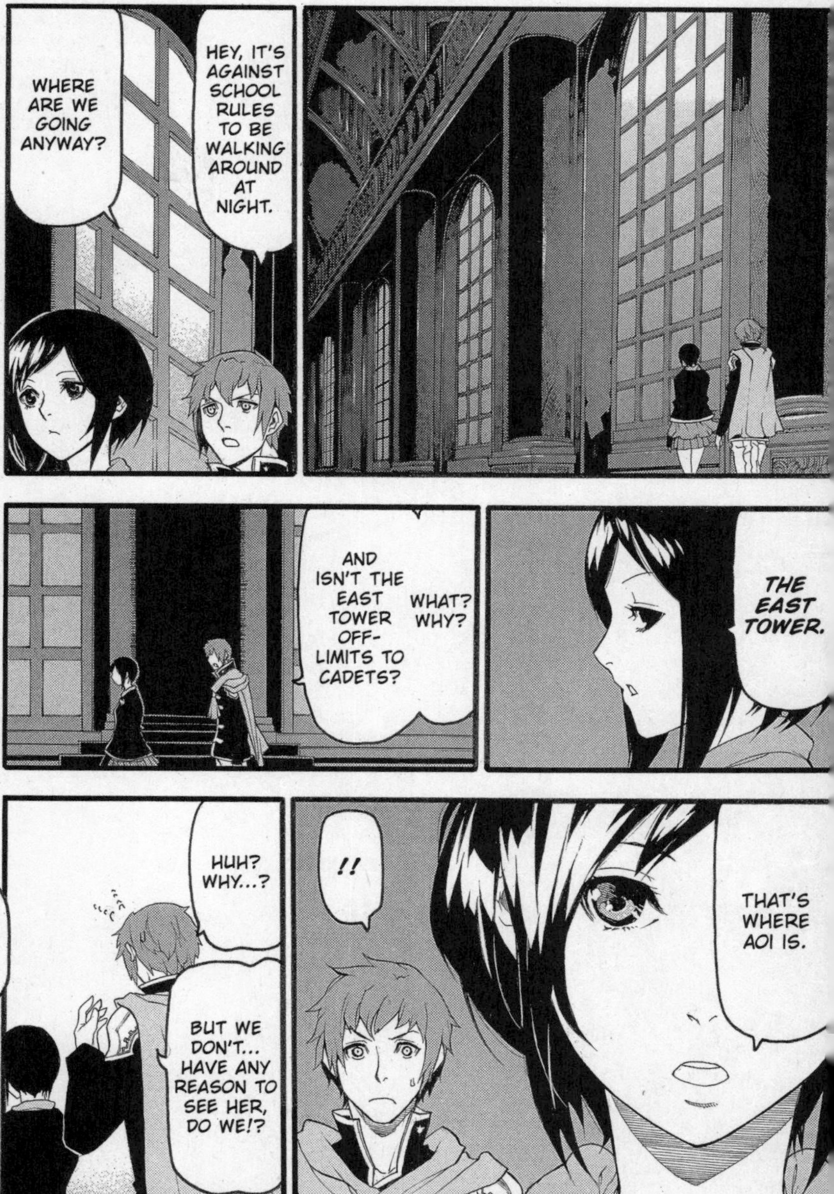
HEY, IT'S AGAINST SCHOOL RULES TO BE WALKING AROUND AT NIGHT.
WHERE ARE WE GOING ANYWAY?
THE EAST TOWER.
WHAT? WHY?
AND ISN'T THE EAST TOWER OFF-LIMITS TO CADETS?
THAT'S WHERE AOI IS.
!!
HUH? WHY...?
BUT WE DON'T... HAVE ANY REASON TO SEE HER, DO WE!?
......

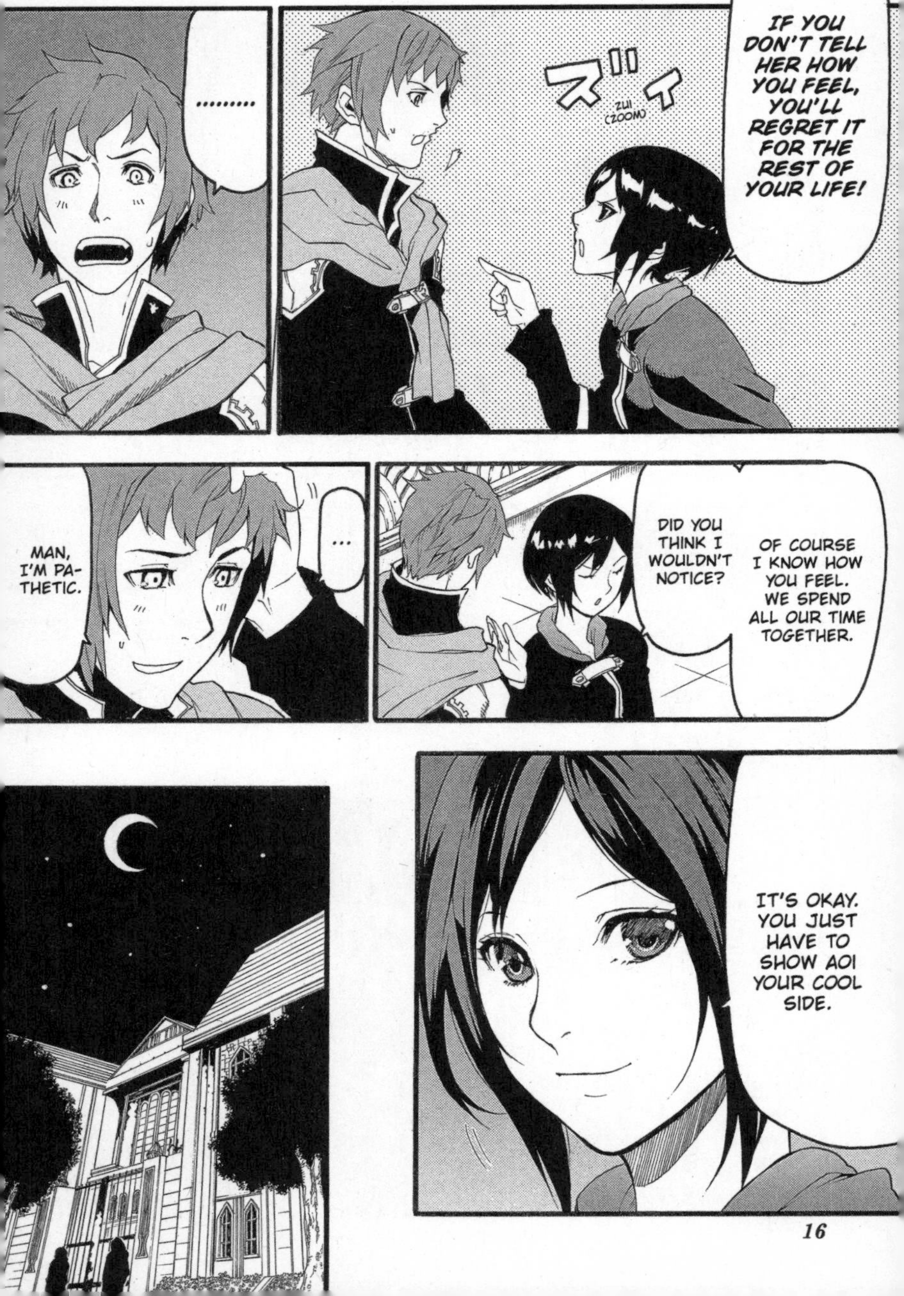
IF YOU DON'T TELL HER HOW YOU FEEL, YOU'LL REGRET IT FOR THE REST OF YOUR LIFE!
ズイ
ZUI (ZOOM)
....
OF COURSE I KNOW HOW YOU FEEL. WE SPEND ALL OUR TIME TOGETHER.
DID YOU THINK I WOULDN'T NOTICE?
...
MAN, I'M PA-THETIC.
IT'S OKAY. YOU JUST HAVE TO SHOW AOI YOUR COOL SIDE.

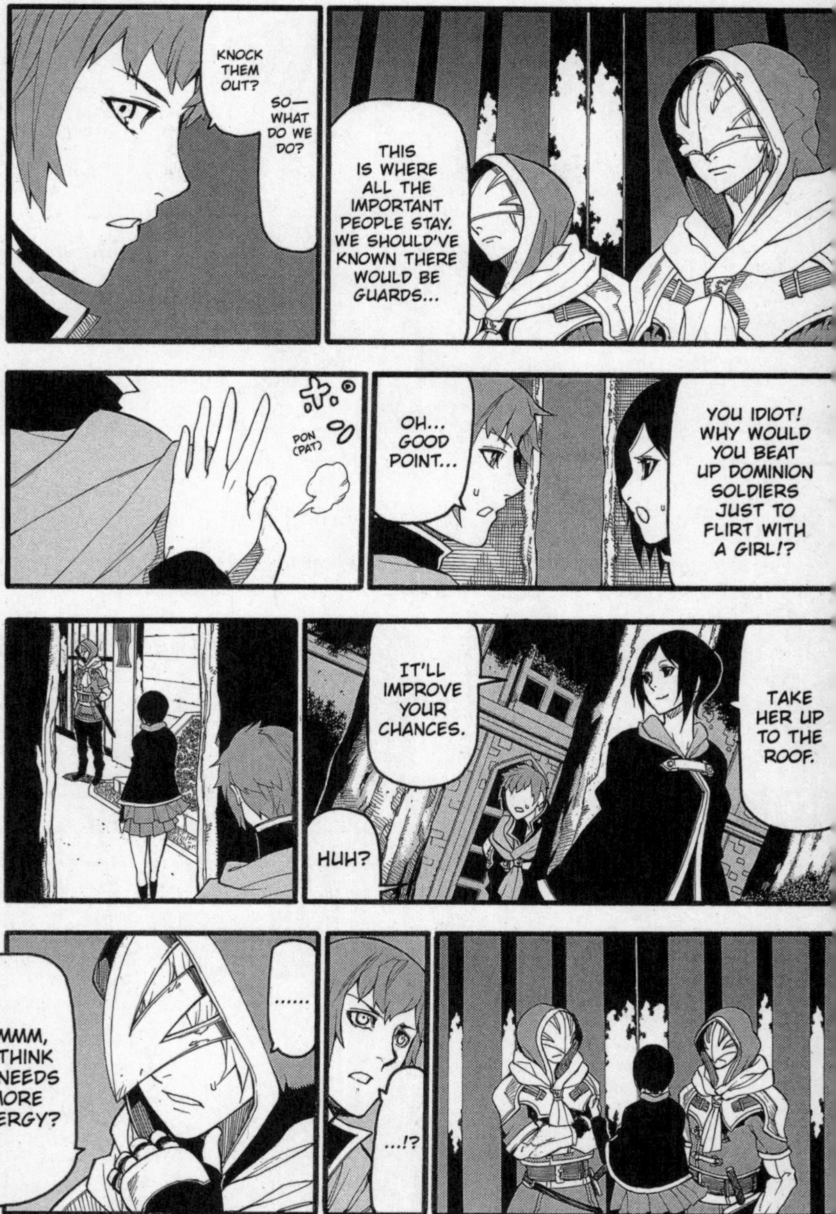
THIS IS WHERE ALL THE IMPORTANT PEOPLE STAY. WE SHOULD'VE KNOWN THERE WOULD BE GUARDS...
KNOCK THEM OUT?
SO— WHAT DO WE DO?
YOU IDIOT! WHY WOULD YOU BEAT UP DOMINION SOLDIERS JUST TO FLIRT WITH A GIRL!?
OH... GOOD POINT...
PON (PAT)
TAKE HER UP TO THE ROOF.
IT'LL IMPROVE YOUR CHANCES.
HUH?
......
...!?
HMMM, I THINK IT NEEDS MORE ENERGY?

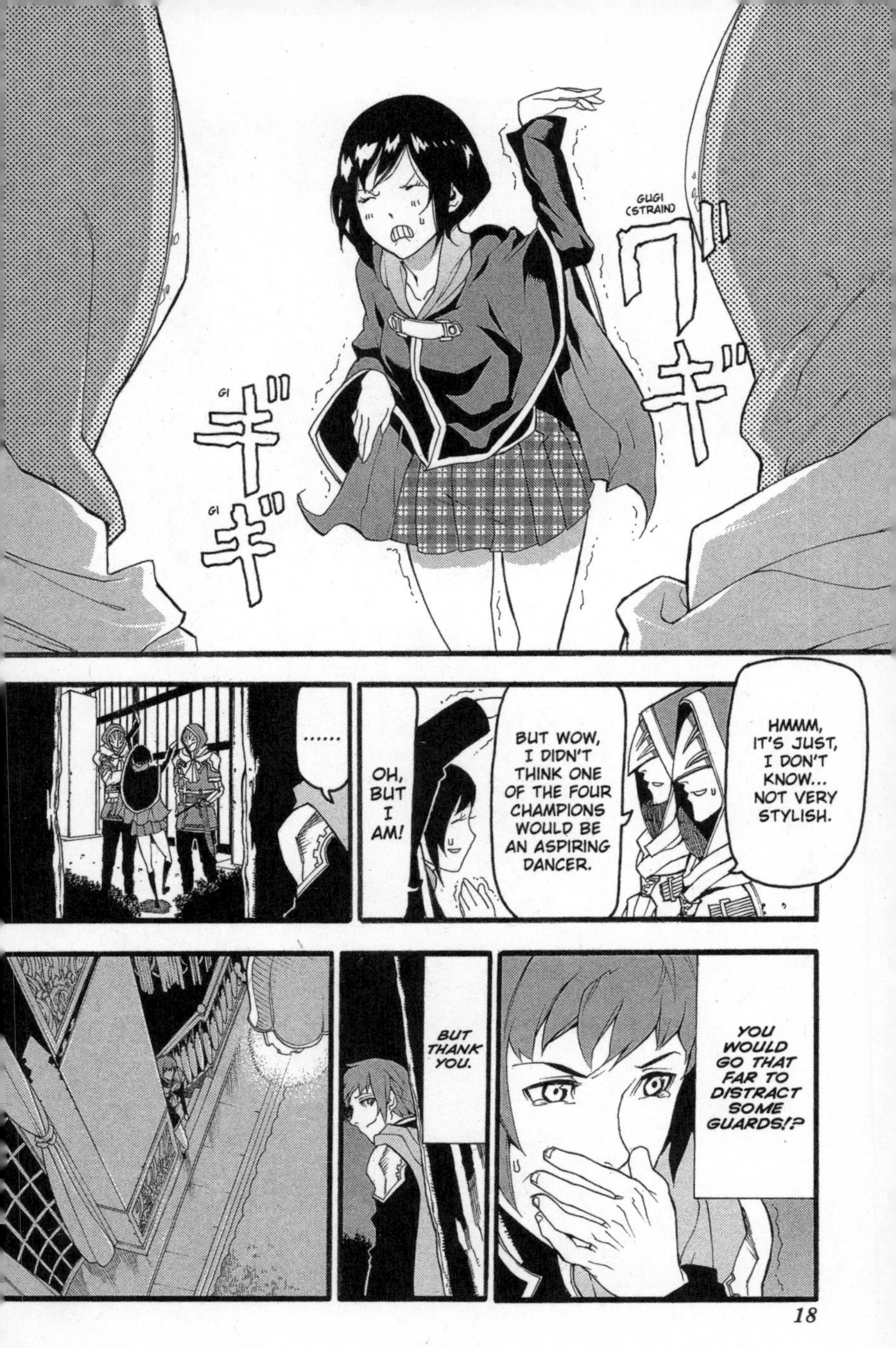
GUGI (STRAIN)
GI
GI
HMMM, IT'S JUST, I DON'T KNOW... NOT VERY STYLISH.
BUT WOW, I DIDN'T THINK ONE OF THE FOUR CHAMPIONS WOULD BE AN ASPIRING DANCER.
OH, BUT I AM!
......
YOU WOULD GO THAT FAR TO DISTRACT SOME GUARDS!?
BUT THANK YOU.

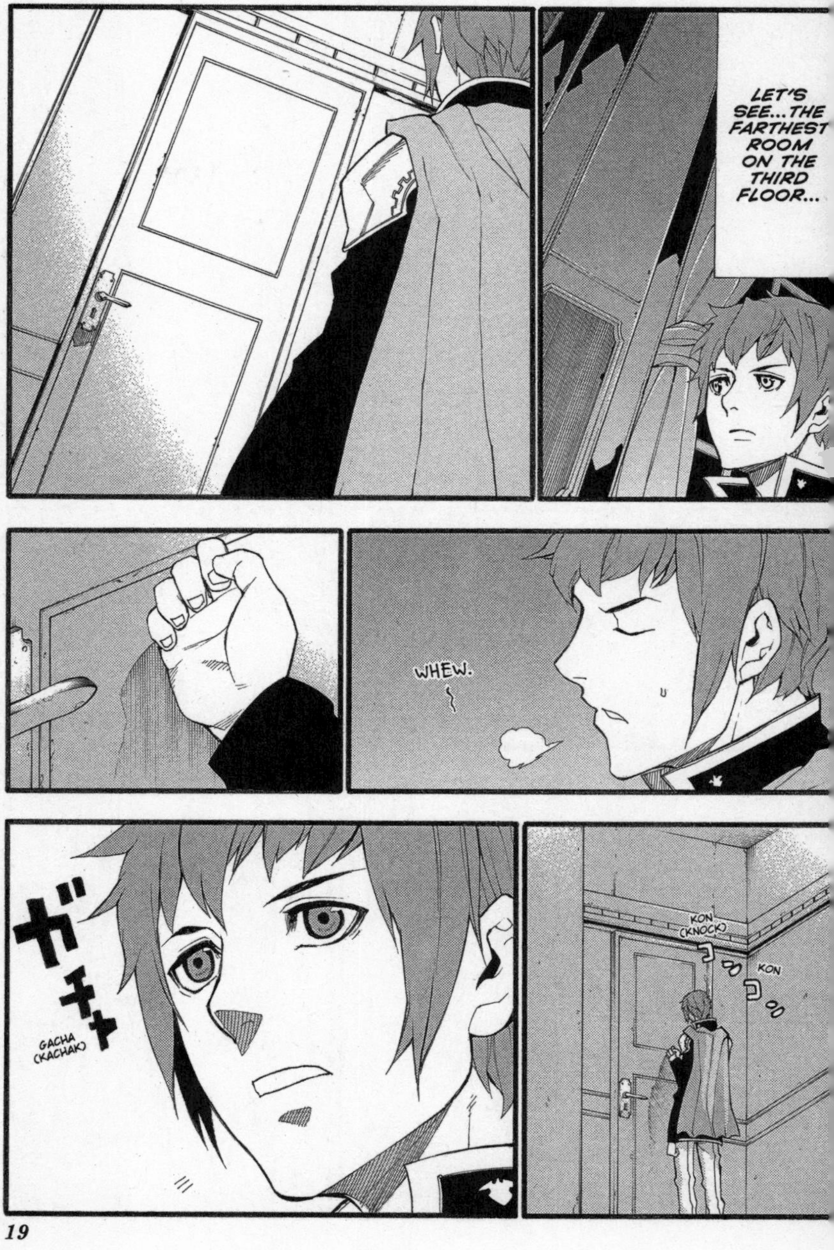
LET'S SEE...THE FARTHEST ROOM ON THE THIRD FLOOR...
WHEW.
KON (KNOCK)
KON
ガチャ
GACHA (KACHAK)

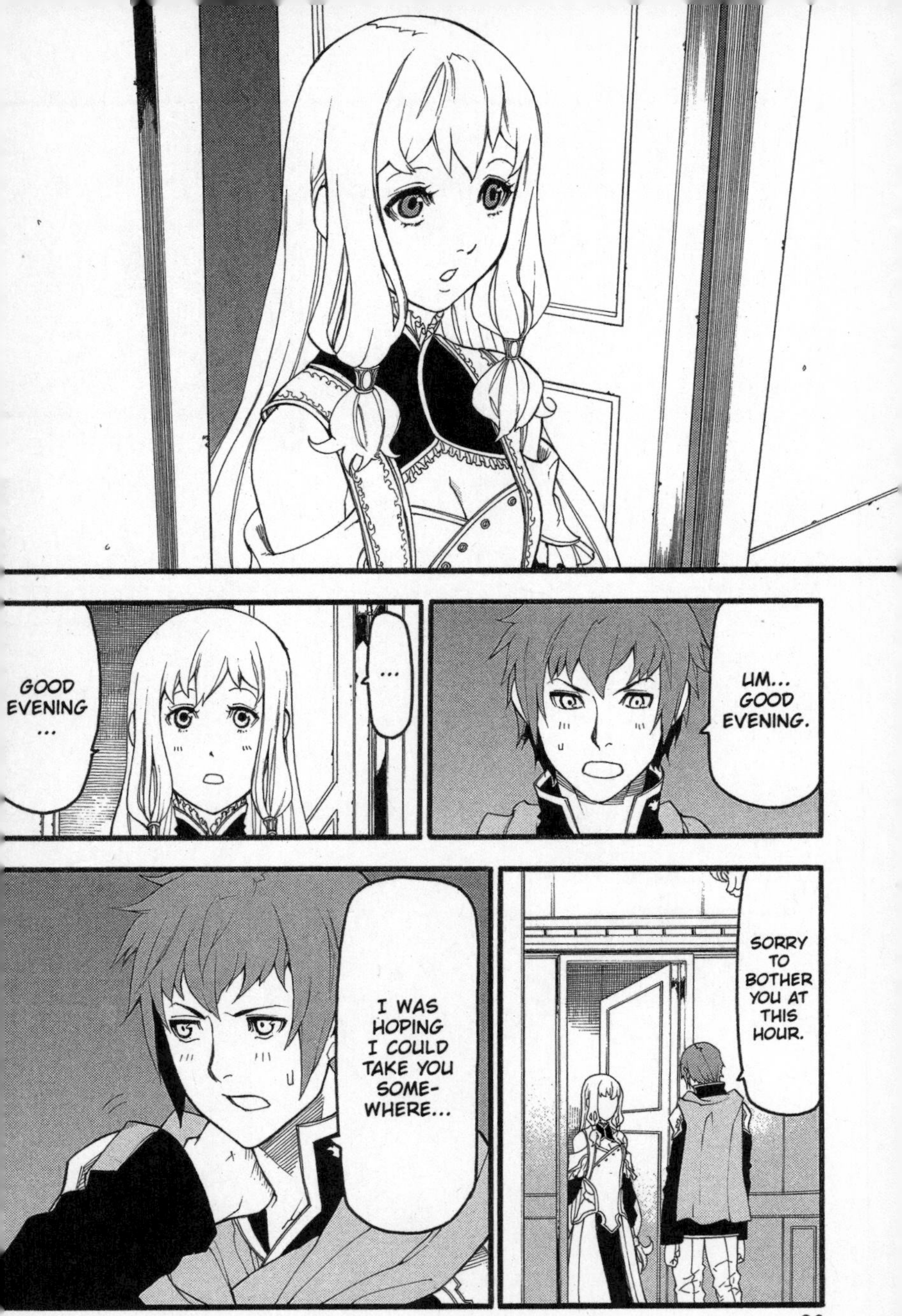
UM... GOOD EVENING.
...
GOOD EVENING ...
SORRY TO BOTHER YOU AT THIS HOUR.
I WAS HOPING I COULD TAKE YOU SOME-WHERE...

......

ALL RIGHT.

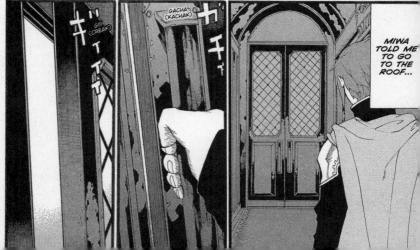

GACHA! (KACHAK)

GIII (CREAK)

MIWA TOLD ME TO GO TO THE ROOF...

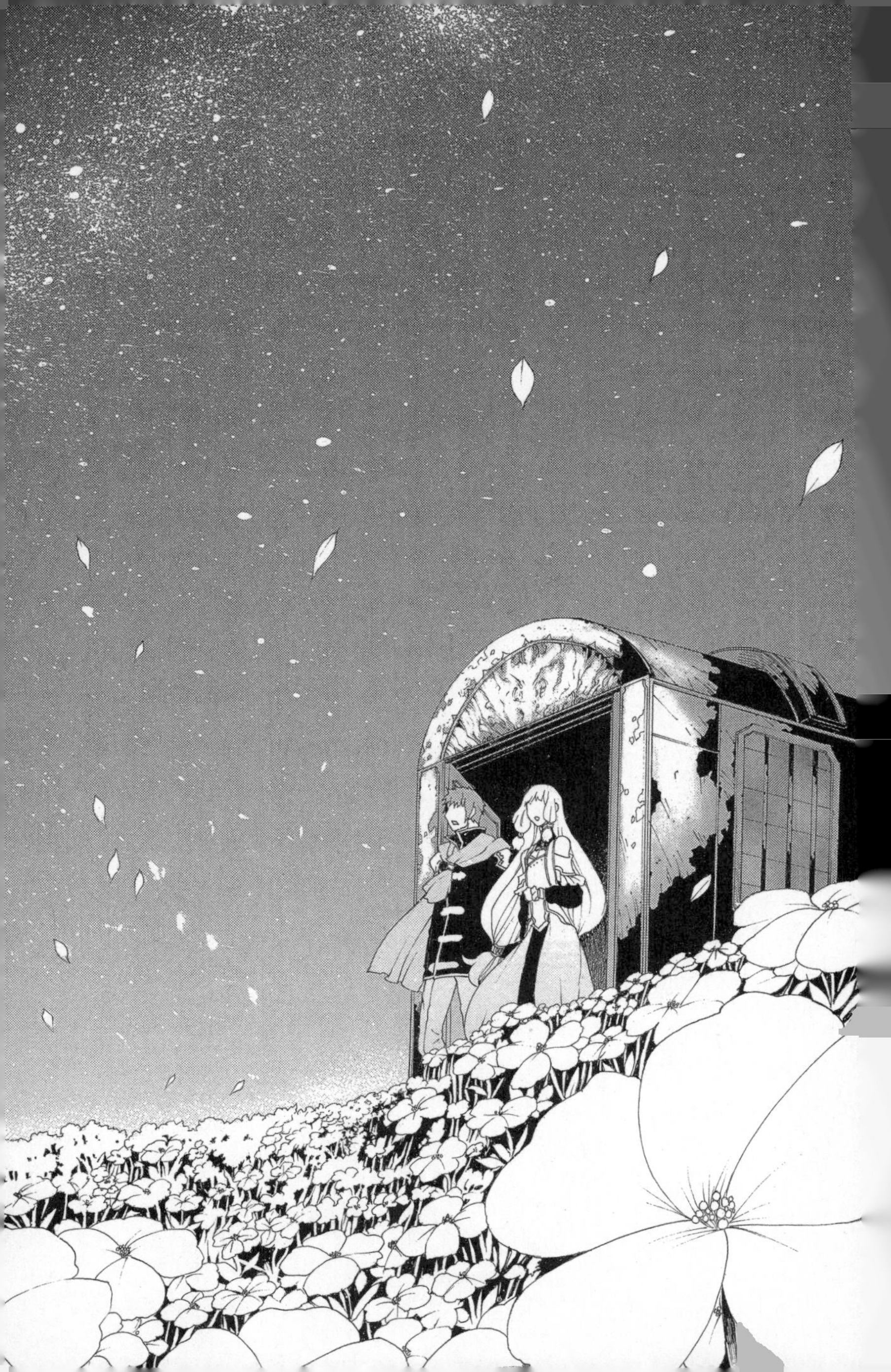

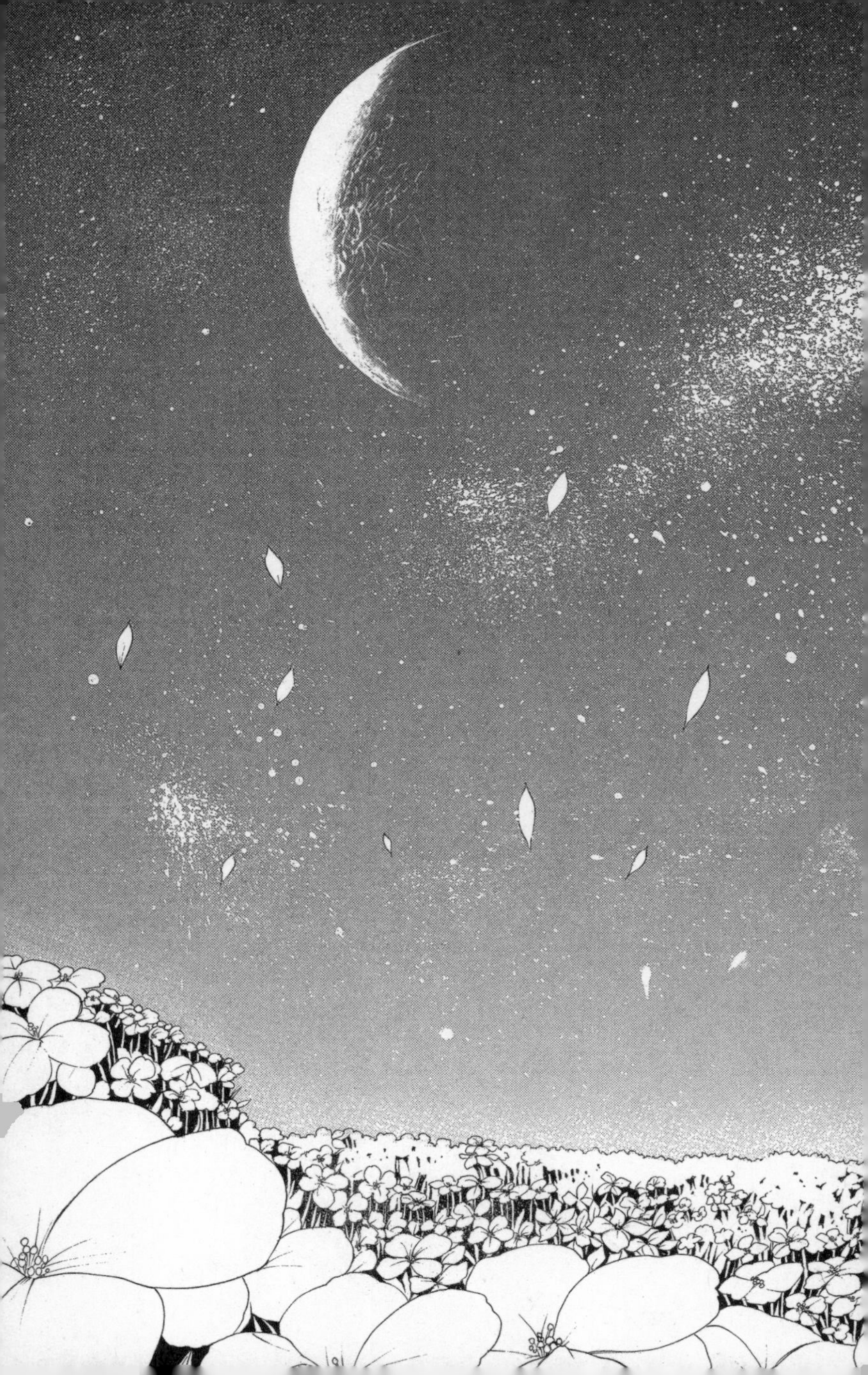

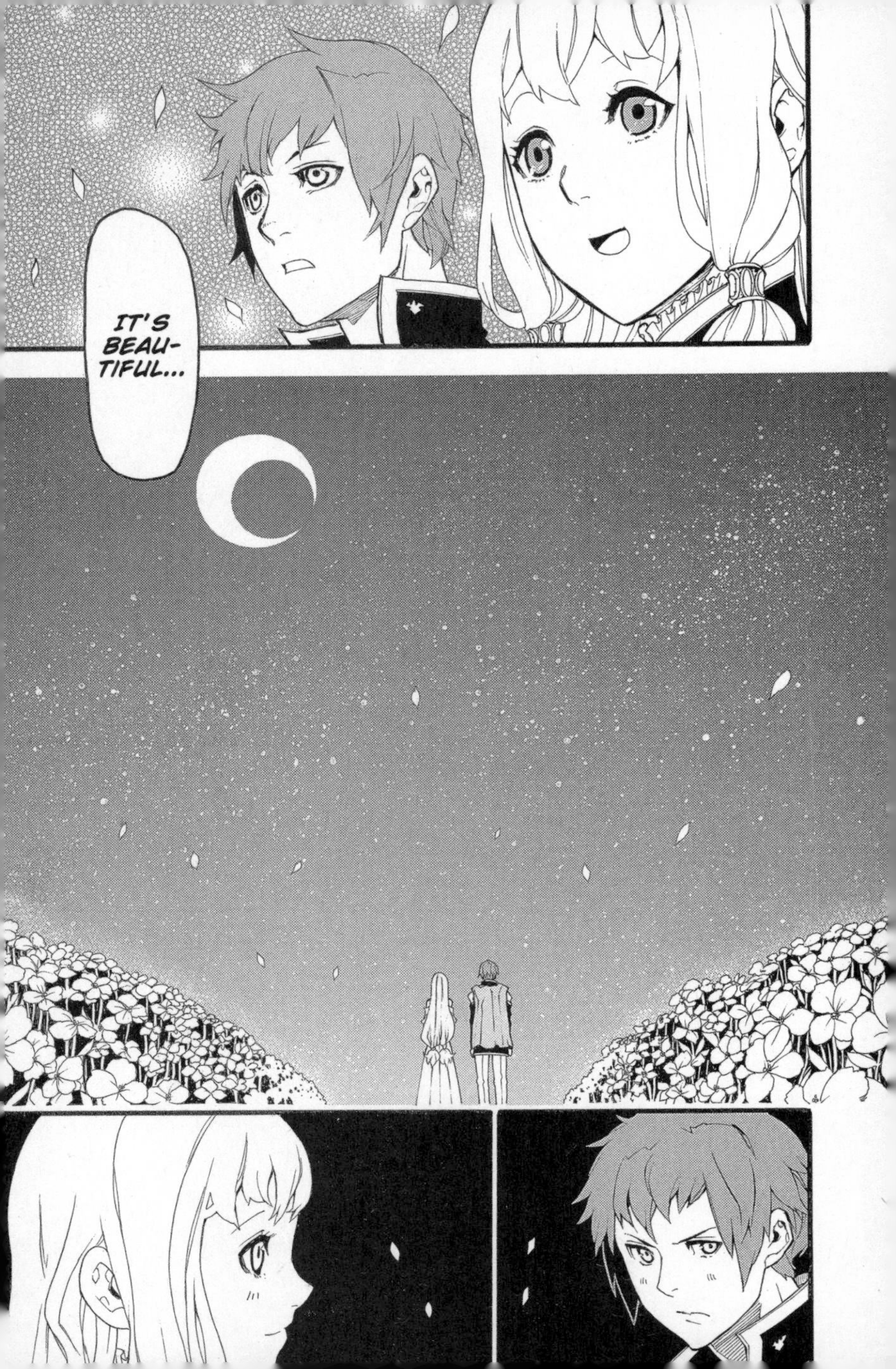
IT'S BEAUTIFUL...

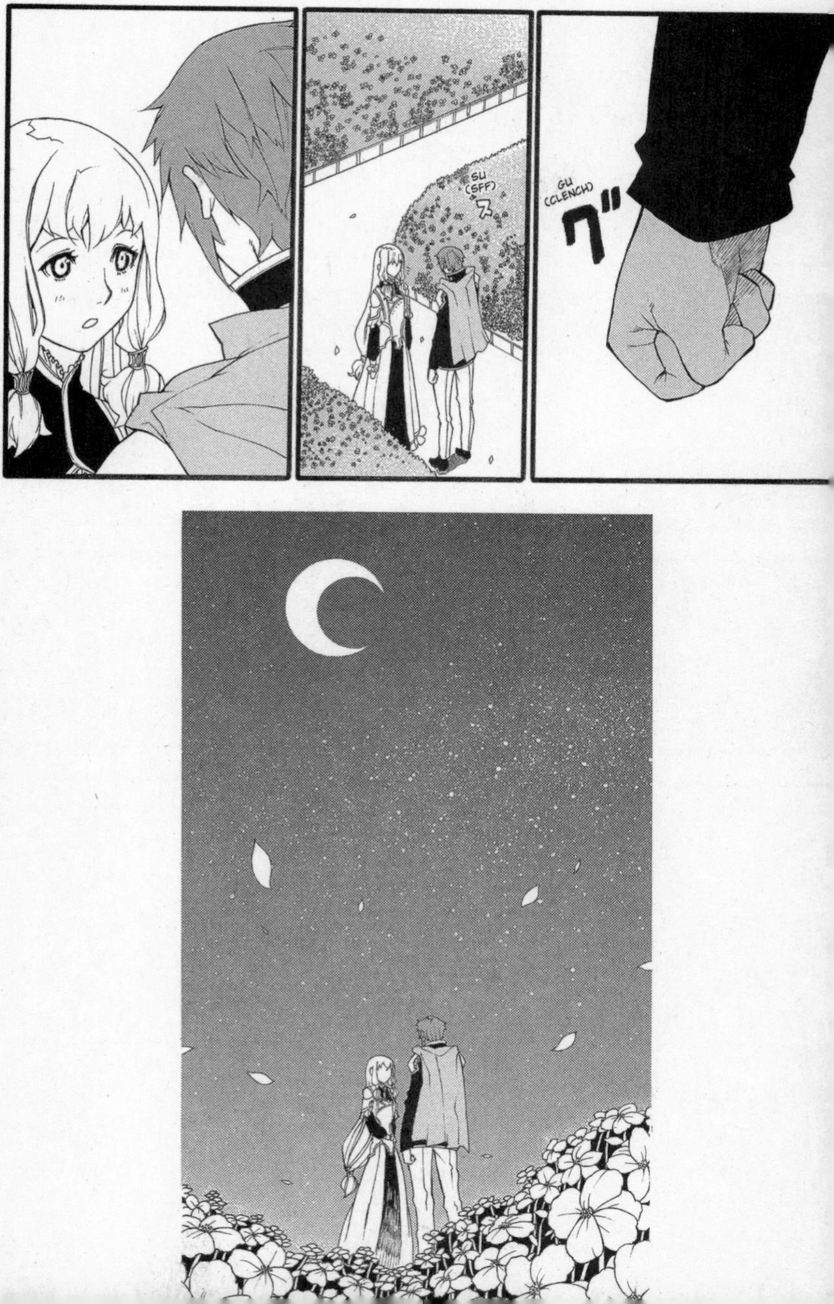
GU (CLENCH)
グ
SU (SFF)
ス

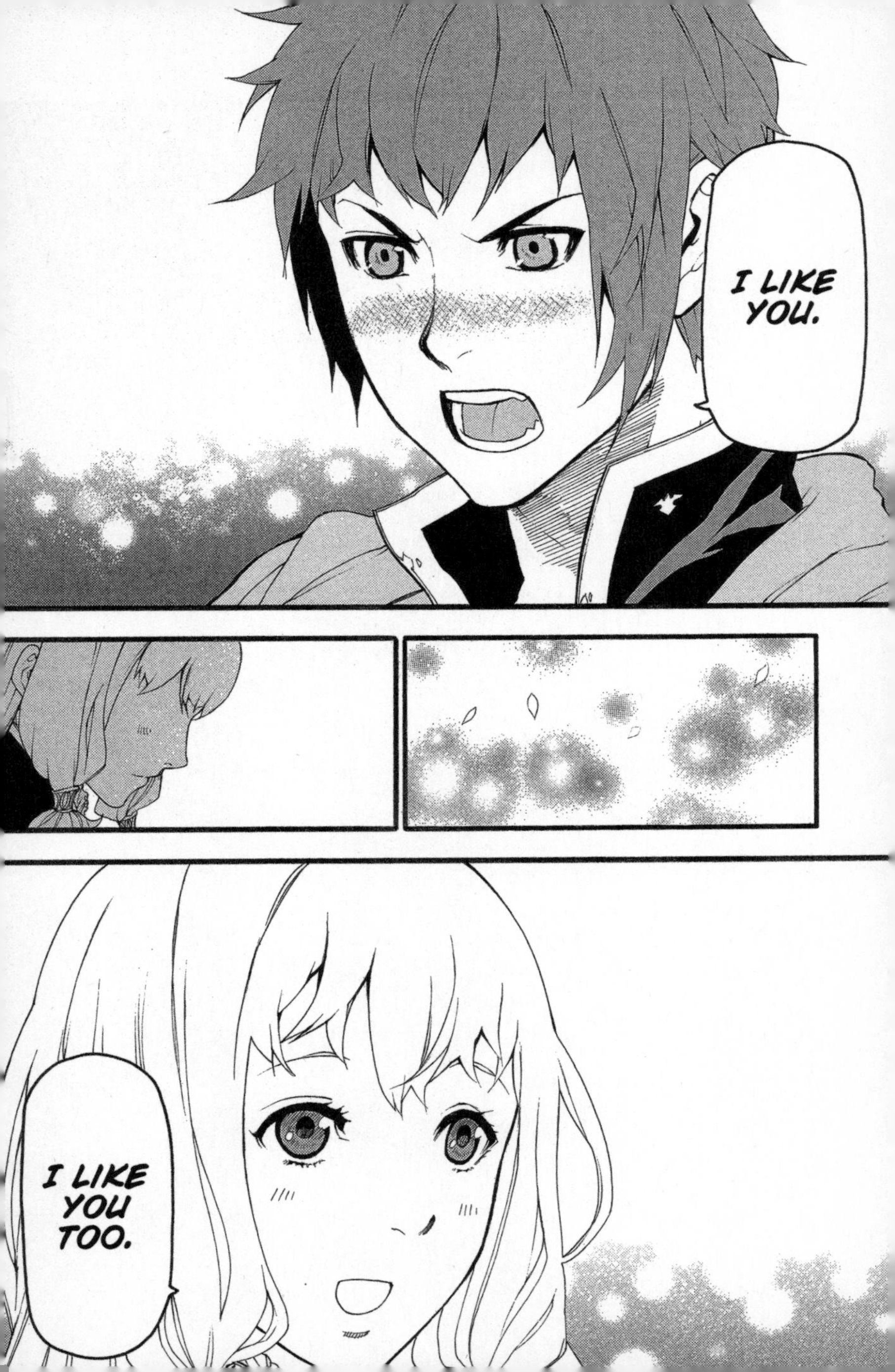
I LIKE YOU.
I LIKE YOU TOO.

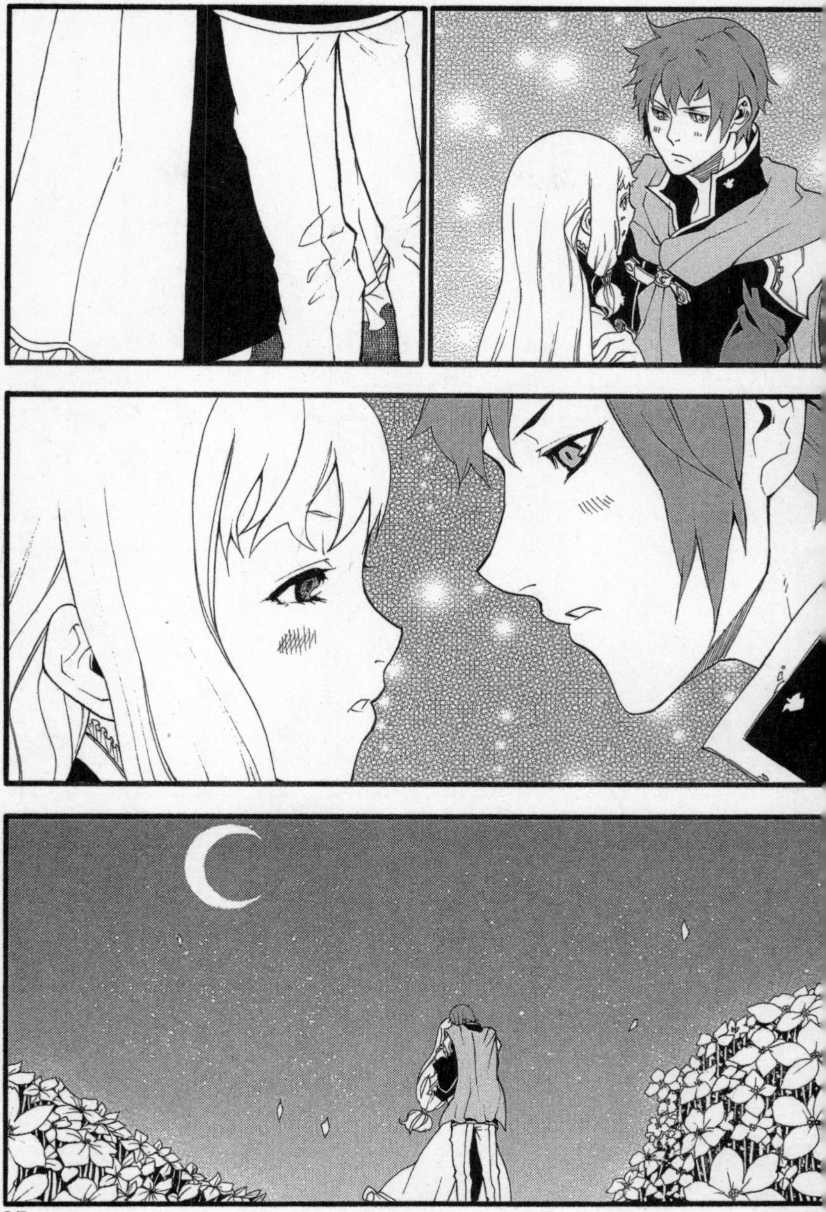

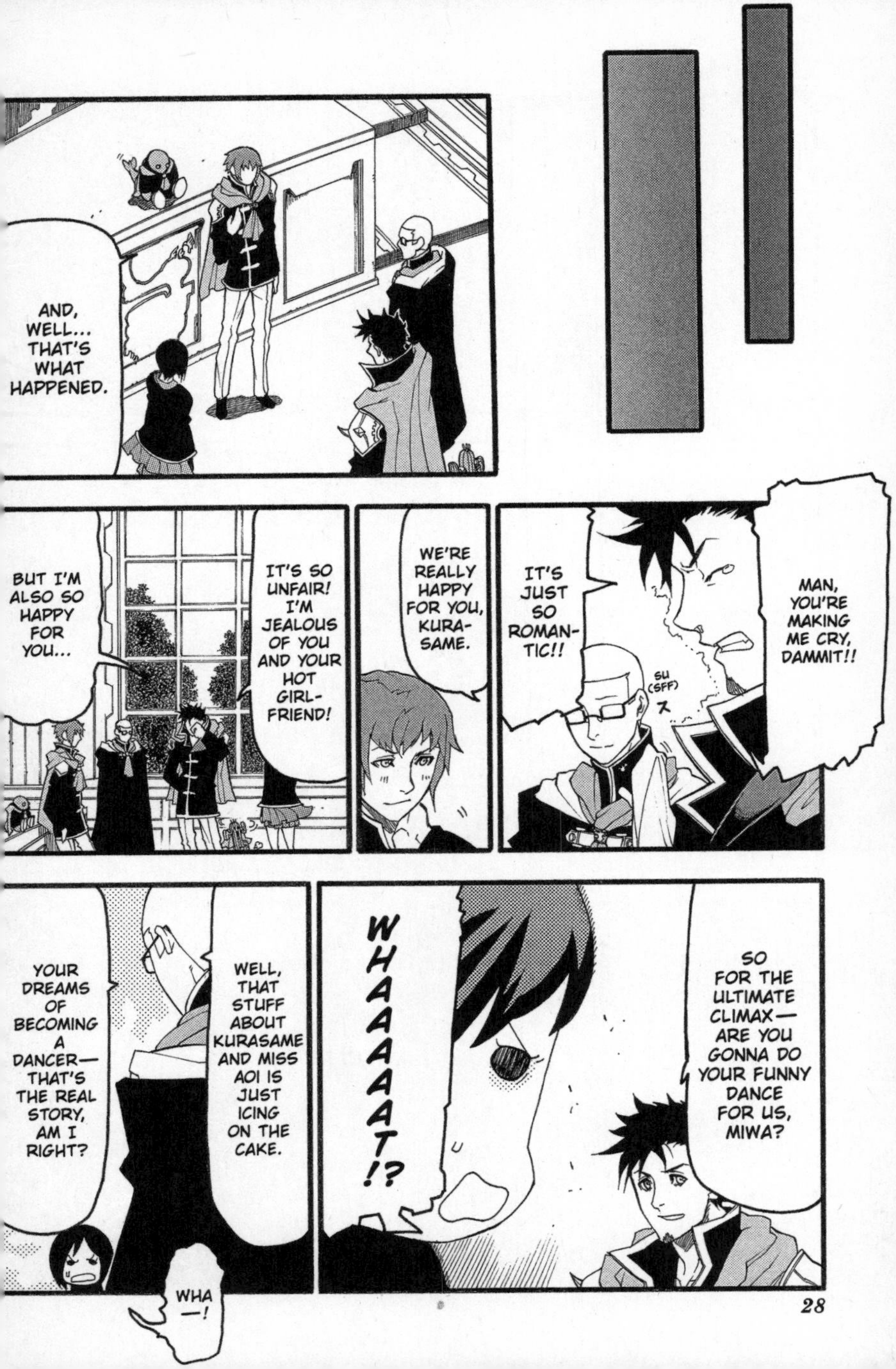
AND, WELL... THAT'S WHAT HAPPENED.
MAN, YOU'RE MAKING ME CRY, DAMMIT!!
IT'S JUST SO ROMANTIC!!
SU (SFF) ス
WE'RE REALLY HAPPY FOR YOU, KURASAME.
IT'S SO UNFAIR! I'M JEALOUS OF YOU AND YOUR HOT GIRLFRIEND!
BUT I'M ALSO SO HAPPY FOR YOU...
SO FOR THE ULTIMATE CLIMAX— ARE YOU GONNA DO YOUR FUNNY DANCE FOR US, MIWA?
WHAAAAAAT!?
WELL, THAT STUFF ABOUT KURASAME AND MISS AOI IS JUST ICING ON THE CAKE.
YOUR DREAMS OF BECOMING A DANCER— THAT'S THE REAL STORY, AM I RIGHT?
WHA—!

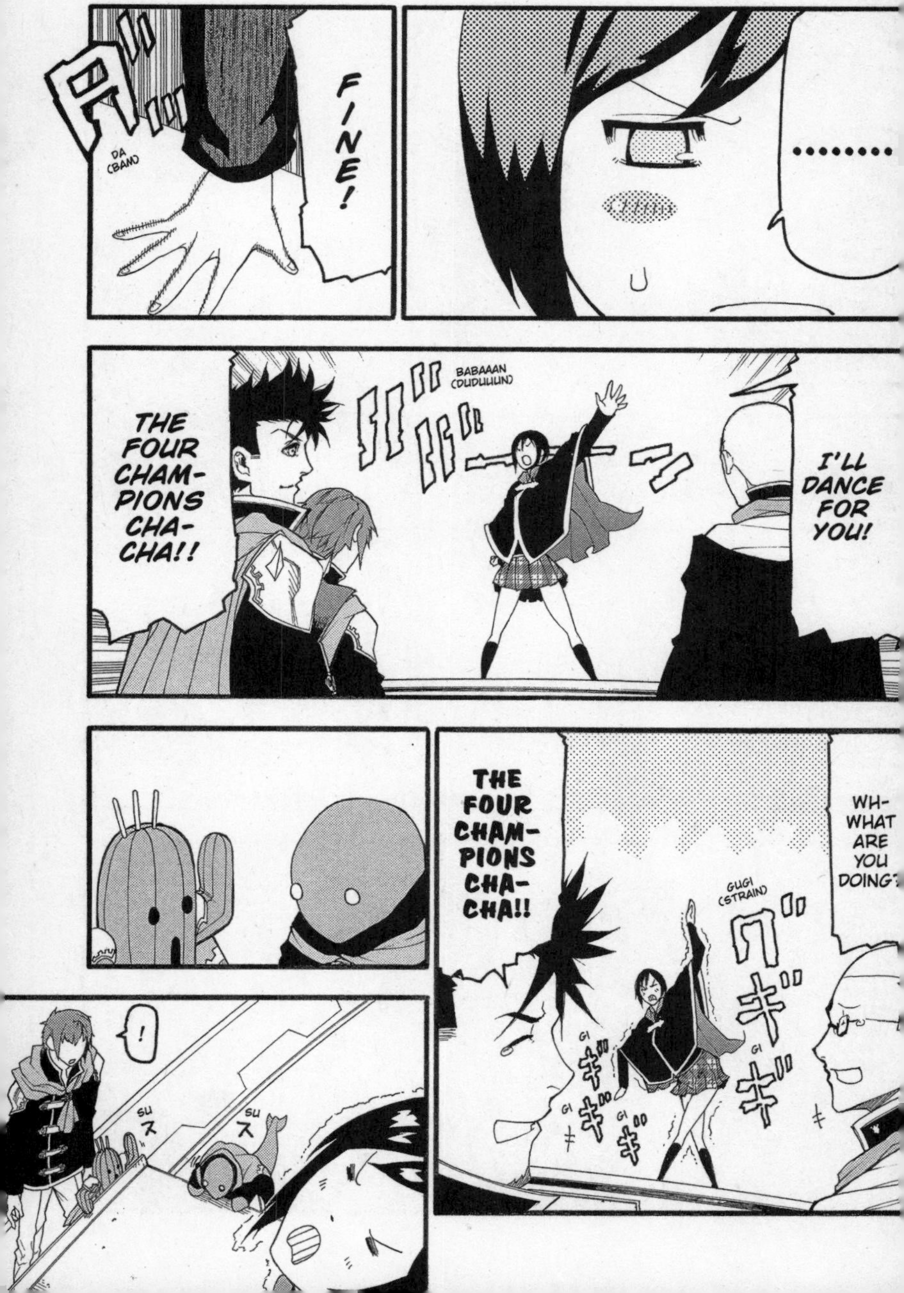
....
FINE!
DA (BAN)
I'LL DANCE FOR YOU!
BABAAAN (DUDUUUN)
THE FOUR CHAMPIONS CHA-CHA!!
WH-WHAT ARE YOU DOING?
GUGI (STRAIN)
THE FOUR CHAMPIONS CHA-CHA!!
GI
GI
GI
GI
!
SU
SU

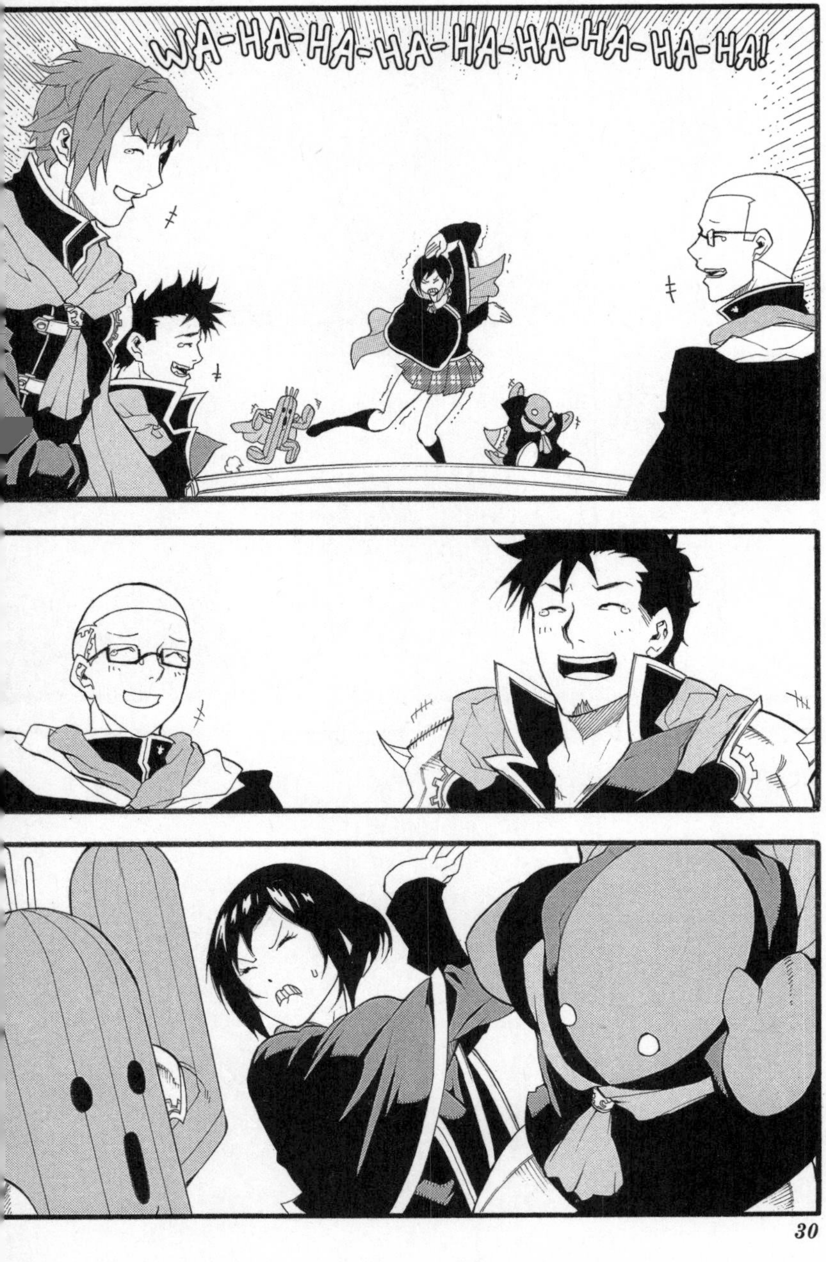
WA-HA-HA-HA-HA-HA-HA-HA-HA!

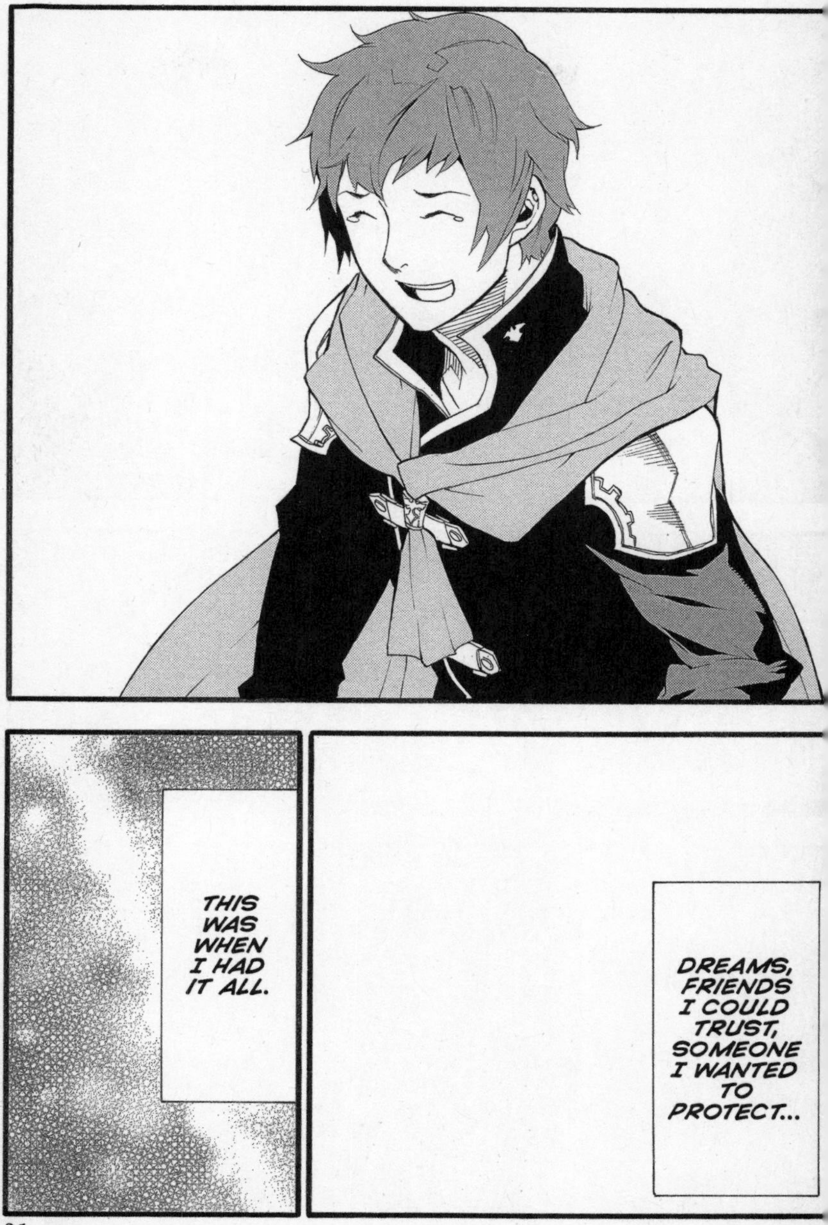
DREAMS, FRIENDS I COULD TRUST, SOMEONE I WANTED TO PROTECT...
THIS WAS WHEN I HAD IT ALL.

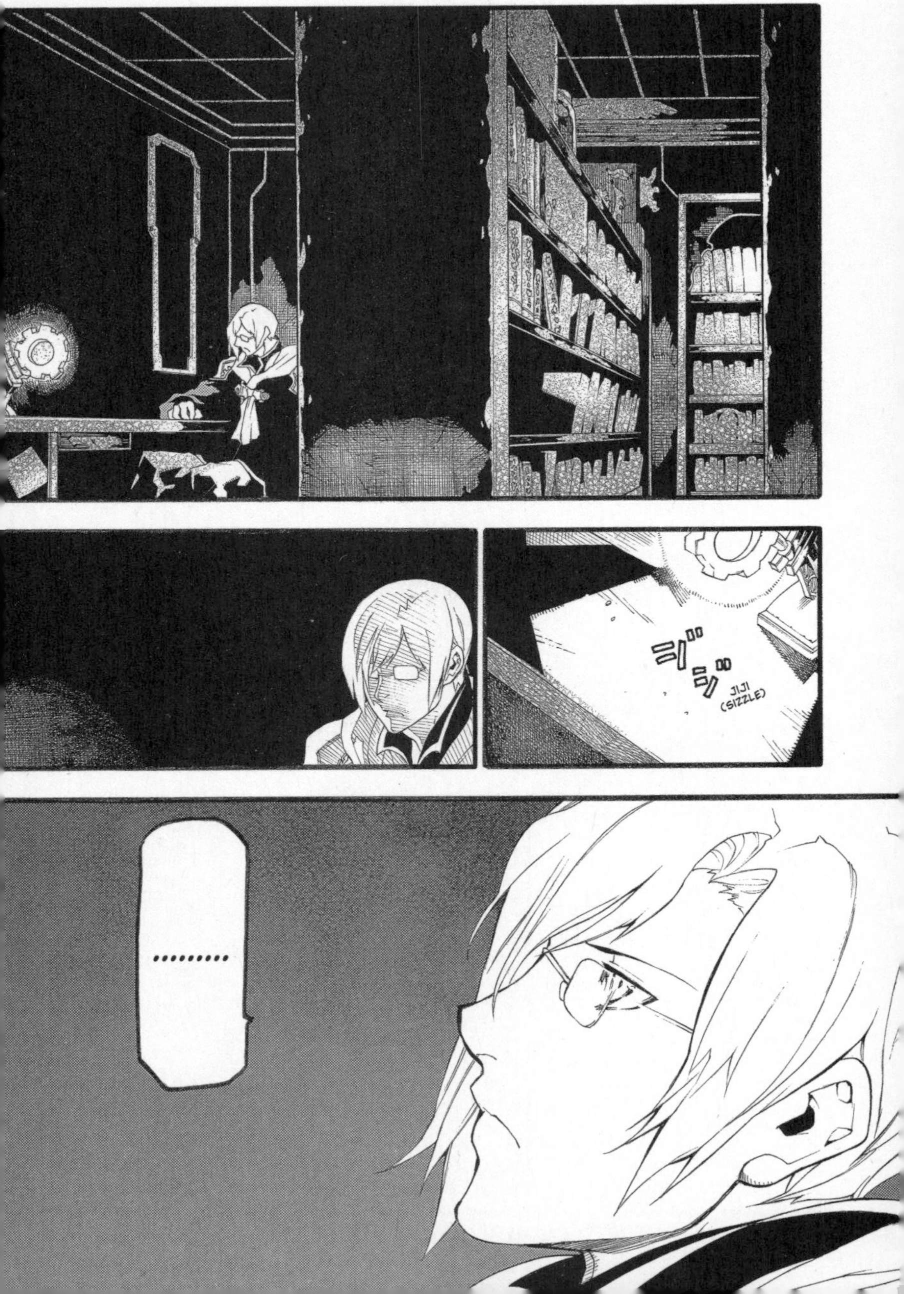
ジジ
JIJI (SIZZLE)
....

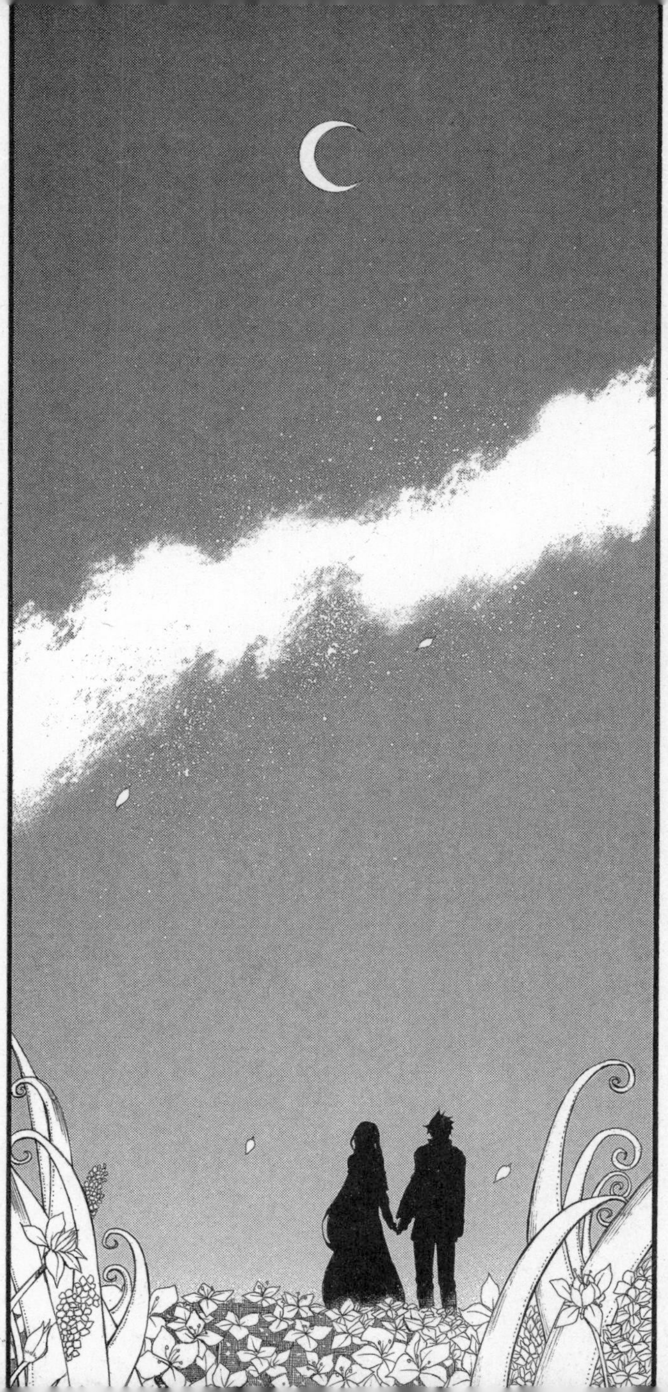

FINAL FANTASY 零式 TYPE-0™

SIDE STORY

The Ice Reaper

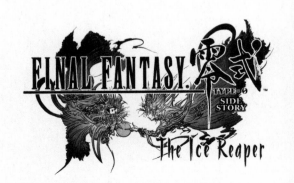

CHAPTER 10: IDEALS AND REALITY

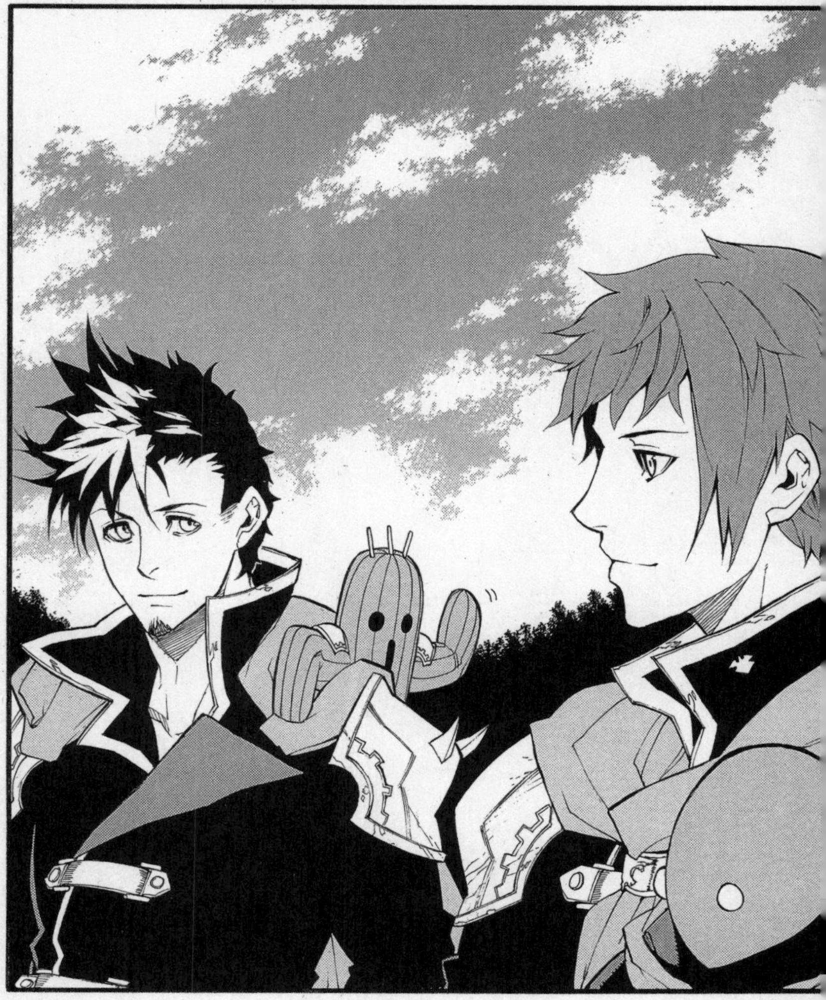

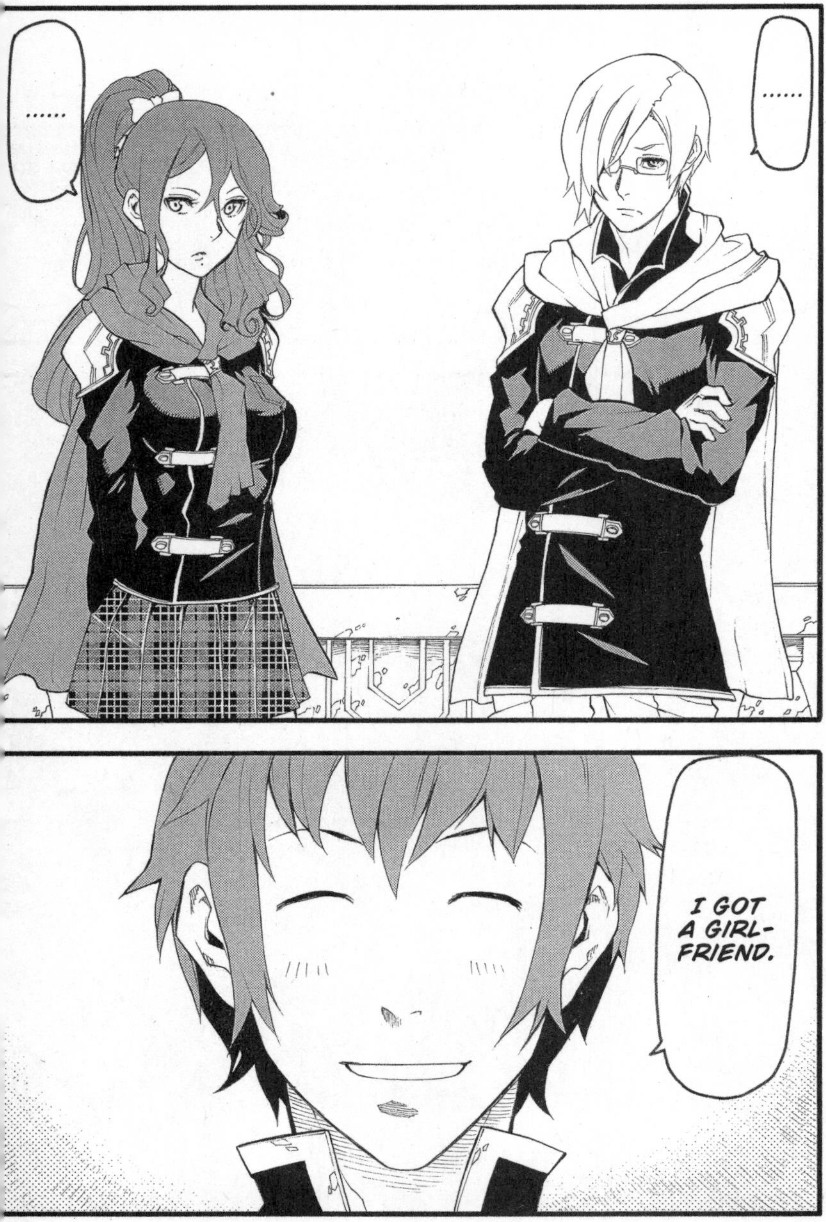
......
......
I GOT A GIRL-FRIEND.

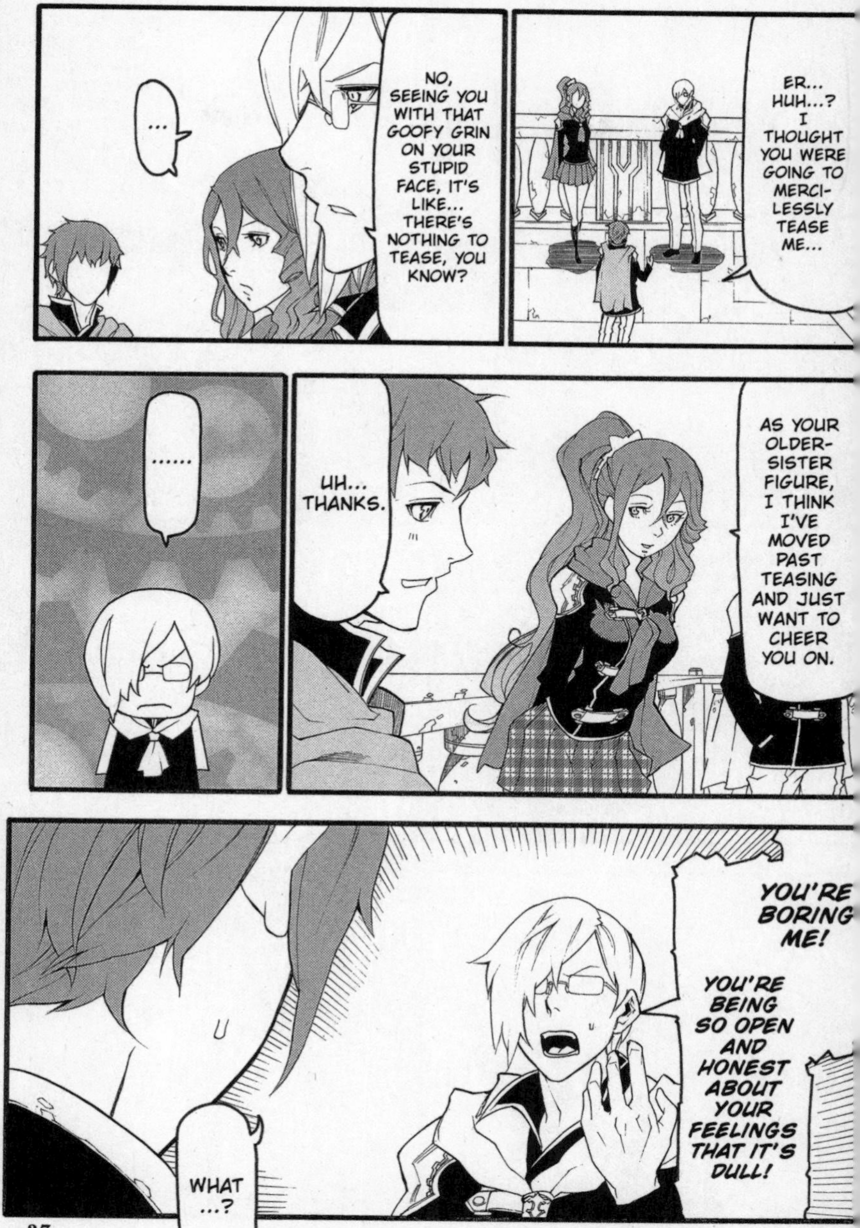
ER... HUH...? I THOUGHT YOU WERE GOING TO MERCILESSLY TEASE ME...
NO, SEEING YOU WITH THAT GOOFY GRIN ON YOUR STUPID FACE, IT'S LIKE... THERE'S NOTHING TO TEASE, YOU KNOW?
...
AS YOUR OLDER-SISTER FIGURE, I THINK I'VE MOVED PAST TEASING AND JUST WANT TO CHEER YOU ON.
UH... THANKS.
......
YOU'RE BORING ME!
YOU'RE BEING SO OPEN AND HONEST ABOUT YOUR FEELINGS THAT IT'S DULL!
WHAT ...?

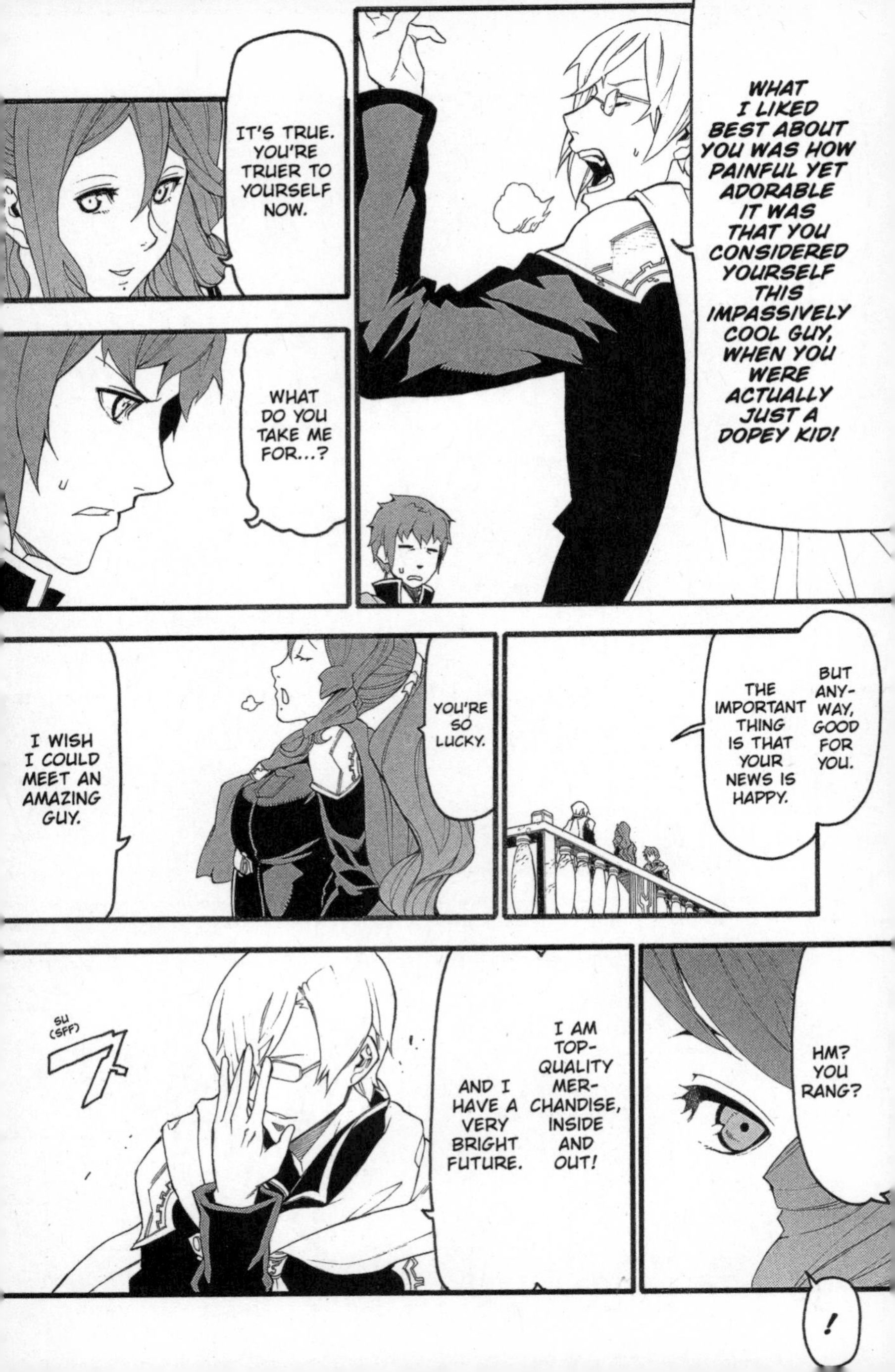
WHAT I LIKED BEST ABOUT YOU WAS HOW PAINFUL YET ADORABLE IT WAS THAT YOU CONSIDERED YOURSELF THIS IMPASSIVELY COOL GUY, WHEN YOU WERE ACTUALLY JUST A DOPEY KID!
IT'S TRUE. YOU'RE TRUER TO YOURSELF NOW.
WHAT DO YOU TAKE ME FOR...?
BUT ANYWAY, GOOD FOR YOU.
THE IMPORTANT THING IS THAT YOUR NEWS IS HAPPY.
YOU'RE SO LUCKY.
I WISH I COULD MEET AN AMAZING GUY.
HM? YOU RANG?
I AM TOP-QUALITY MERCHANDISE, INSIDE AND OUT!
AND I HAVE A VERY BRIGHT FUTURE.
SU (SFF)
!

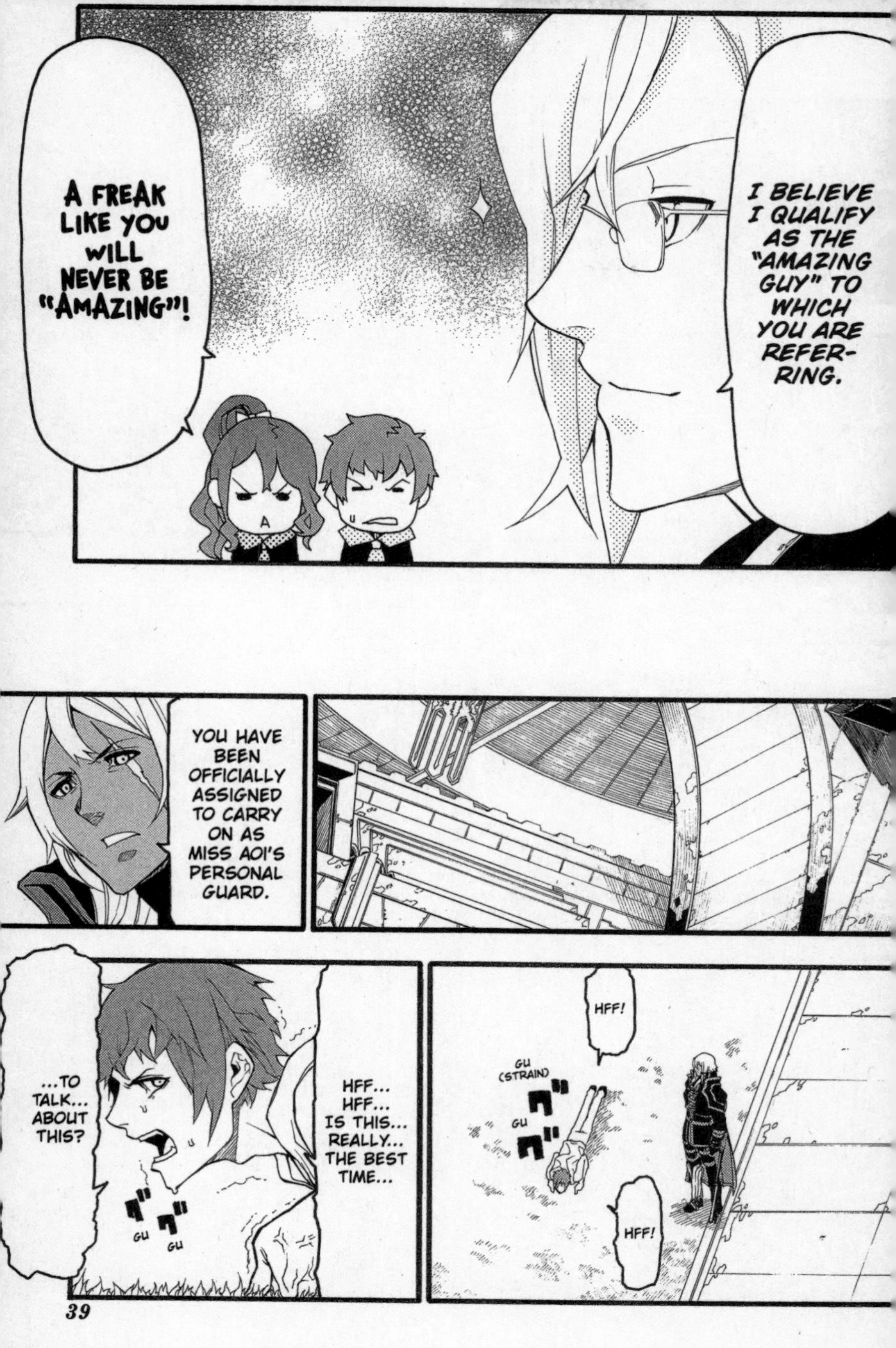
I BELIEVE I QUALIFY AS THE "AMAZING GUY" TO WHICH YOU ARE REFER-RING.
A FREAK LIKE YOU WILL NEVER BE "AMAZING"!
YOU HAVE BEEN OFFICIALLY ASSIGNED TO CARRY ON AS MISS AOI'S PERSONAL GUARD.
HFF!
GU (STRAIN)
GU
HFF!
HFF... HFF... IS THIS... REALLY... THE BEST TIME...
...TO TALK... ABOUT THIS?
GU
GU

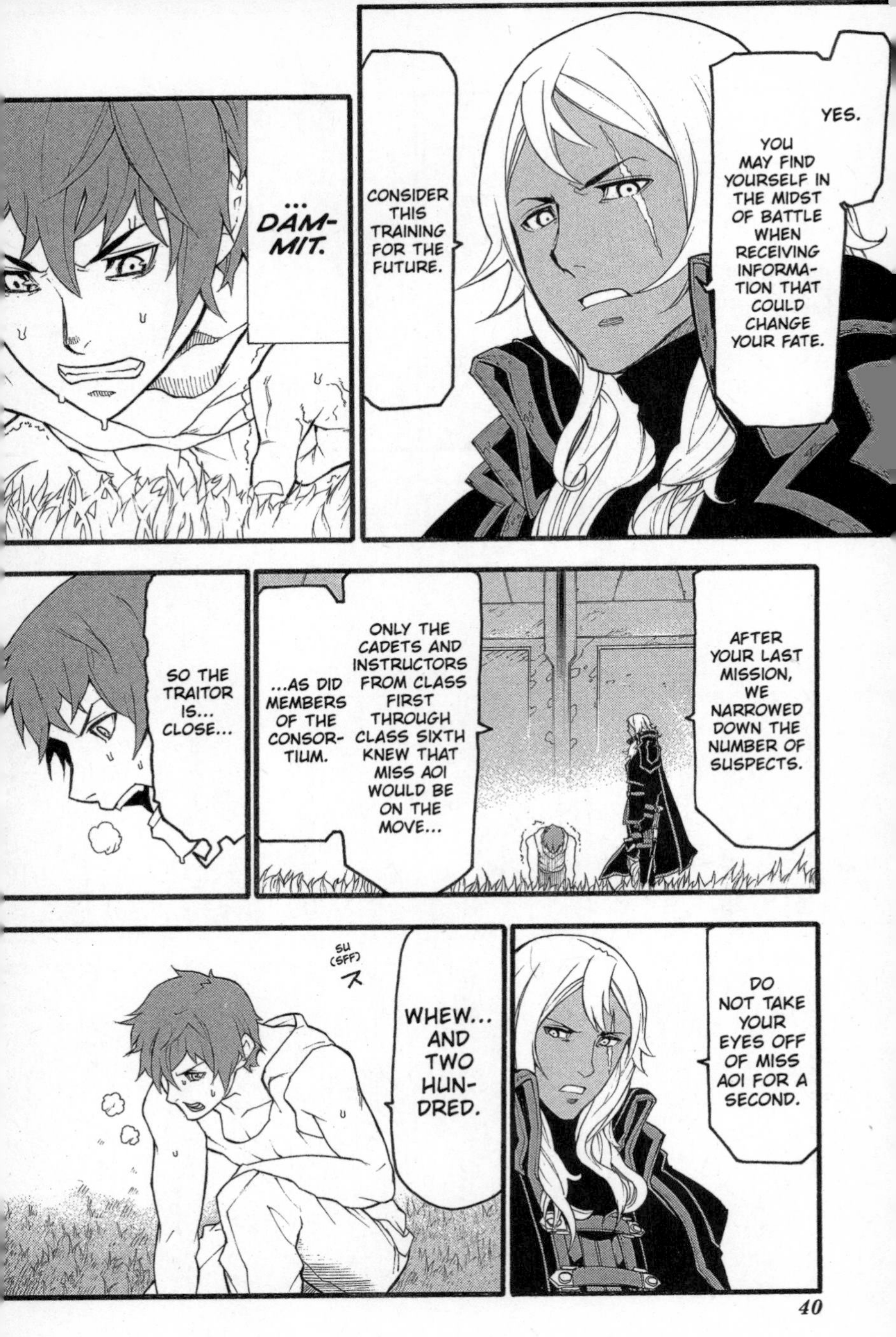
YES.
YOU MAY FIND YOURSELF IN THE MIDST OF BATTLE WHEN RECEIVING INFORMATION THAT COULD CHANGE YOUR FATE.
CONSIDER THIS TRAINING FOR THE FUTURE.
...DAM-MIT.
AFTER YOUR LAST MISSION, WE NARROWED DOWN THE NUMBER OF SUSPECTS.
ONLY THE CADETS AND INSTRUCTORS FROM CLASS FIRST THROUGH CLASS SIXTH KNEW THAT MISS AOI WOULD BE ON THE MOVE...
...AS DID MEMBERS OF THE CONSOR-TIUM.
SO THE TRAITOR IS... CLOSE...
DO NOT TAKE YOUR EYES OFF OF MISS AOI FOR A SECOND.
SU (SFF) ス
WHEW... AND TWO HUN-DRED.

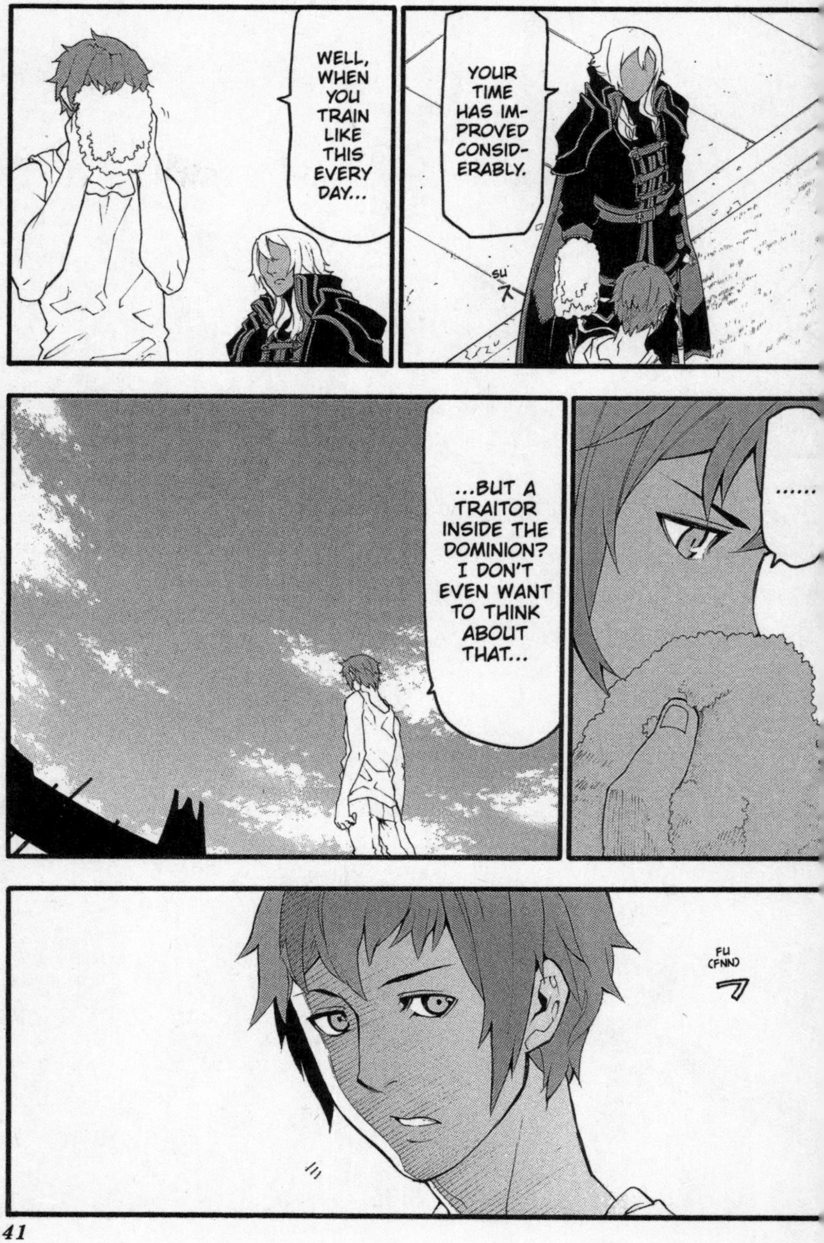
YOUR TIME HAS IMPROVED CONSIDERABLY.
SU
WELL, WHEN YOU TRAIN LIKE THIS EVERY DAY...
......
...BUT A TRAITOR INSIDE THE DOMINION? I DON'T EVEN WANT TO THINK ABOUT THAT...
FU (FNN)

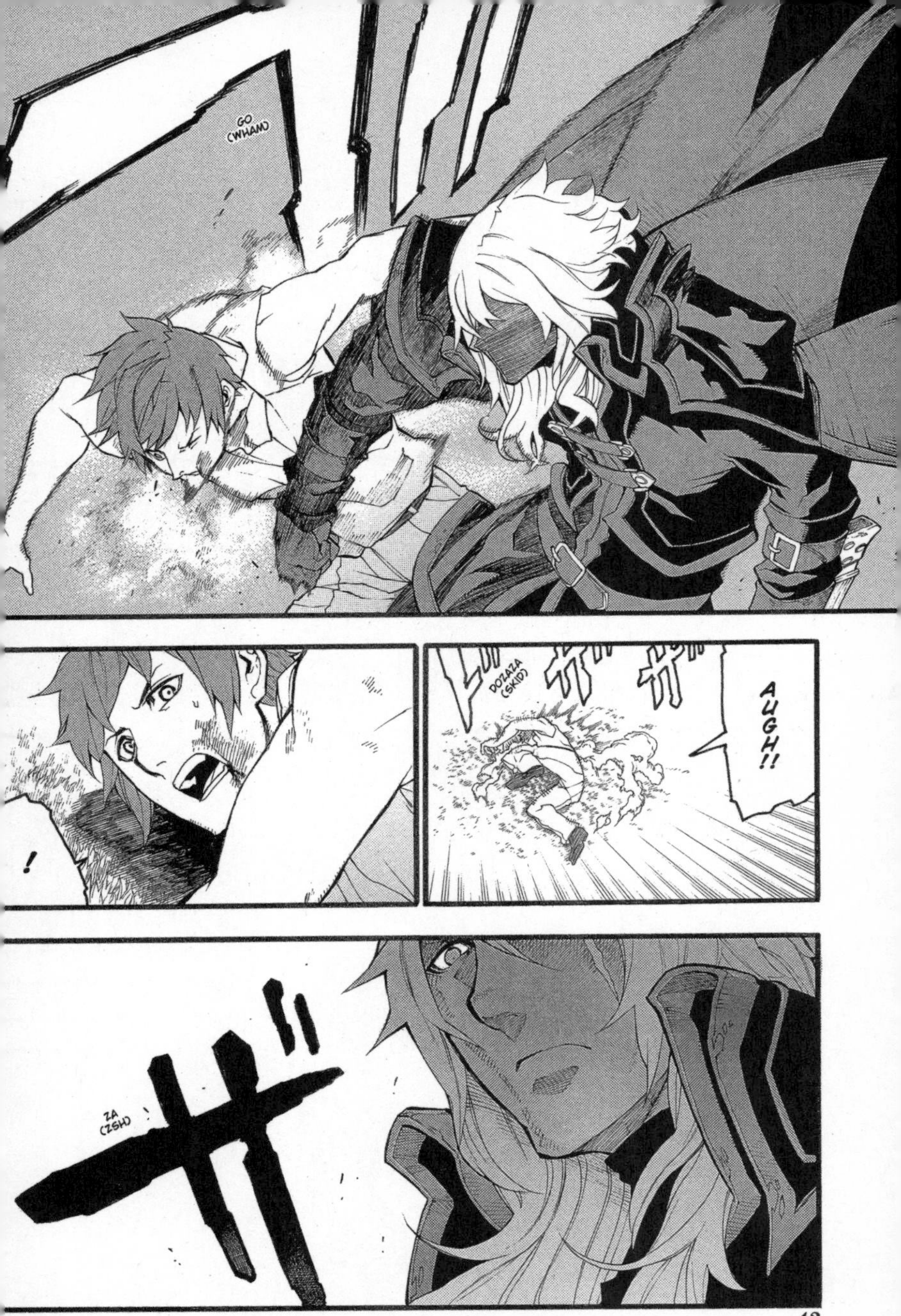
GO
(WHAM)
AUGH!!
DOZAZA
(SKID)
!
ZA
(ZSH)

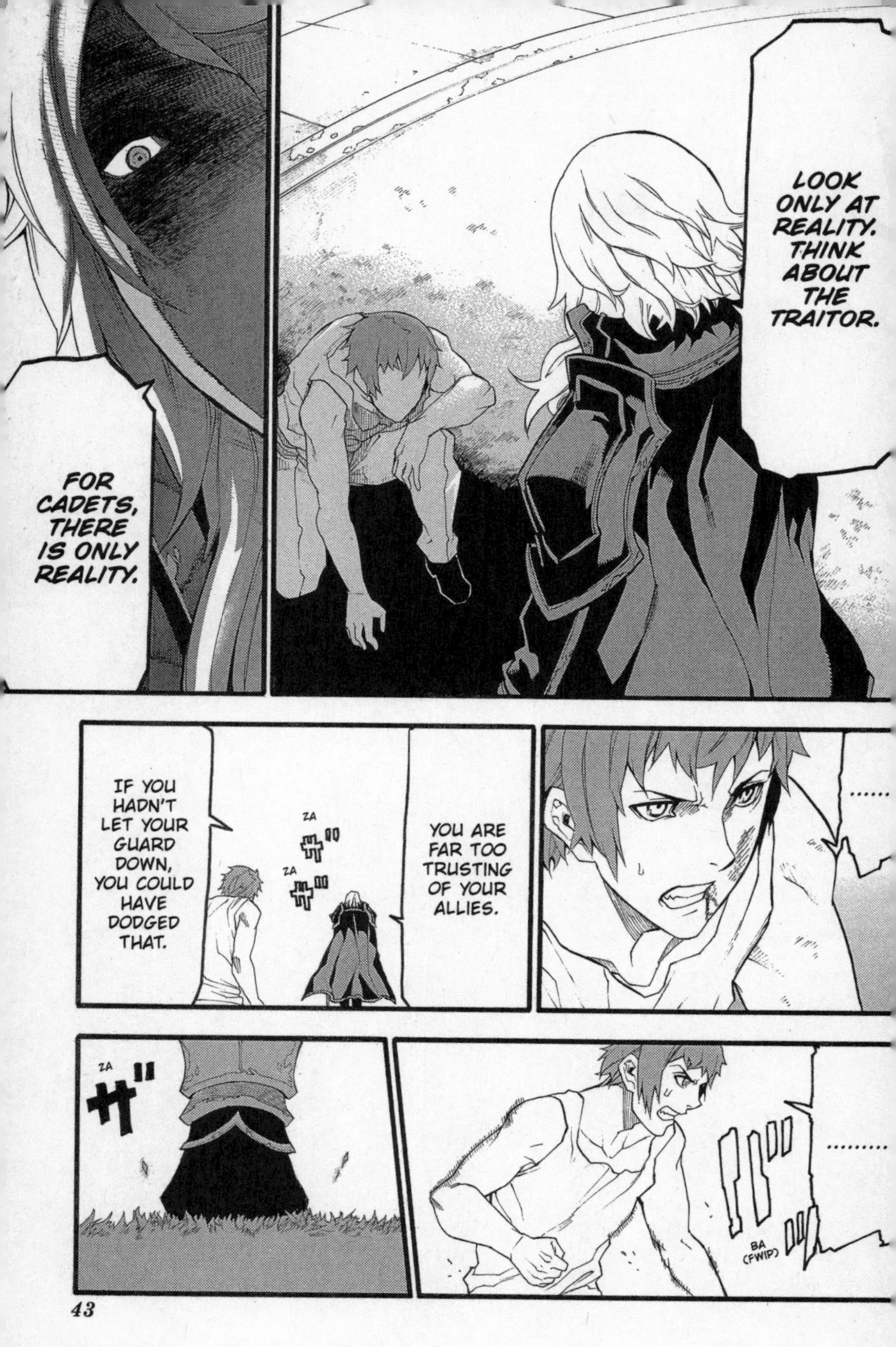
LOOK ONLY AT REALITY. THINK ABOUT THE TRAITOR.
FOR CADETS, THERE IS ONLY REALITY.
......
YOU ARE FAR TOO TRUSTING OF YOUR ALLIES.
ZA
ZA
IF YOU HADN'T LET YOUR GUARD DOWN, YOU COULD HAVE DODGED THAT.
....
BA (FWIP)
ZA

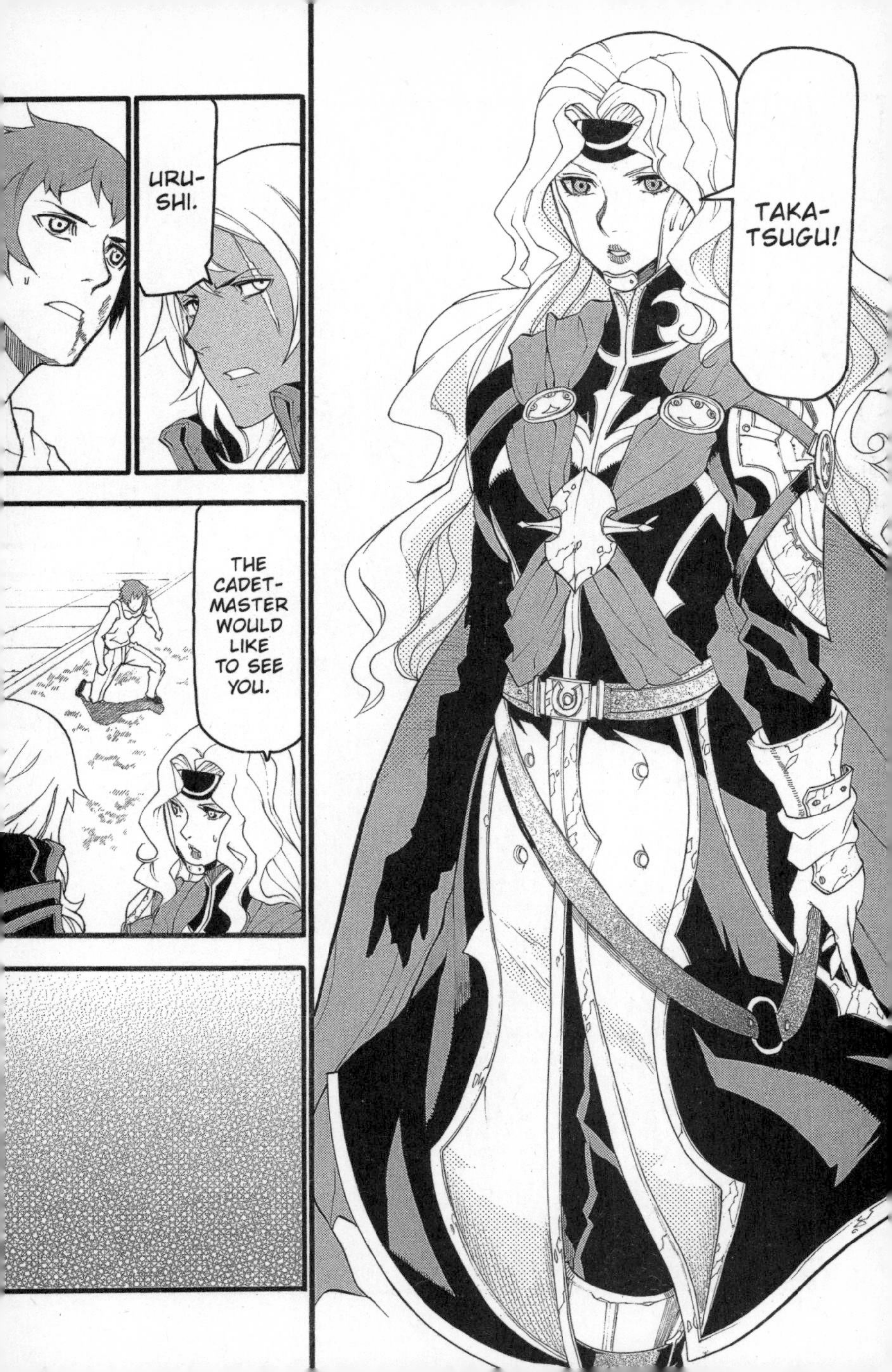
TAKA-
TSUGU!
URU-
SHI.
THE
CADET-
MASTER
WOULD
LIKE
TO SEE
YOU.

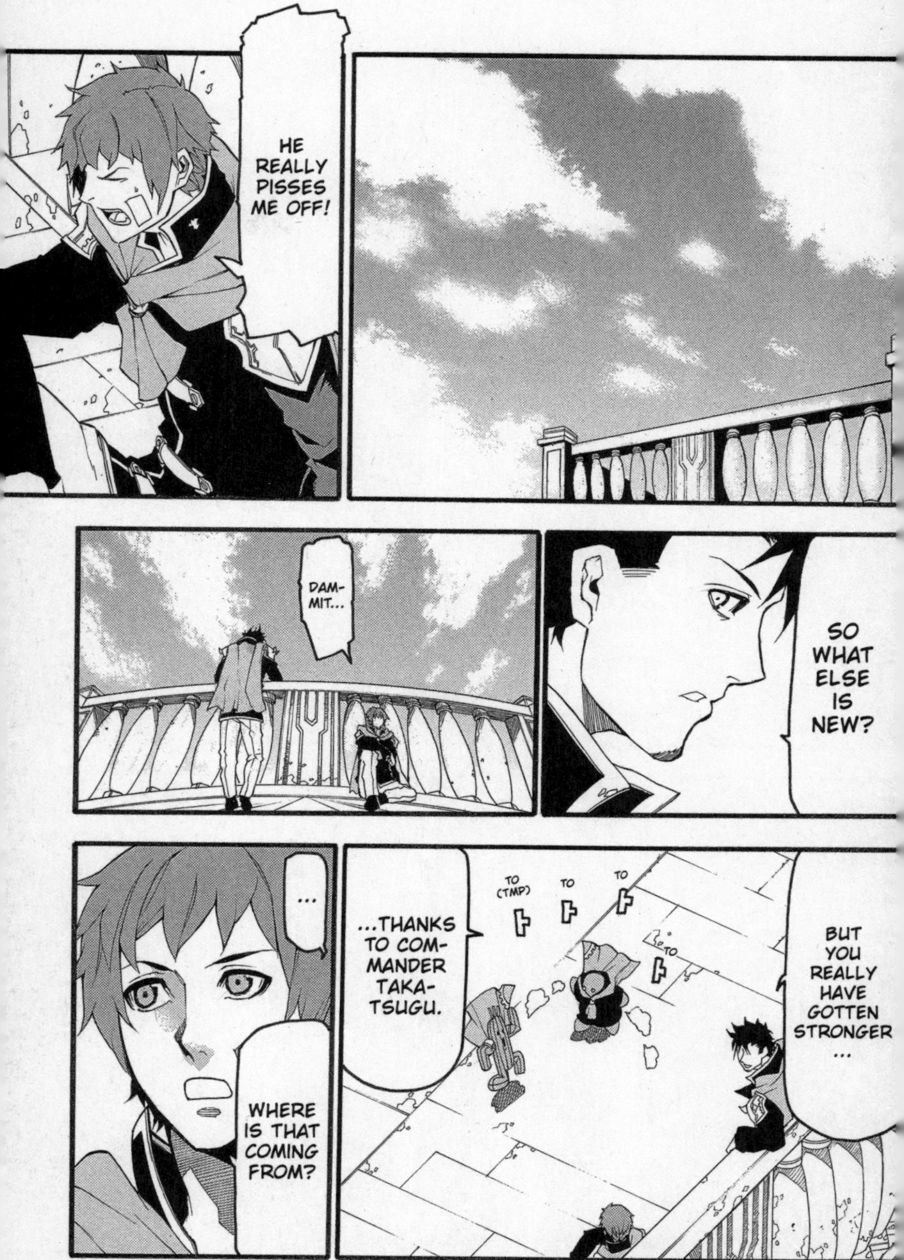
HE REALLY PISSES ME OFF!
SO WHAT ELSE IS NEW?
DAM-MIT...
BUT YOU REALLY HAVE GOTTEN STRONGER ...
TO ト
TO ト
TO ト
TO (TMP) ト
...THANKS TO COM-MANDER TAKA-TSUGU.
...
WHERE IS THAT COMING FROM?

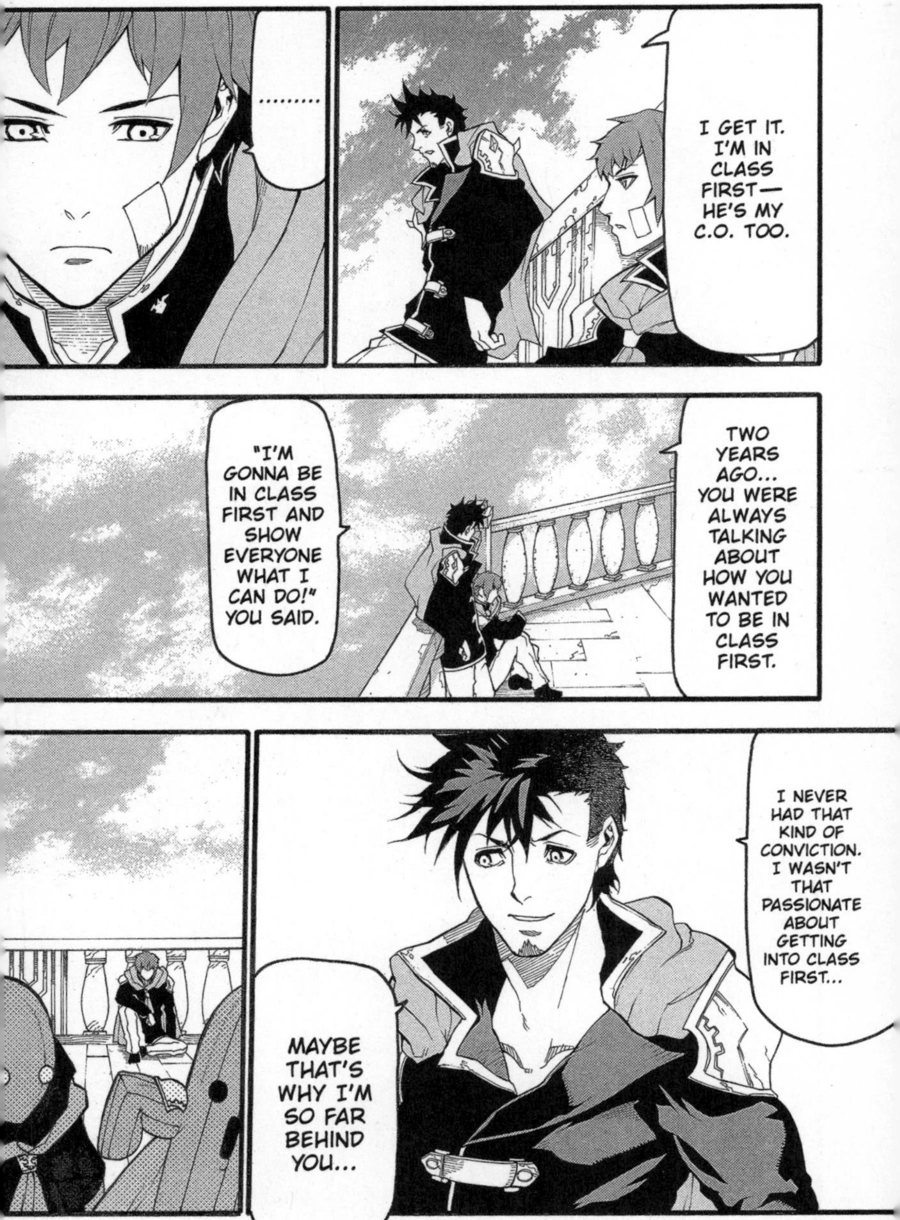
I GET IT. I'M IN CLASS FIRST— HE'S MY C.O. TOO.
....
TWO YEARS AGO... YOU WERE ALWAYS TALKING ABOUT HOW YOU WANTED TO BE IN CLASS FIRST.
"I'M GONNA BE IN CLASS FIRST AND SHOW EVERYONE WHAT I CAN DO!" YOU SAID.
I NEVER HAD THAT KIND OF CONVICTION. I WASN'T THAT PASSIONATE ABOUT GETTING INTO CLASS FIRST...
MAYBE THAT'S WHY I'M SO FAR BEHIND YOU...

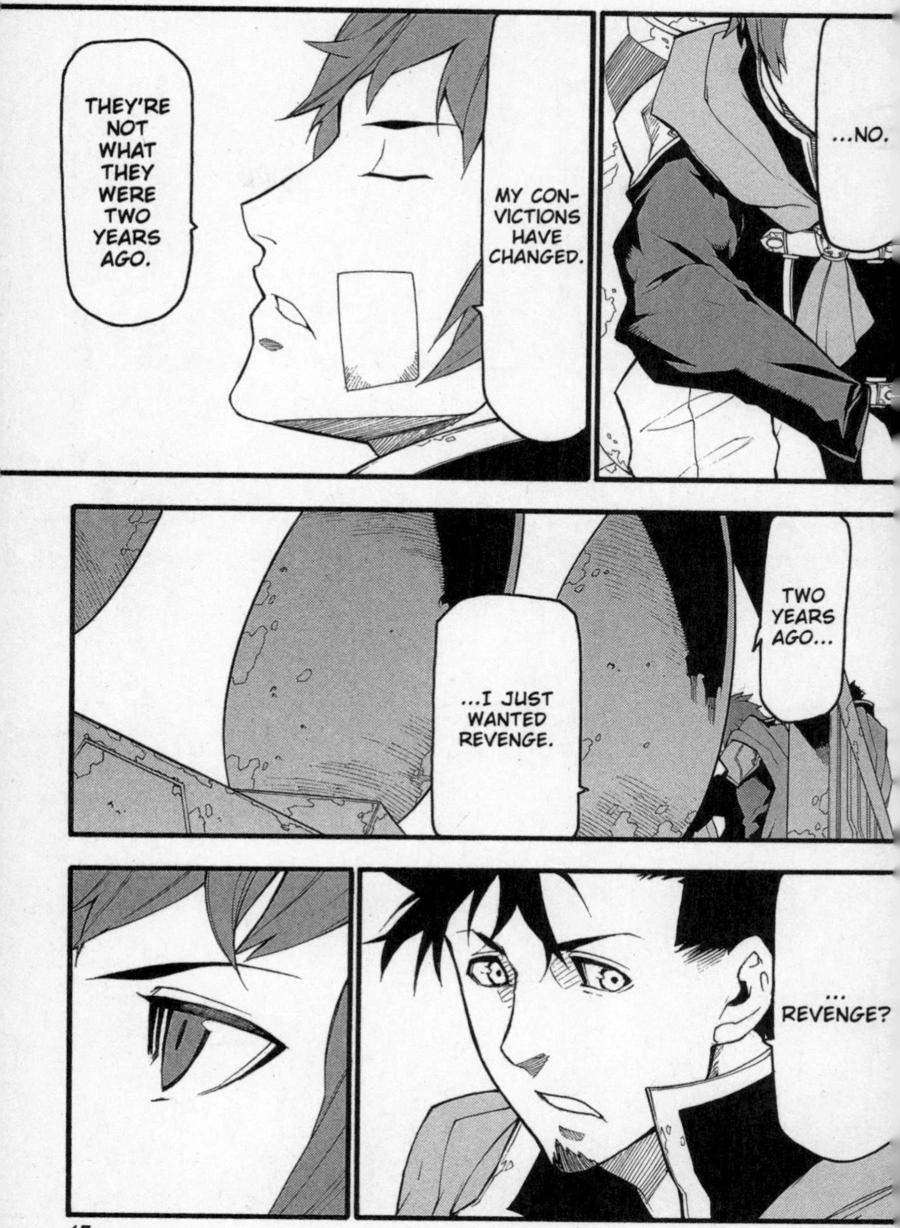
...NO.
MY CON-VICTIONS HAVE CHANGED.
THEY'RE NOT WHAT THEY WERE TWO YEARS AGO.
TWO YEARS AGO...
...I JUST WANTED REVENGE.
... REVENGE?

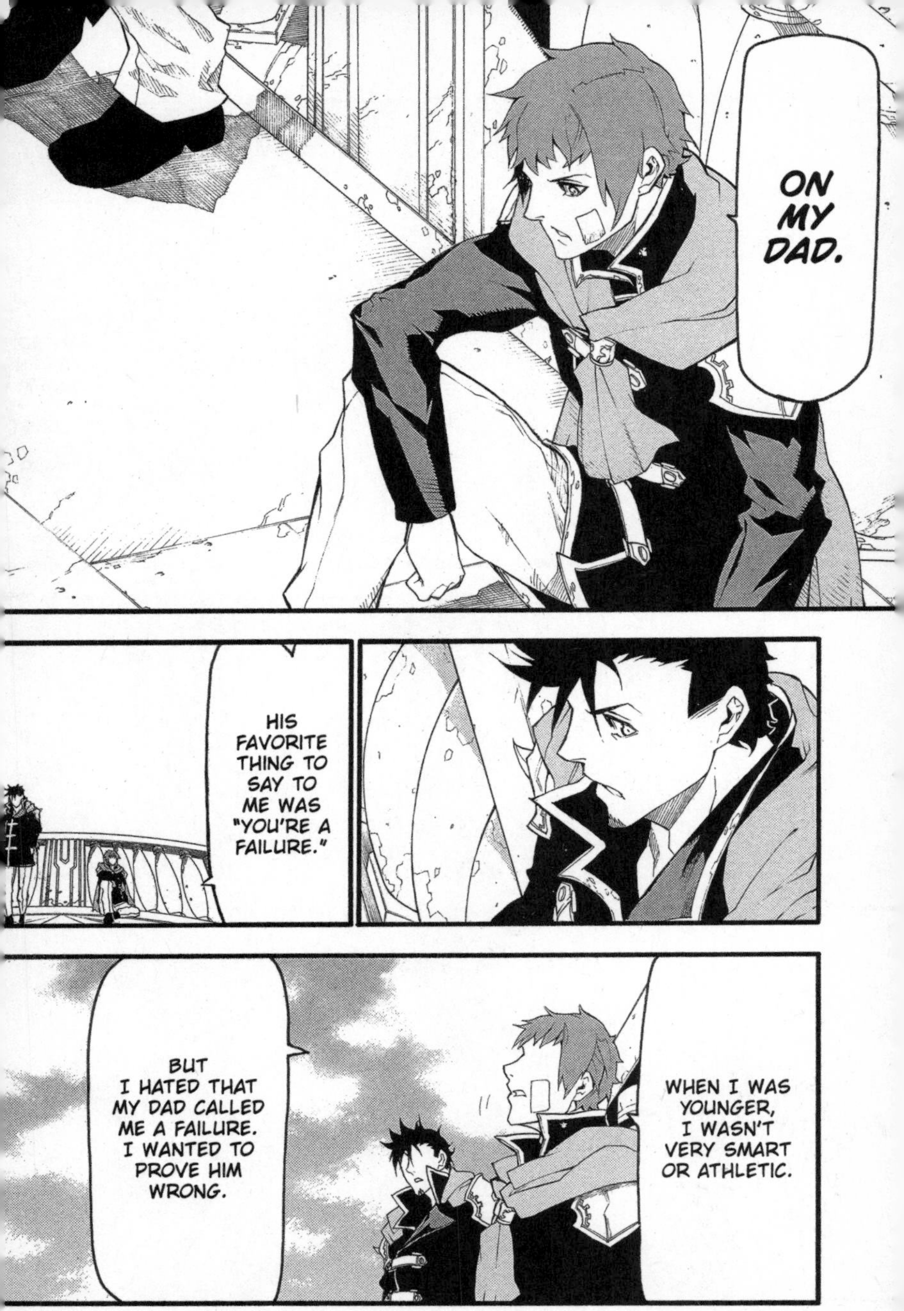
ON MY DAD.
HIS FAVORITE THING TO SAY TO ME WAS "YOU'RE A FAILURE."
WHEN I WAS YOUNGER, I WASN'T VERY SMART OR ATHLETIC.
BUT I HATED THAT MY DAD CALLED ME A FAILURE. I WANTED TO PROVE HIM WRONG.

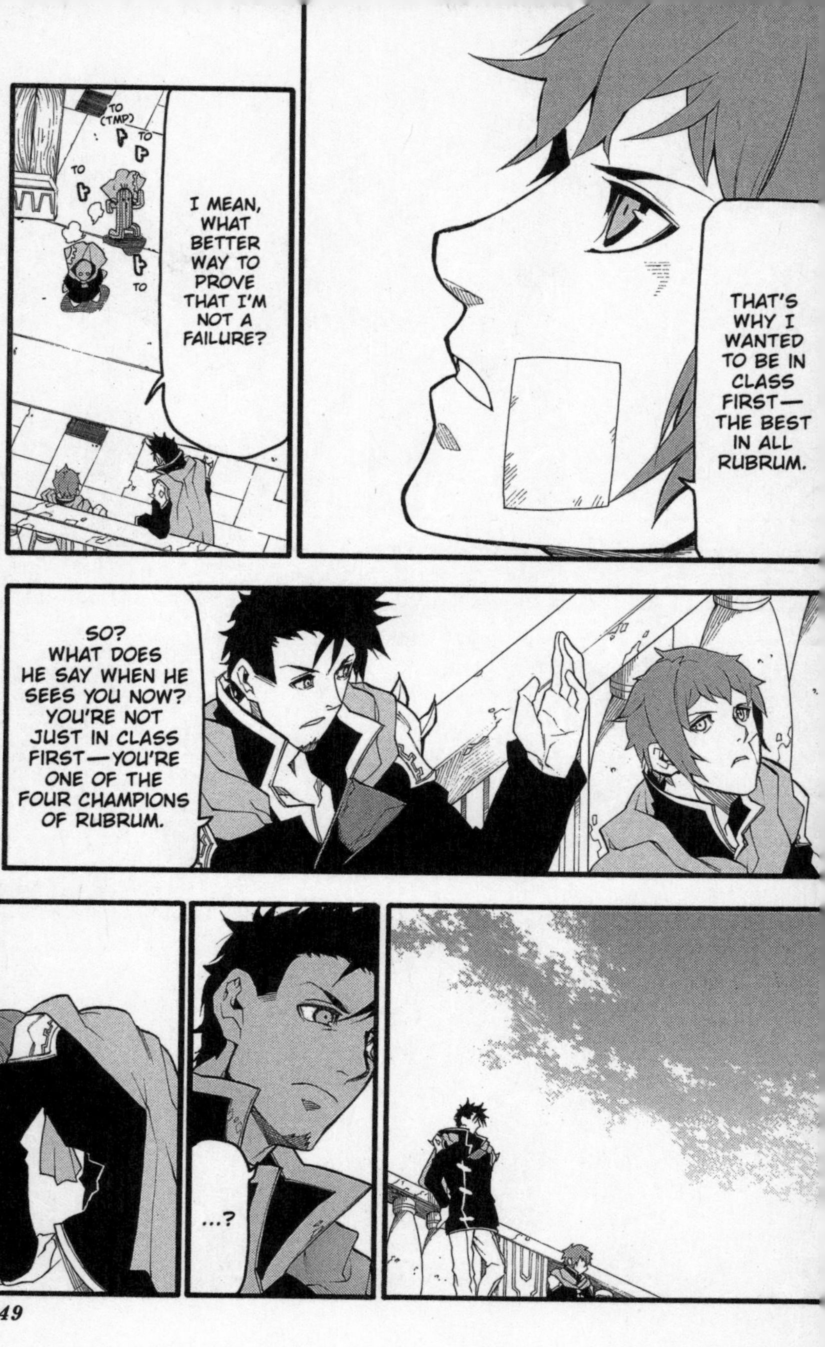
THAT'S WHY I WANTED TO BE IN CLASS FIRST— THE BEST IN ALL RUBRUM.
TO (TMP)
TO
TO
TO
I MEAN, WHAT BETTER WAY TO PROVE THAT I'M NOT A FAILURE?
SO? WHAT DOES HE SAY WHEN HE SEES YOU NOW? YOU'RE NOT JUST IN CLASS FIRST—YOU'RE ONE OF THE FOUR CHAMPIONS OF RUBRUM.
...?
ス SU (SFF)

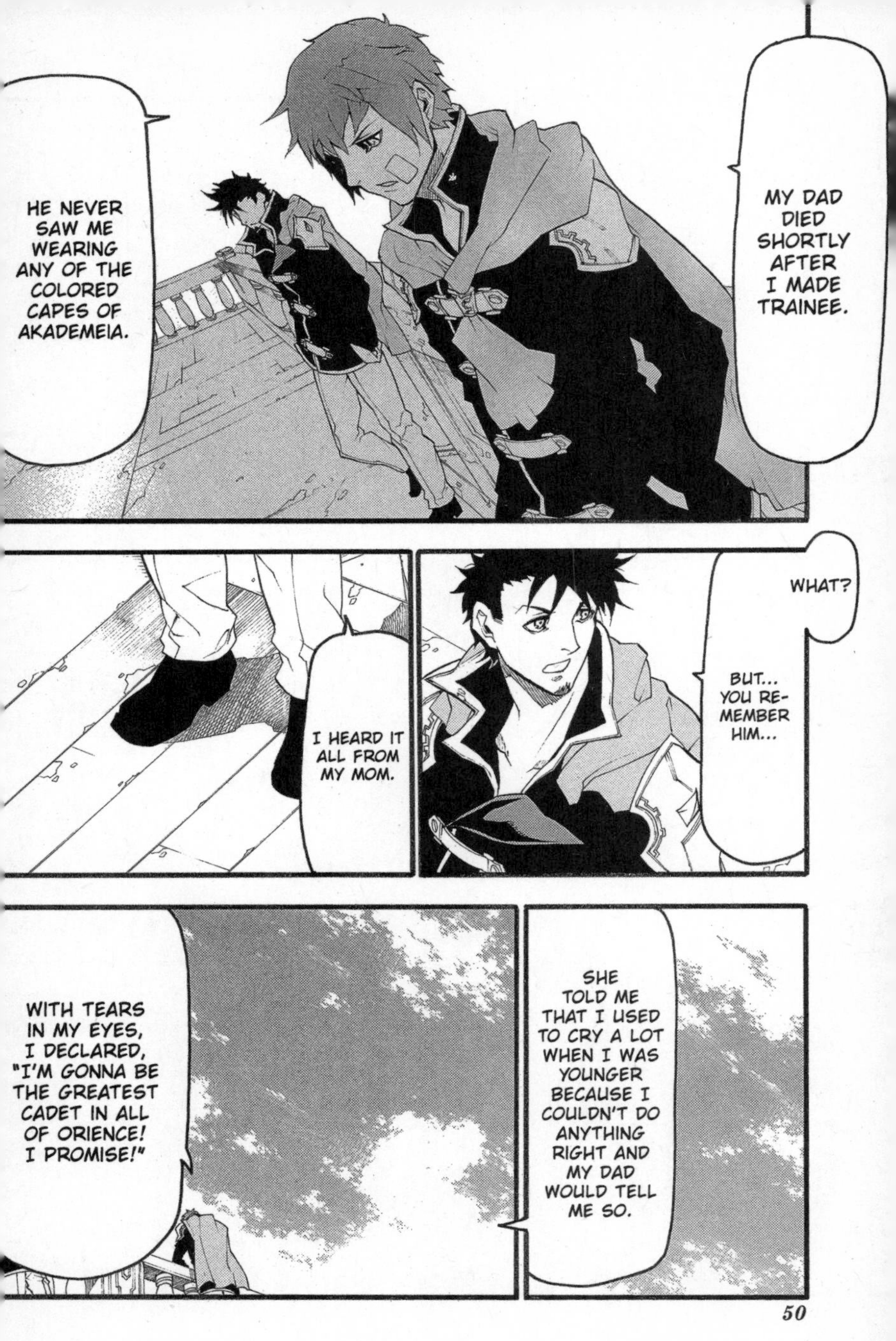
MY DAD DIED SHORTLY AFTER I MADE TRAINEE.
HE NEVER SAW ME WEARING ANY OF THE COLORED CAPES OF AKADEMEIA.
WHAT?
BUT... YOU RE-MEMBER HIM...
I HEARD IT ALL FROM MY MOM.
SHE TOLD ME THAT I USED TO CRY A LOT WHEN I WAS YOUNGER BECAUSE I COULDN'T DO ANYTHING RIGHT AND MY DAD WOULD TELL ME SO.
WITH TEARS IN MY EYES, I DECLARED, "I'M GONNA BE THE GREATEST CADET IN ALL OF ORIENCE! I PROMISE!"

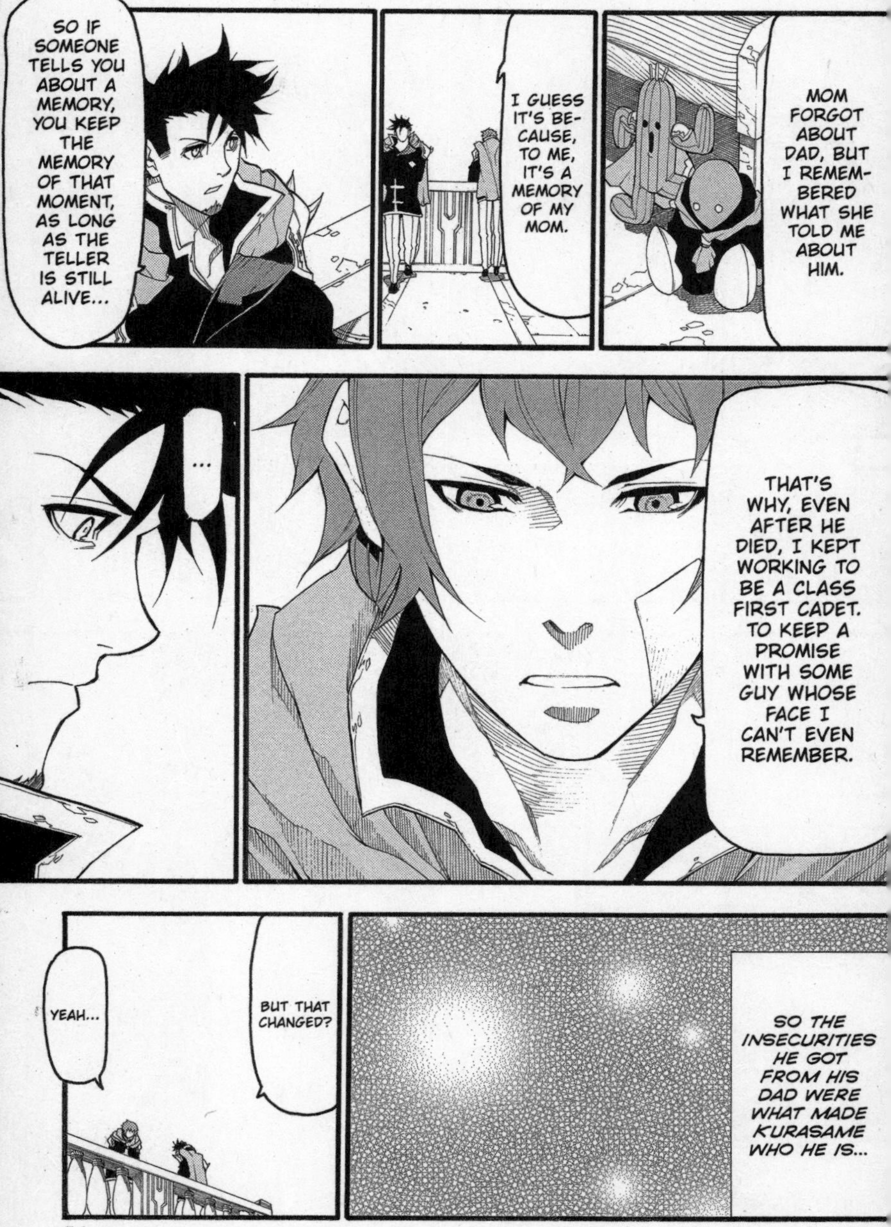
MOM FORGOT ABOUT DAD, BUT I REMEMBERED WHAT SHE TOLD ME ABOUT HIM.
I GUESS IT'S BECAUSE, TO ME, IT'S A MEMORY OF MY MOM.
SO IF SOMEONE TELLS YOU ABOUT A MEMORY, YOU KEEP THE MEMORY OF THAT MOMENT, AS LONG AS THE TELLER IS STILL ALIVE...
THAT'S WHY, EVEN AFTER HE DIED, I KEPT WORKING TO BE A CLASS FIRST CADET. TO KEEP A PROMISE WITH SOME GUY WHOSE FACE I CAN'T EVEN REMEMBER.
...
SO THE INSECURITIES HE GOT FROM HIS DAD WERE WHAT MADE KURASAME WHO HE IS...
BUT THAT CHANGED?
YEAH...

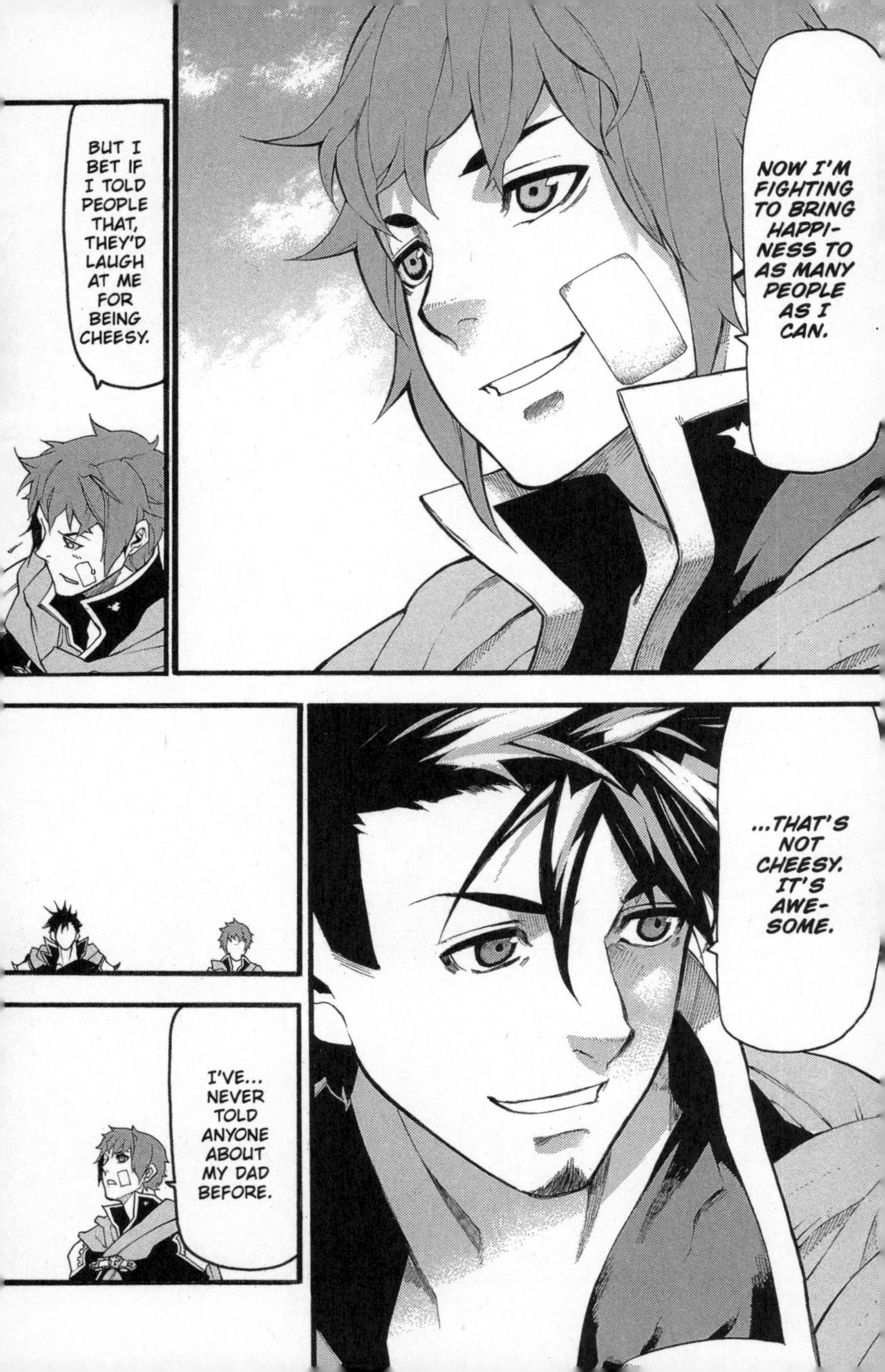
NOW I'M FIGHTING TO BRING HAPPINESS TO AS MANY PEOPLE AS I CAN.
BUT I BET IF I TOLD PEOPLE THAT, THEY'D LAUGH AT ME FOR BEING CHEESY.
...THAT'S NOT CHEESY. IT'S AWESOME.
I'VE... NEVER TOLD ANYONE ABOUT MY DAD BEFORE.

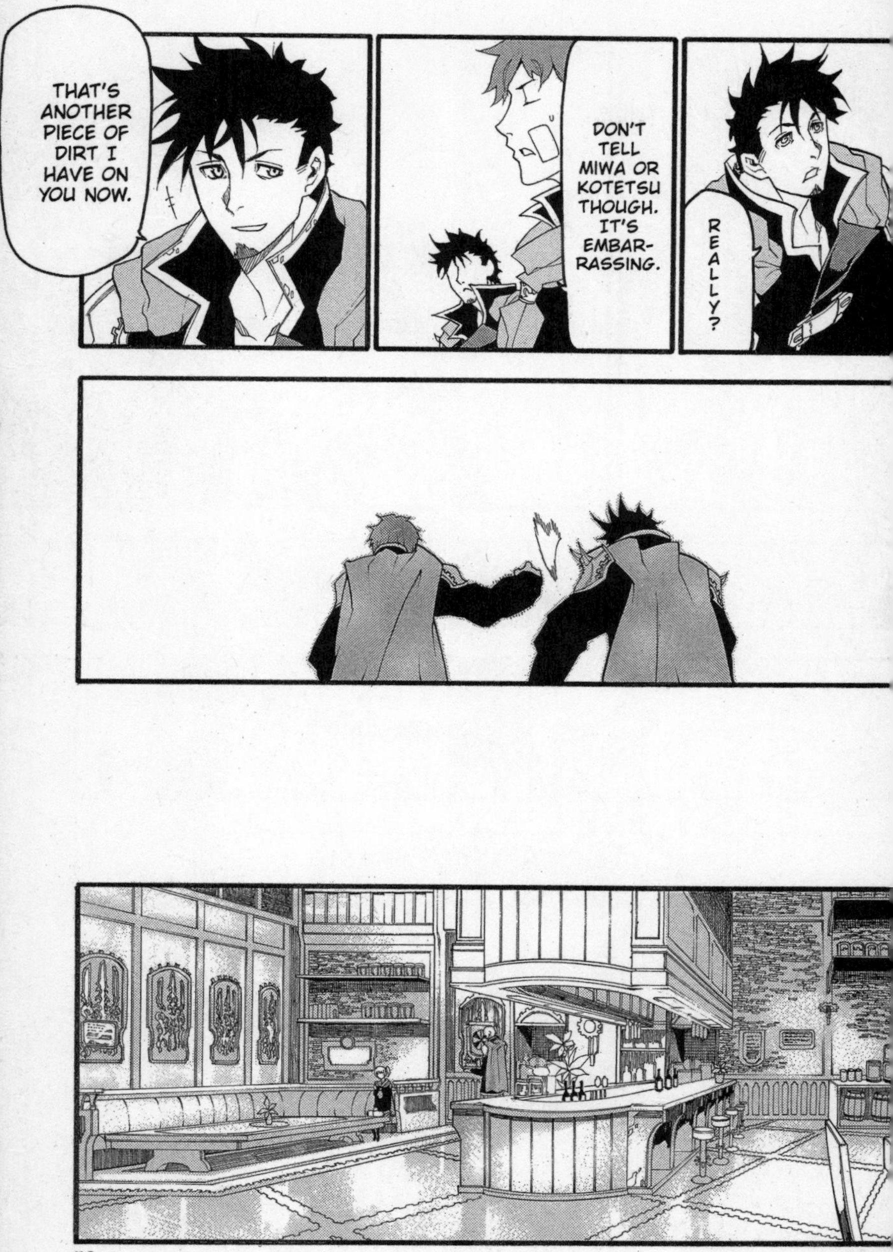
REALLY?
DON'T TELL MIWA OR KOTETSU THOUGH. IT'S EMBARRASSING.
THAT'S ANOTHER PIECE OF DIRT I HAVE ON YOU NOW.

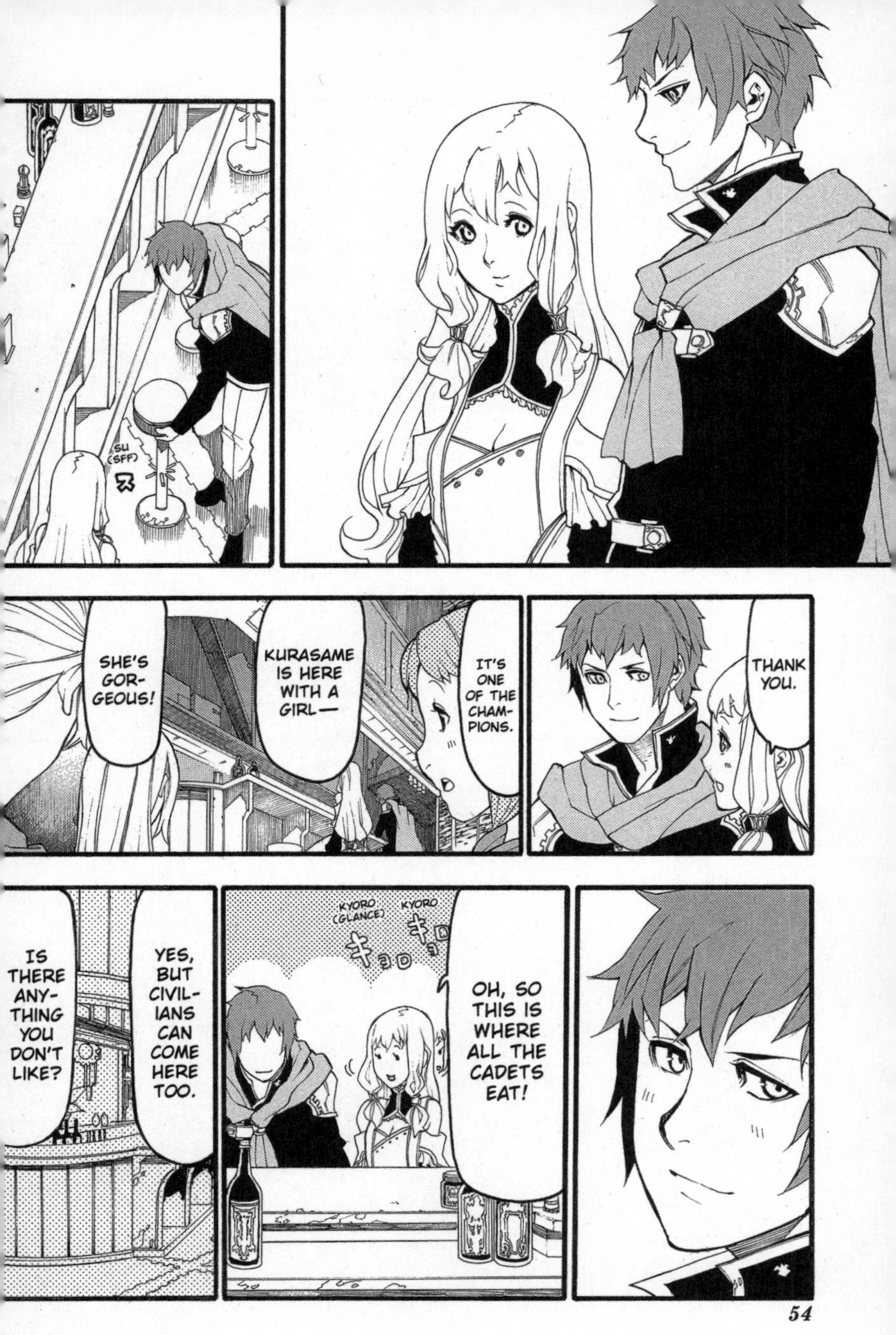
SU (SFF)
THANK YOU.
IT'S ONE OF THE CHAMPIONS.
KURASAME IS HERE WITH A GIRL—
SHE'S GORGEOUS!
KYORO (GLANCE) KYORO
OH, SO THIS IS WHERE ALL THE CADETS EAT!
YES, BUT CIVILIANS CAN COME HERE TOO.
IS THERE ANYTHING YOU DON'T LIKE?

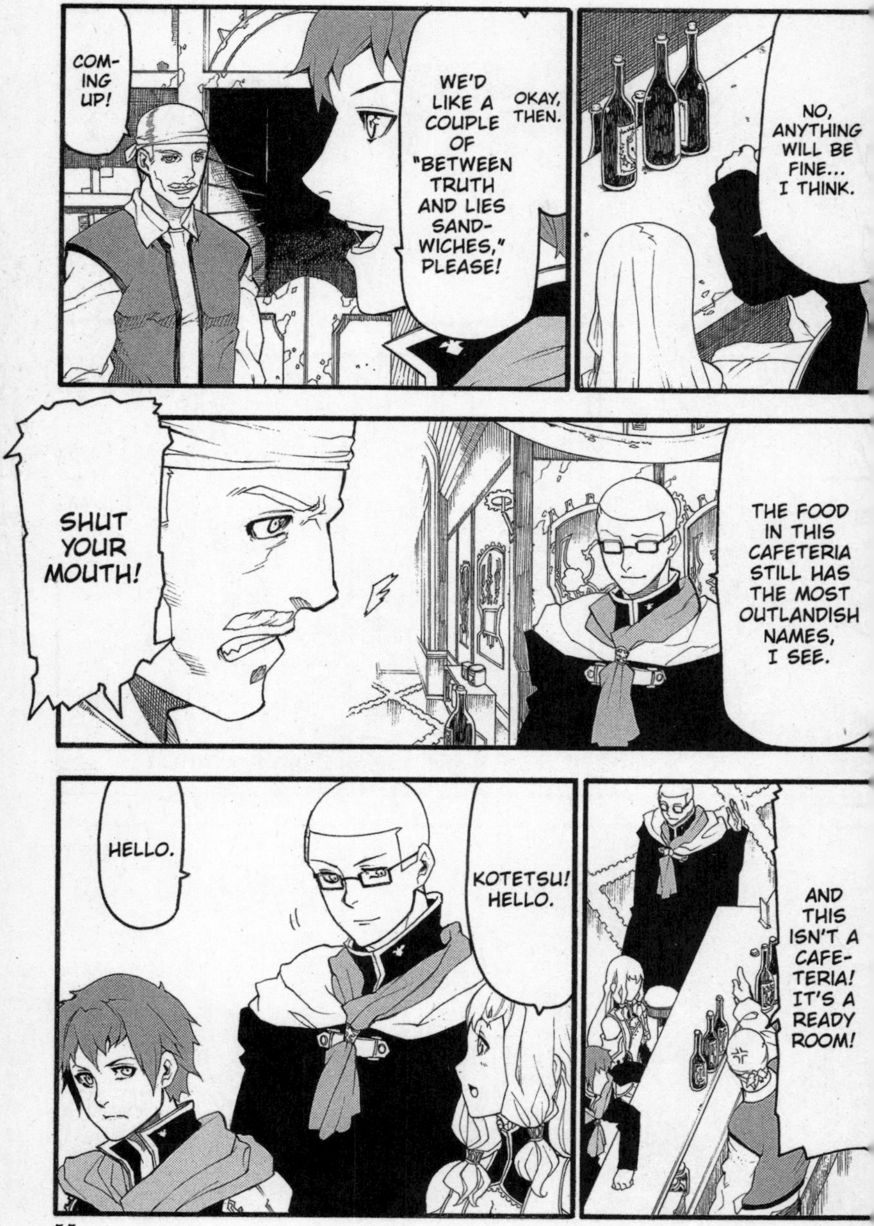
NO, ANYTHING WILL BE FINE... I THINK.
OKAY, THEN.
WE'D LIKE A COUPLE OF "BETWEEN TRUTH AND LIES SAND-WICHES," PLEASE!
COM-ING UP!
THE FOOD IN THIS CAFETERIA STILL HAS THE MOST OUTLANDISH NAMES, I SEE.
SHUT YOUR MOUTH!
AND THIS ISN'T A CAFE-TERIA! IT'S A READY ROOM!
KOTETSU! HELLO.
HELLO.

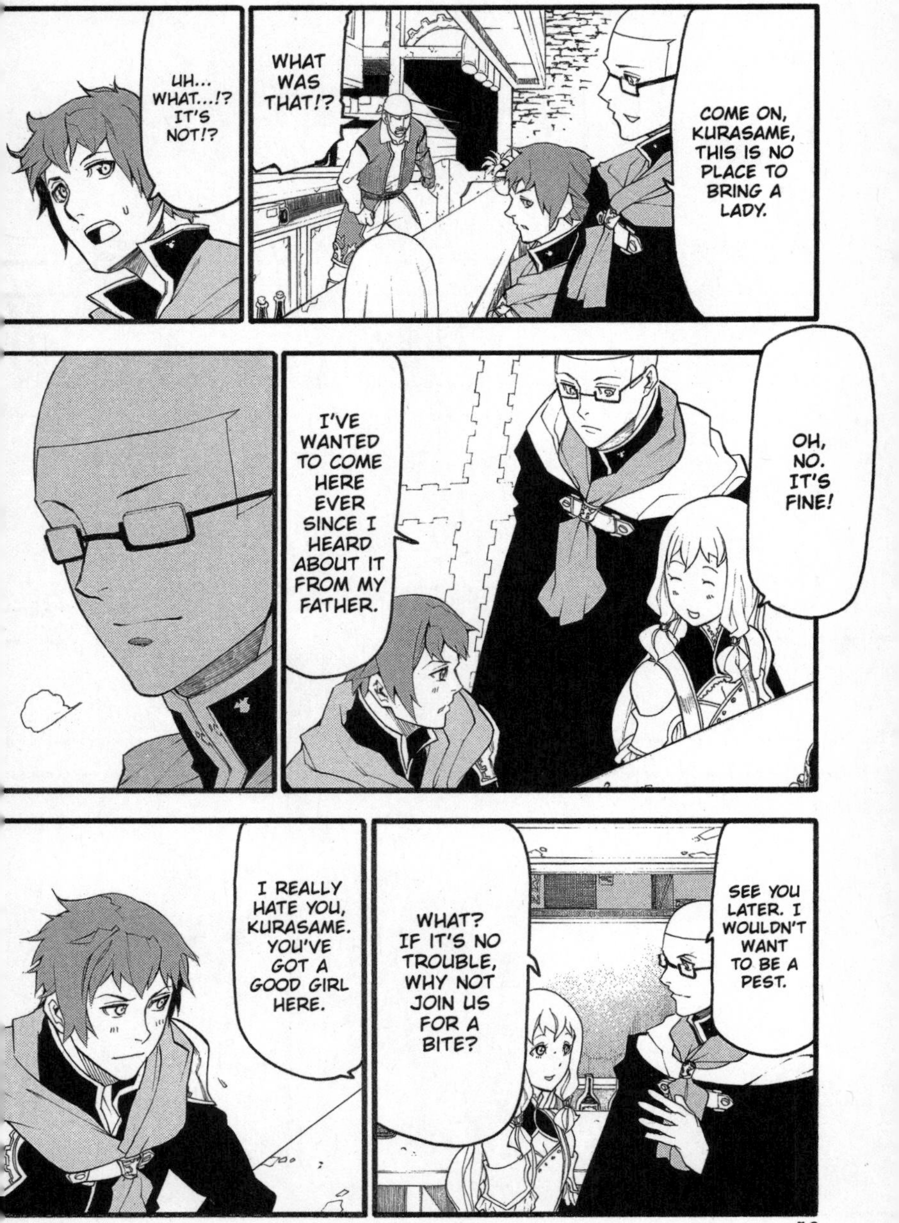
COME ON, KURASAME, THIS IS NO PLACE TO BRING A LADY.
WHAT WAS THAT!?
UH... WHAT...!? IT'S NOT!?
OH, NO. IT'S FINE!
I'VE WANTED TO COME HERE EVER SINCE I HEARD ABOUT IT FROM MY FATHER.
SEE YOU LATER. I WOULDN'T WANT TO BE A PEST.
WHAT? IF IT'S NO TROUBLE, WHY NOT JOIN US FOR A BITE?
I REALLY HATE YOU, KURASAME. YOU'VE GOT A GOOD GIRL HERE.

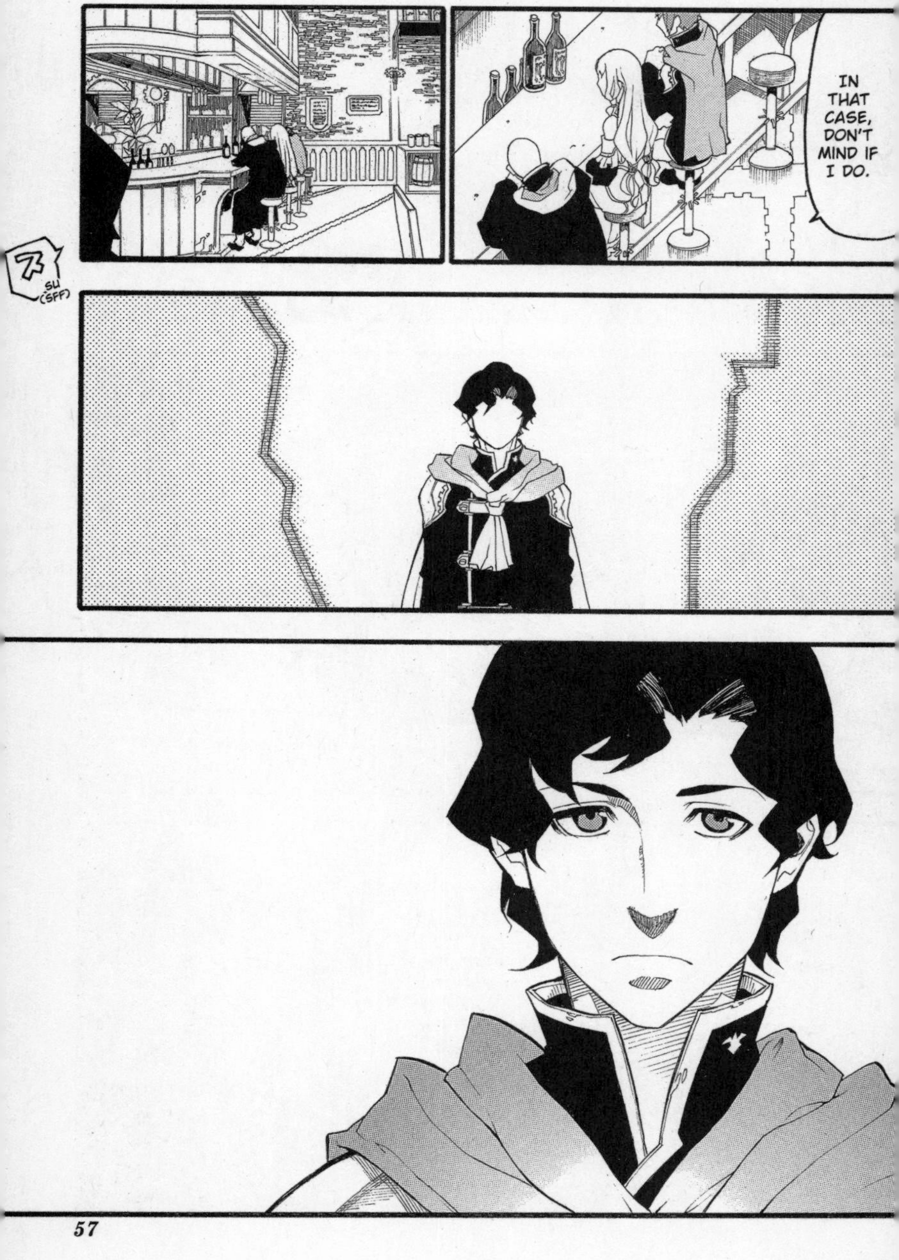
IN THAT CASE, DON'T MIND IF I DO.
SU (SFF)

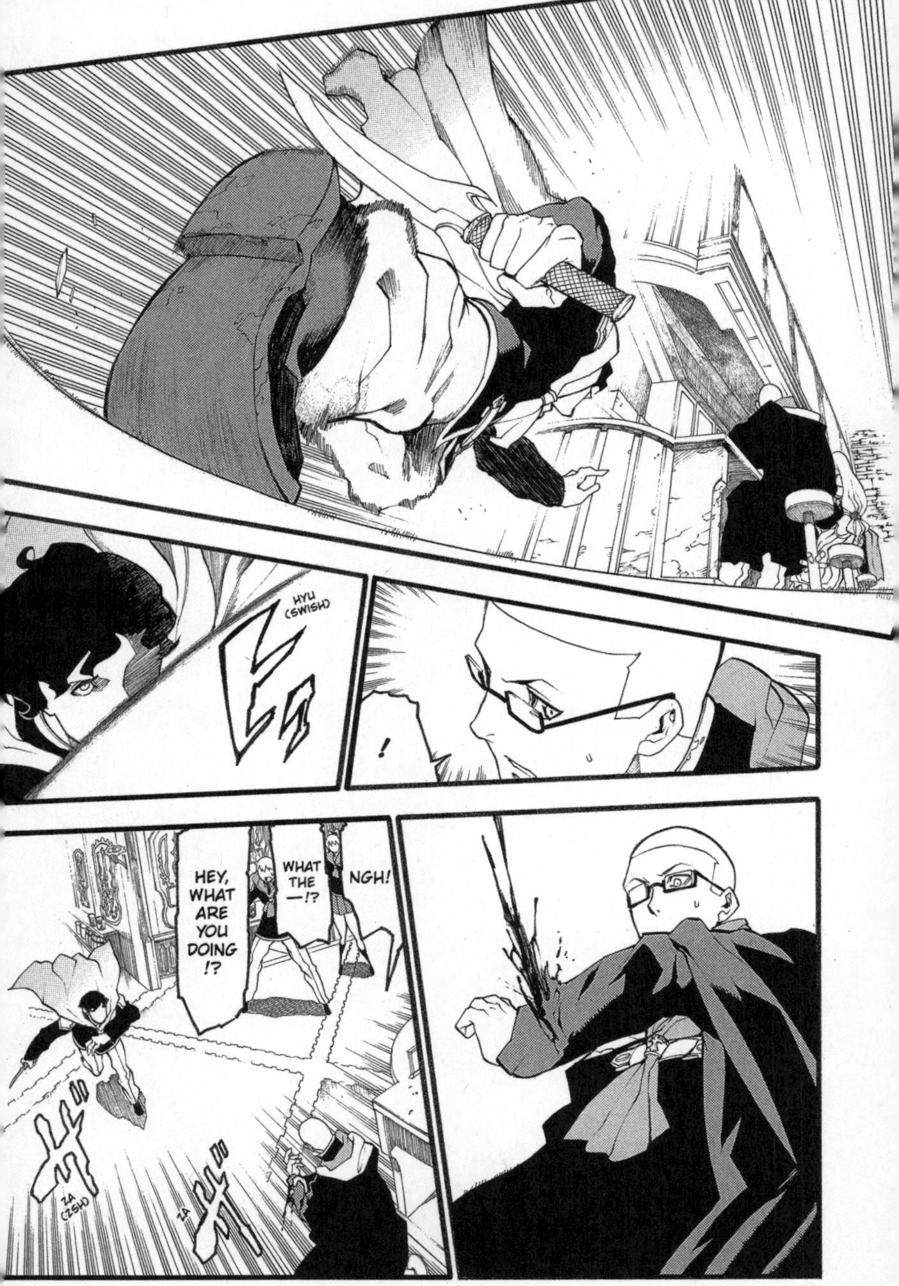

!
HYU (SWISH)
NGH!
WHAT THE—!?
HEY, WHAT ARE YOU DOING!?
ZA (ZSH)
ZA

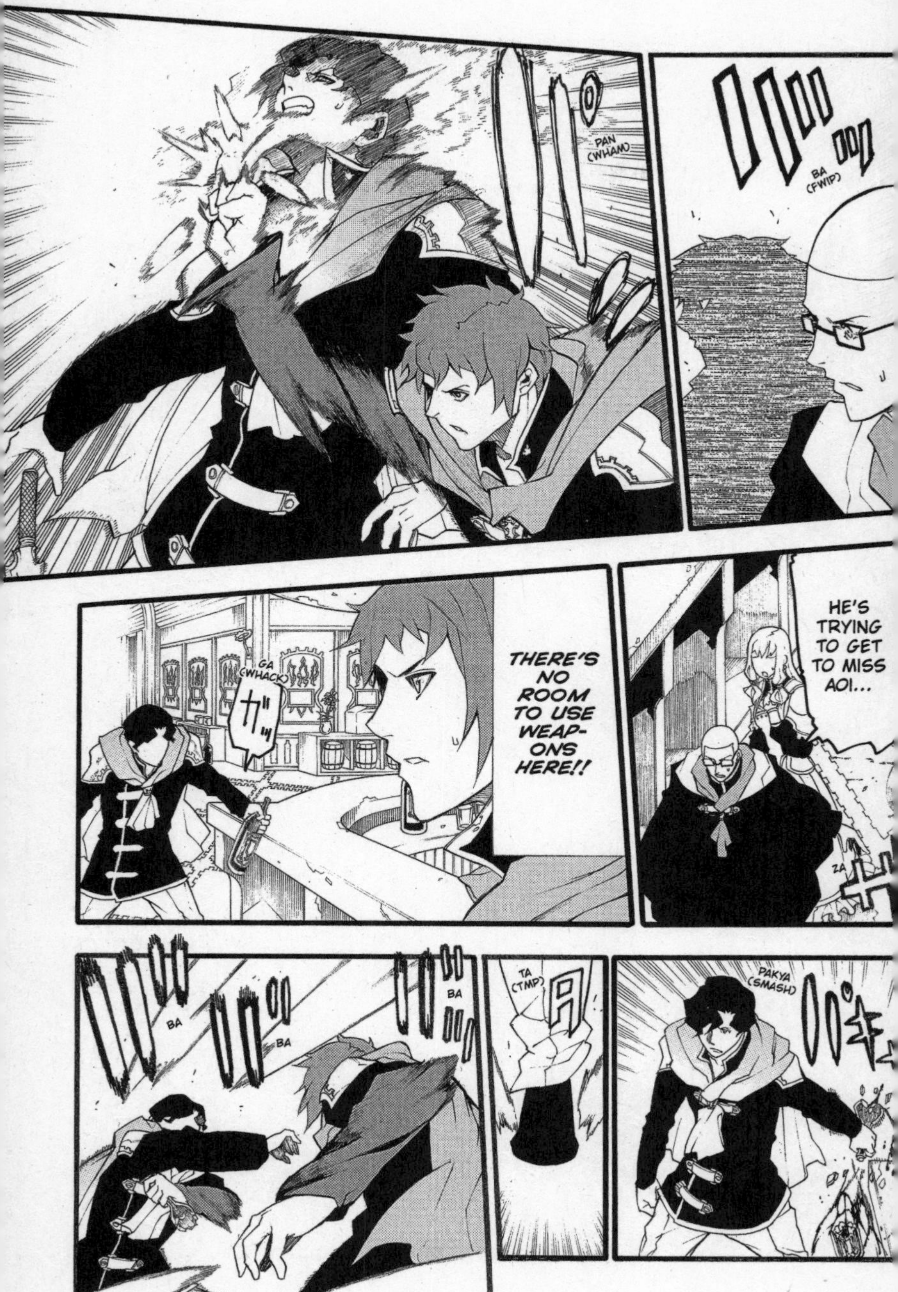
BA
(FWIP)
PAN
(WHAM)
HE'S TRYING TO GET TO MISS AOI...
ZA
THERE'S NO ROOM TO USE WEAP-ONS HERE!!
GA
(WHACK)
ガッ
PAKYA
(SMASH)
TA
(TMP)
BA
BA
BA

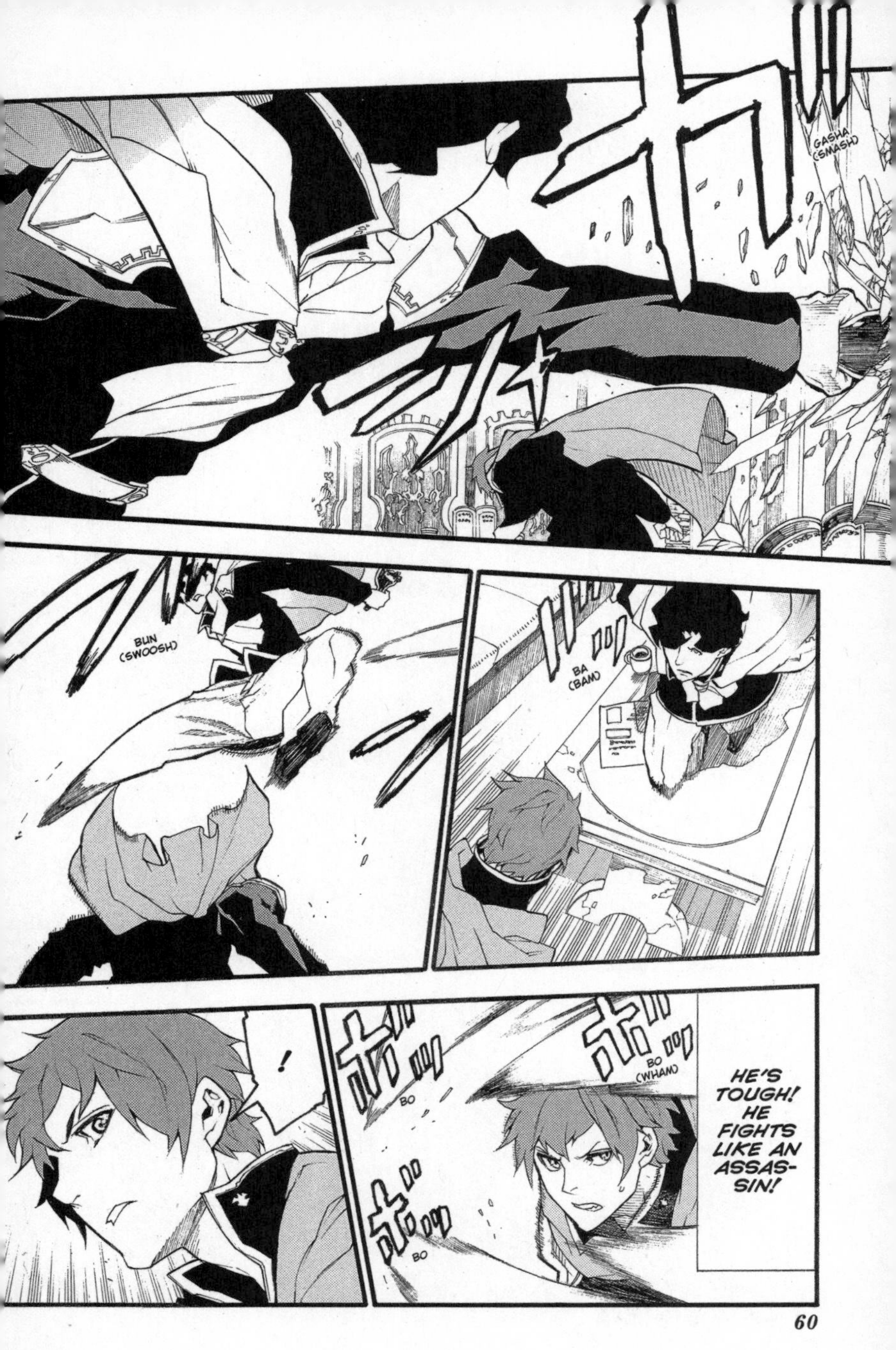
GASHA (SMASH)
BA (BAM)
BUN (SWOOSH)
HE'S TOUGH! HE FIGHTS LIKE AN ASSAS-SIN!
BO (WHAM)
BO
BO
!

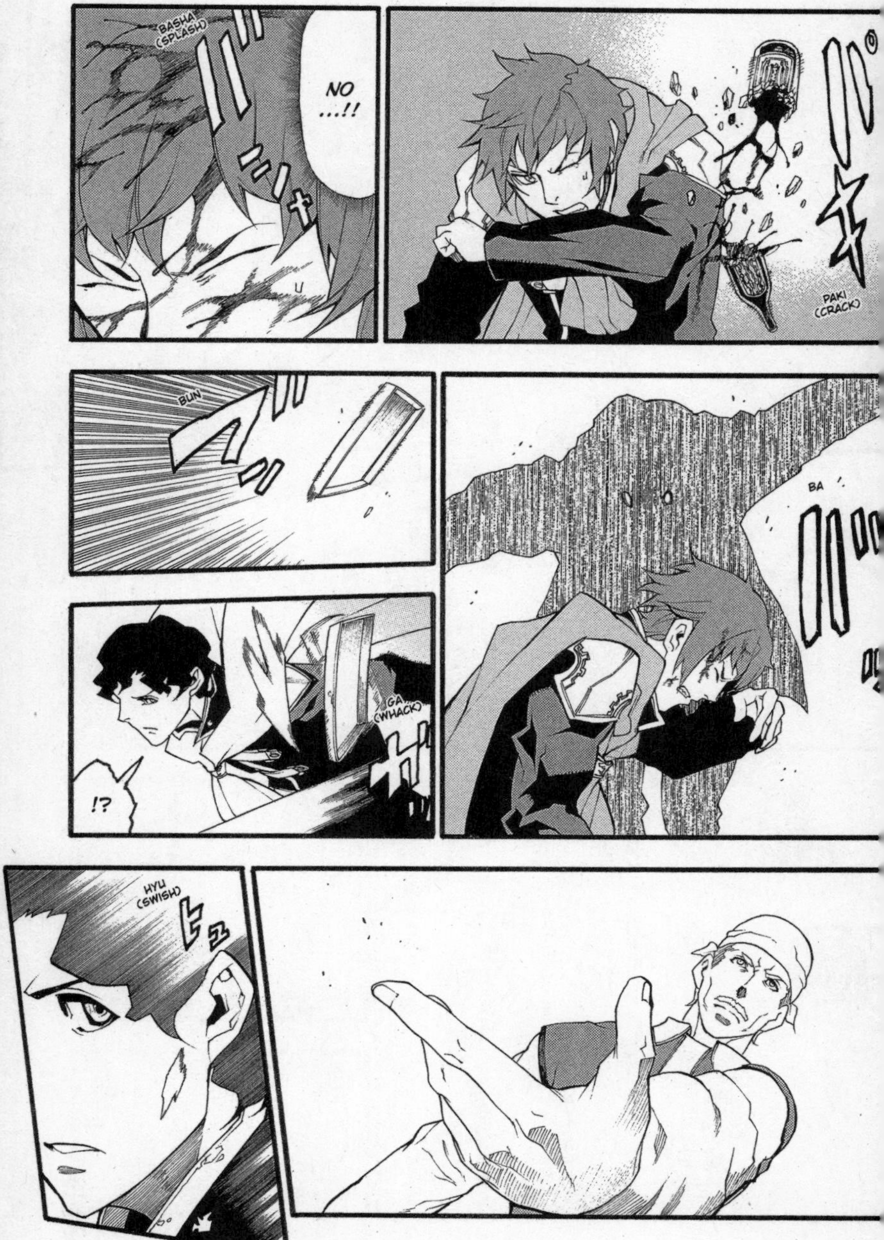
PAKI
(CRACK)
BASHA
(SPLASH)
NO ...!!
BA
BUN
GA
(WHACK)
!?
HYU
(SWISH)

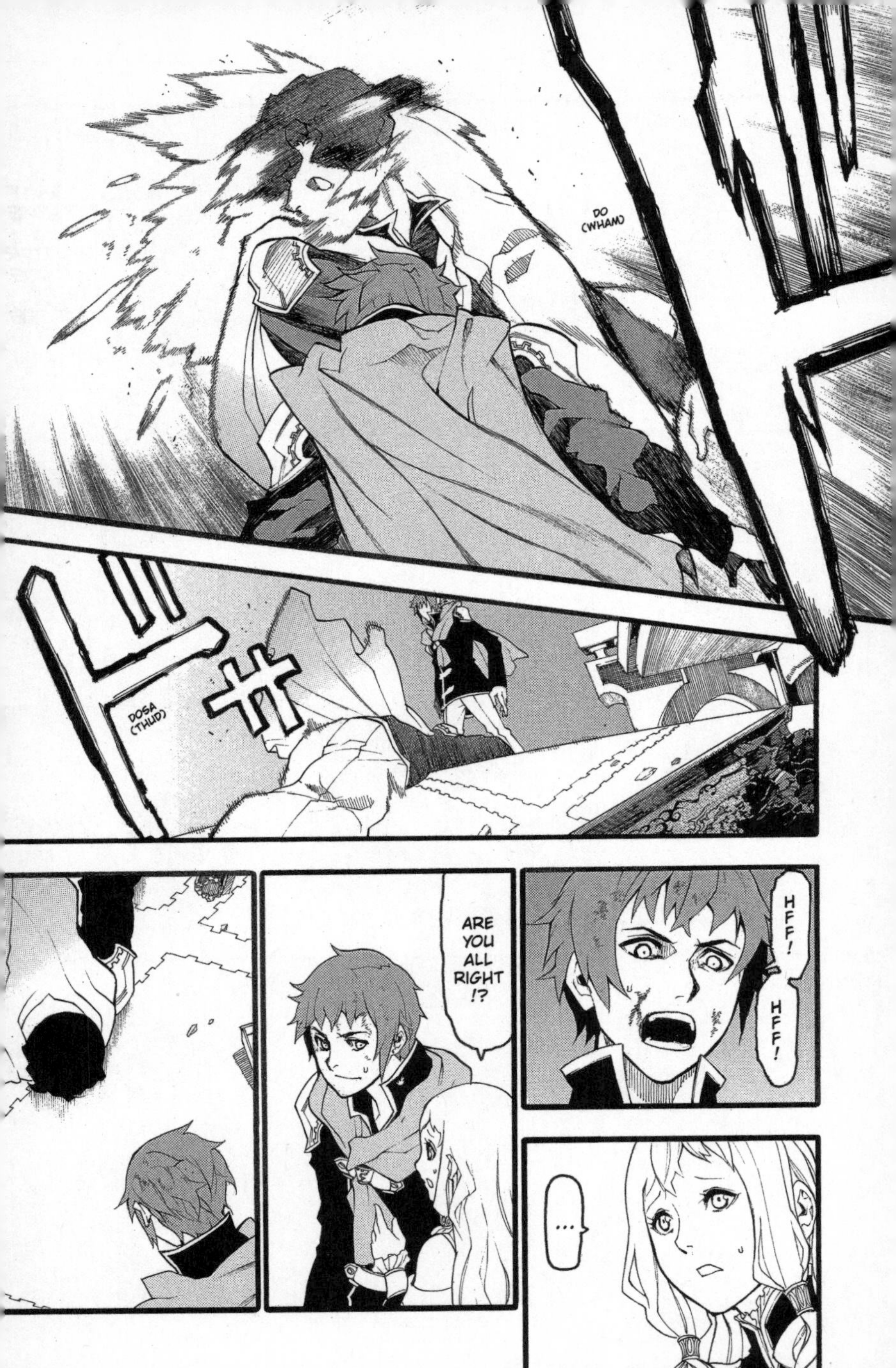
DO (WHAM)
DOSA (THUD)
HFF! HFF!
...
ARE YOU ALL RIGHT!?

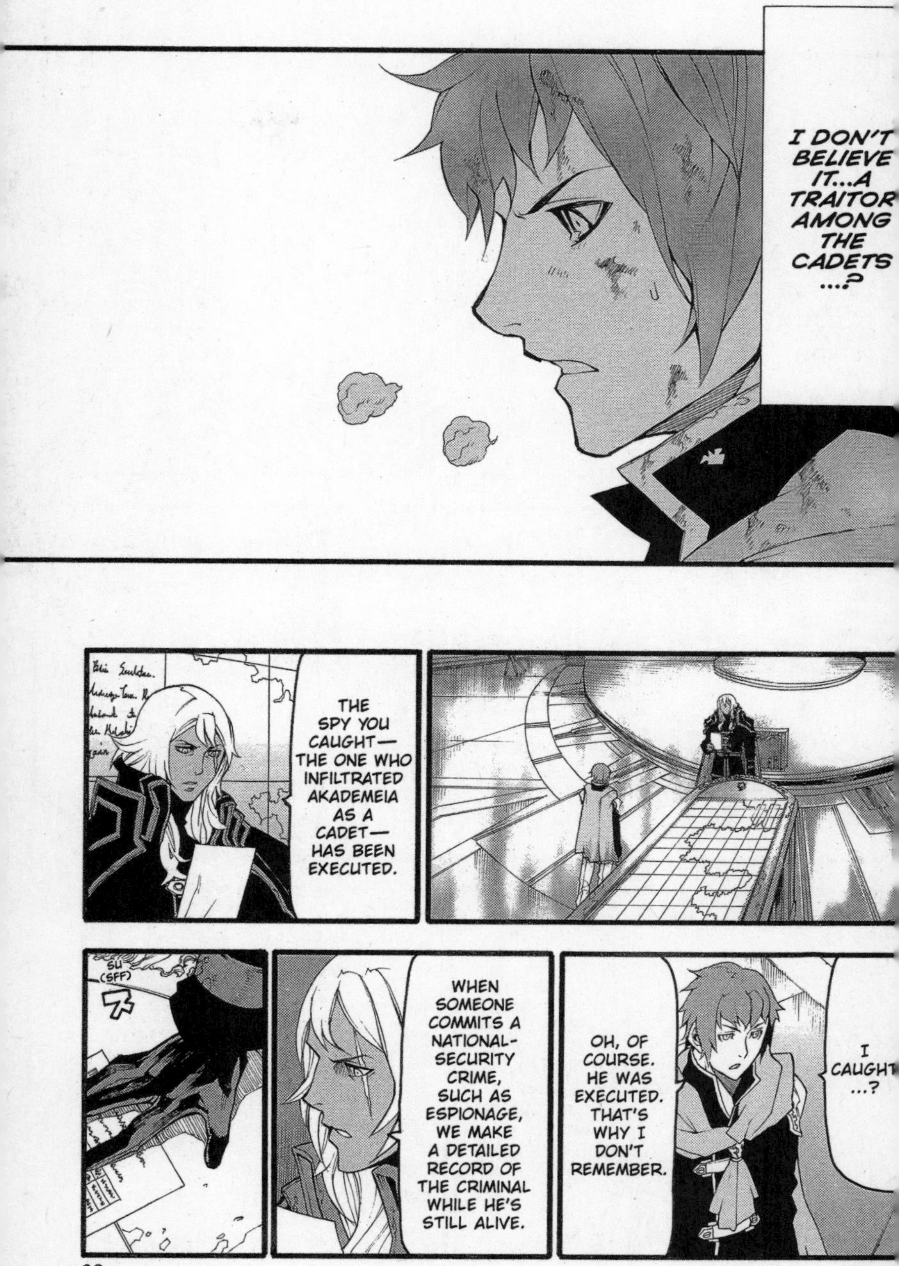
I DON'T BELIEVE IT...A TRAITOR AMONG THE CADETS ...?
THE SPY YOU CAUGHT— THE ONE WHO INFILTRATED AKADEMEIA AS A CADET— HAS BEEN EXECUTED.
I CAUGHT ...?
OH, OF COURSE. HE WAS EXECUTED. THAT'S WHY I DON'T REMEMBER.
WHEN SOMEONE COMMITS A NATIONAL-SECURITY CRIME, SUCH AS ESPIONAGE, WE MAKE A DETAILED RECORD OF THE CRIMINAL WHILE HE'S STILL ALIVE.
SU (SFF)

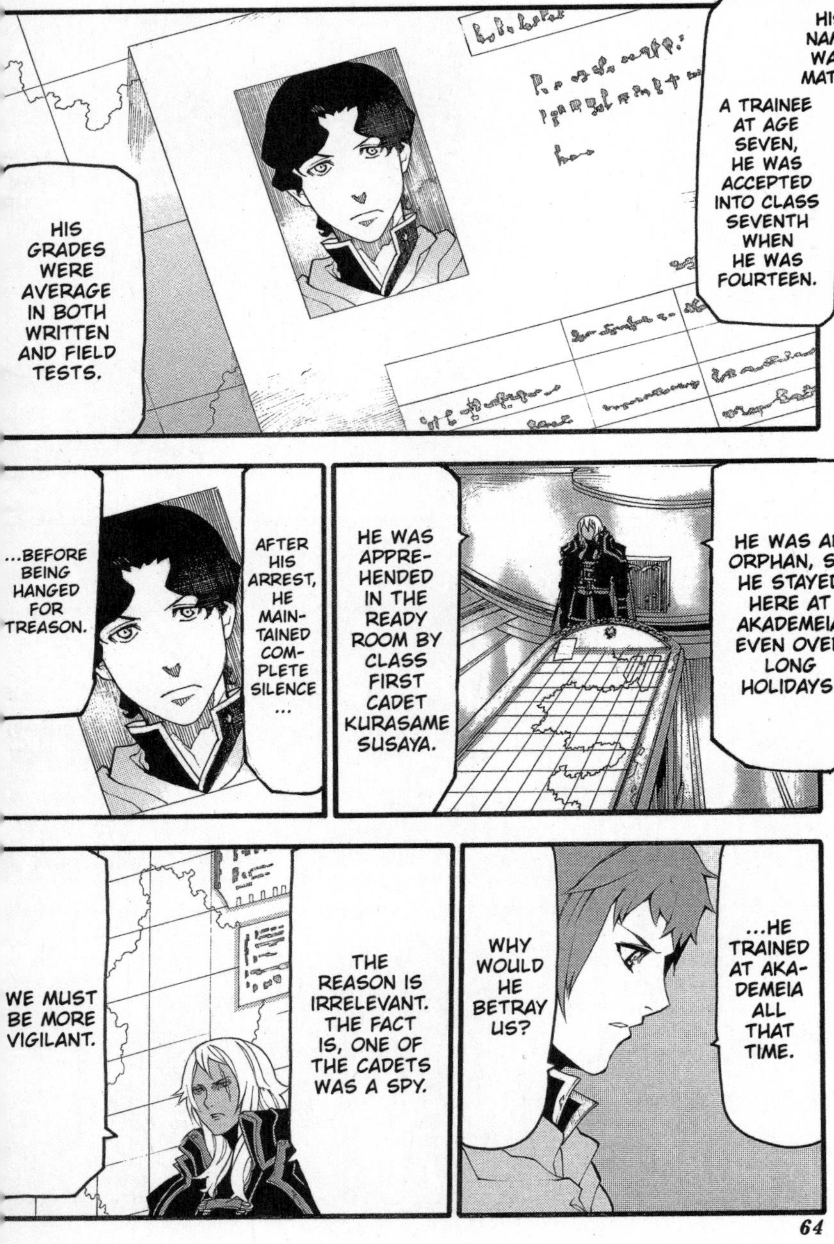
HIS NAME WAS MATIN.
A TRAINEE AT AGE SEVEN, HE WAS ACCEPTED INTO CLASS SEVENTH WHEN HE WAS FOURTEEN.
HIS GRADES WERE AVERAGE IN BOTH WRITTEN AND FIELD TESTS.
HE WAS AN ORPHAN, SO HE STAYED HERE AT AKADEMEIA EVEN OVER LONG HOLIDAYS.
HE WAS APPREHENDED IN THE READY ROOM BY CLASS FIRST CADET KURASAME SUSAYA.
AFTER HIS ARREST, HE MAINTAINED COMPLETE SILENCE...
...BEFORE BEING HANGED FOR TREASON.
...HE TRAINED AT AKADEMEIA ALL THAT TIME.
WHY WOULD HE BETRAY US?
THE REASON IS IRRELEVANT. THE FACT IS, ONE OF THE CADETS WAS A SPY.
WE MUST BE MORE VIGILANT.

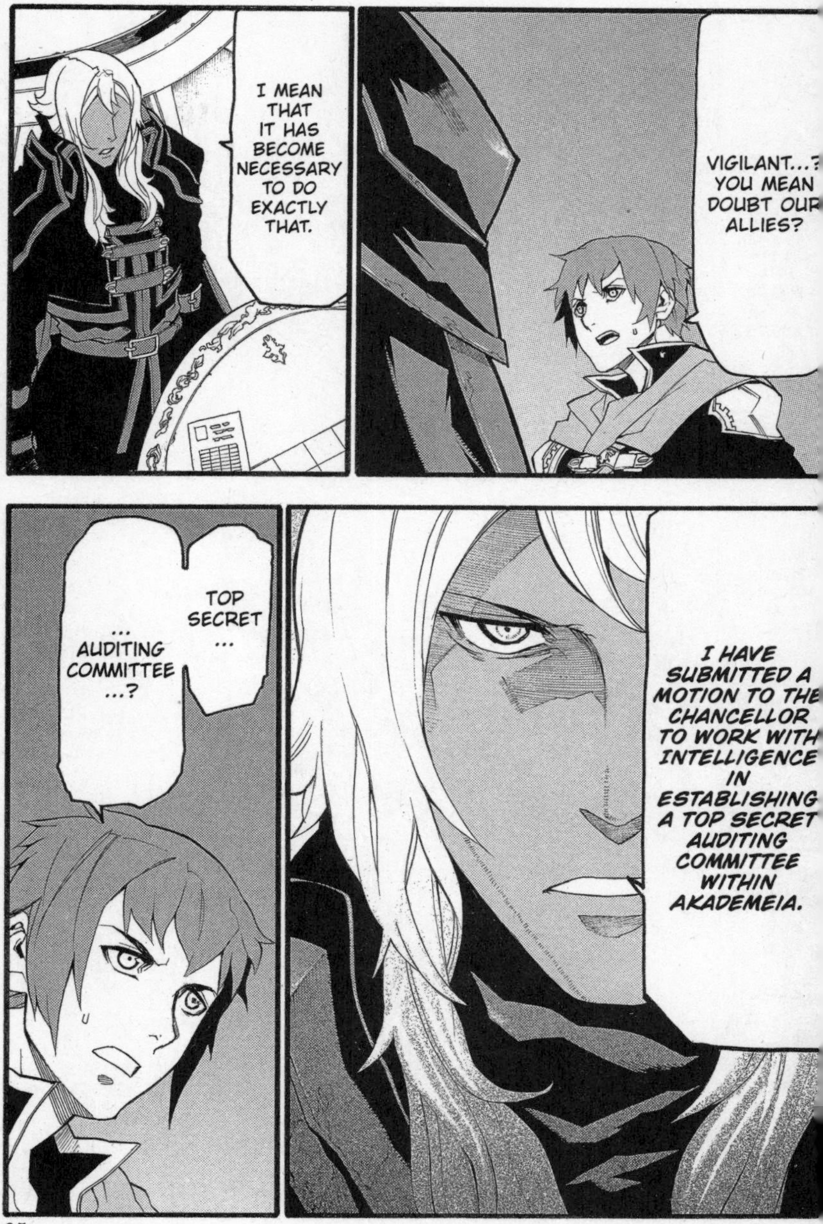
VIGILANT...? YOU MEAN DOUBT OUR ALLIES?
I MEAN THAT IT HAS BECOME NECESSARY TO DO EXACTLY THAT.
I HAVE SUBMITTED A MOTION TO THE CHANCELLOR TO WORK WITH INTELLIGENCE IN ESTABLISHING A TOP SECRET AUDITING COMMITTEE WITHIN AKADEMEIA.
TOP SECRET ...
... AUDITING COMMITTEE ...?

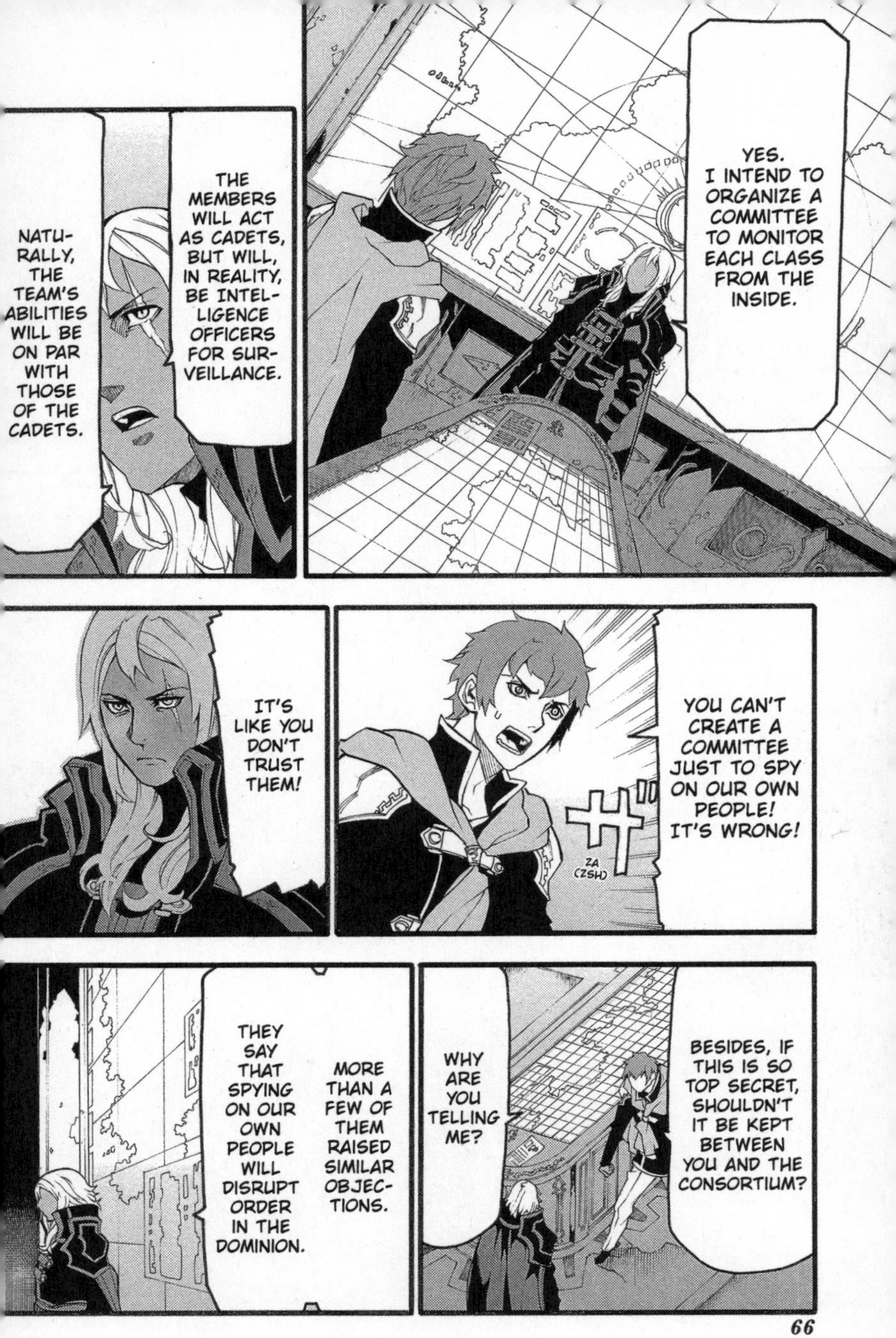
YES. I INTEND TO ORGANIZE A COMMITTEE TO MONITOR EACH CLASS FROM THE INSIDE.
THE MEMBERS WILL ACT AS CADETS, BUT WILL, IN REALITY, BE INTELLIGENCE OFFICERS FOR SURVEILLANCE.
NATURALLY, THE TEAM'S ABILITIES WILL BE ON PAR WITH THOSE OF THE CADETS.
YOU CAN'T CREATE A COMMITTEE JUST TO SPY ON OUR OWN PEOPLE! IT'S WRONG!
ZA (ZSH)
IT'S LIKE YOU DON'T TRUST THEM!
BESIDES, IF THIS IS SO TOP SECRET, SHOULDN'T IT BE KEPT BETWEEN YOU AND THE CONSORTIUM?
WHY ARE YOU TELLING ME?
MORE THAN A FEW OF THEM RAISED SIMILAR OBJECTIONS.
THEY SAY THAT SPYING ON OUR OWN PEOPLE WILL DISRUPT ORDER IN THE DOMINION.

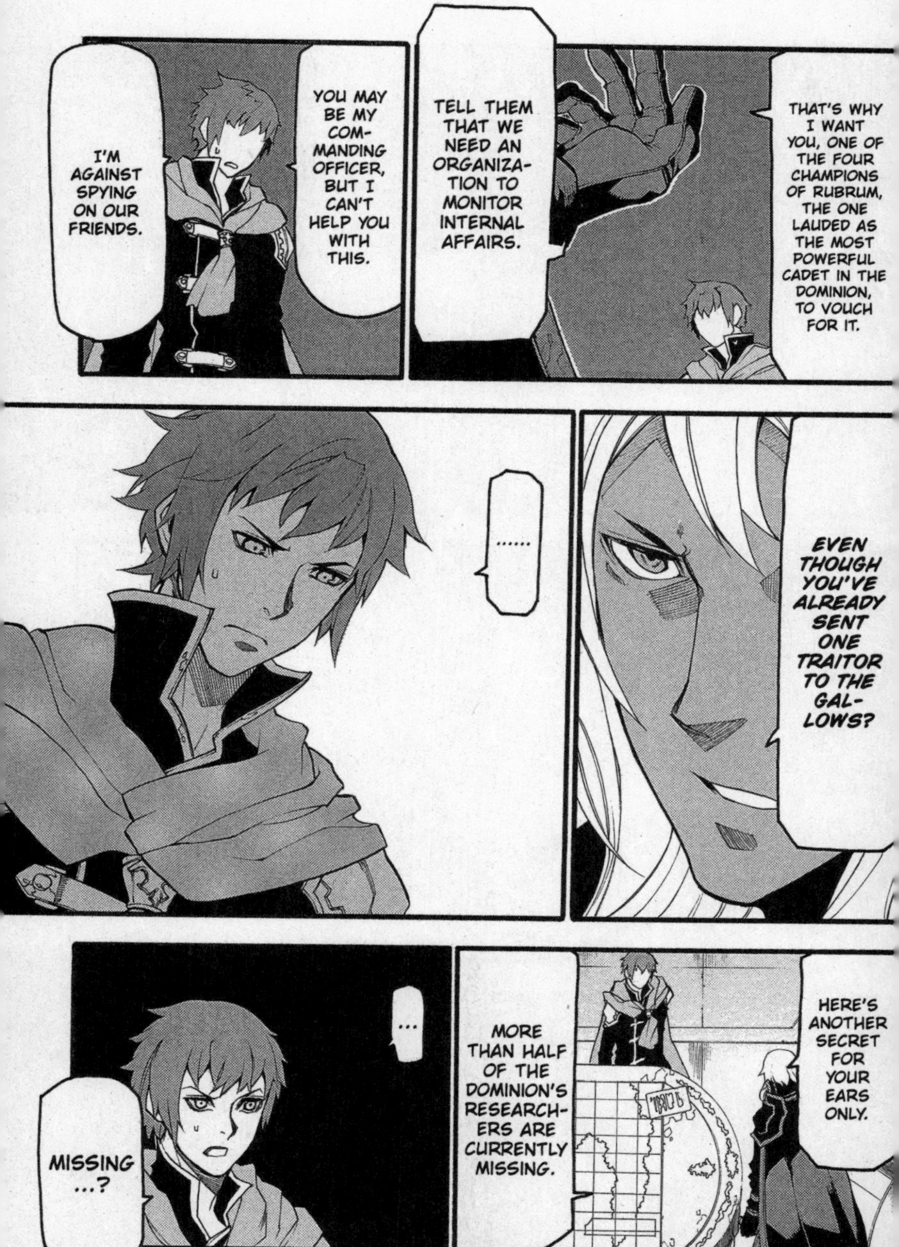
THAT'S WHY I WANT YOU, ONE OF THE FOUR CHAMPIONS OF RUBRUM, THE ONE LAUDED AS THE MOST POWERFUL CADET IN THE DOMINION, TO VOUCH FOR IT.
TELL THEM THAT WE NEED AN ORGANIZATION TO MONITOR INTERNAL AFFAIRS.
YOU MAY BE MY COMMANDING OFFICER, BUT I CAN'T HELP YOU WITH THIS.
I'M AGAINST SPYING ON OUR FRIENDS.
EVEN THOUGH YOU'VE ALREADY SENT ONE TRAITOR TO THE GALLOWS?
......
HERE'S ANOTHER SECRET FOR YOUR EARS ONLY.
MORE THAN HALF OF THE DOMINION'S RESEARCHERS ARE CURRENTLY MISSING.
...
MISSING...?

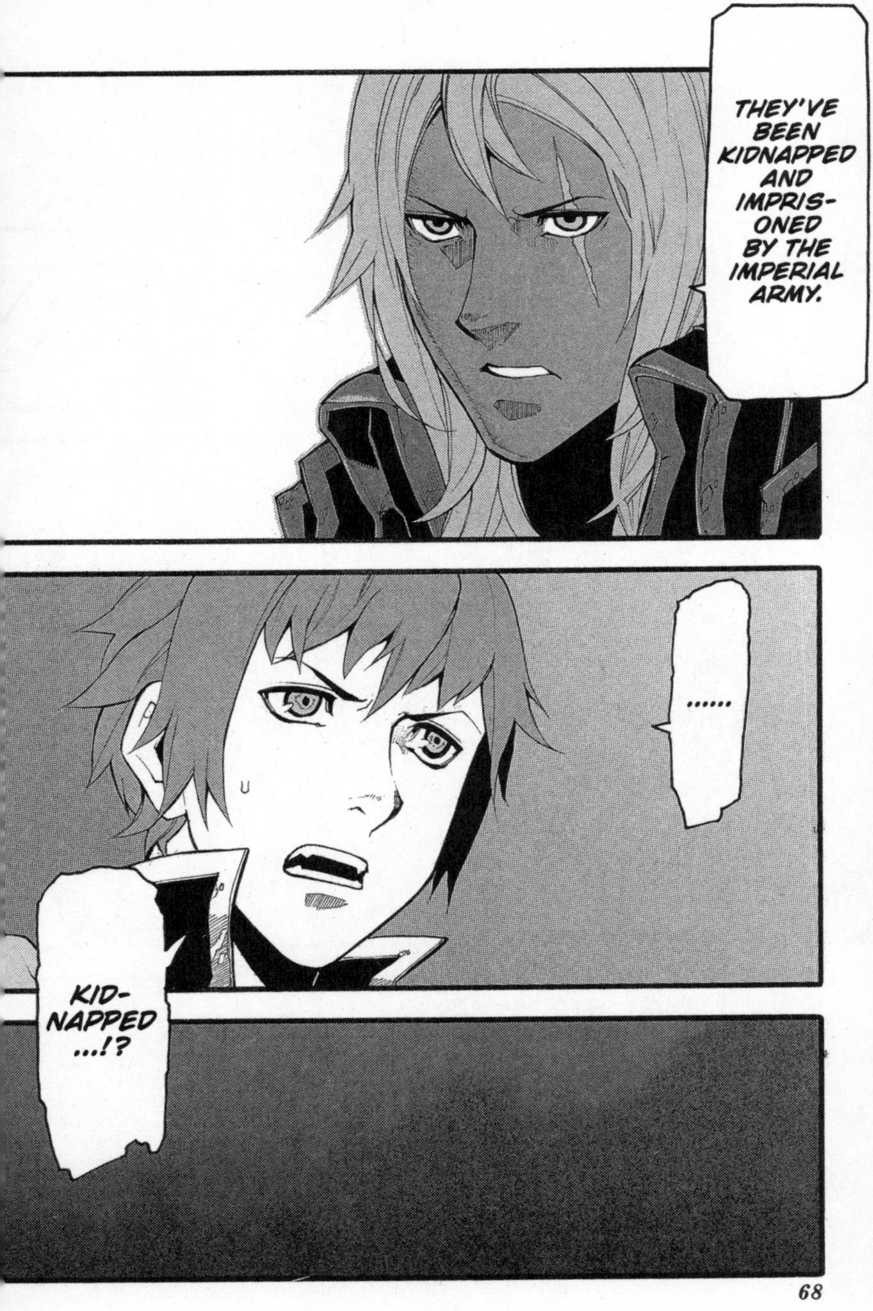
THEY'VE BEEN KIDNAPPED AND IMPRIS-ONED BY THE IMPERIAL ARMY.
......
KID-NAPPED ...!?

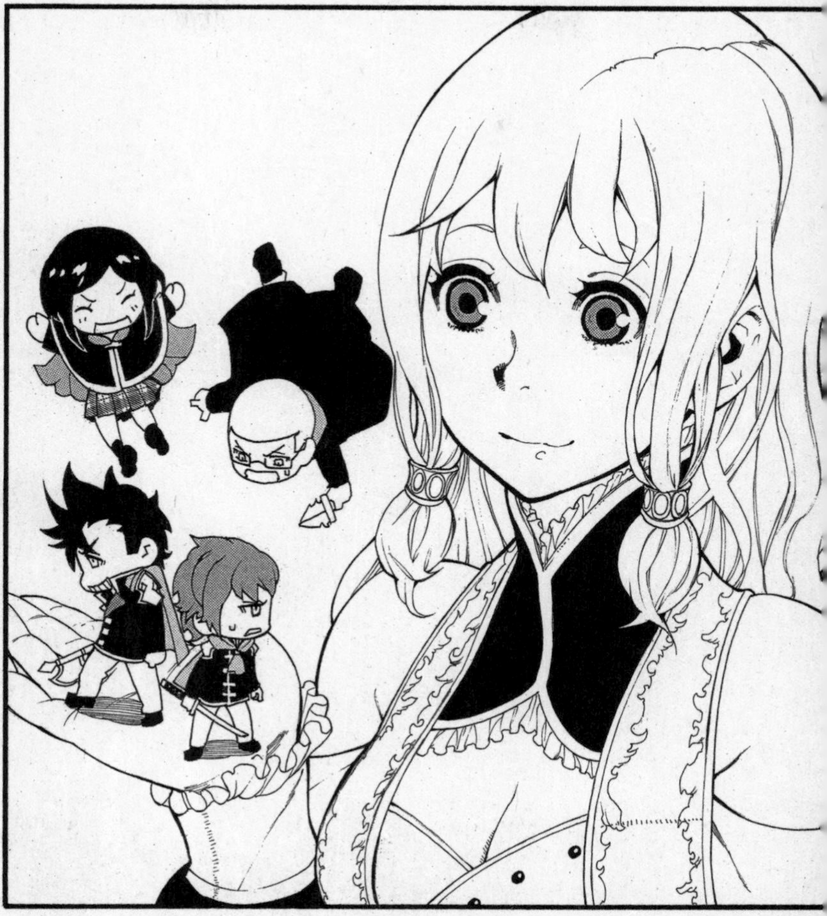

FINAL FANTASY 零式 TYPE-0™

SIDE STORY

The Ice Reaper

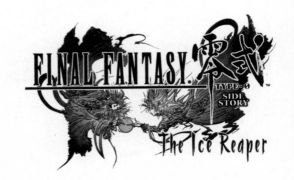

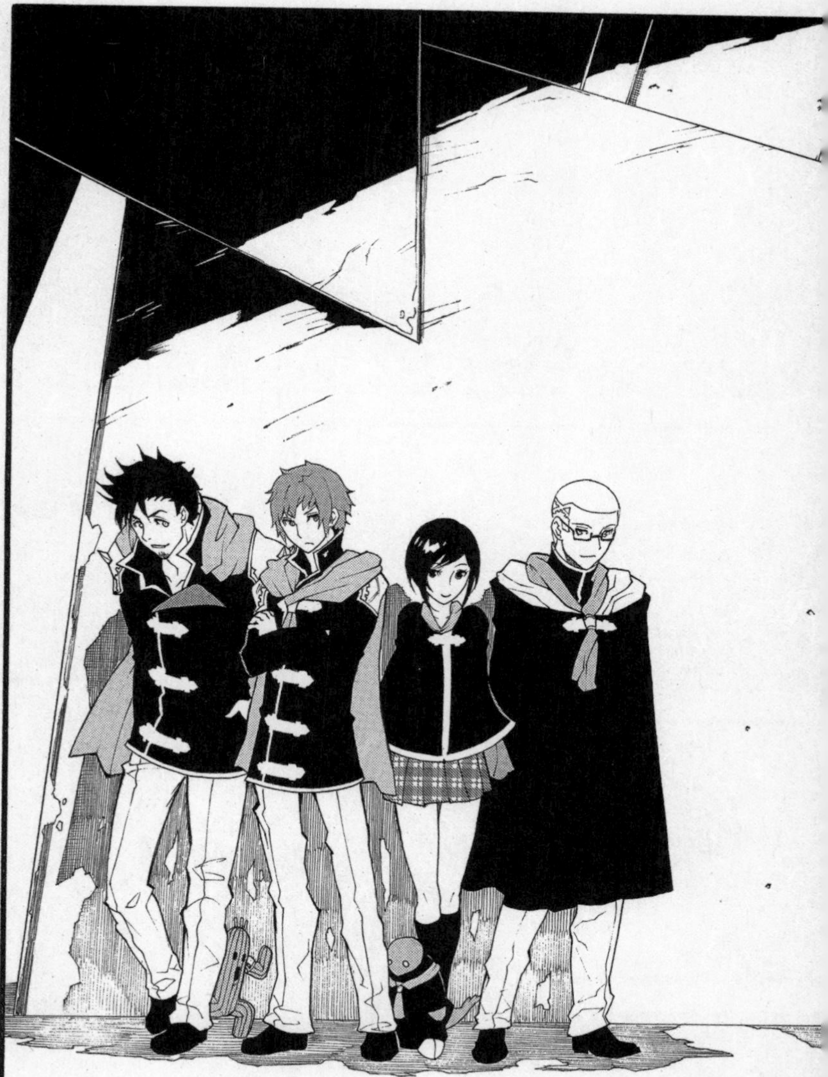

CHAPTER 11: DECISION

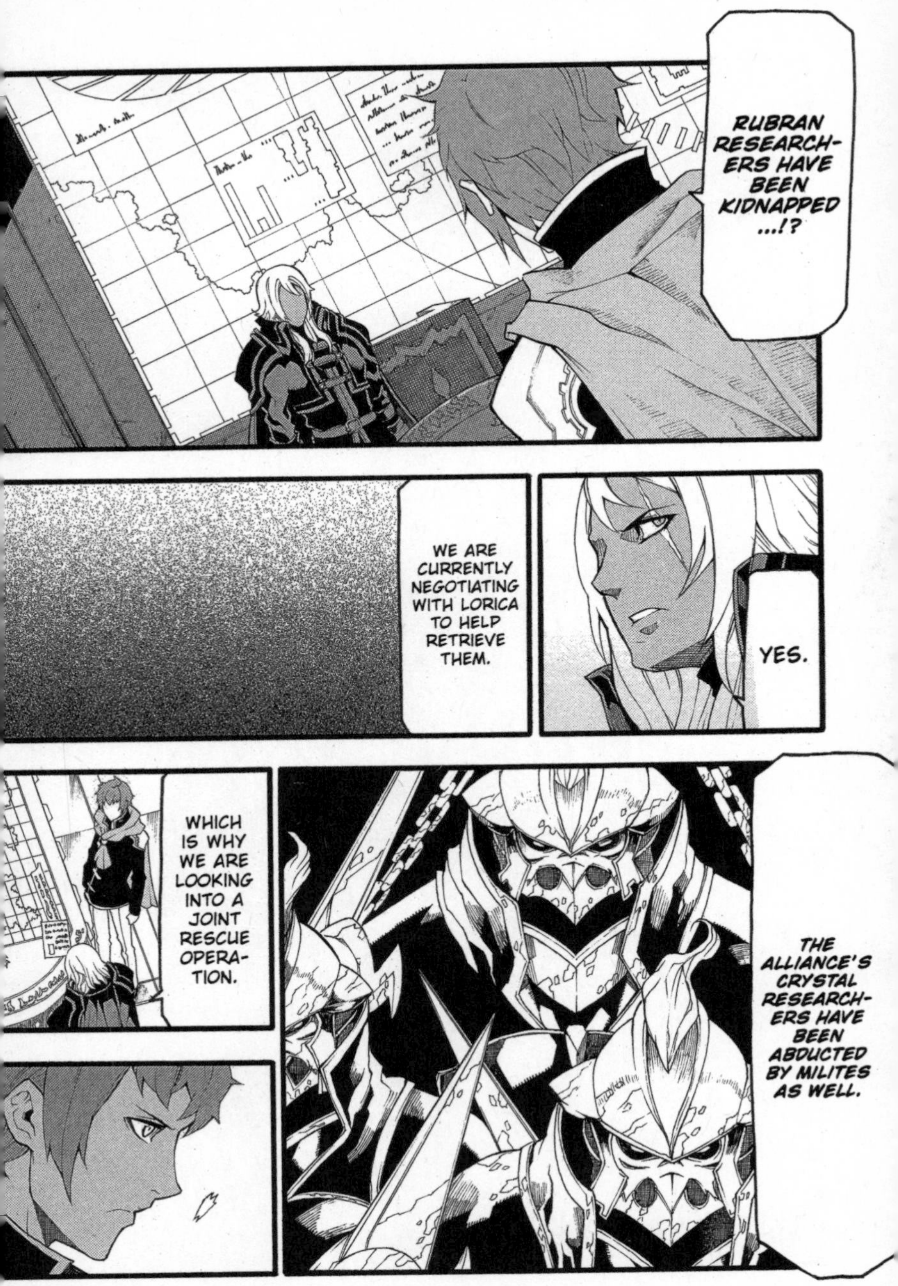
RUBRAN RESEARCHERS HAVE BEEN KIDNAPPED ...!?
YES.
WE ARE CURRENTLY NEGOTIATING WITH LORICA TO HELP RETRIEVE THEM.
THE ALLIANCE'S CRYSTAL RESEARCHERS HAVE BEEN ABDUCTED BY MILITES AS WELL.
WHICH IS WHY WE ARE LOOKING INTO A JOINT RESCUE OPERATION.

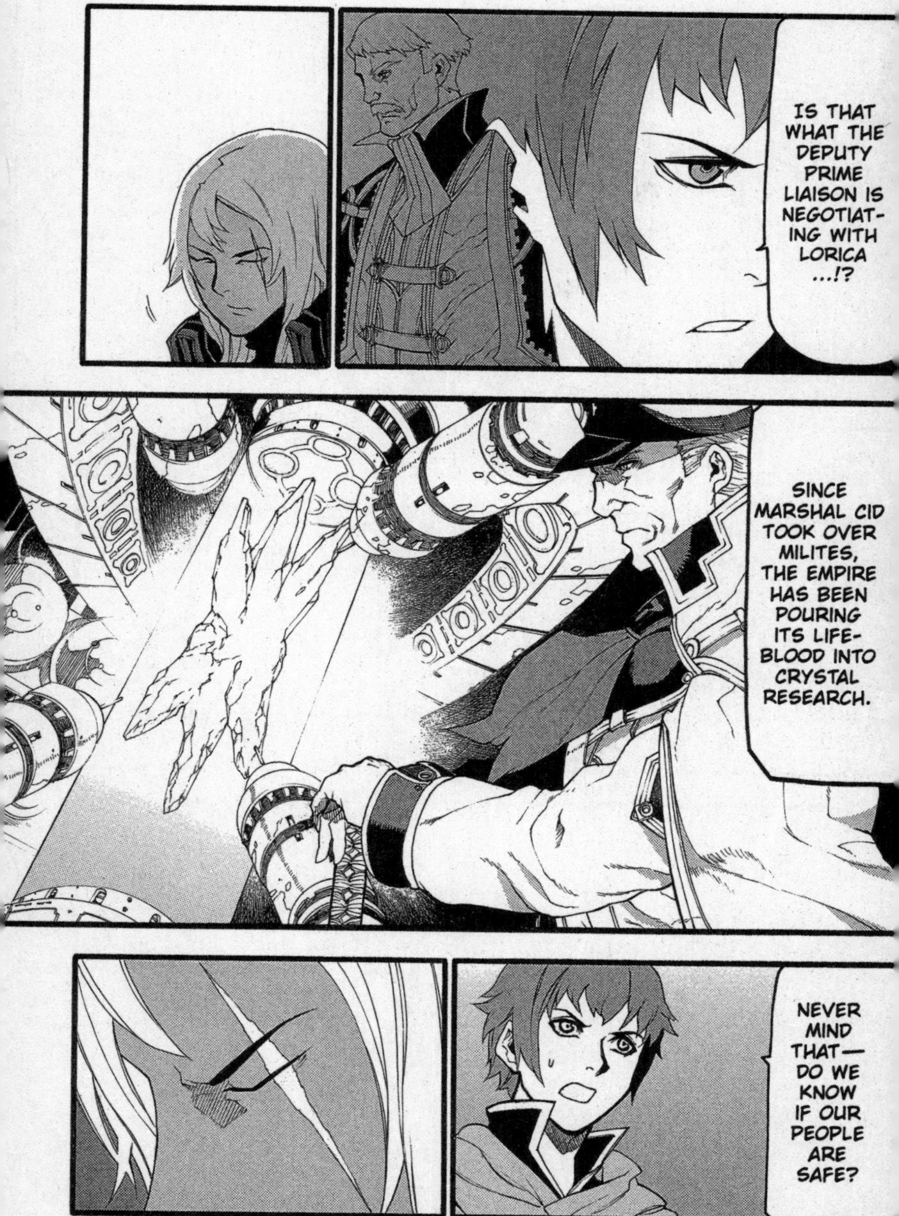
IS THAT WHAT THE DEPUTY PRIME LIAISON IS NEGOTIATING WITH LORICA ...!?
SINCE MARSHAL CID TOOK OVER MILITES, THE EMPIRE HAS BEEN POURING ITS LIFE-BLOOD INTO CRYSTAL RESEARCH.
NEVER MIND THAT—DO WE KNOW IF OUR PEOPLE ARE SAFE?

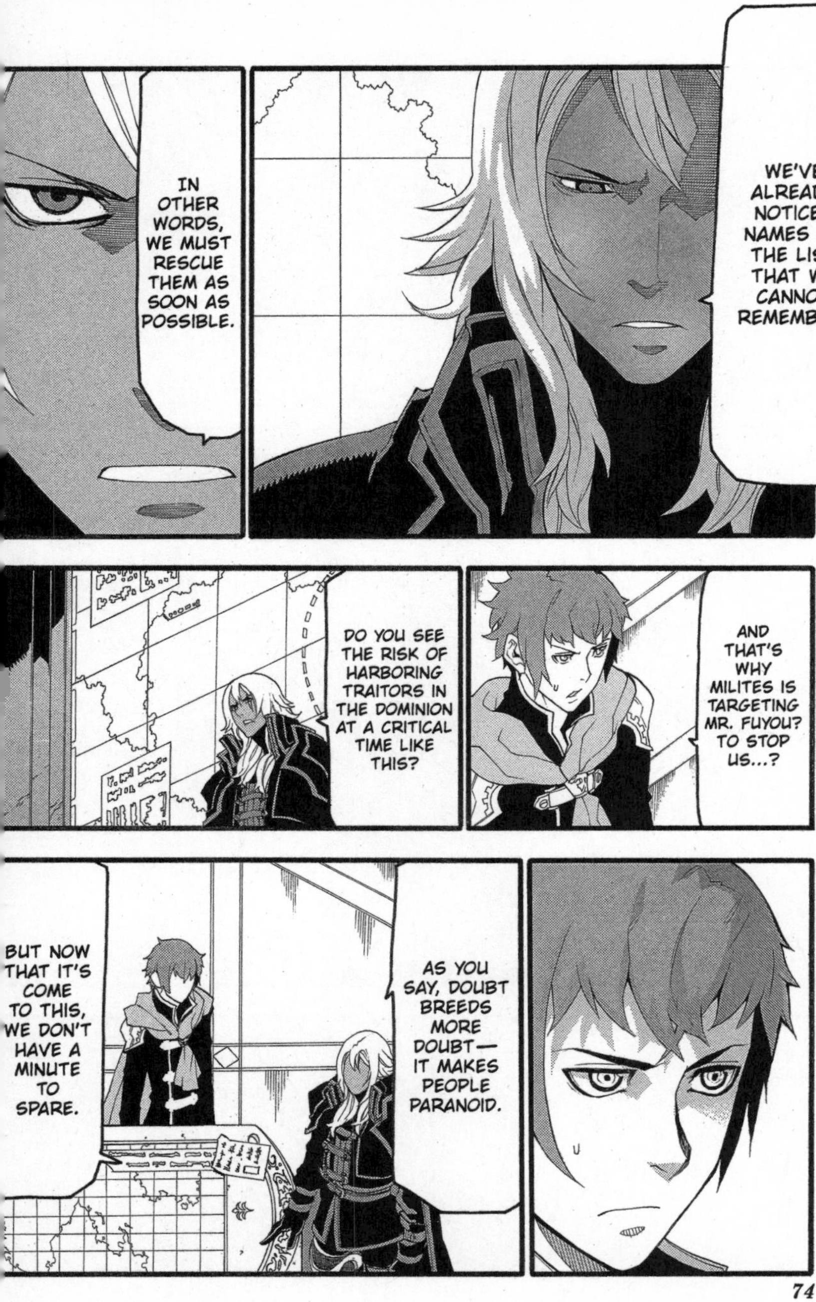
WE'VE ALREADY NOTICED NAMES ON THE LIST THAT WE CANNOT REMEMBER.
IN OTHER WORDS, WE MUST RESCUE THEM AS SOON AS POSSIBLE.
AND THAT'S WHY MILITES IS TARGETING MR. FUYOU? TO STOP US...?
DO YOU SEE THE RISK OF HARBORING TRAITORS IN THE DOMINION AT A CRITICAL TIME LIKE THIS?
AS YOU SAY, DOUBT BREEDS MORE DOUBT— IT MAKES PEOPLE PARANOID.
BUT NOW THAT IT'S COME TO THIS, WE DON'T HAVE A MINUTE TO SPARE.

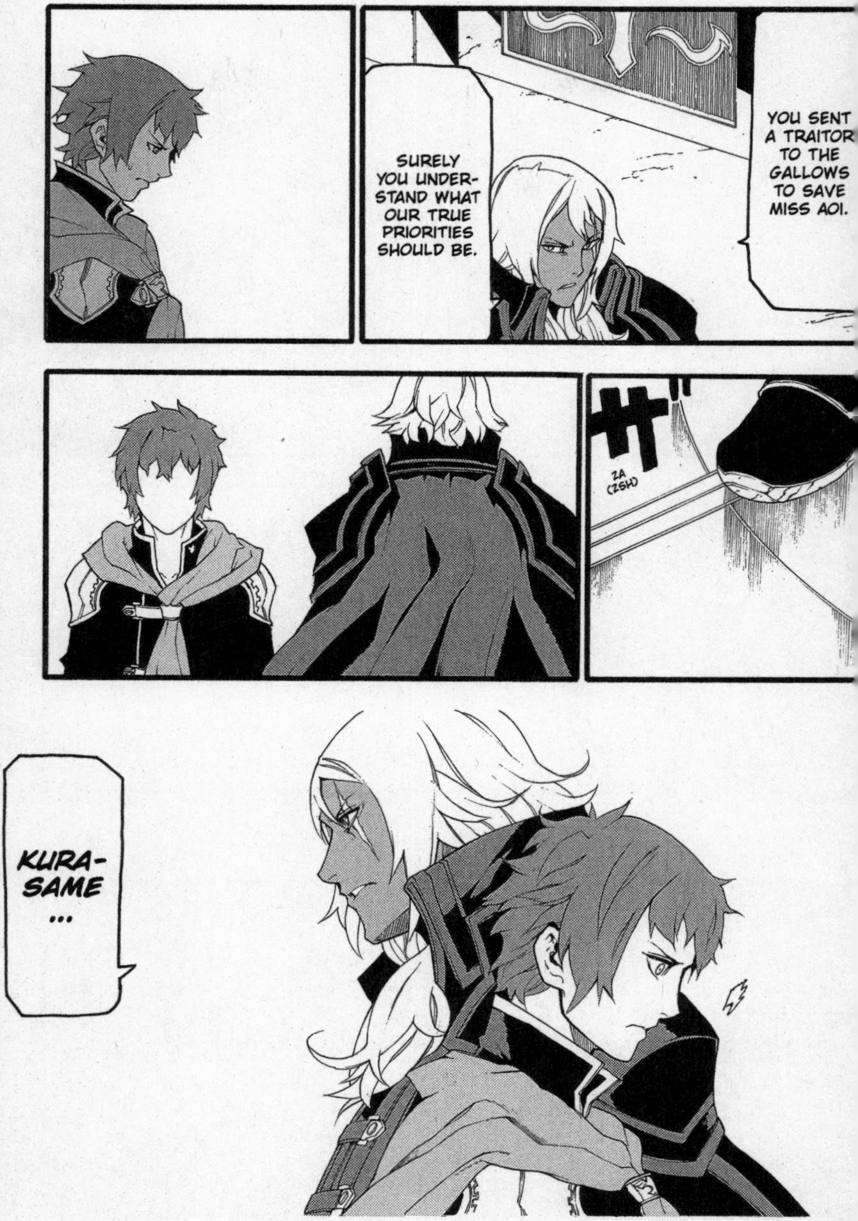
YOU SENT A TRAITOR TO THE GALLOWS TO SAVE MISS AOI.
SURELY YOU UNDERSTAND WHAT OUR TRUE PRIORITIES SHOULD BE.
ZA (ZSH)
KURA-SAME...

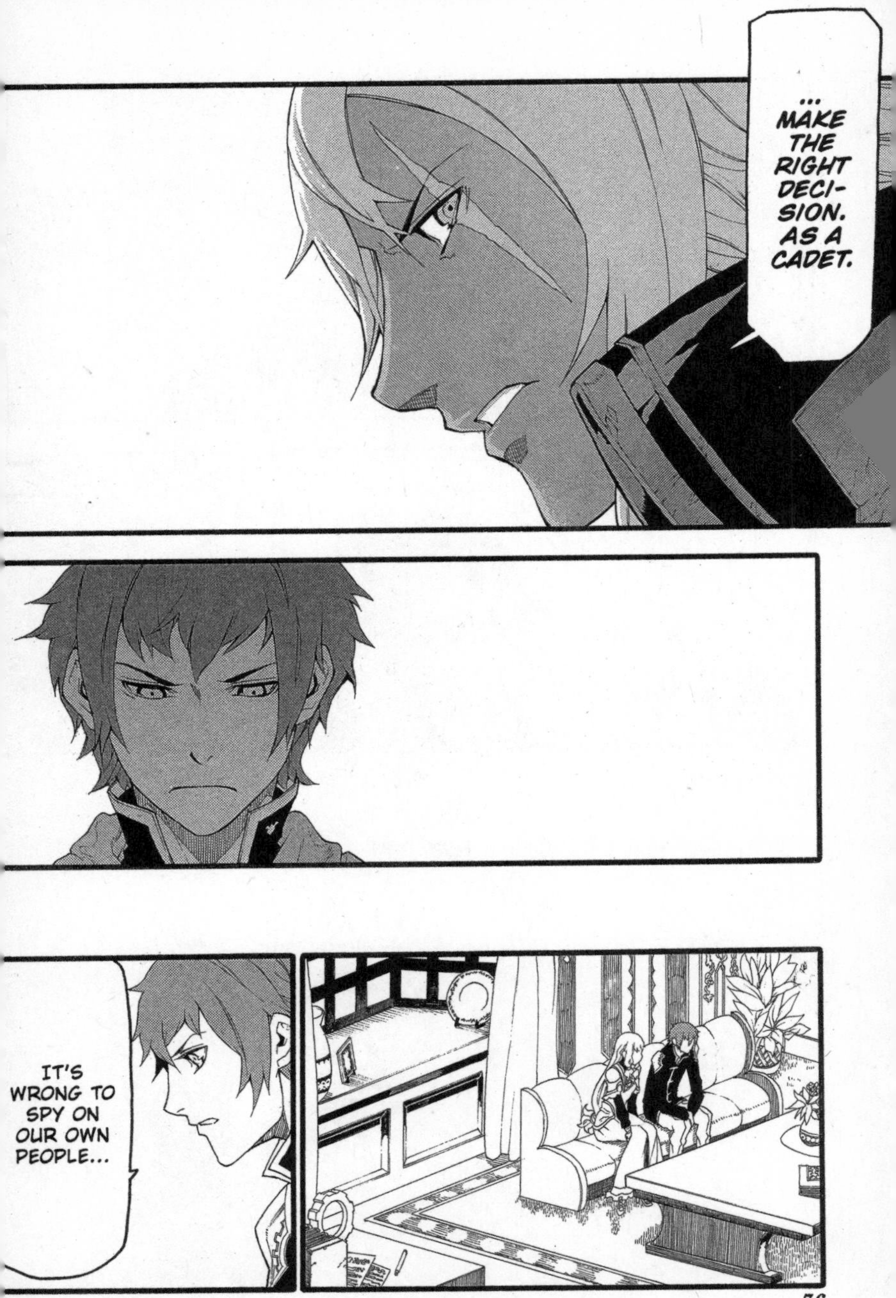
... MAKE THE RIGHT DECI-SION. AS A CADET.
IT'S WRONG TO SPY ON OUR OWN PEOPLE...

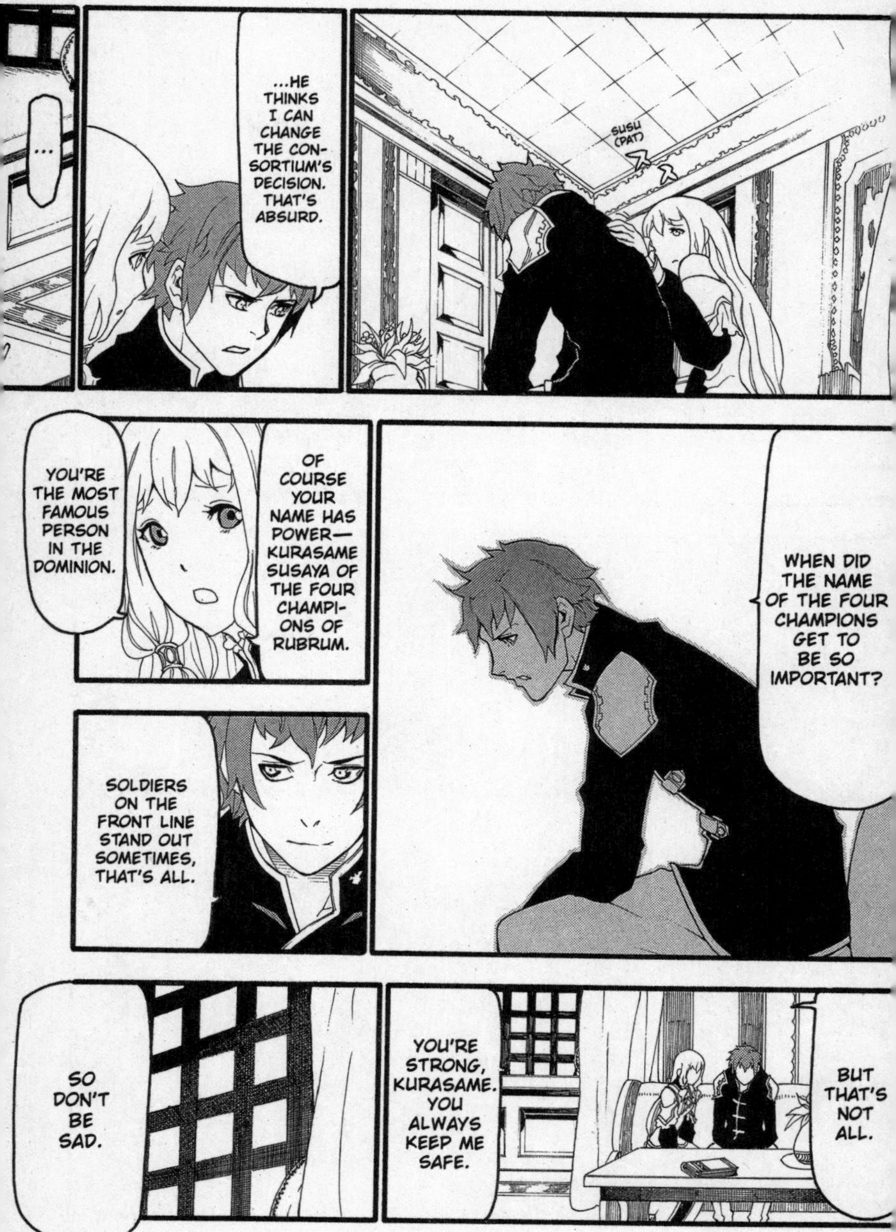
SUSU (PAT)
...HE THINKS I CAN CHANGE THE CON-SORTIUM'S DECISION. THAT'S ABSURD.
...
WHEN DID THE NAME OF THE FOUR CHAMPIONS GET TO BE SO IMPORTANT?
OF COURSE YOUR NAME HAS POWER—KURASAME SUSAYA OF THE FOUR CHAMPI-ONS OF RUBRUM.
YOU'RE THE MOST FAMOUS PERSON IN THE DOMINION.
SOLDIERS ON THE FRONT LINE STAND OUT SOMETIMES, THAT'S ALL.
BUT THAT'S NOT ALL.
YOU'RE STRONG, KURASAME. YOU ALWAYS KEEP ME SAFE.
SO DON'T BE SAD.

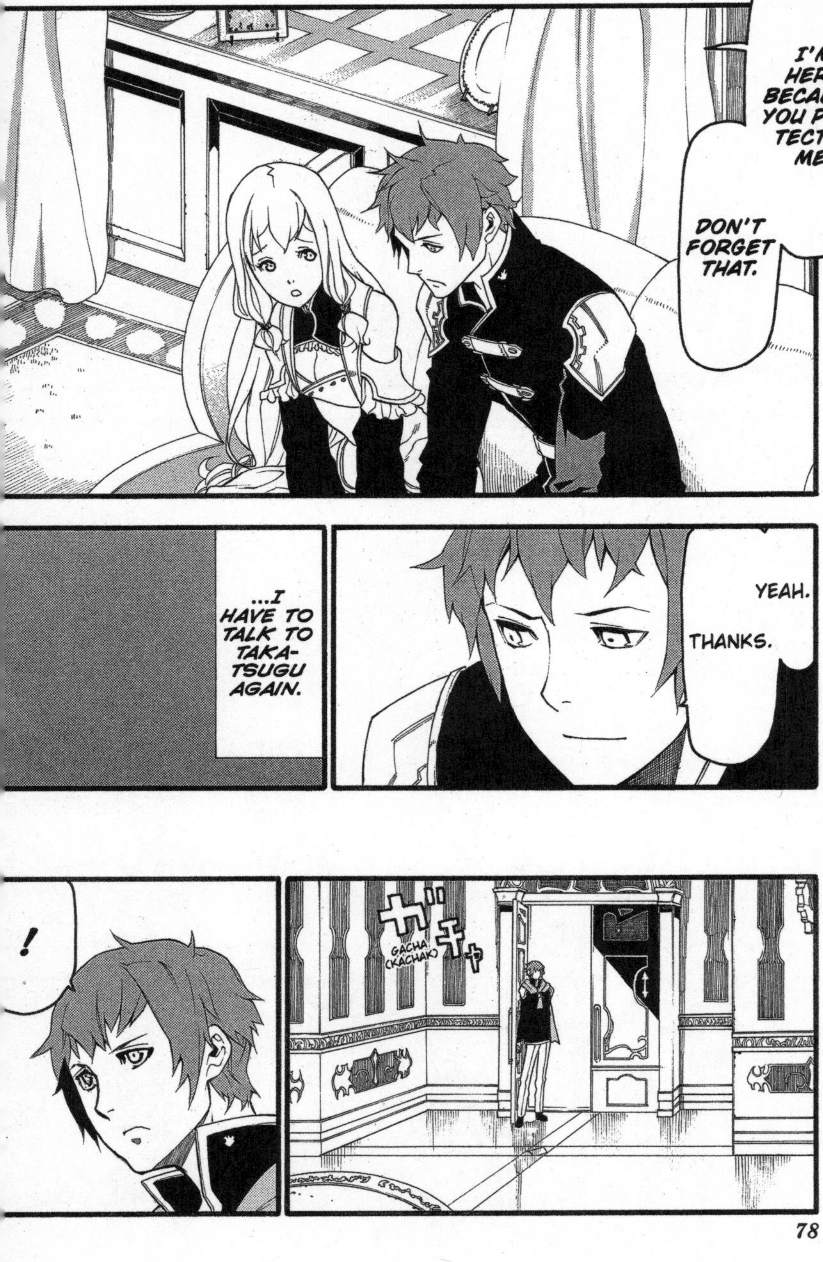
I'M HERE BECAUSE YOU PRO-TECTED ME.
DON'T FORGET THAT.
YEAH.
THANKS.
...I HAVE TO TALK TO TAKA-TSUGU AGAIN.
ガチャ
GACHA (KACHAK)
!

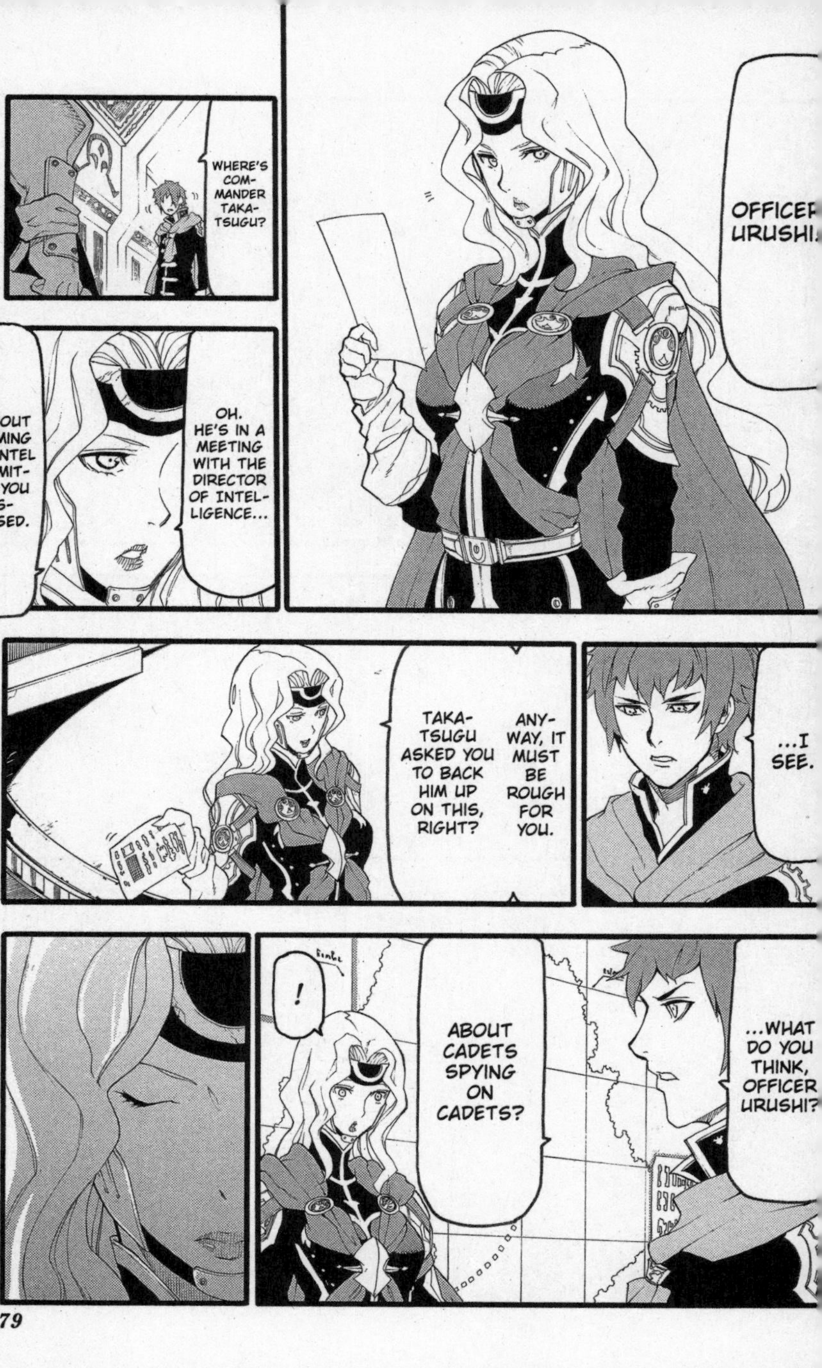
OFFICER URUSHI.
WHERE'S COMMANDER TAKATSUGU?
OH. HE'S IN A MEETING WITH THE DIRECTOR OF INTELLIGENCE...
...ABOUT FORMING THE INTEL COMMITTEE YOU DISCUSSED.
...I SEE.
ANYWAY, IT MUST BE ROUGH FOR YOU.
TAKATSUGU ASKED YOU TO BACK HIM UP ON THIS, RIGHT?
...WHAT DO YOU THINK, OFFICER URUSHI?
ABOUT CADETS SPYING ON CADETS?
!

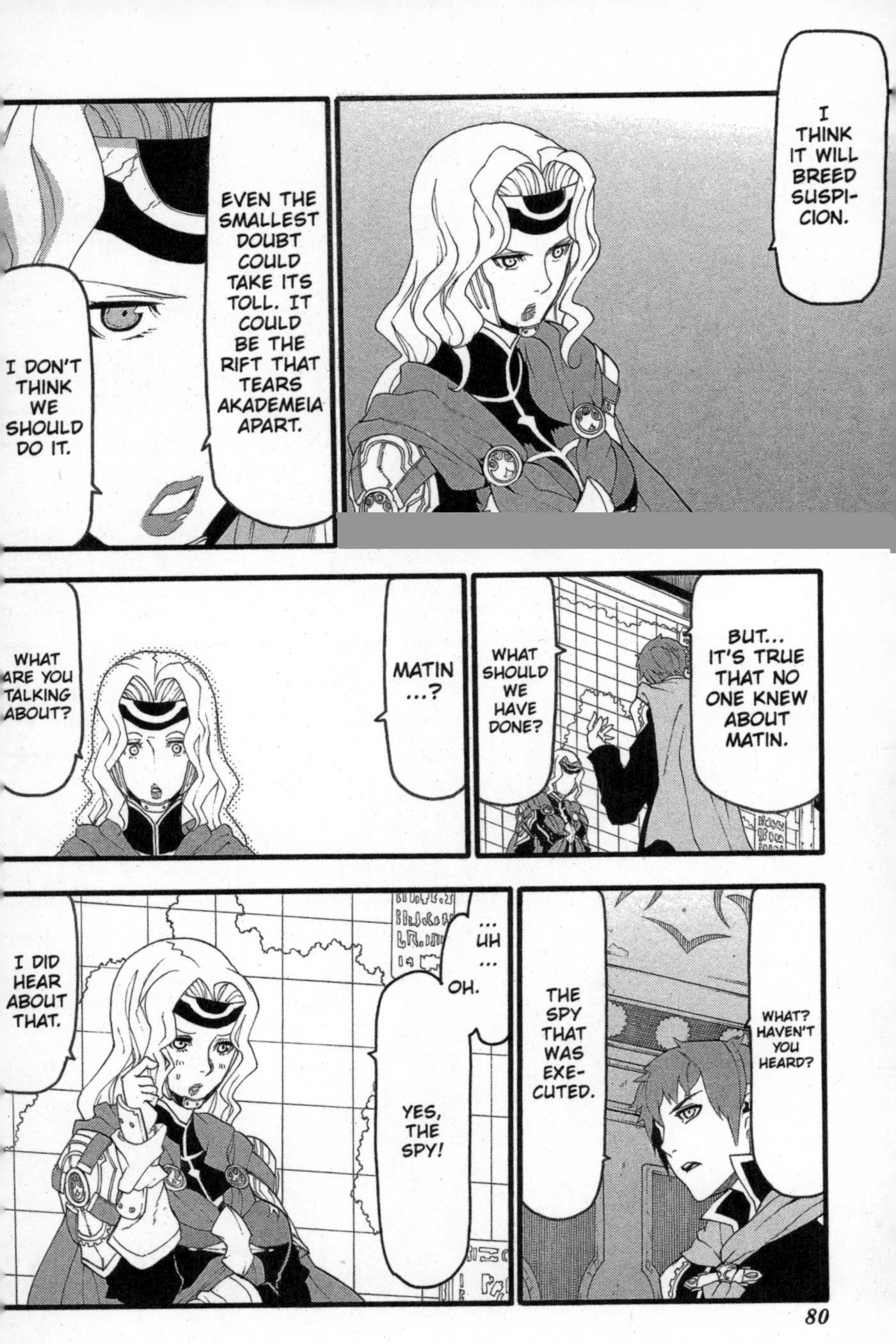

I THINK IT WILL BREED SUSPICION.
EVEN THE SMALLEST DOUBT COULD TAKE ITS TOLL. IT COULD BE THE RIFT THAT TEARS AKADEMEIA APART.
I DON'T THINK WE SHOULD DO IT.
BUT... IT'S TRUE THAT NO ONE KNEW ABOUT MATIN.
WHAT SHOULD WE HAVE DONE?
MATIN ...?
WHAT ARE YOU TALKING ABOUT?
WHAT? HAVEN'T YOU HEARD?
THE SPY THAT WAS EXECUTED.
... UH ...
OH.
YES, THE SPY!
I DID HEAR ABOUT THAT.

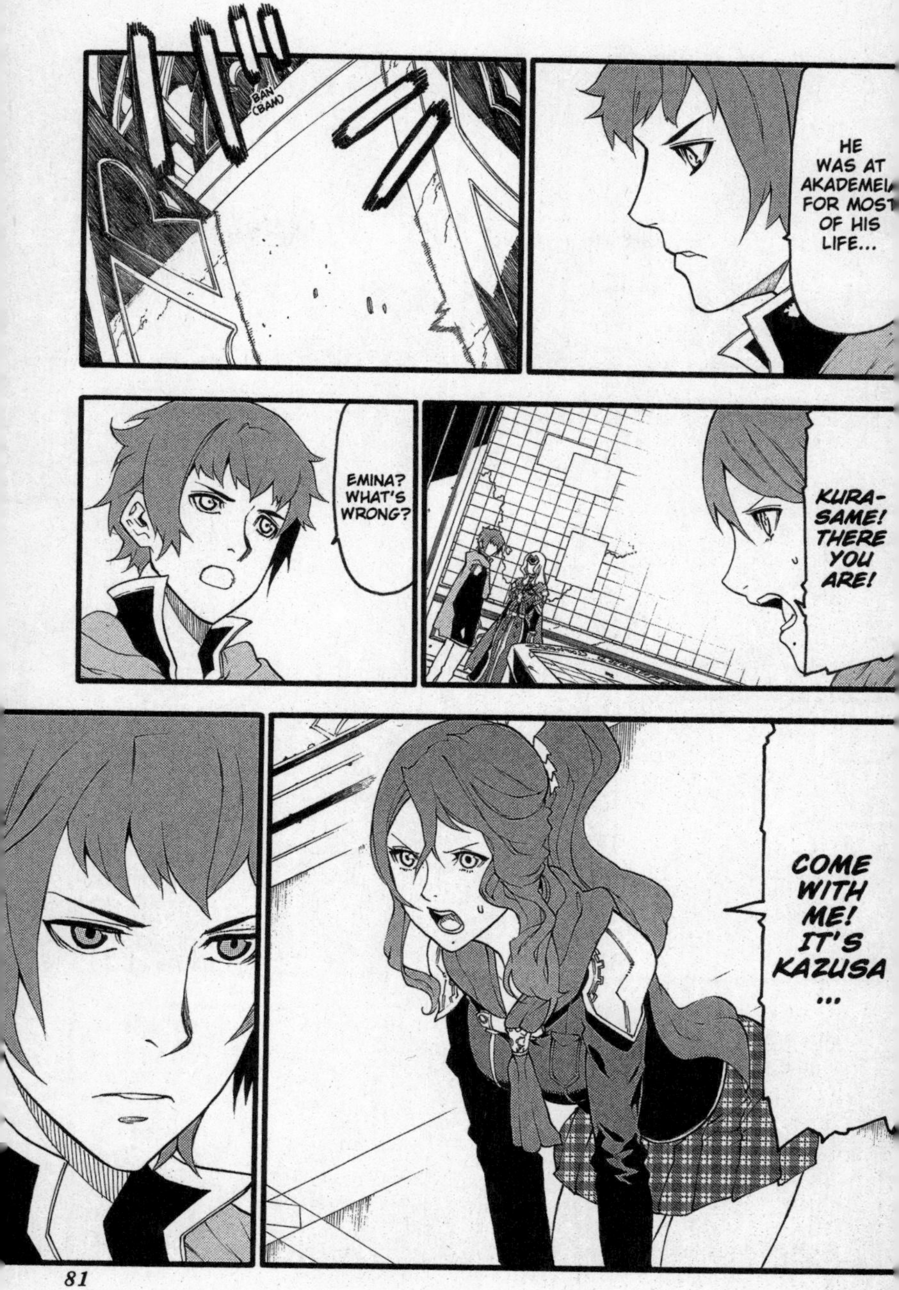
HE WAS AT AKADEMEIA FOR MOST OF HIS LIFE...
BAN (BAM)
KURA-SAME! THERE YOU ARE!
EMINA? WHAT'S WRONG?
COME WITH ME! IT'S KAZUSA ...

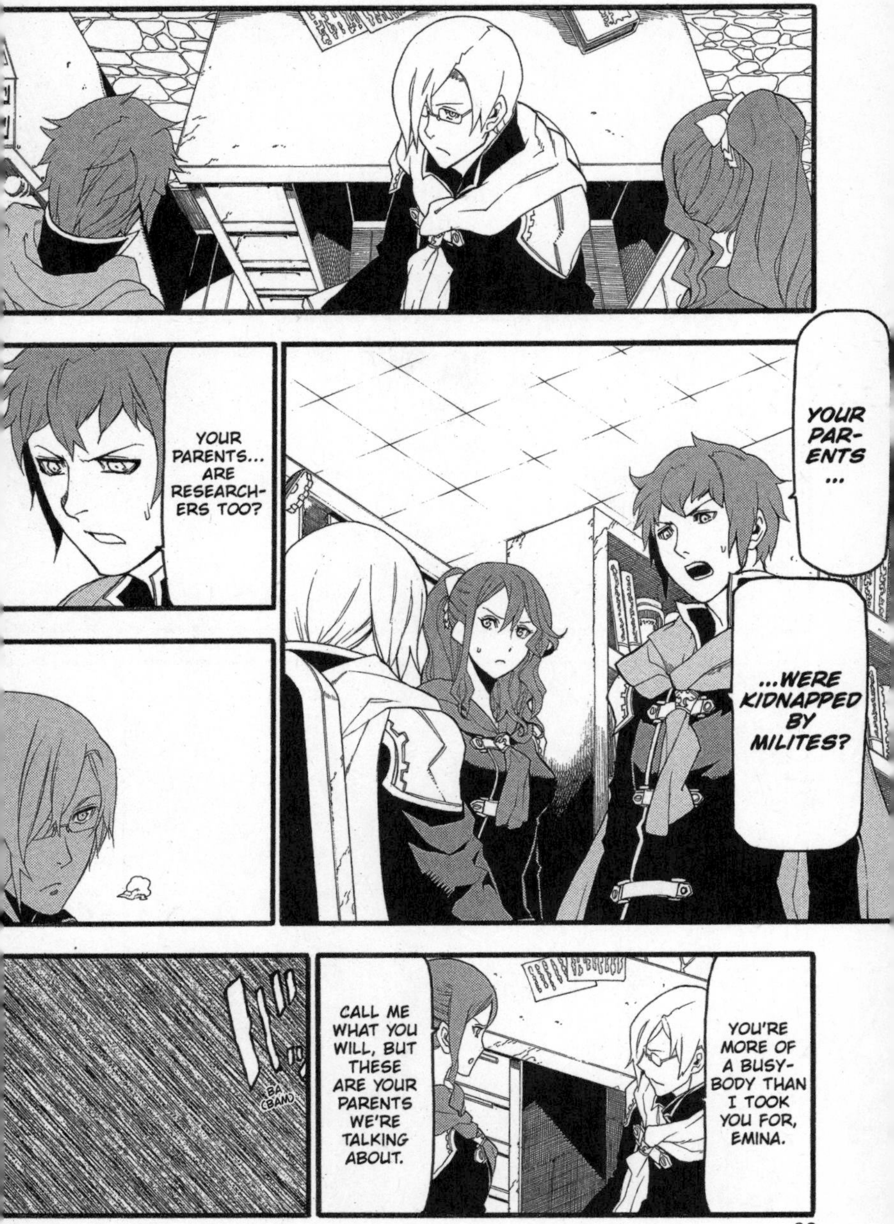
YOUR PARENTS...
...WERE KIDNAPPED BY MILITES?
YOUR PARENTS... ARE RESEARCHERS TOO?
YOU'RE MORE OF A BUSYBODY THAN I TOOK YOU FOR, EMINA.
CALL ME WHAT YOU WILL, BUT THESE ARE YOUR PARENTS WE'RE TALKING ABOUT.
BA (BAM)

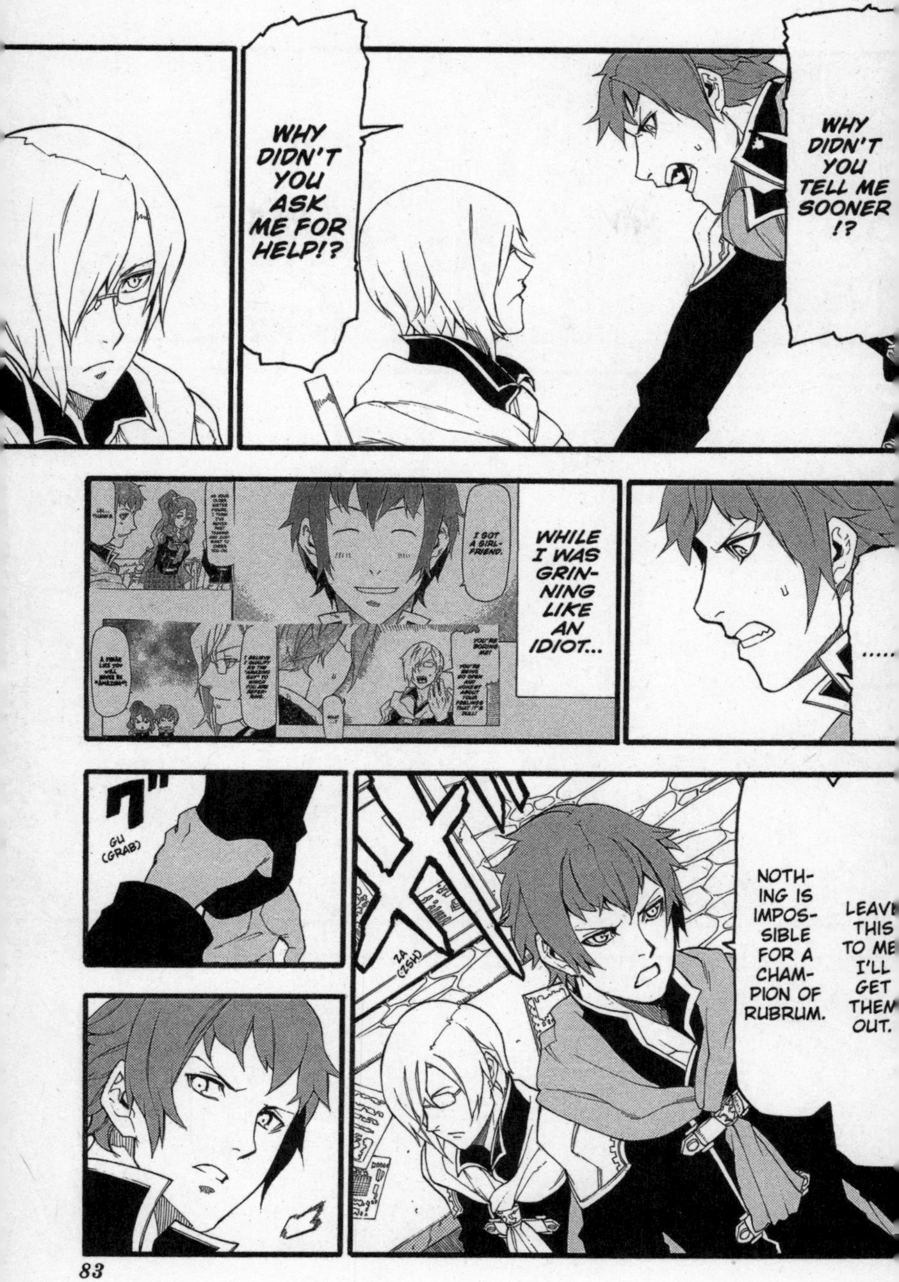
WHY DIDN'T YOU TELL ME SOONER !?
WHY DIDN'T YOU ASK ME FOR HELP!?
.....
WHILE I WAS GRINNING LIKE AN IDIOT...
I GOT A GIRL-FRIEND.
LEAV THIS TO ME I'LL GET THEM OUT.
NOTH-ING IS IMPOS-SIBLE FOR A CHAM-PION OF RUBRUM.
ZA (ZSH)
GU (GRAB)

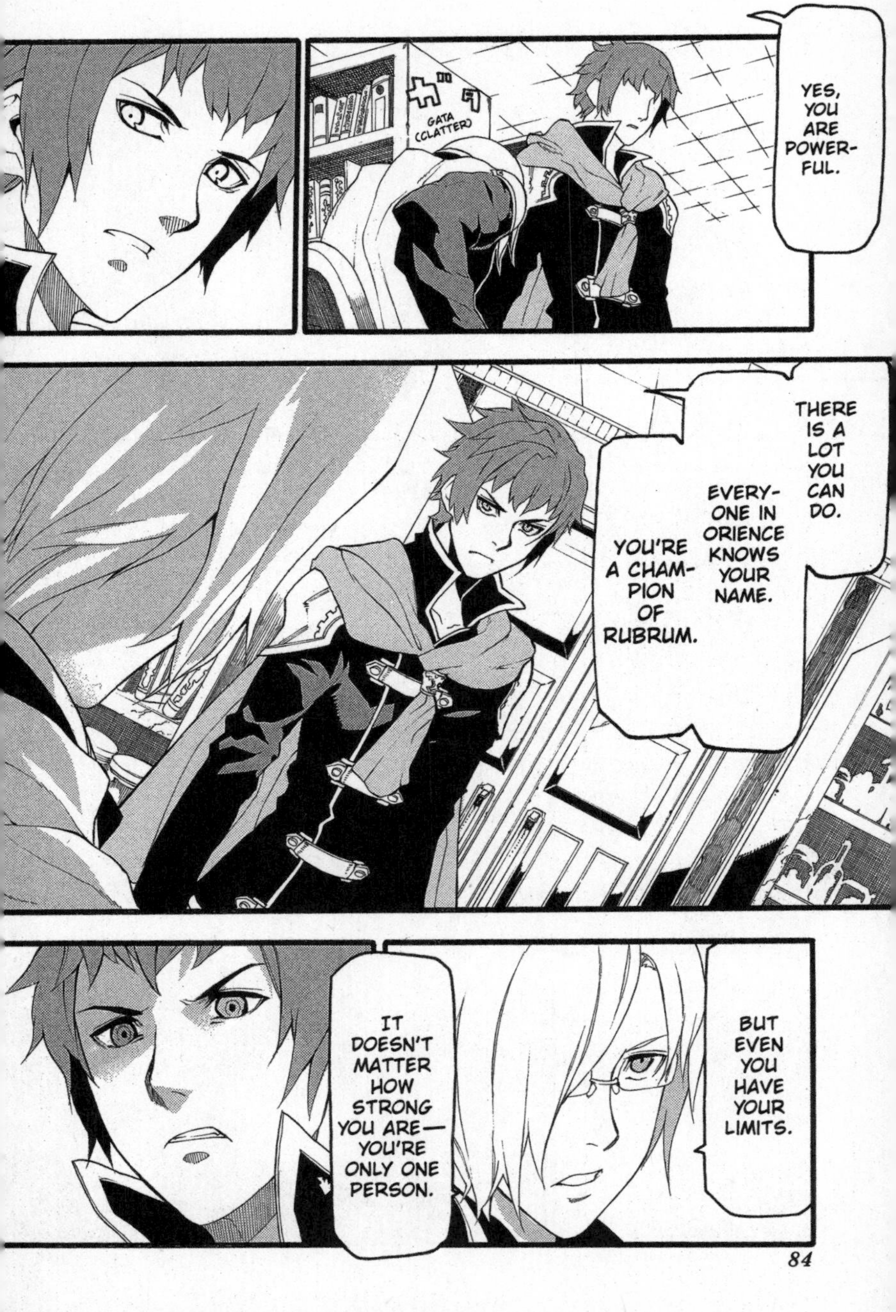
YES, YOU ARE POWERFUL.
GATA (CLATTER)
THERE IS A LOT YOU CAN DO.
EVERYONE IN ORIENCE KNOWS YOUR NAME.
YOU'RE A CHAMPION OF RUBRUM.
BUT EVEN YOU HAVE YOUR LIMITS.
IT DOESN'T MATTER HOW STRONG YOU ARE—YOU'RE ONLY ONE PERSON.

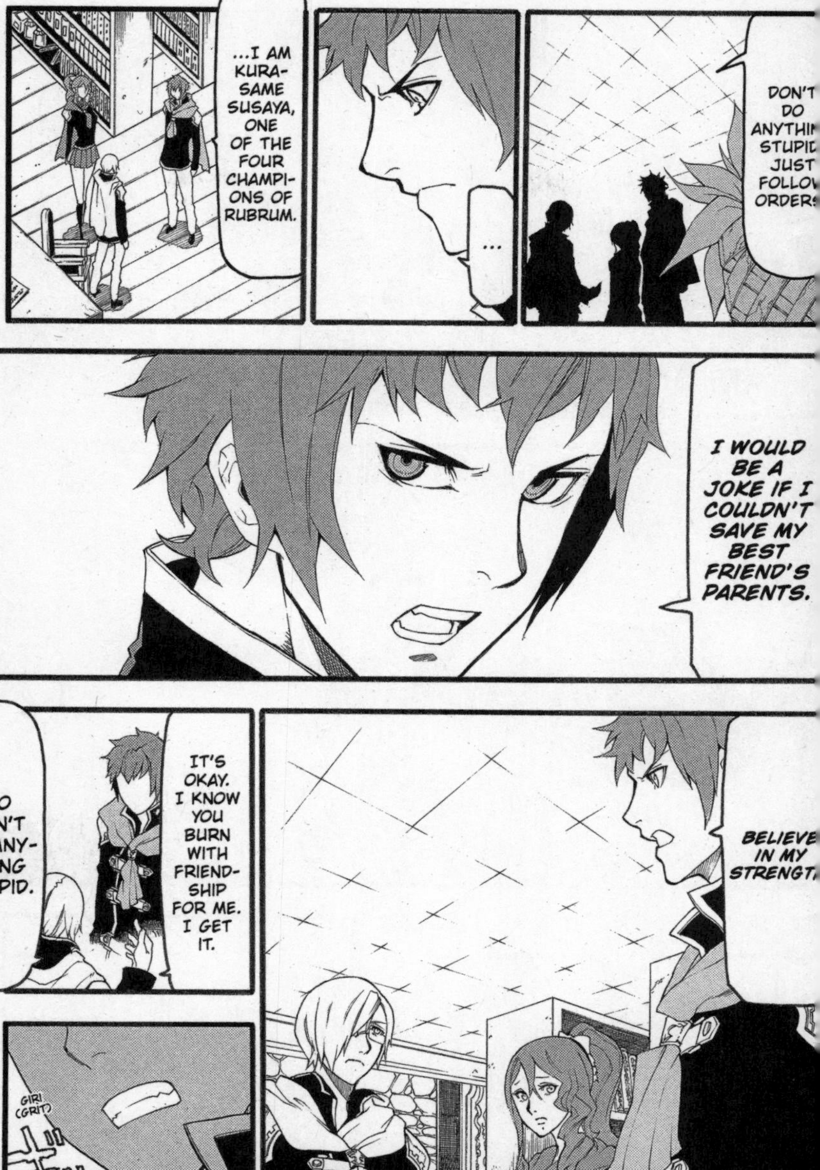
DON'T DO ANYTHIN STUPID JUST FOLLOW ORDERS
...
...I AM KURA-SAME SUSAYA, ONE OF THE FOUR CHAMPI-ONS OF RUBRUM.
I WOULD BE A JOKE IF I COULDN'T SAVE MY BEST FRIEND'S PARENTS.
BELIEVE IN MY STRENGT
IT'S OKAY. I KNOW YOU BURN WITH FRIEND-SHIP FOR ME. I GET IT.
SO DON'T DO ANY-THING STUPID.
GIRI (GRIT)

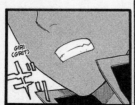

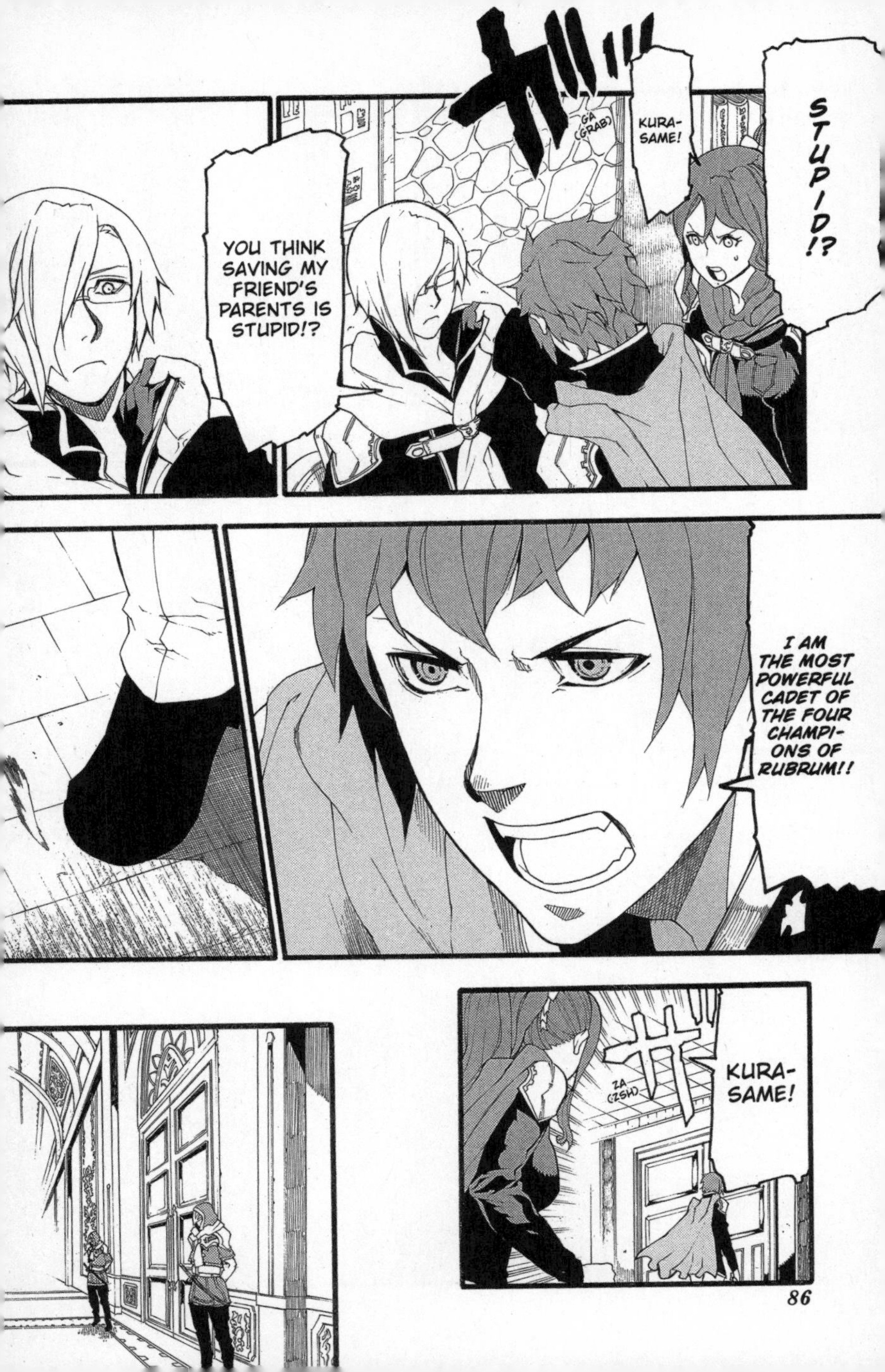
STUPID!?
KURA-SAME!
GA (GRAB)
YOU THINK SAVING MY FRIEND'S PARENTS IS STUPID!?
I AM THE MOST POWERFUL CADET OF THE FOUR CHAMPIONS OF RUBRUM!!
KURA-SAME!
ZA (ZSH)

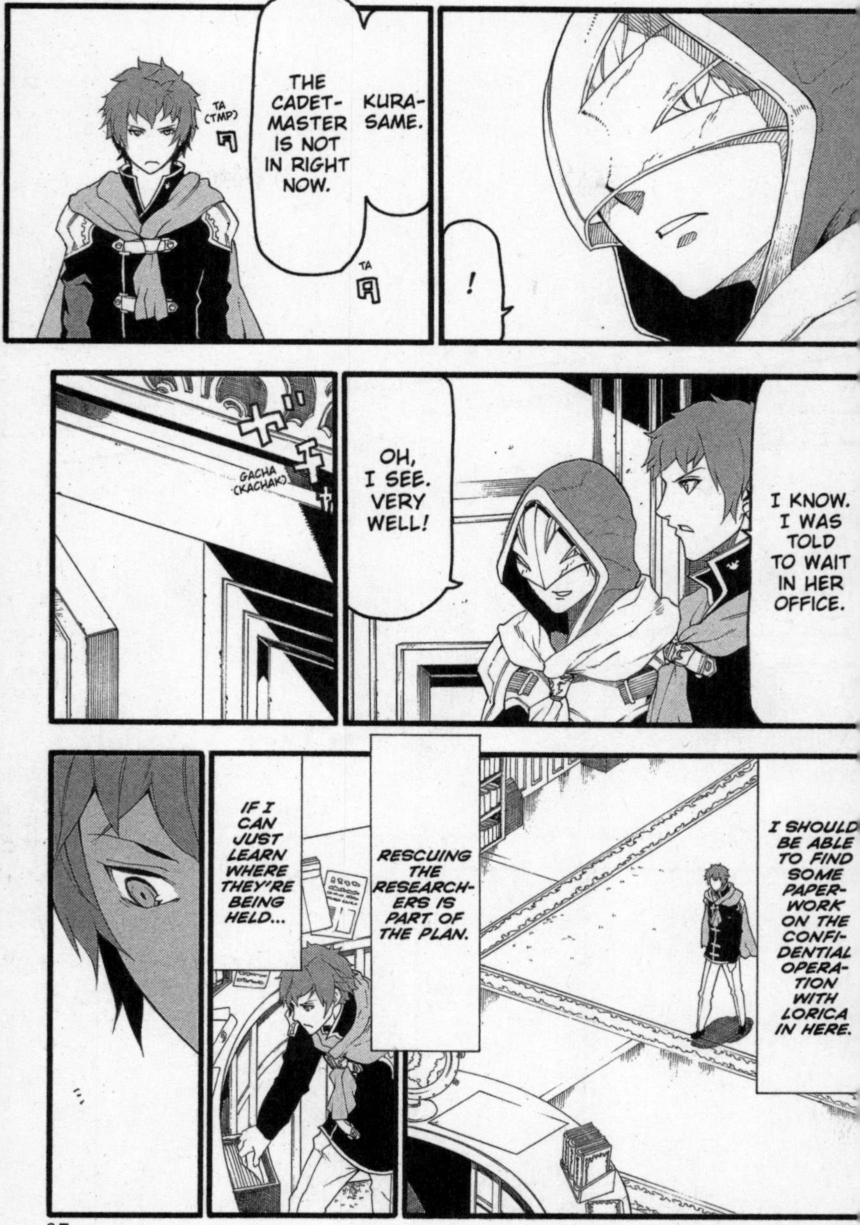
!
KURA-SAME.
THE CADET-MASTER IS NOT IN RIGHT NOW.
TA (TMP)
TA
I KNOW. I WAS TOLD TO WAIT IN HER OFFICE.
OH, I SEE. VERY WELL!
GACHA (KACHAK)
I SHOULD BE ABLE TO FIND SOME PAPERWORK ON THE CONFIDENTIAL OPERATION WITH LORICA IN HERE.
RESCUING THE RESEARCHERS IS PART OF THE PLAN.
IF I CAN JUST LEARN WHERE THEY'RE BEING HELD...

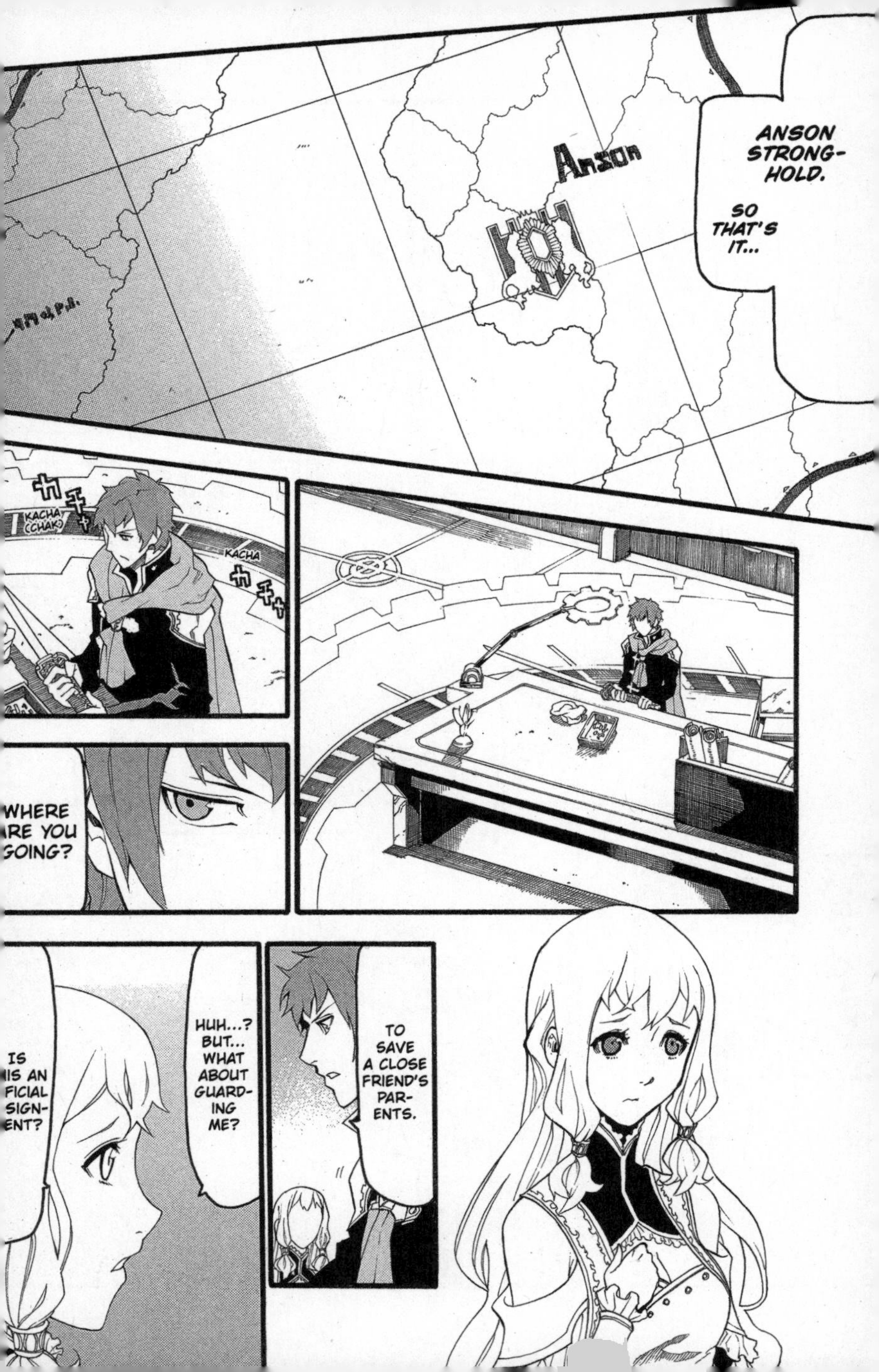

Anson
ANSON STRONG-HOLD.
SO THAT'S IT...
カチャ
KACHA (CHAK)
KACHA
カチャ
WHERE ARE YOU GOING?
TO SAVE A CLOSE FRIEND'S PAR-ENTS.
HUH...? BUT... WHAT ABOUT GUARD-ING ME?
IS IS AN FICIAL SIGN-ENT?

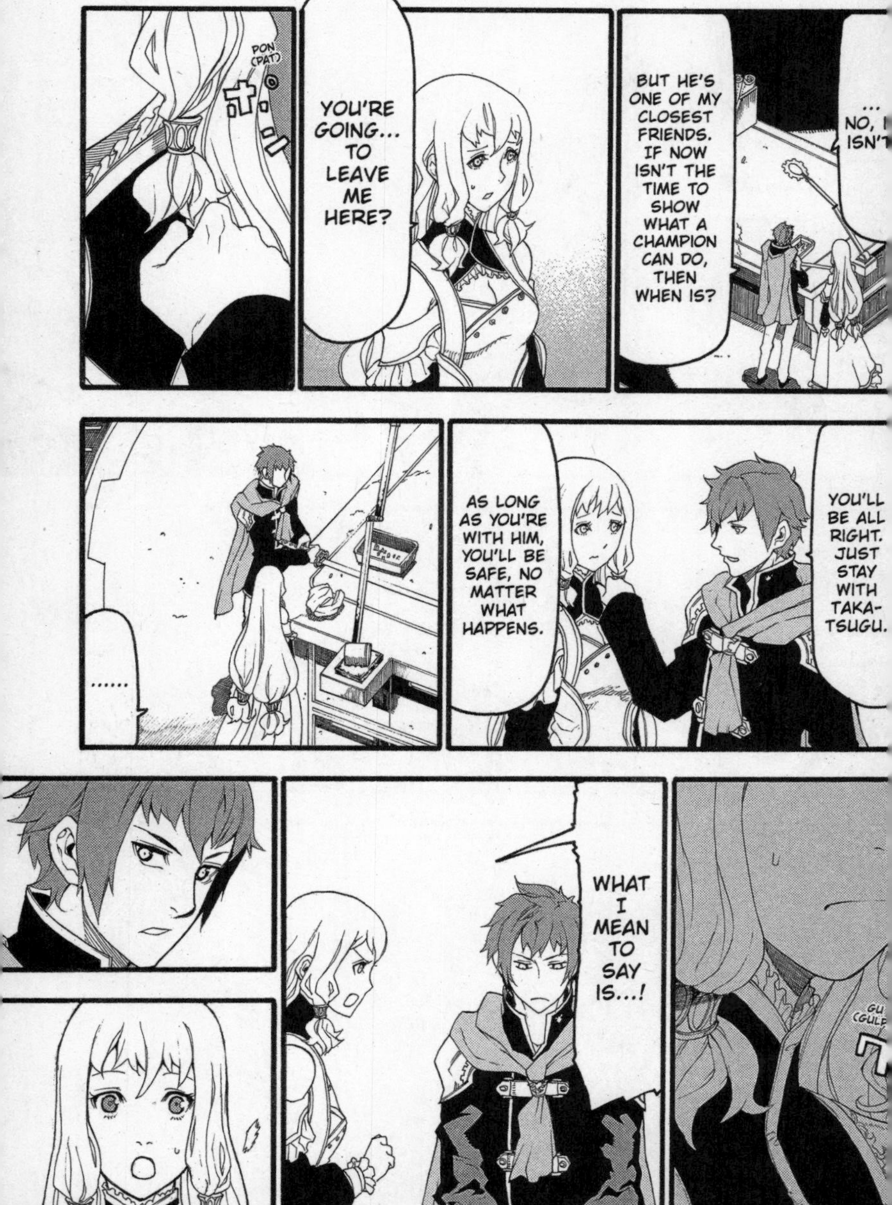

... NO, I ISN'
BUT HE'S ONE OF MY CLOSEST FRIENDS. IF NOW ISN'T THE TIME TO SHOW WHAT A CHAMPION CAN DO, THEN WHEN IS?
YOU'RE GOING... TO LEAVE ME HERE?
PON (PAT)
YOU'LL BE ALL RIGHT. JUST STAY WITH TAKA-TSUGU.
AS LONG AS YOU'RE WITH HIM, YOU'LL BE SAFE, NO MATTER WHAT HAPPENS.
......
GU (GULP)
WHAT I MEAN TO SAY IS...!

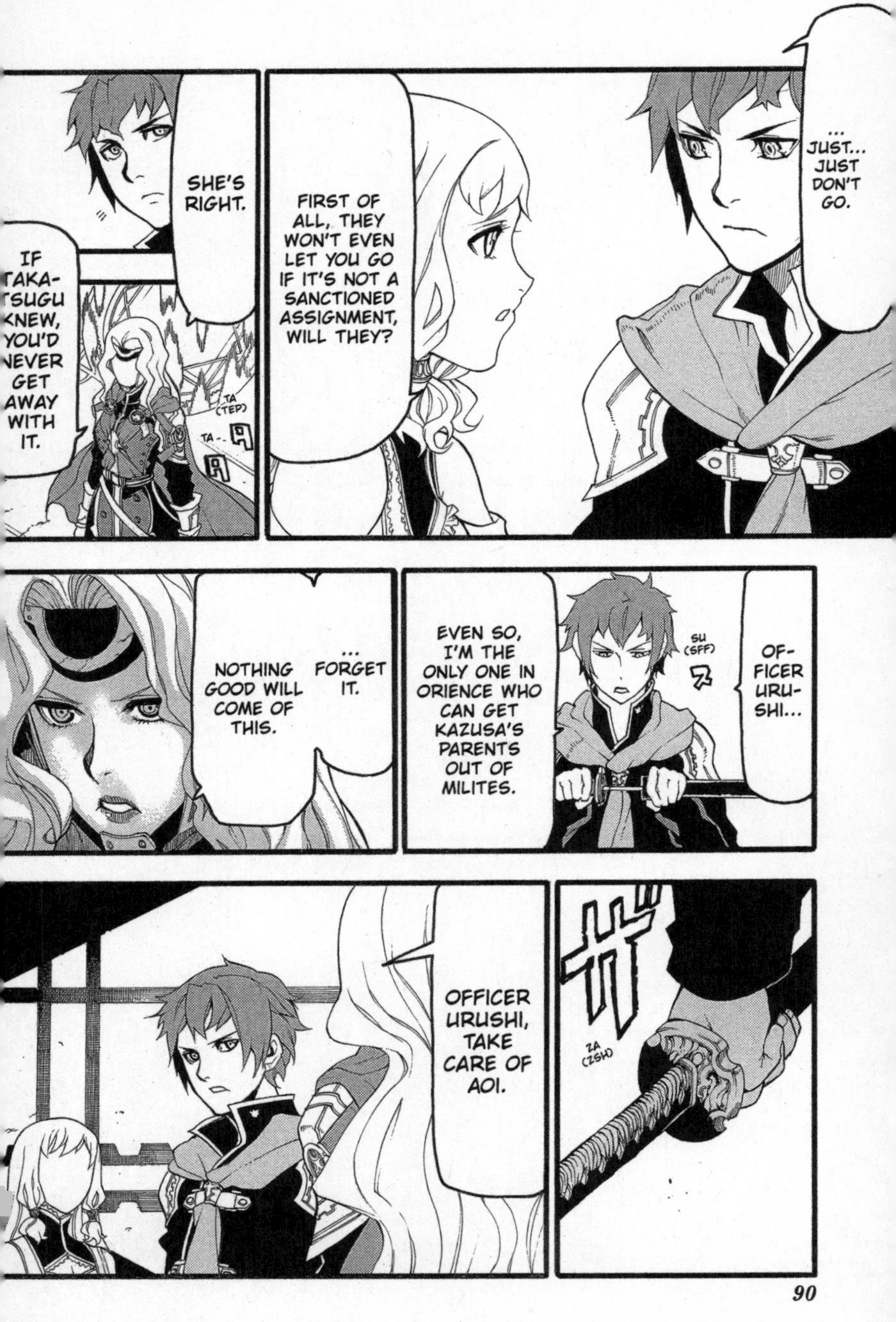
... JUST... JUST DON'T GO.
FIRST OF ALL, THEY WON'T EVEN LET YOU GO IF IT'S NOT A SANCTIONED ASSIGNMENT, WILL THEY?
SHE'S RIGHT.
IF TAKA-TSUGU KNEW, YOU'D NEVER GET AWAY WITH IT.
TA (TEP)
TA-..
OF-FICER URU-SHI...
SU (SFF)
EVEN SO, I'M THE ONLY ONE IN ORIENCE WHO CAN GET KAZUSA'S PARENTS OUT OF MILITES.
... FORGET IT.
NOTHING GOOD WILL COME OF THIS.
ZA (ZSH)
OFFICER URUSHI, TAKE CARE OF AOI.

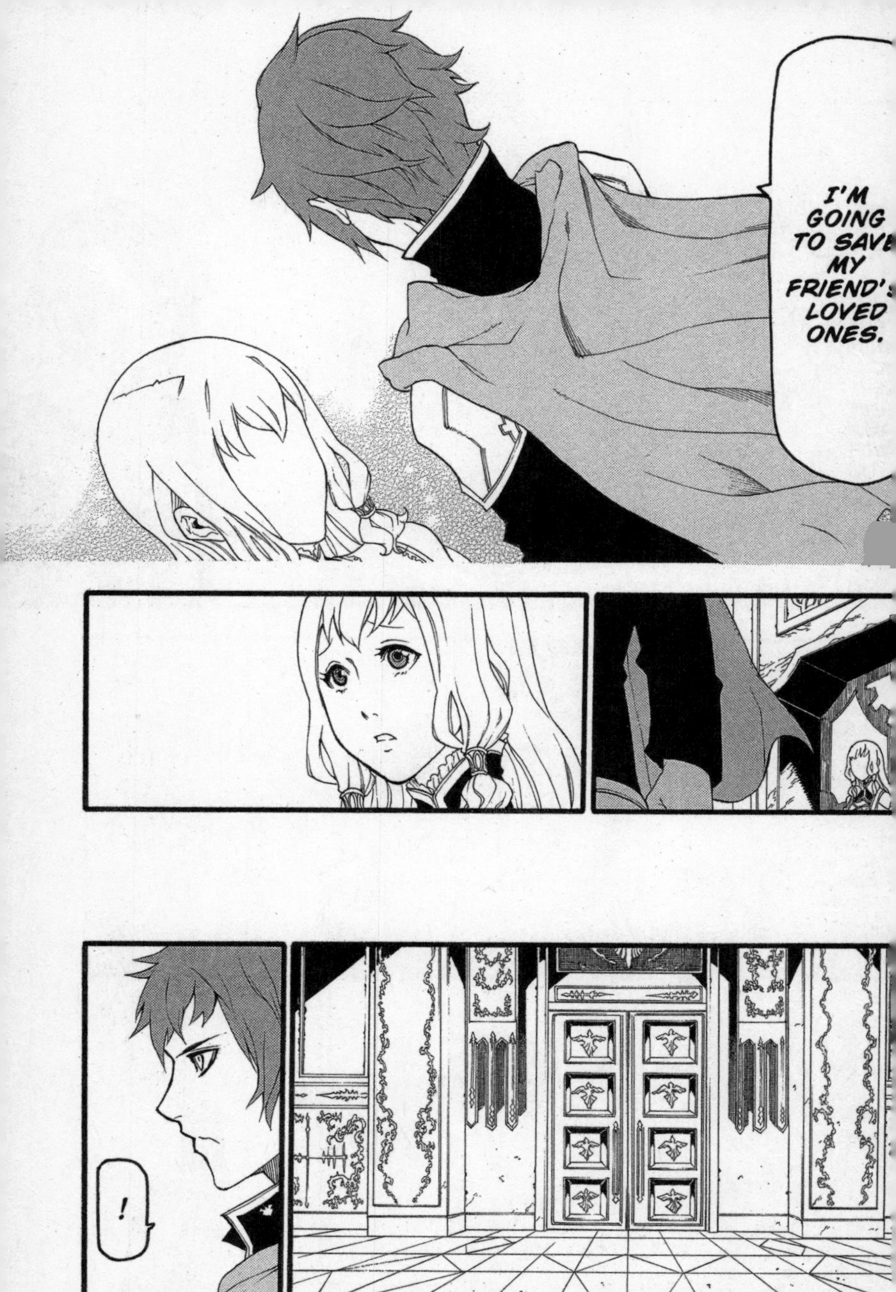
I'M GOING TO SAVE MY FRIEND'S LOVED ONES.
!

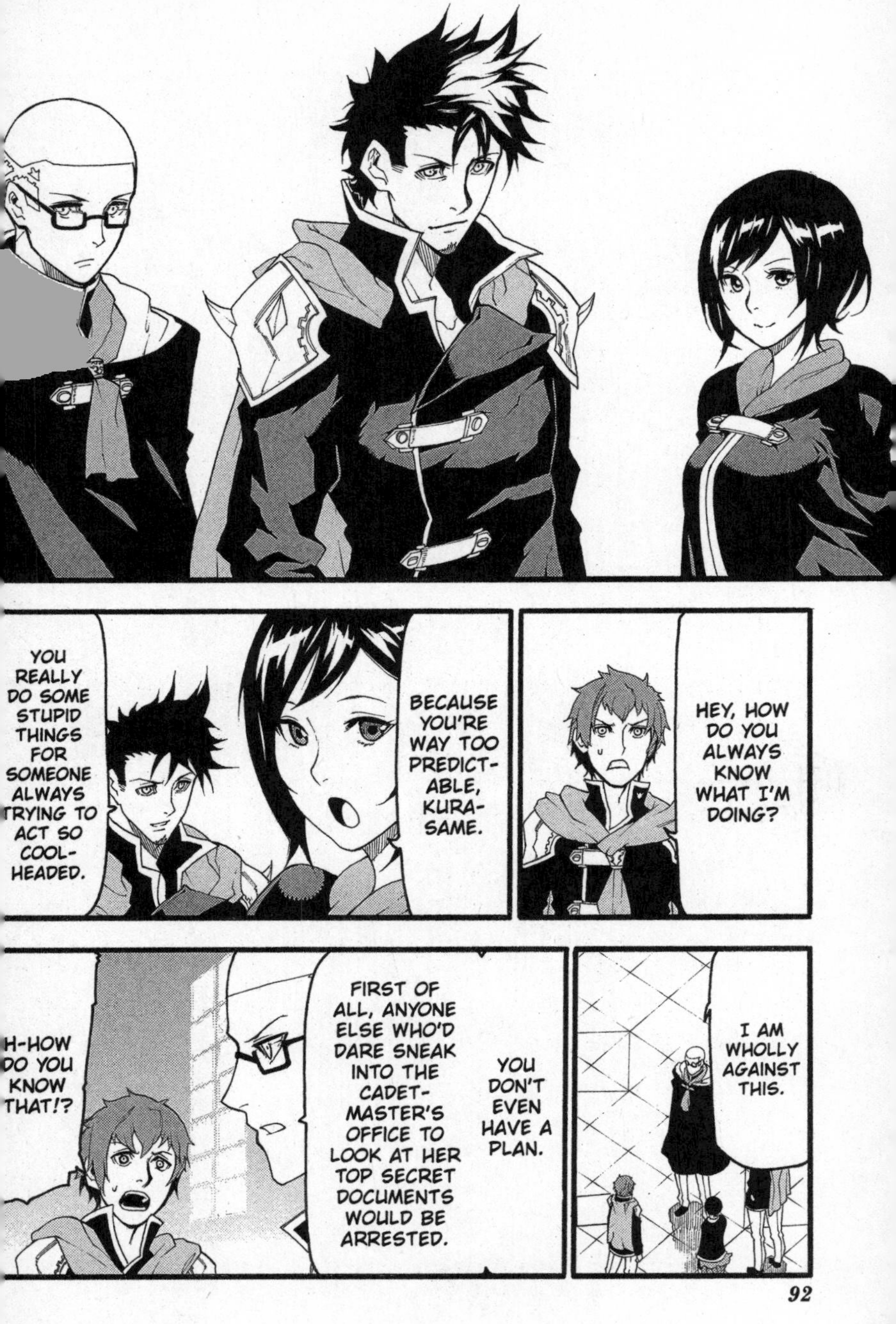
HEY, HOW DO YOU ALWAYS KNOW WHAT I'M DOING?
BECAUSE YOU'RE WAY TOO PREDICTABLE, KURASAME.
YOU REALLY DO SOME STUPID THINGS FOR SOMEONE ALWAYS TRYING TO ACT SO COOL-HEADED.
I AM WHOLLY AGAINST THIS.
YOU DON'T EVEN HAVE A PLAN.
FIRST OF ALL, ANYONE ELSE WHO'D DARE SNEAK INTO THE CADET-MASTER'S OFFICE TO LOOK AT HER TOP SECRET DOCUMENTS WOULD BE ARRESTED.
H-HOW DO YOU KNOW THAT!?

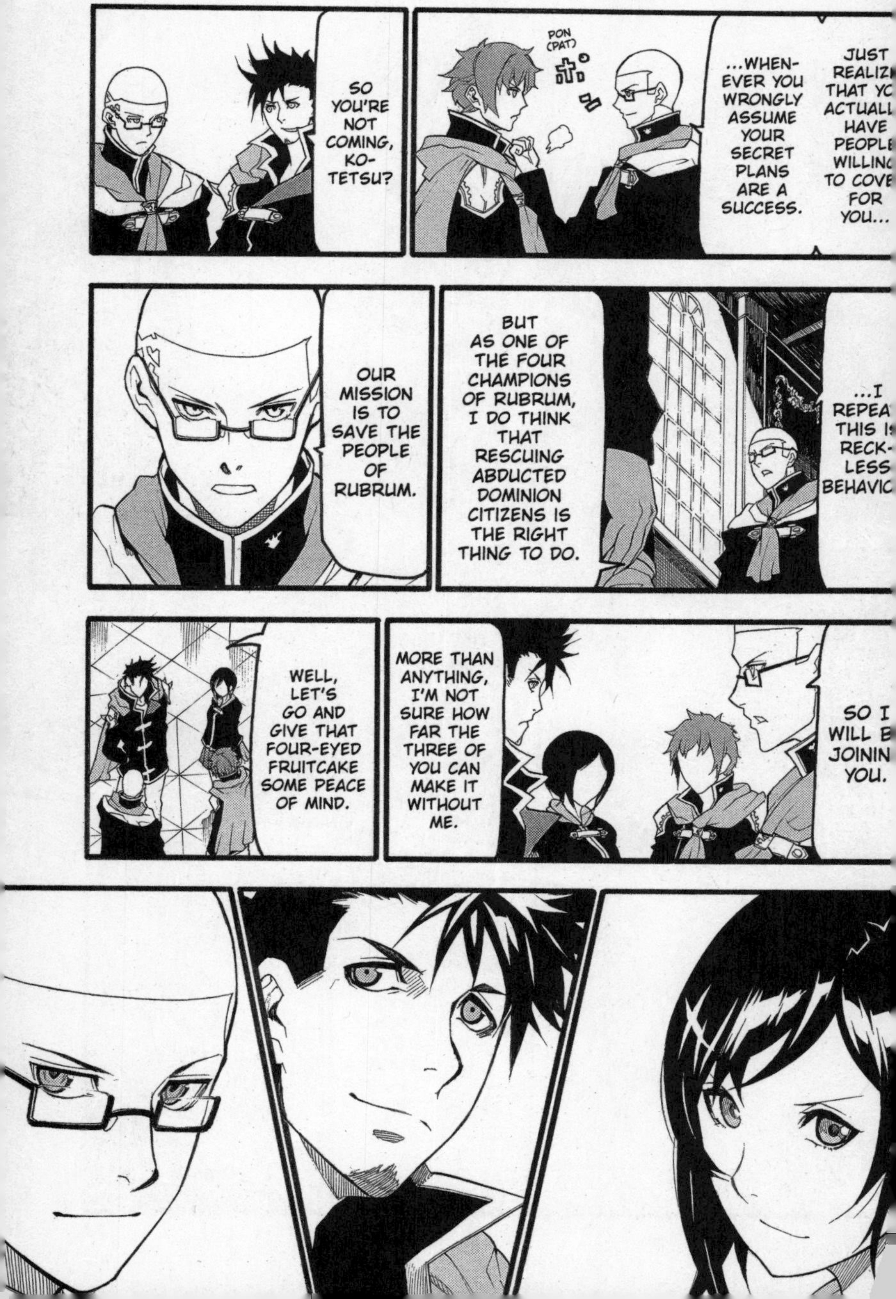
JUST REALIZ THAT YO ACTUALL HAVE PEOPLE WILLING TO COVE FOR YOU...
...WHEN-EVER YOU WRONGLY ASSUME YOUR SECRET PLANS ARE A SUCCESS.
PON (PAT)
ポン
SO YOU'RE NOT COMING, KO-TETSU?
...I REPEA THIS I RECK-LESS BEHAVIO
BUT AS ONE OF THE FOUR CHAMPIONS OF RUBRUM, I DO THINK THAT RESCUING ABDUCTED DOMINION CITIZENS IS THE RIGHT THING TO DO.
OUR MISSION IS TO SAVE THE PEOPLE OF RUBRUM.
SO I WILL B JOININ YOU.
MORE THAN ANYTHING, I'M NOT SURE HOW FAR THE THREE OF YOU CAN MAKE IT WITHOUT ME.
WELL, LET'S GO AND GIVE THAT FOUR-EYED FRUITCAKE SOME PEACE OF MIND.

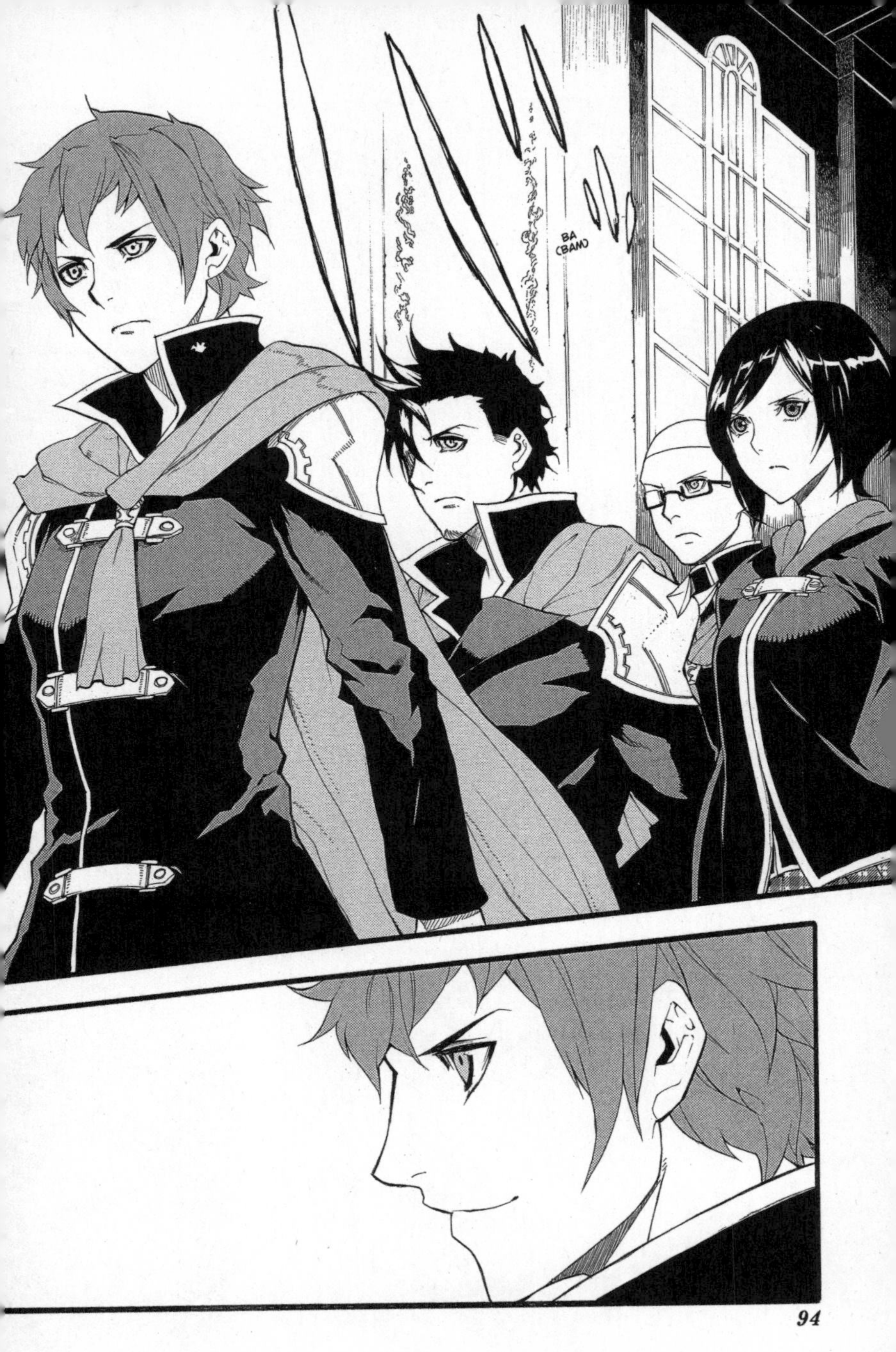
BA
(BAM)

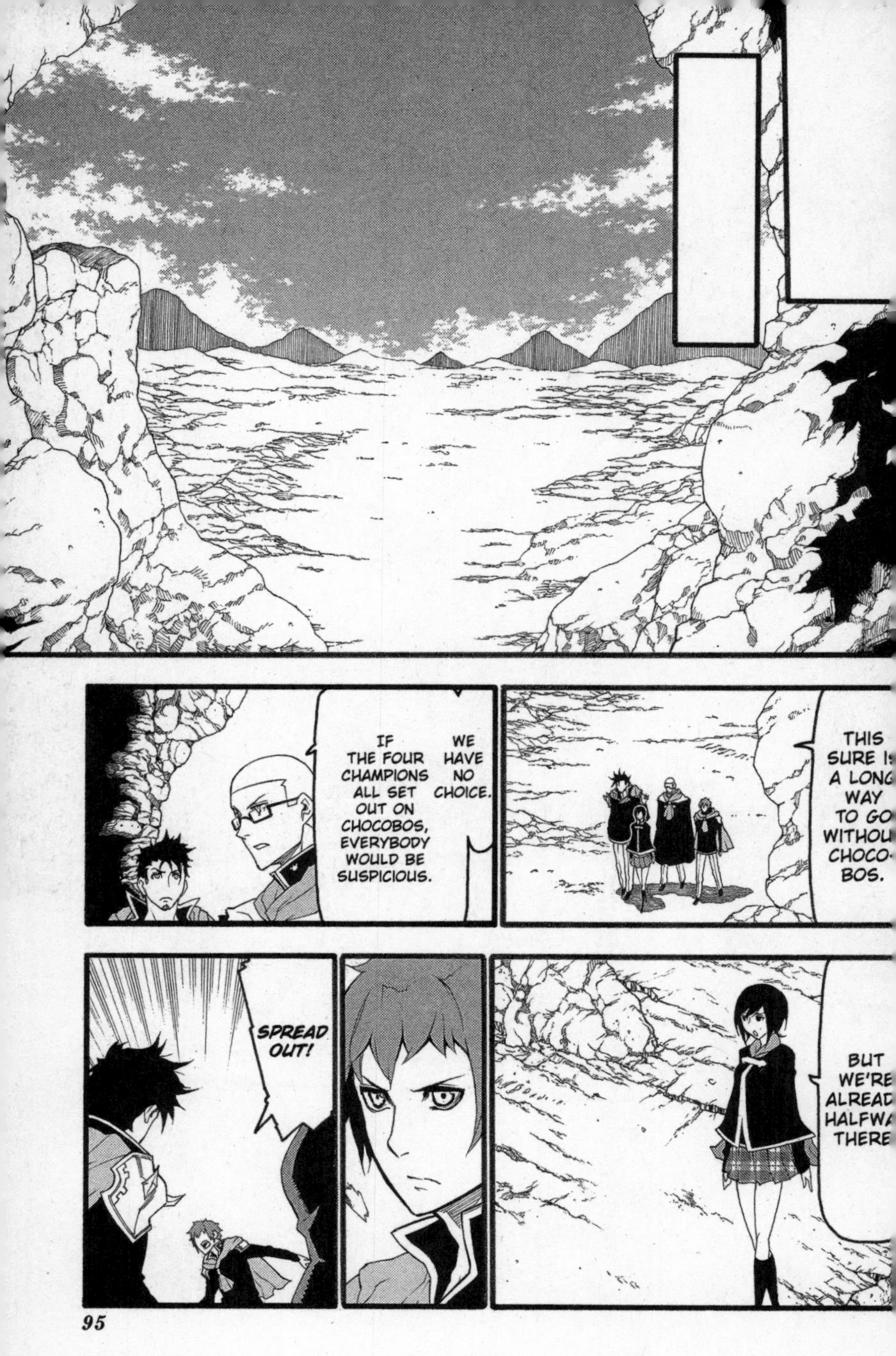
THIS SURE IS A LONG WAY TO GO WITHOU CHOCO-BOS.
WE HAVE NO CHOICE.
IF THE FOUR CHAMPIONS ALL SET OUT ON CHOCOBOS, EVERYBODY WOULD BE SUSPICIOUS.
BUT WE'RE ALREAD HALFWA THERE
SPREAD OUT!

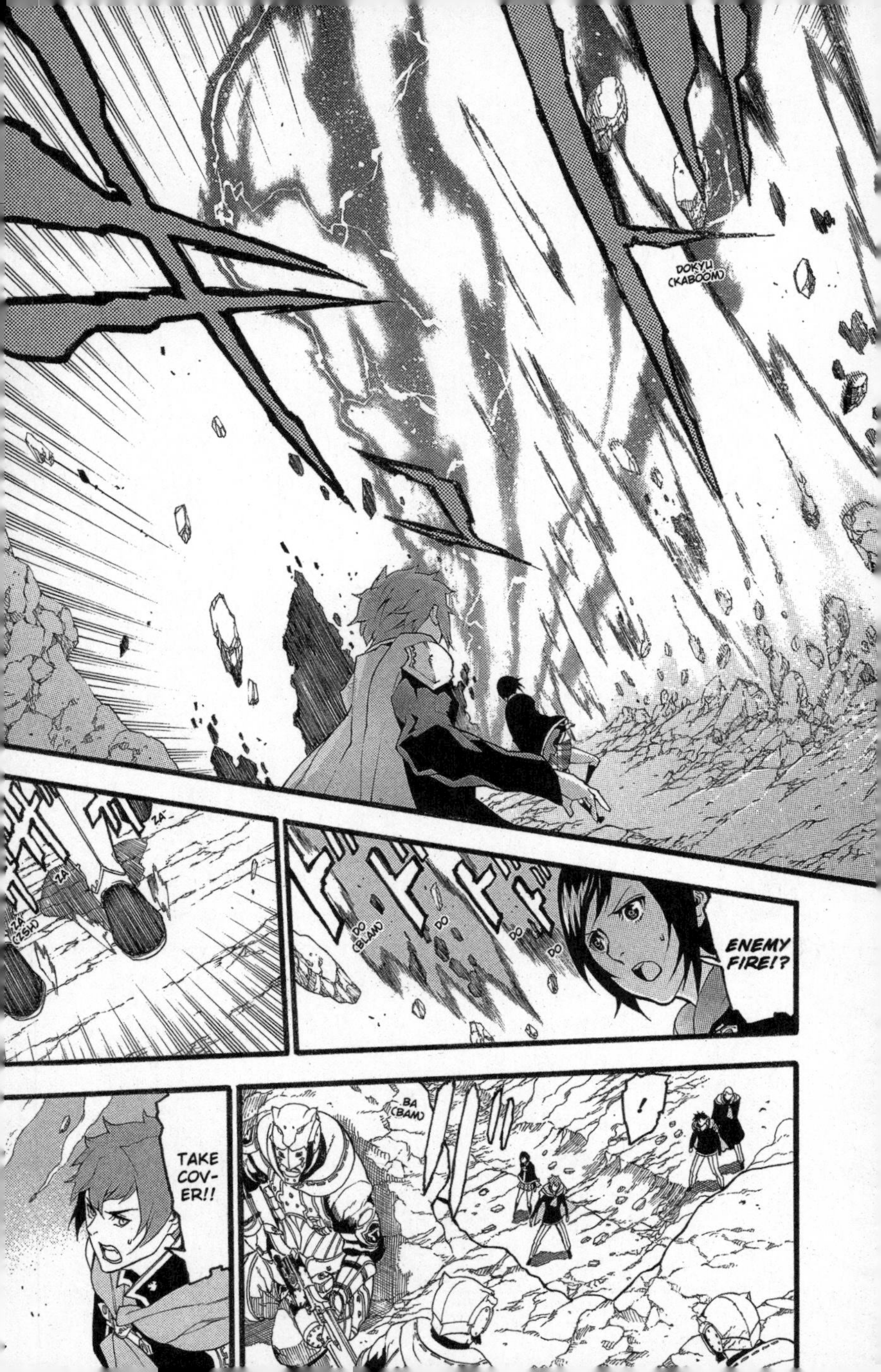
DOKYU
(KABOOM)
ENEMY FIRE!?
DO
DO
DO
DO
(BLAM)
ZA
ZA
ZA
(ZSH)
!
BA
(BAM)
TAKE COVER!!

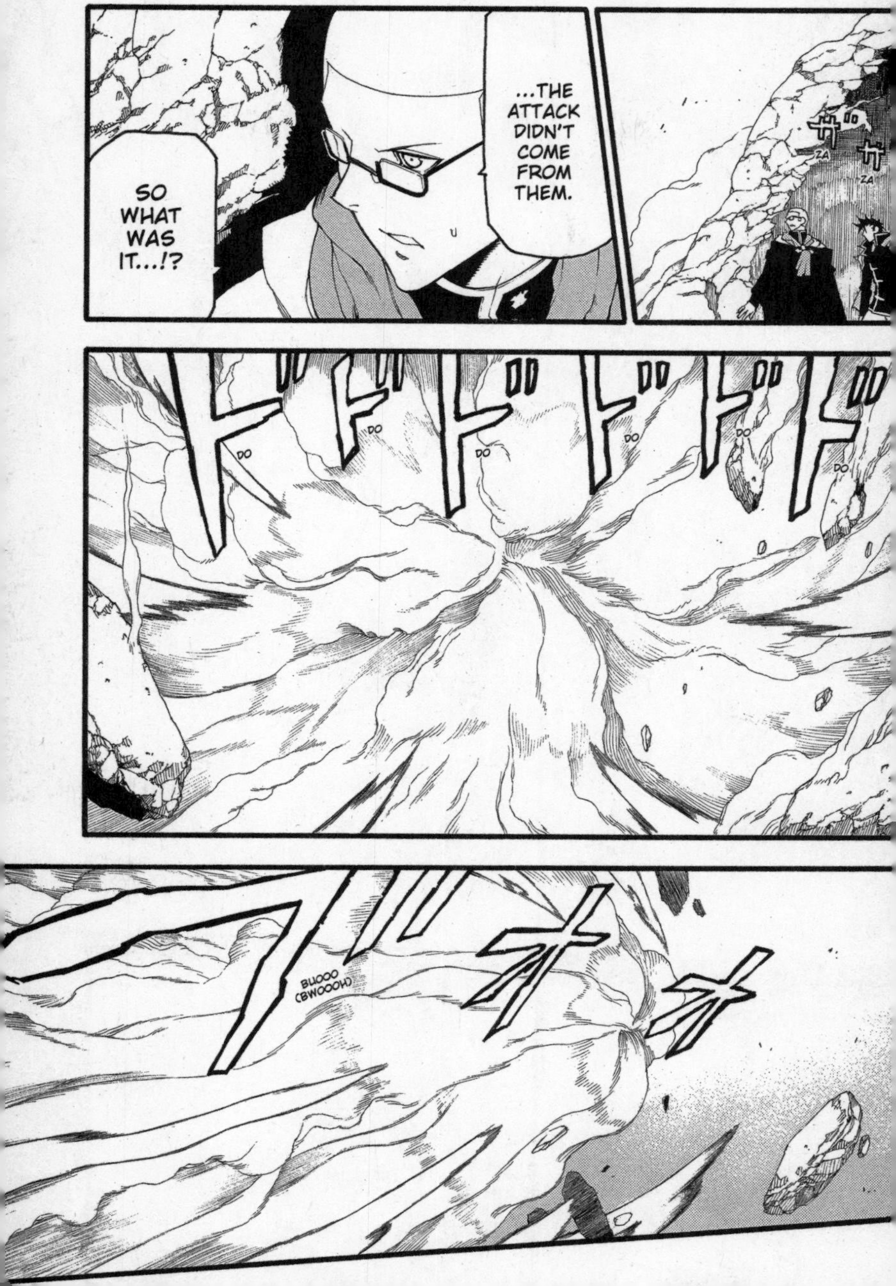
ZA
ZA
...THE ATTACK DIDN'T COME FROM THEM.
SO WHAT WAS IT...!?
DO
DO
DO
DO
DO
DO
BUOOO (BWOOOH)

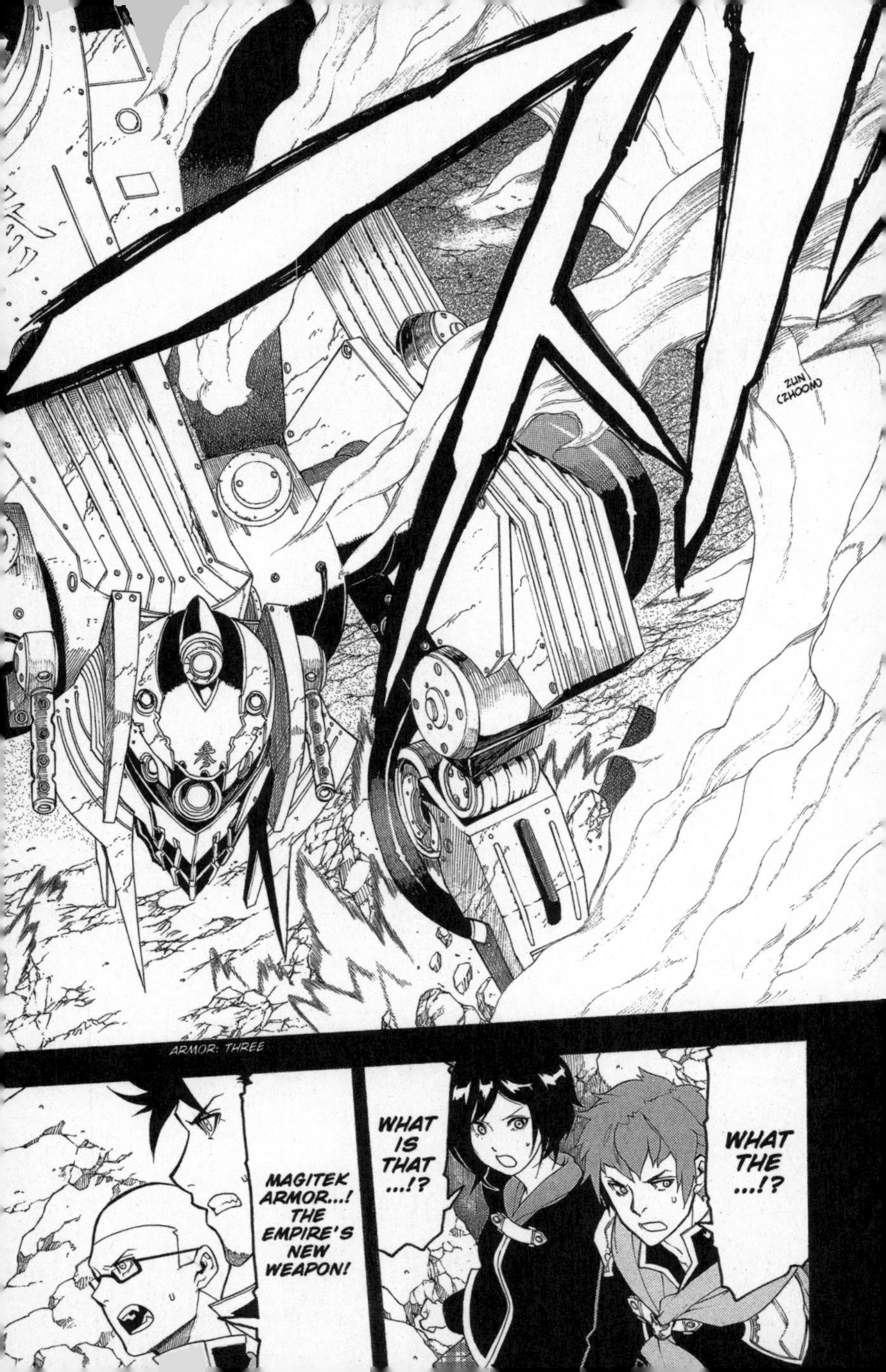
ZUN (ZHOOM)
ARMOR: THREE
WHAT THE ...!?
WHAT IS THAT ...!?
MAGITEK ARMOR...! THE EMPIRE'S NEW WEAPON!

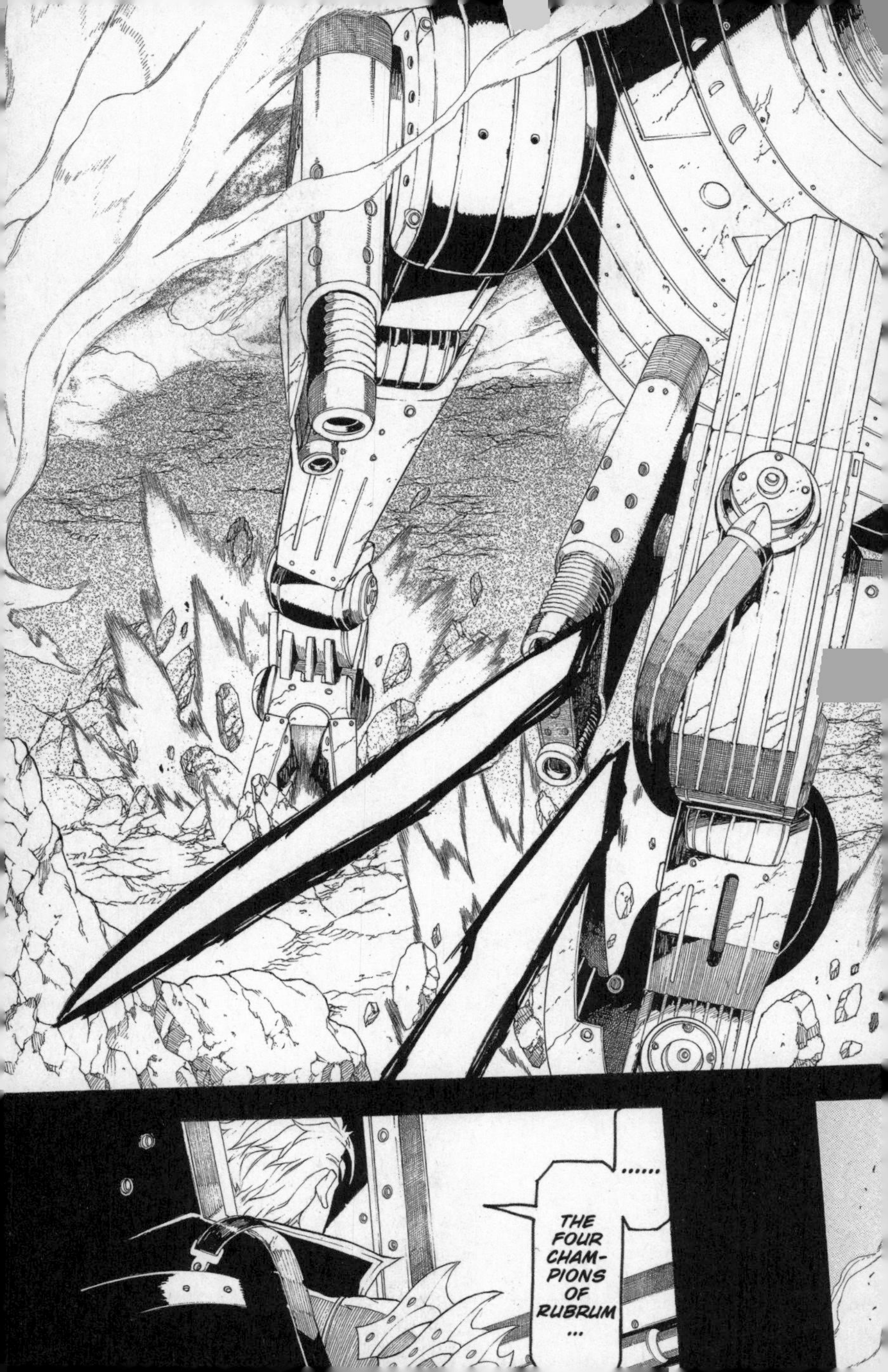
......
THE FOUR CHAMPIONS OF RUBRUM ...

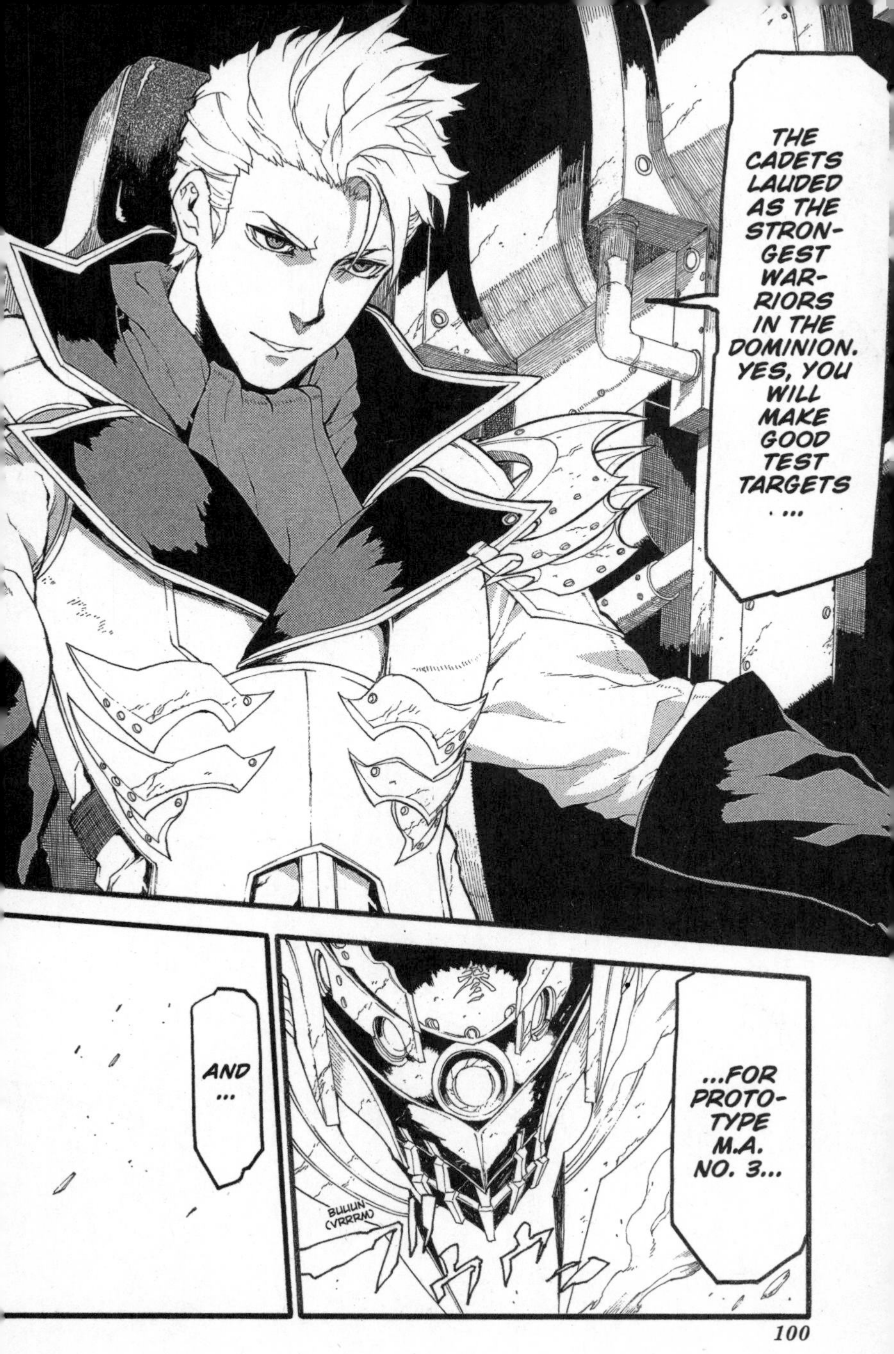
THE CADETS LAUDED AS THE STRONGEST WARRIORS IN THE DOMINION. YES, YOU WILL MAKE GOOD TEST TARGETS ...
...FOR PROTOTYPE M.A. NO. 3...
BULUN (VRRRM)
AND ...

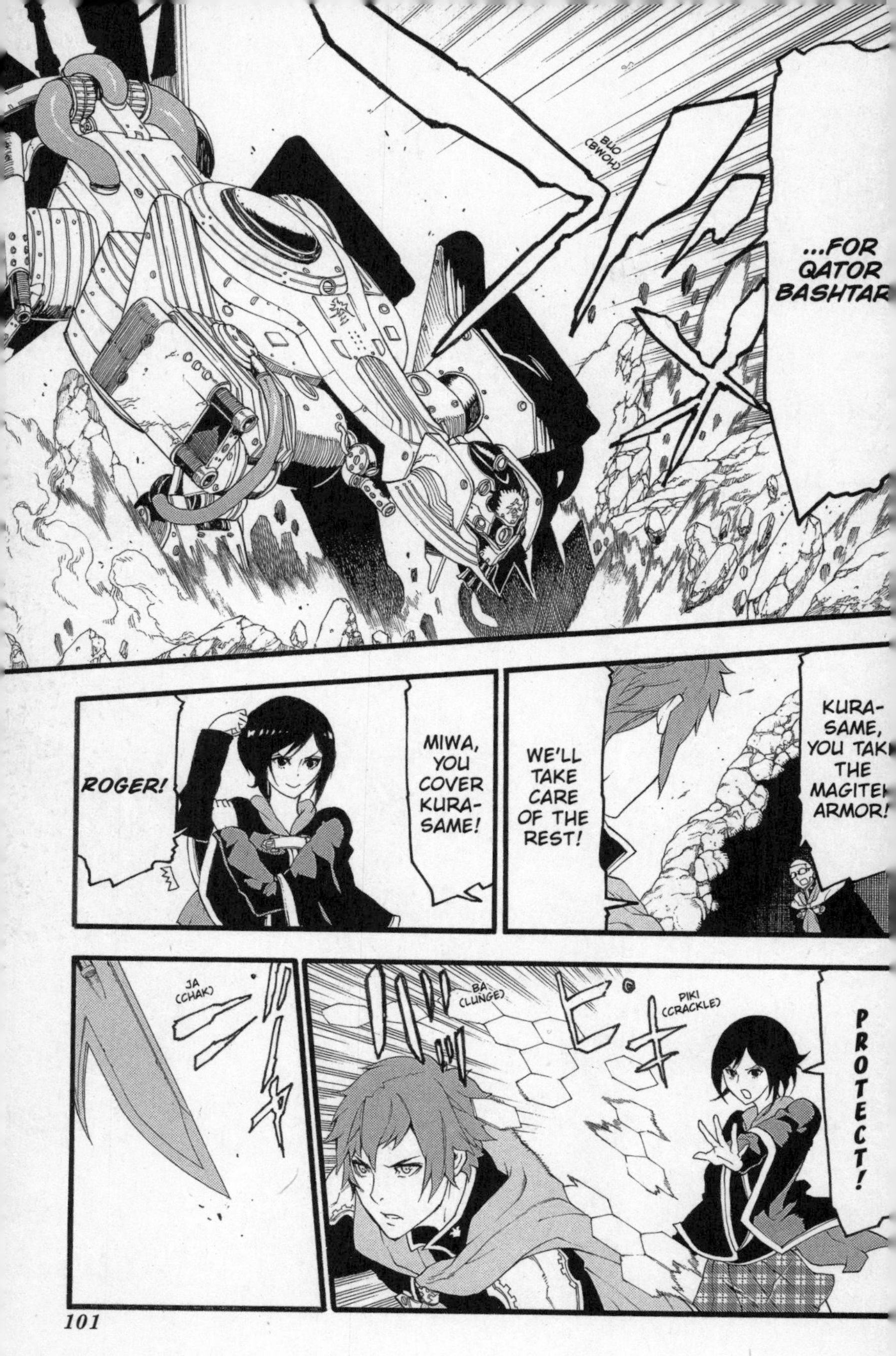
...FOR QATOR BASHTAR
BUO (BWOH)
KURA-SAME, YOU TAK THE MAGITEK ARMOR!
WE'LL TAKE CARE OF THE REST!
MIWA, YOU COVER KURA-SAME!
ROGER!
PROTECT!
PIKI (CRACKLE)
BA (LUNGE)
JA (CHAK)

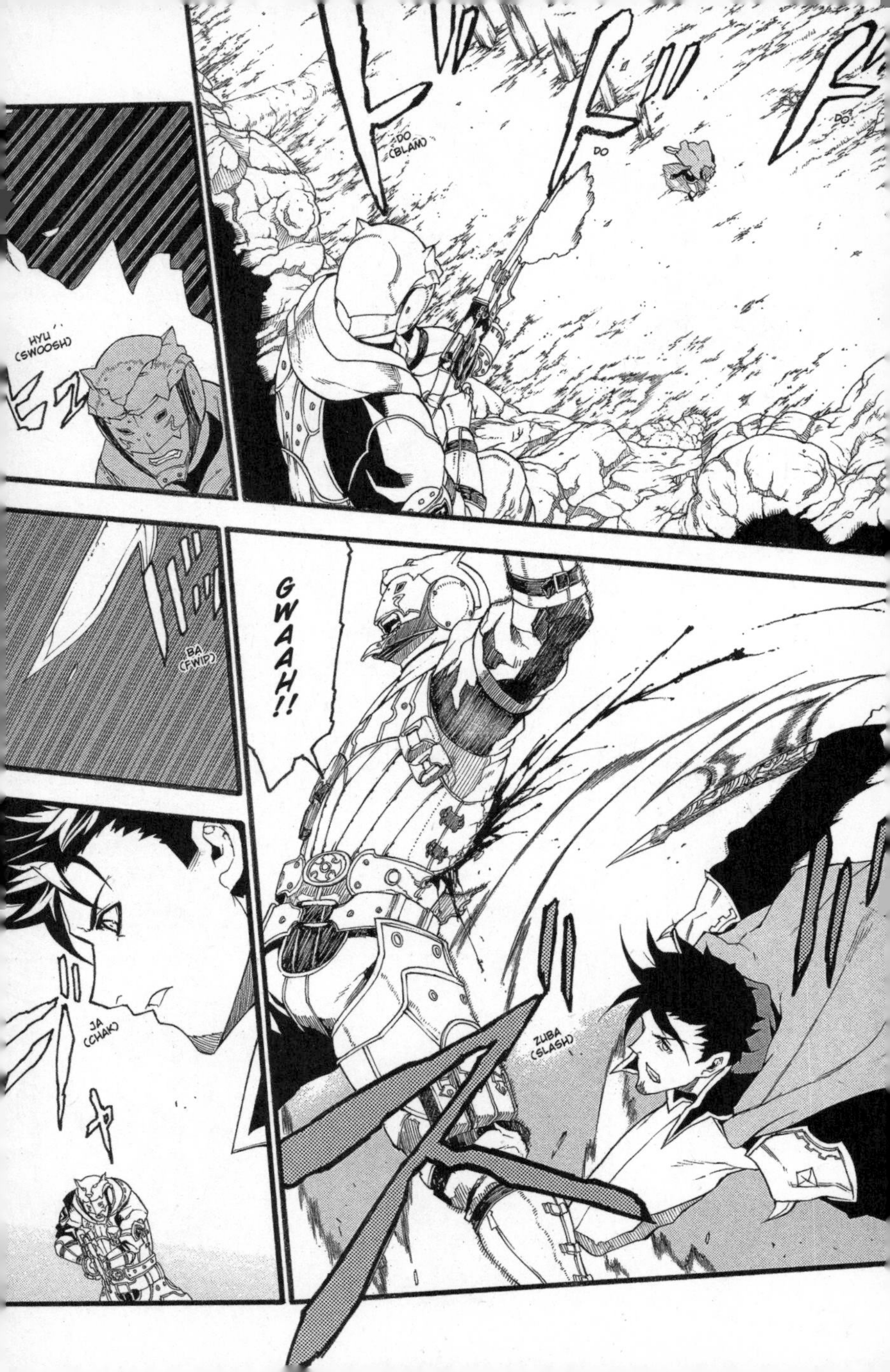
DO
DO
DO (BLAM)
HYU (SWOOSH)
GWAAAH!!
ZUBA (SLASH)
BA (FWIP)
JA (CHAK)

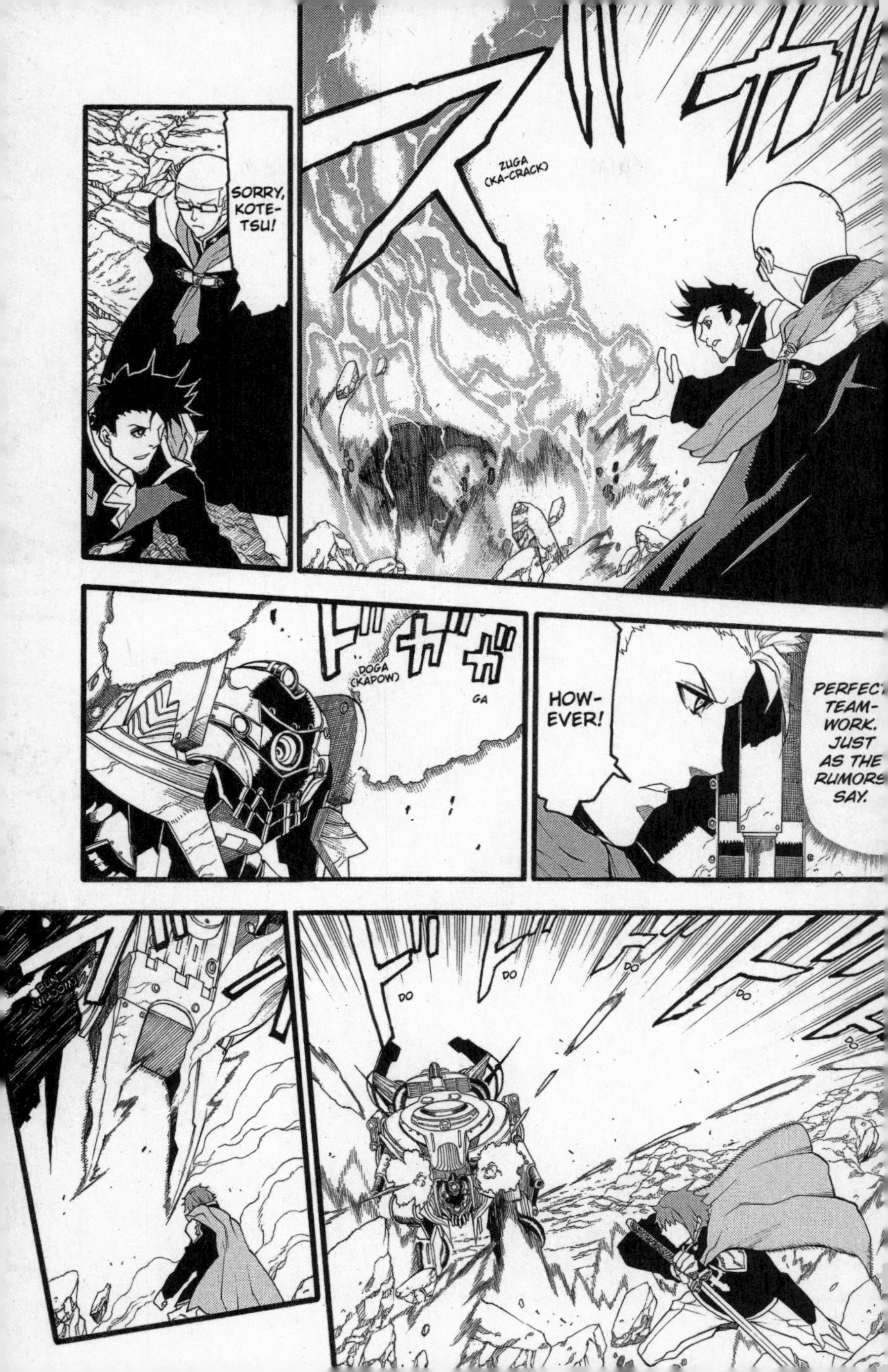
ZUGA (KA-CRACK)
SORRY, KOTE-TSU!
PERFECT TEAM-WORK. JUST AS THE RUMORS SAY.
HOW-EVER!
DOGA (KAPOW)
GA
DO
DO
DO
DO
DO
BUN (WHOOM)

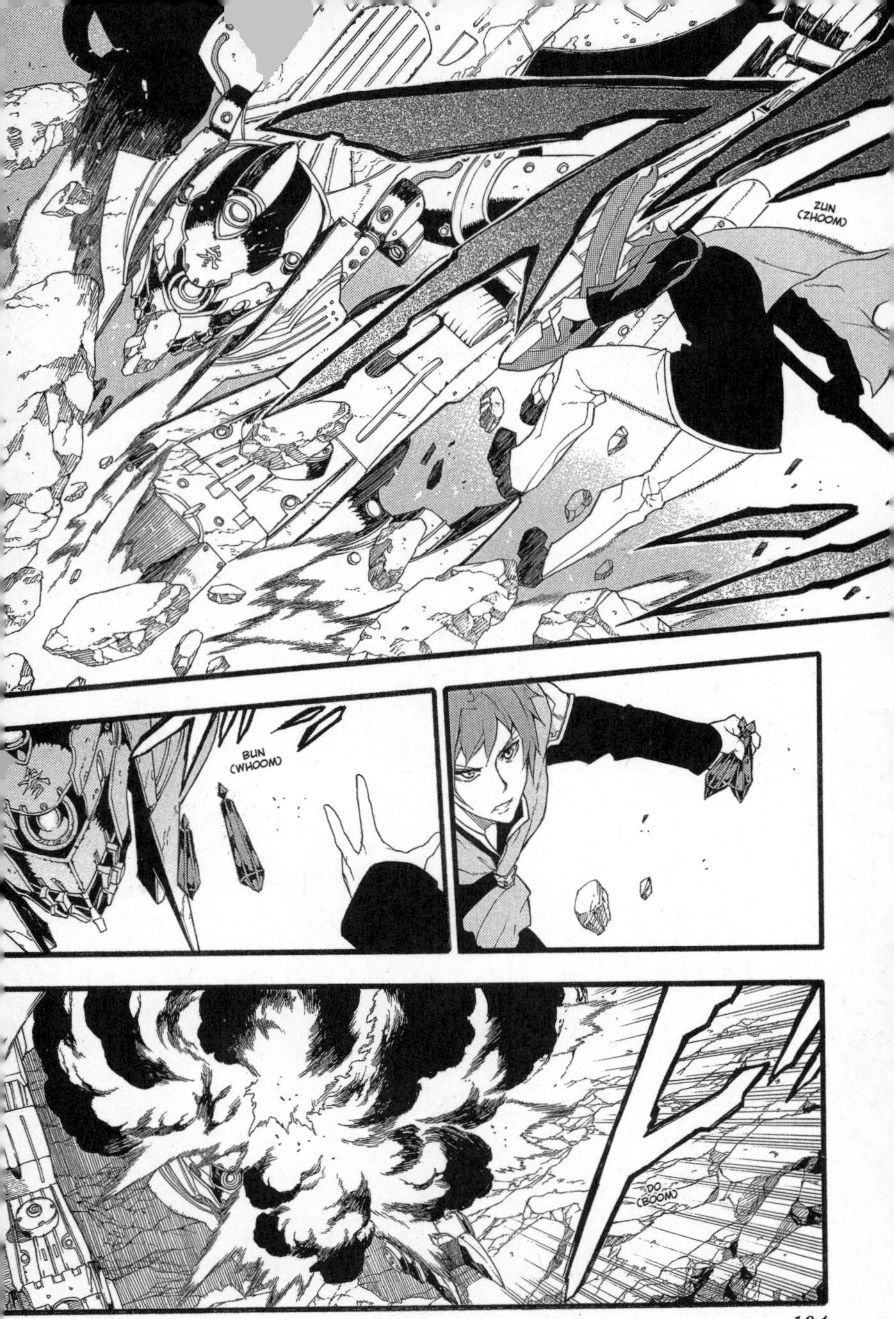
ZUN
(ZHOOM)
BUN
(WHOOM)
DO
(BOOM)

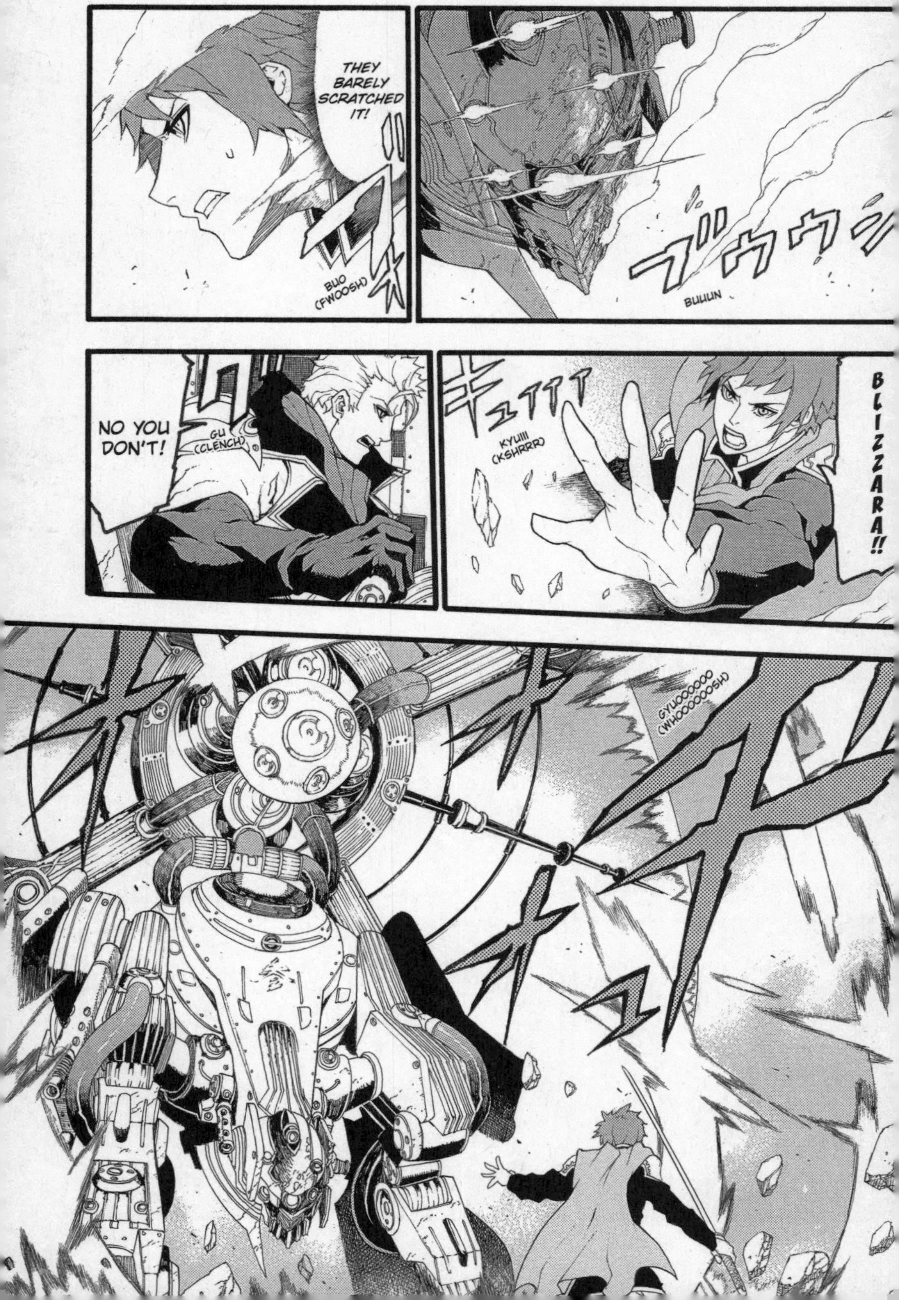
BUUUN
THEY BARELY SCRATCHED IT!
BUO (FWOOSH)
BLIZZARA!!
KYUIII (KSHRRR)
NO YOU DON'T!
GU (CLENCH)
GYUOOOOOO (WHOOOOOOSH)

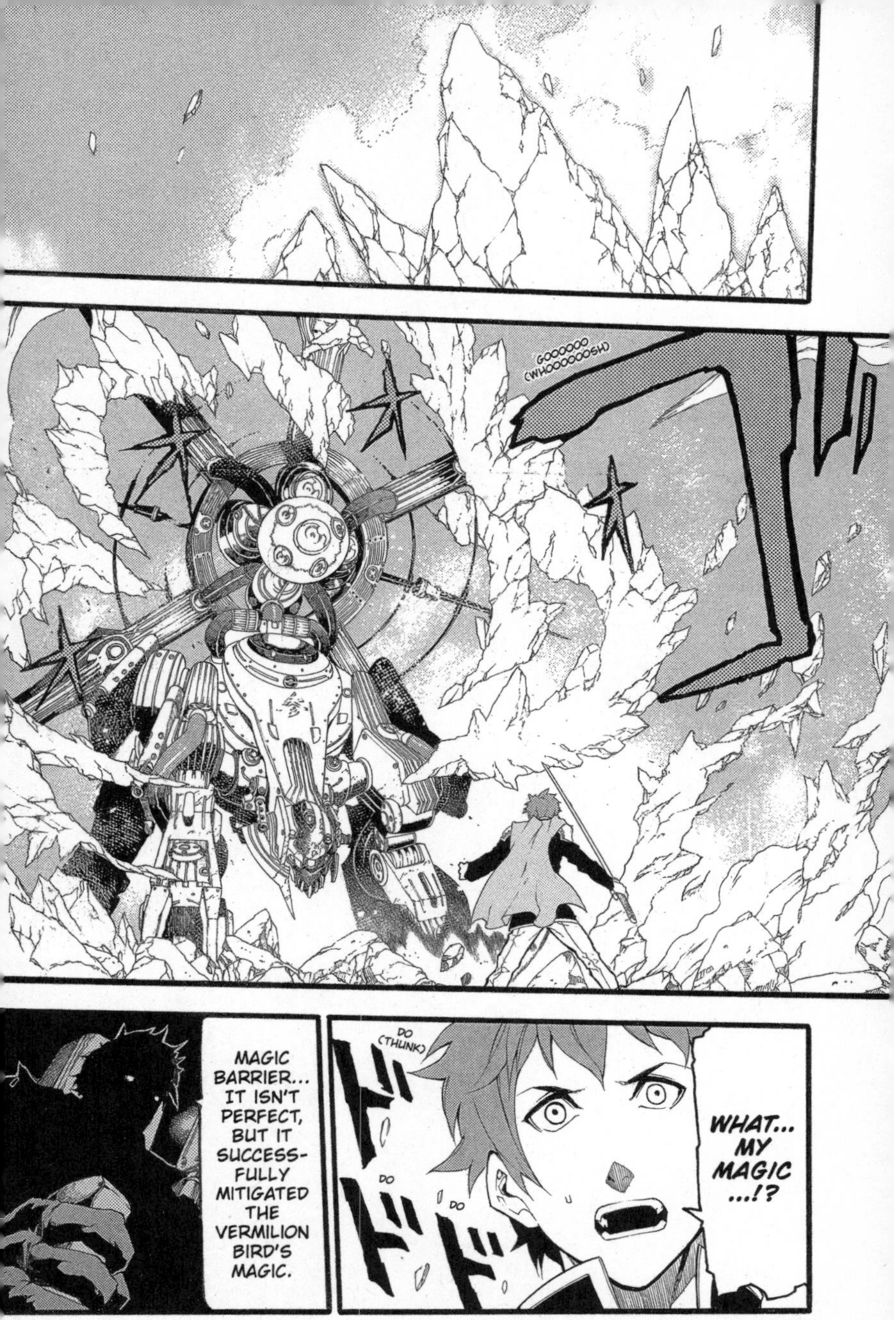
GOOOOOO
(WHOOOOOOSH)
DO
(THUNK)
WHAT... MY MAGIC ...!?
DO
DO
MAGIC BARRIER... IT ISN'T PERFECT, BUT IT SUCCESS-FULLY MITIGATED THE VERMILION BIRD'S MAGIC.

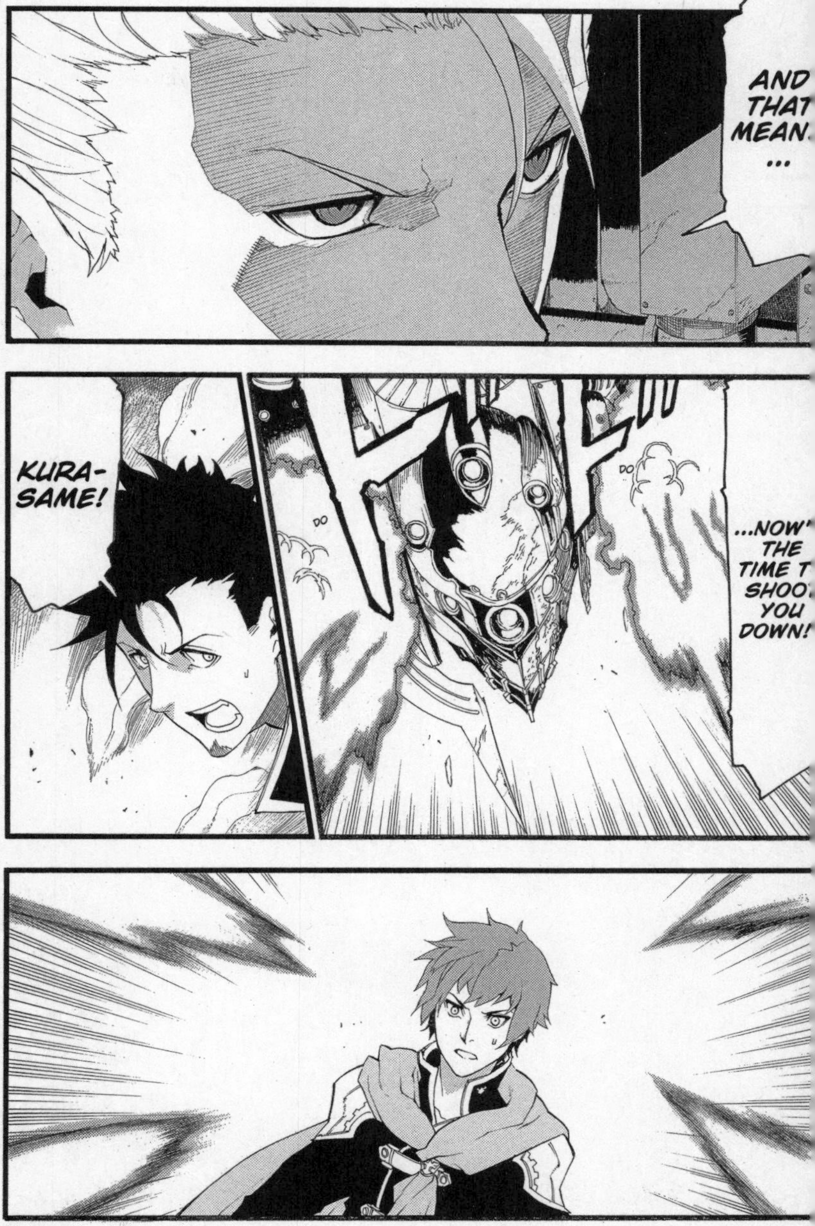
AND THAT MEAN
...
...NOW THE TIME T SHOO YOU DOWN!
DO
DO
KURA-SAME!

FINAL FANTASY 零式 TYPE-0™
SIDE STORY
The Ice Reaper

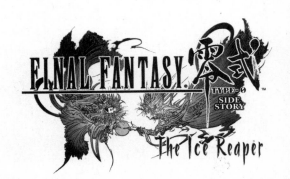

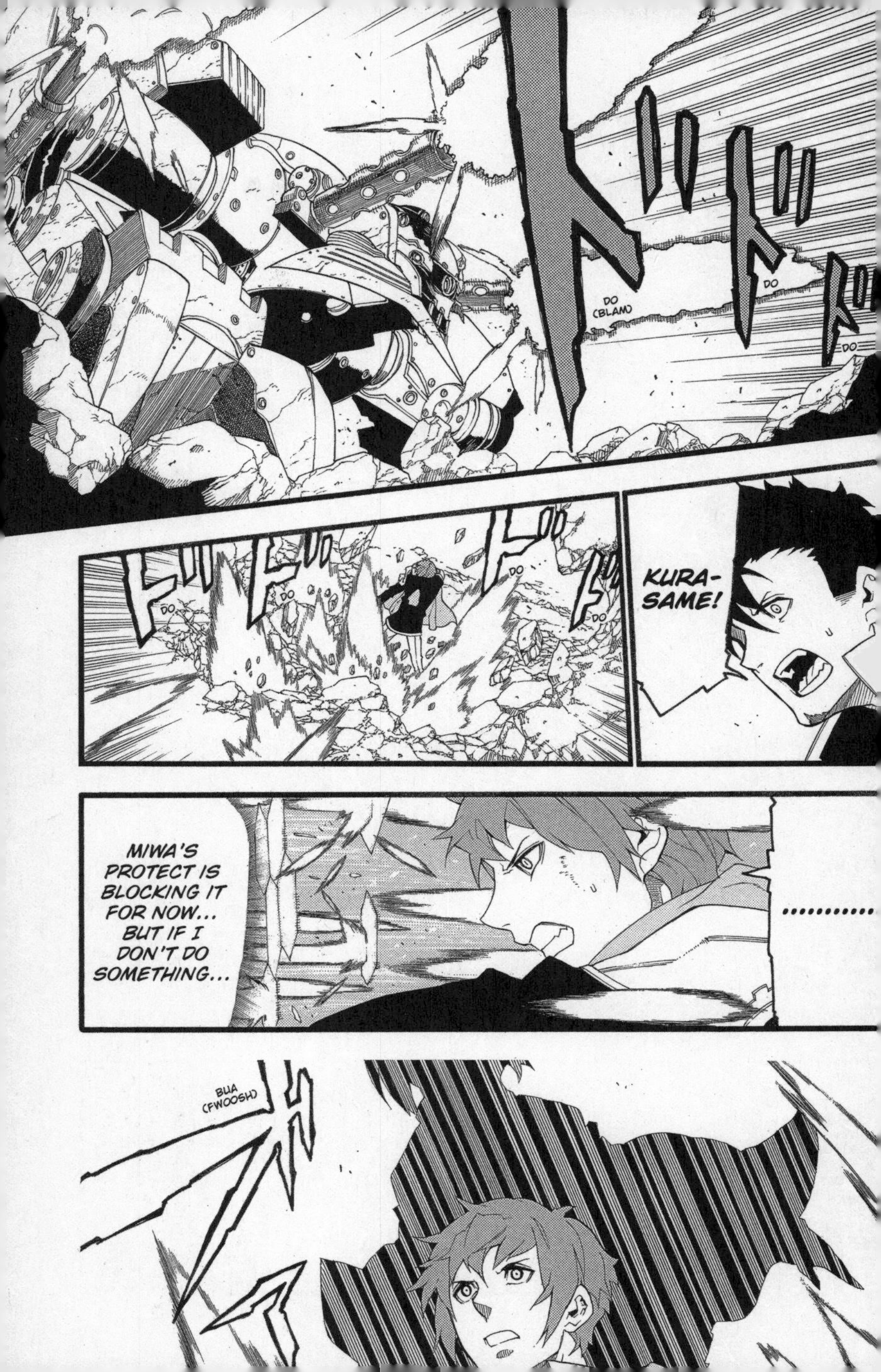
DO (BLAM)
DO
DO
KURA-SAME!
DO
DO
DO
DO
....
MIWA'S PROTECT IS BLOCKING IT FOR NOW... BUT IF I DON'T DO SOMETHING...
BUA (FWOOSH)

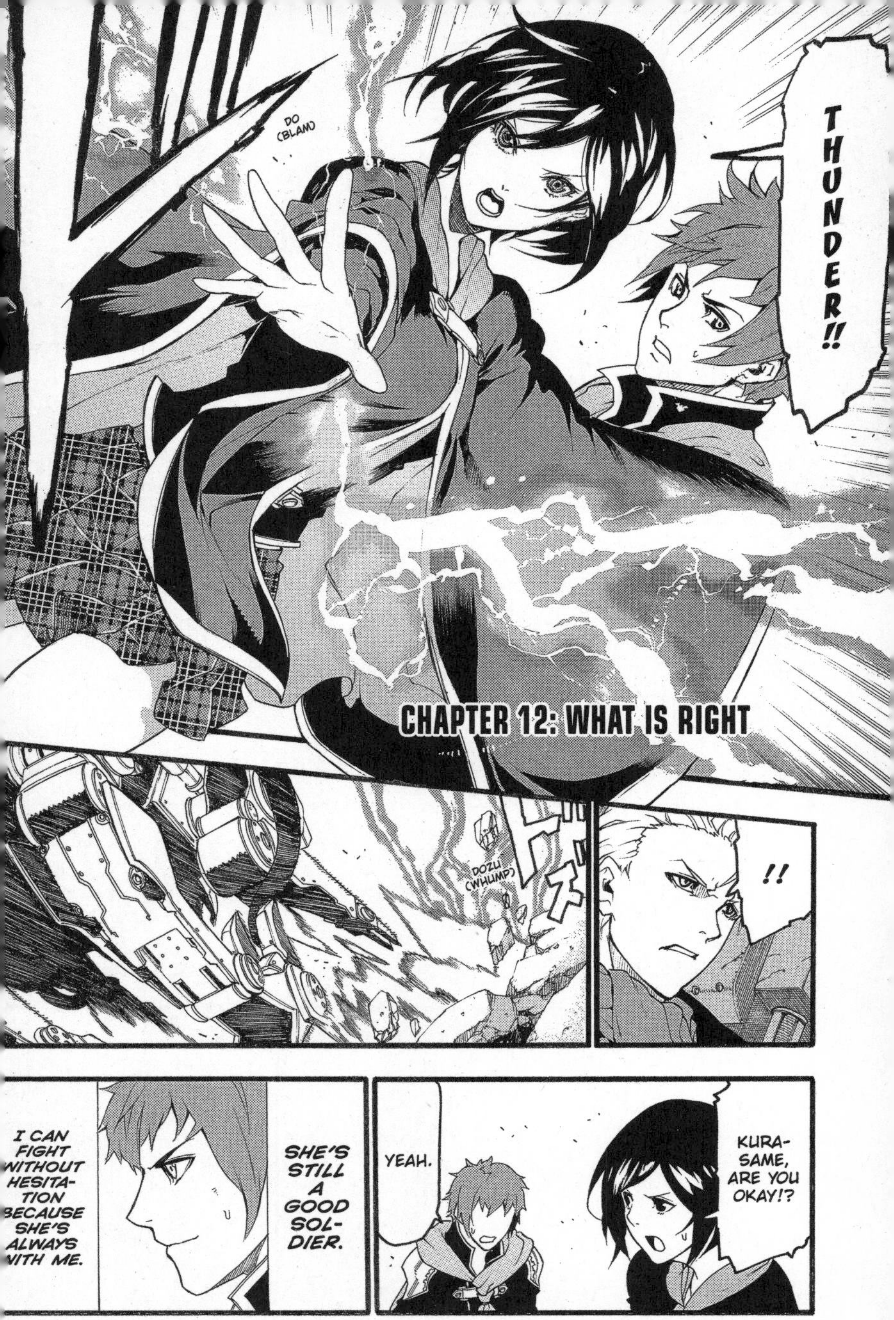
THUNDER!!
DO (BLAM)
CHAPTER 12: WHAT IS RIGHT
!!
DOZU (WHUMP)
KURA-SAME, ARE YOU OKAY!?
YEAH.
SHE'S STILL A GOOD SOL-DIER.
I CAN FIGHT WITHOUT HESITA-TION BECAUSE SHE'S ALWAYS WITH ME.

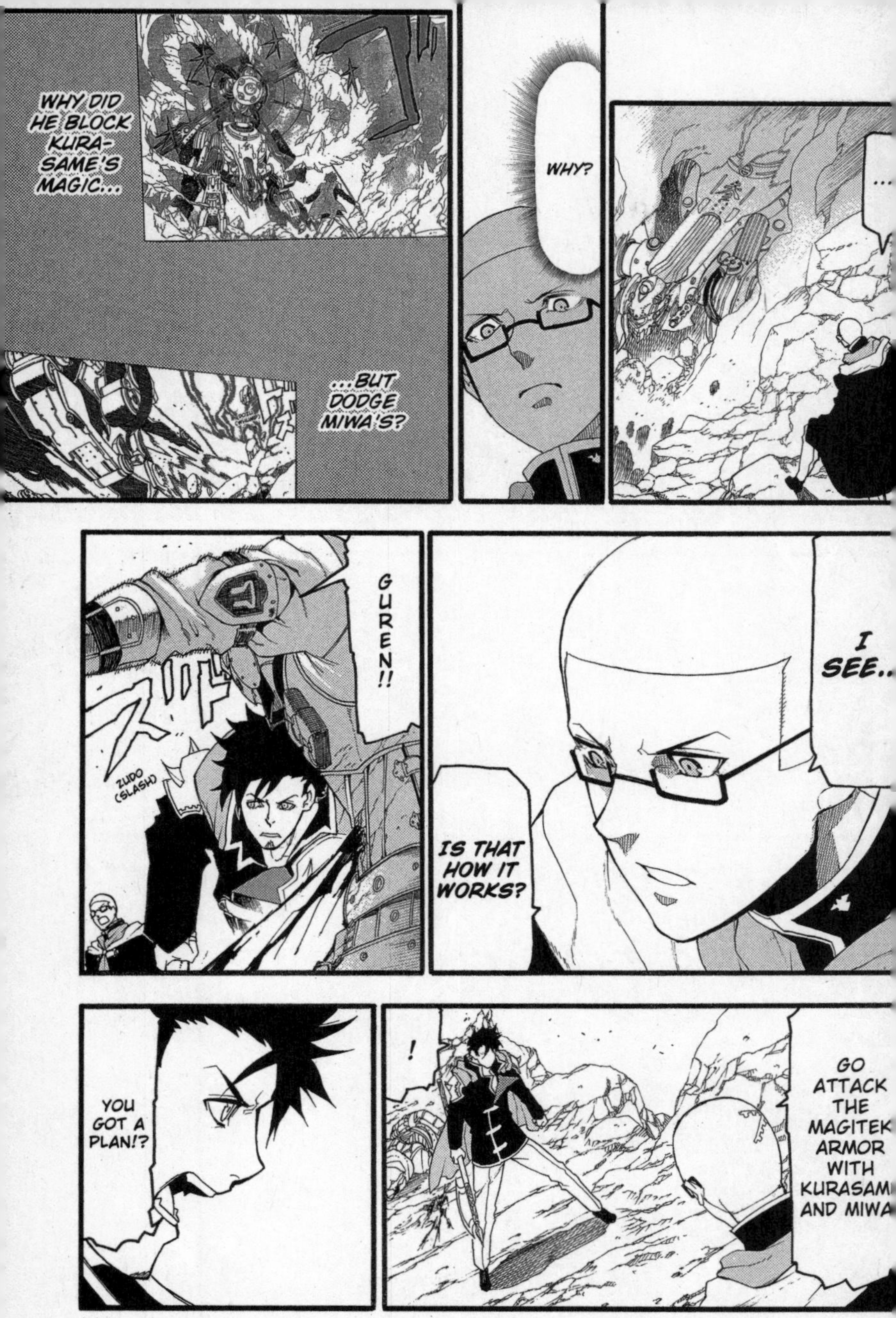
...
WHY?
WHY DID HE BLOCK KURA-SAME'S MAGIC...
...BUT DODGE MIWA'S?
I SEE...
IS THAT HOW IT WORKS?
GUREN!!
ZUDO (SLASH)
GO ATTACK THE MAGITEK ARMOR WITH KURASAM AND MIWA
!
YOU GOT A PLAN!?

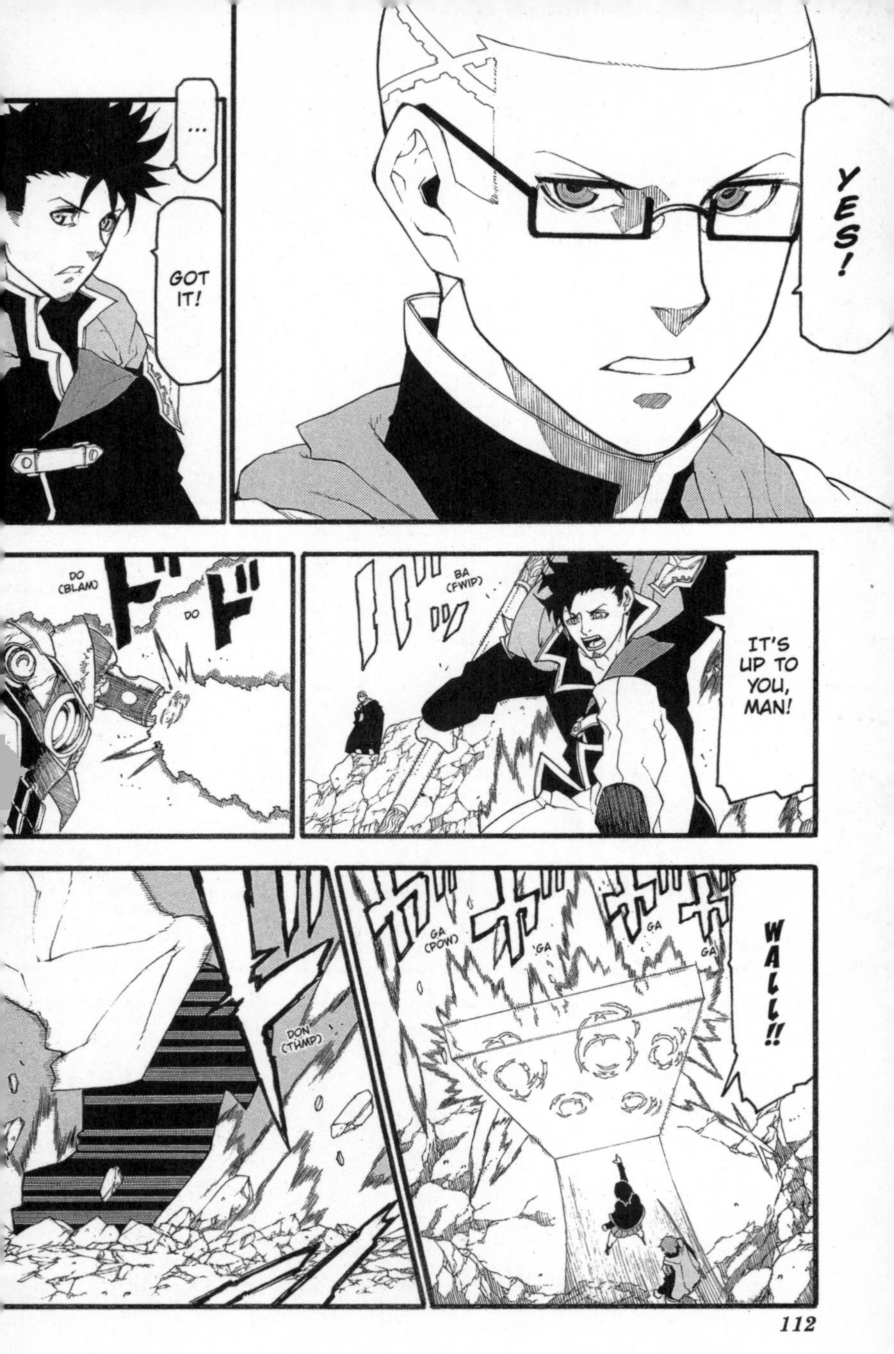
YES!
...
GOT IT!
BA (FWIP)
IT'S UP TO YOU, MAN!
DO (BLAM)
DO
GA
GA
GA
GA (POW)
WALL!!
...
DON (THMP)

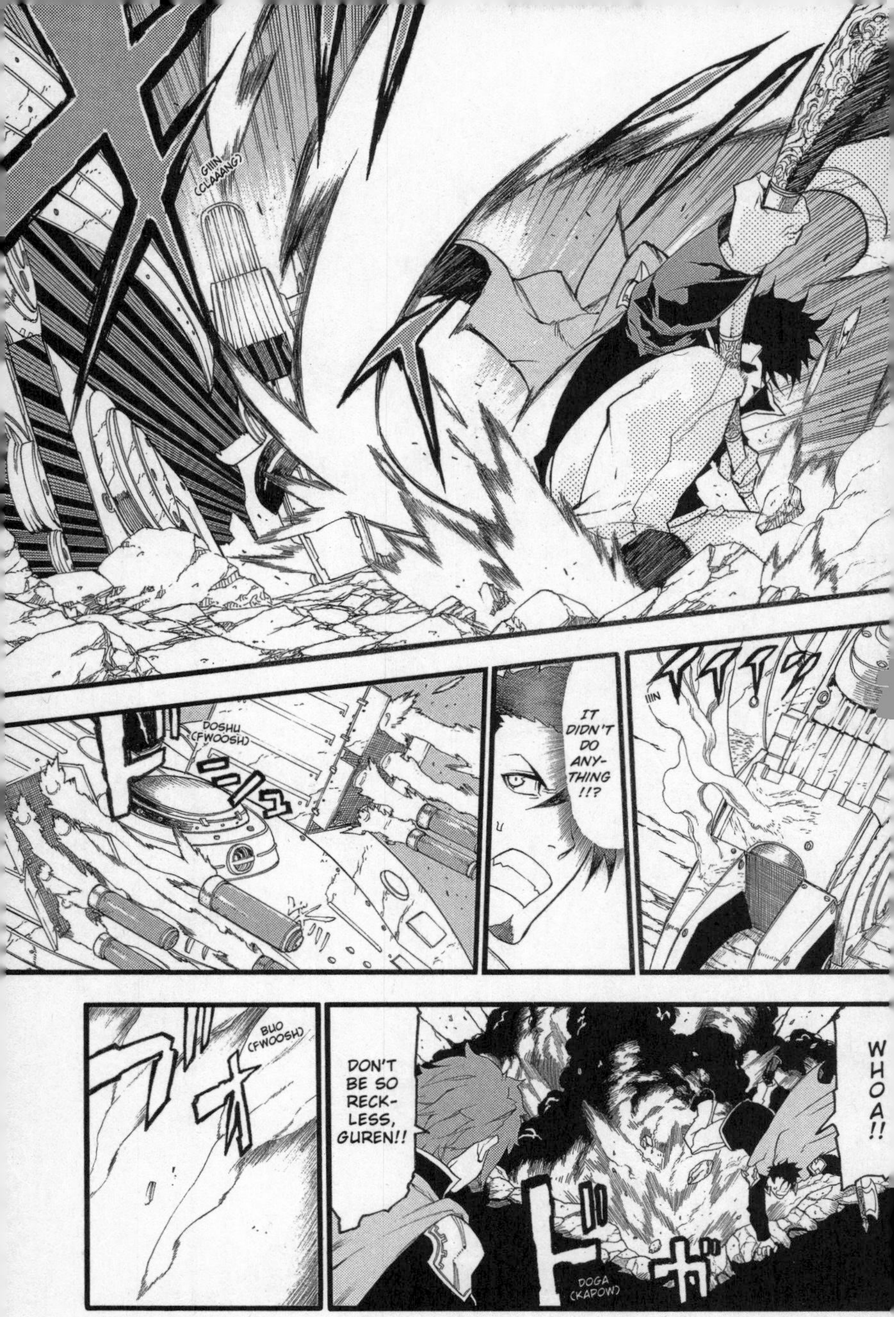
GIIIN (CLAAANG)
IIIN
IT DIDN'T DO ANY-THING!!?
DOSHU (FWOOSH)
WHOA!!
DON'T BE SO RECK-LESS, GUREN!!
DOGA (KAPOW)
BUO (FWOOSH)

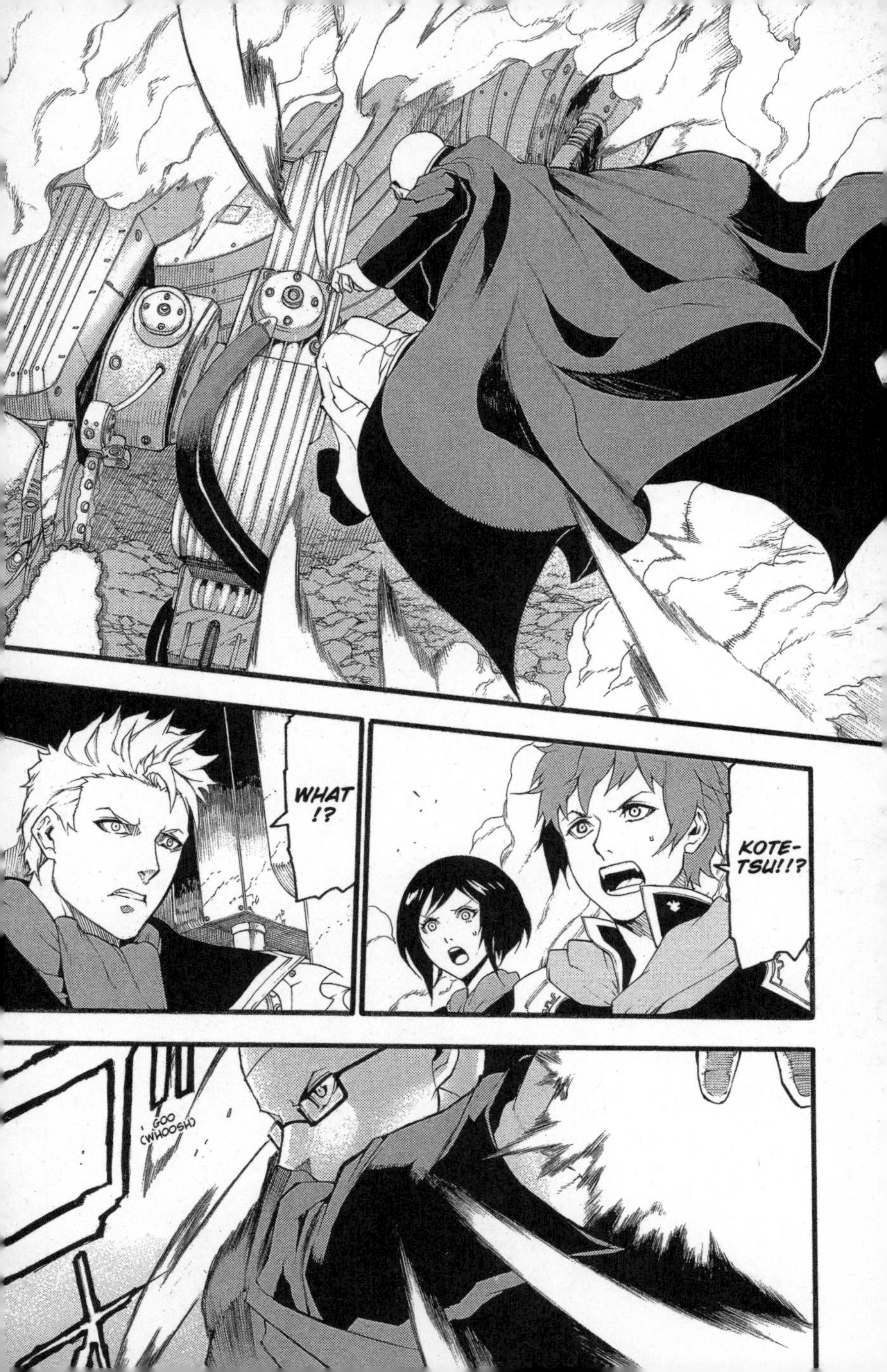
KOTE-TSU!!?
WHAT !?
GOO (WHOOSH)

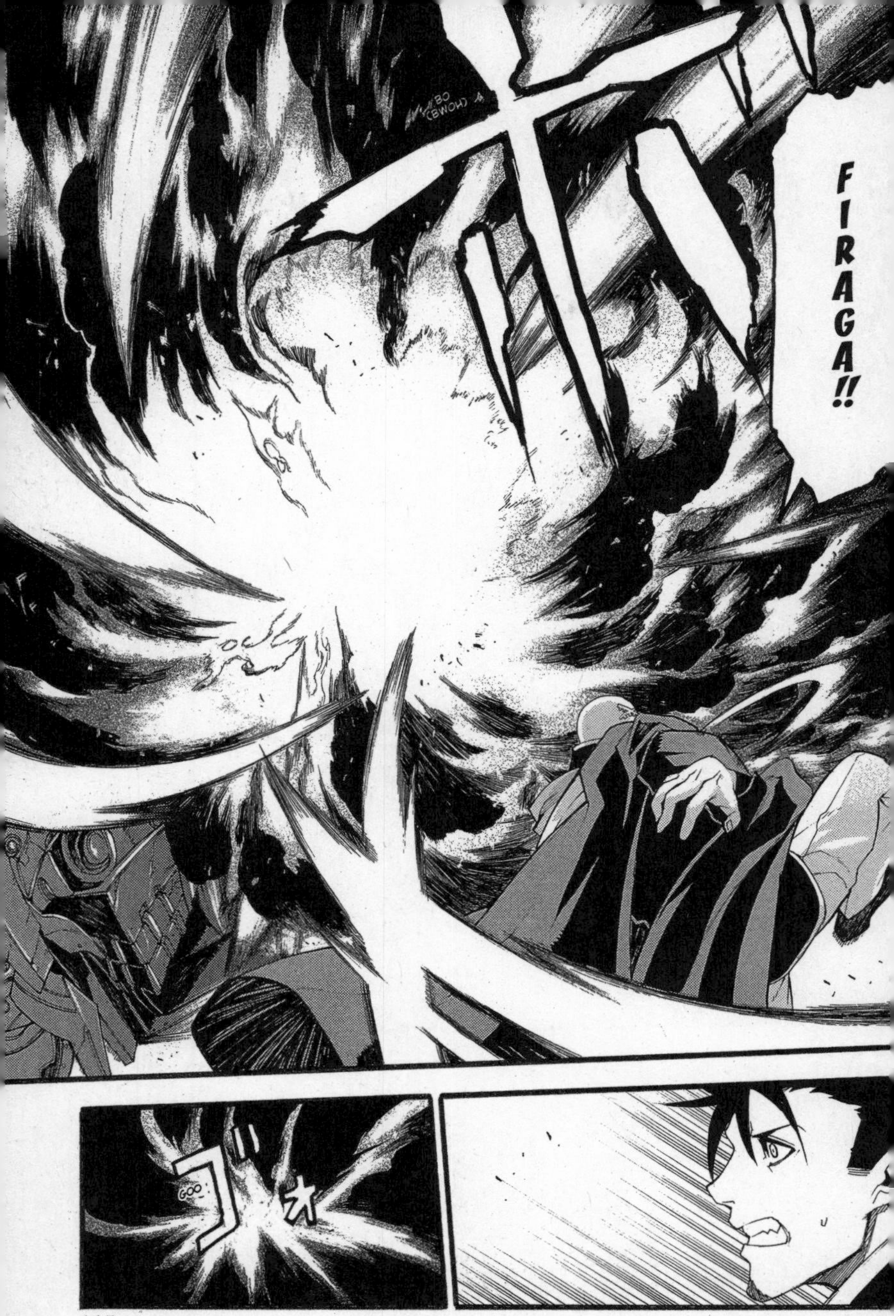
FIRAGA!!
BO
(BWOH)
GOO

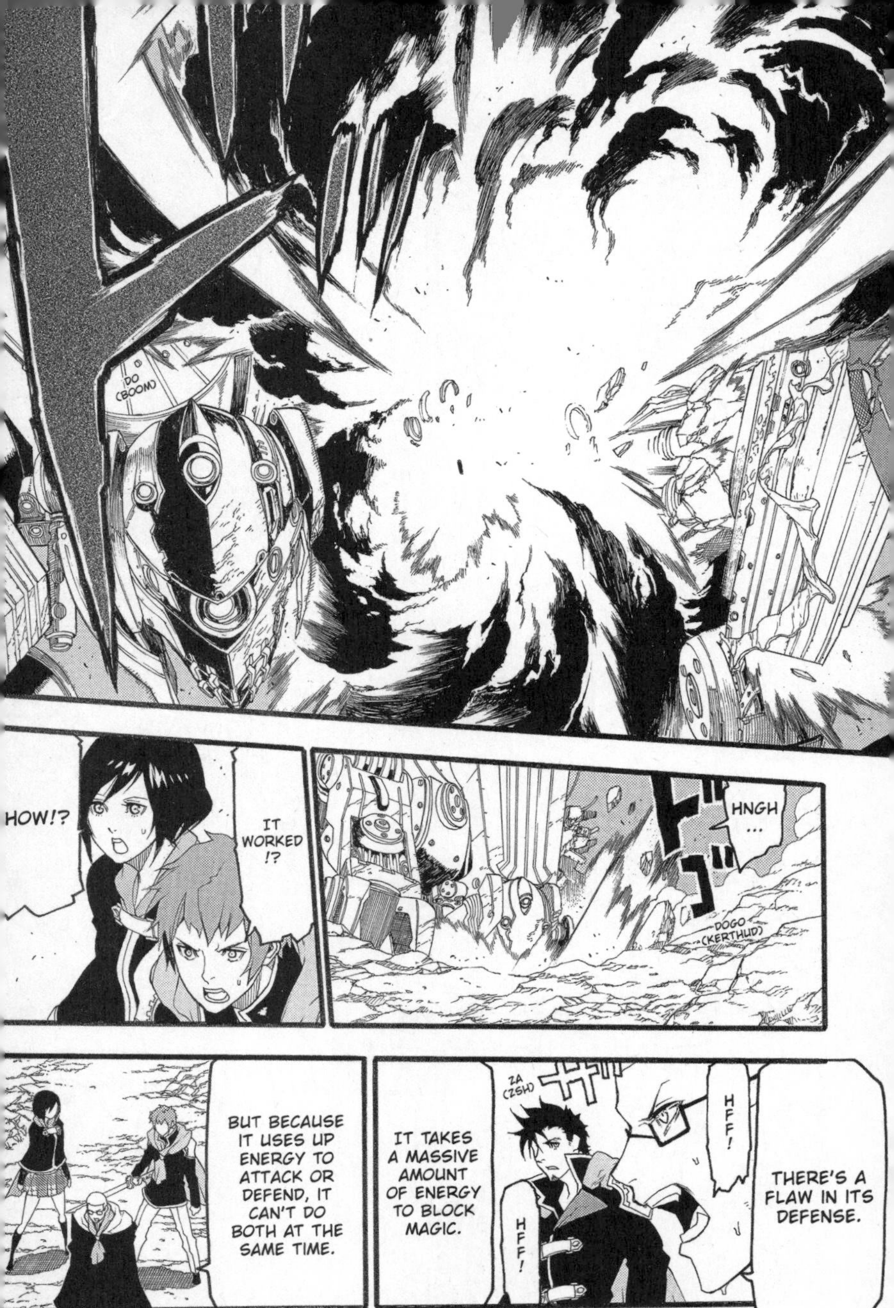
DO (BOOM)
HNGH ...
DOGO (KERTHUD)
IT WORKED !?
HOW!?
THERE'S A FLAW IN ITS DEFENSE.
HFF!
HFF!
ZA (ZSH)
IT TAKES A MASSIVE AMOUNT OF ENERGY TO BLOCK MAGIC.
BUT BECAUSE IT USES UP ENERGY TO ATTACK OR DEFEND, IT CAN'T DO BOTH AT THE SAME TIME.

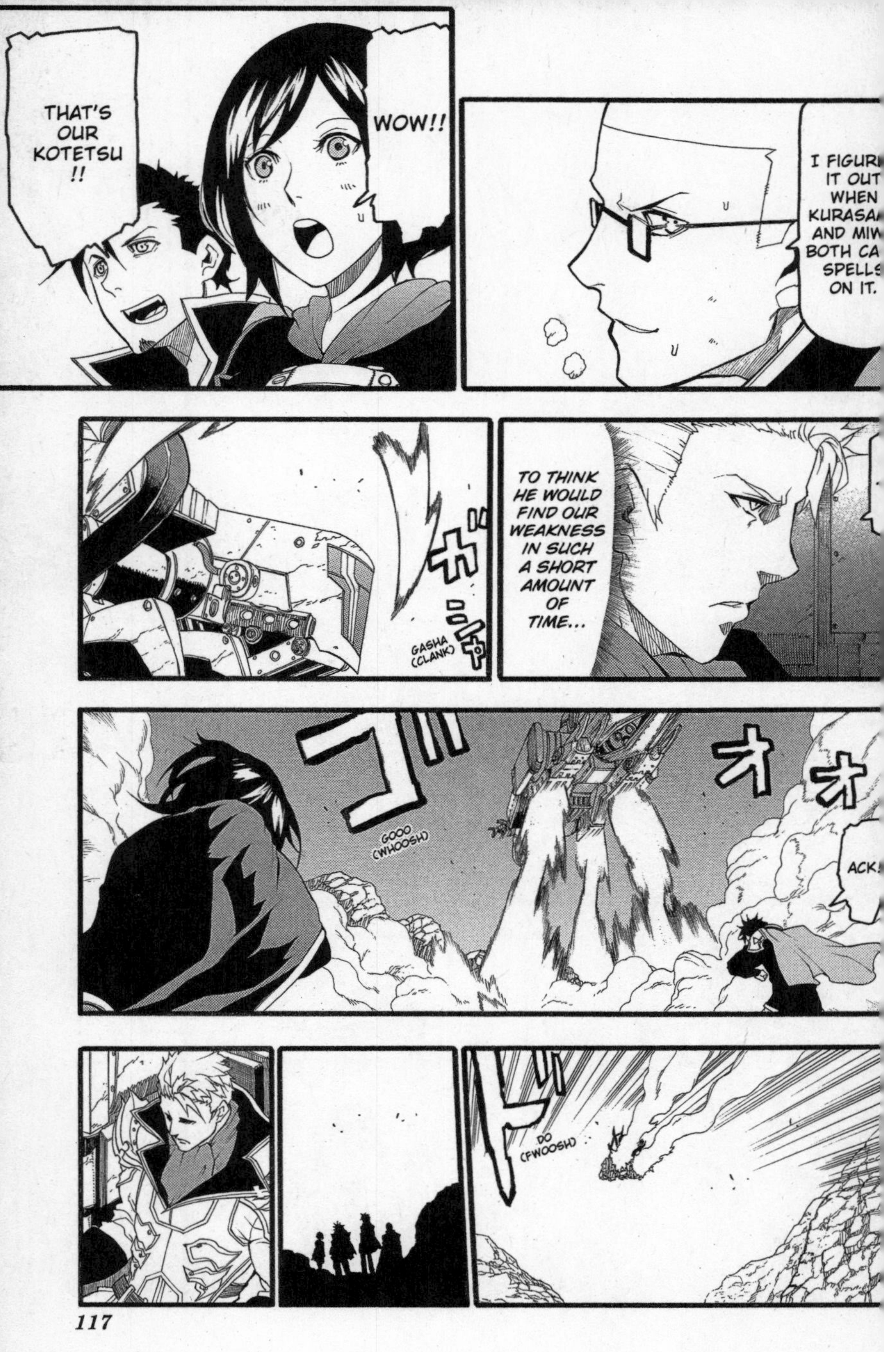
I FIGUR
IT OUT
WHEN
KURASA
AND MIW
BOTH CA
SPELLS
ON IT.
WOW!!
THAT'S OUR KOTETSU!!
TO THINK HE WOULD FIND OUR WEAKNESS IN SUCH A SHORT AMOUNT OF TIME...
GASHA (CLANK)
ACK
GOOO (WHOOSH)
DO (FWOOSH)

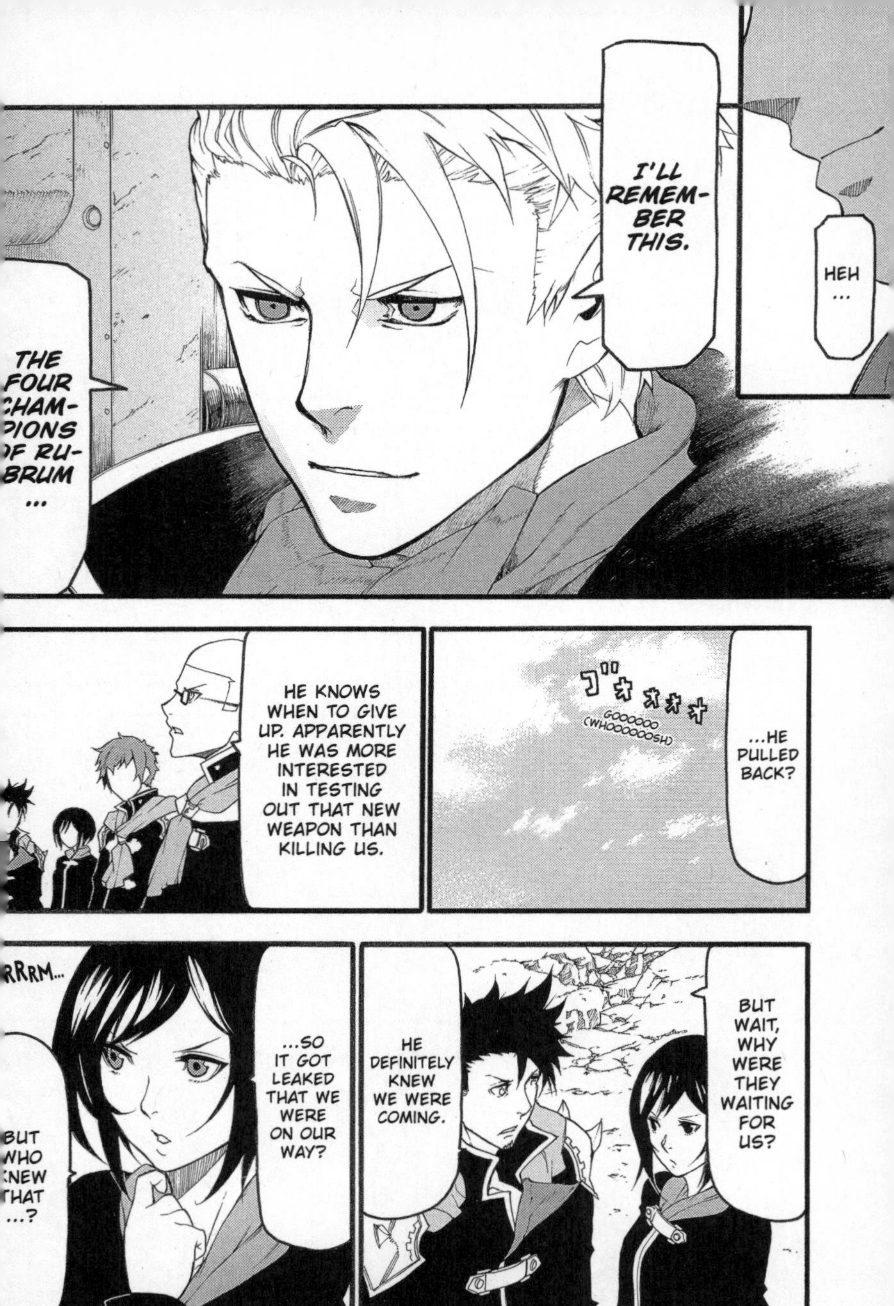
HEH...
I'LL REMEMBER THIS.
THE FOUR CHAMPIONS OF RUBRUM...
ゴオオオオ
GOOOOOO (WHOOOOOOSH)
...HE PULLED BACK?
HE KNOWS WHEN TO GIVE UP. APPARENTLY HE WAS MORE INTERESTED IN TESTING OUT THAT NEW WEAPON THAN KILLING US.
BUT WAIT, WHY WERE THEY WAITING FOR US?
HE DEFINITELY KNEW WE WERE COMING.
...SO IT GOT LEAKED THAT WE WERE ON OUR WAY?
RRRM...
BUT WHO KNEW THAT...?

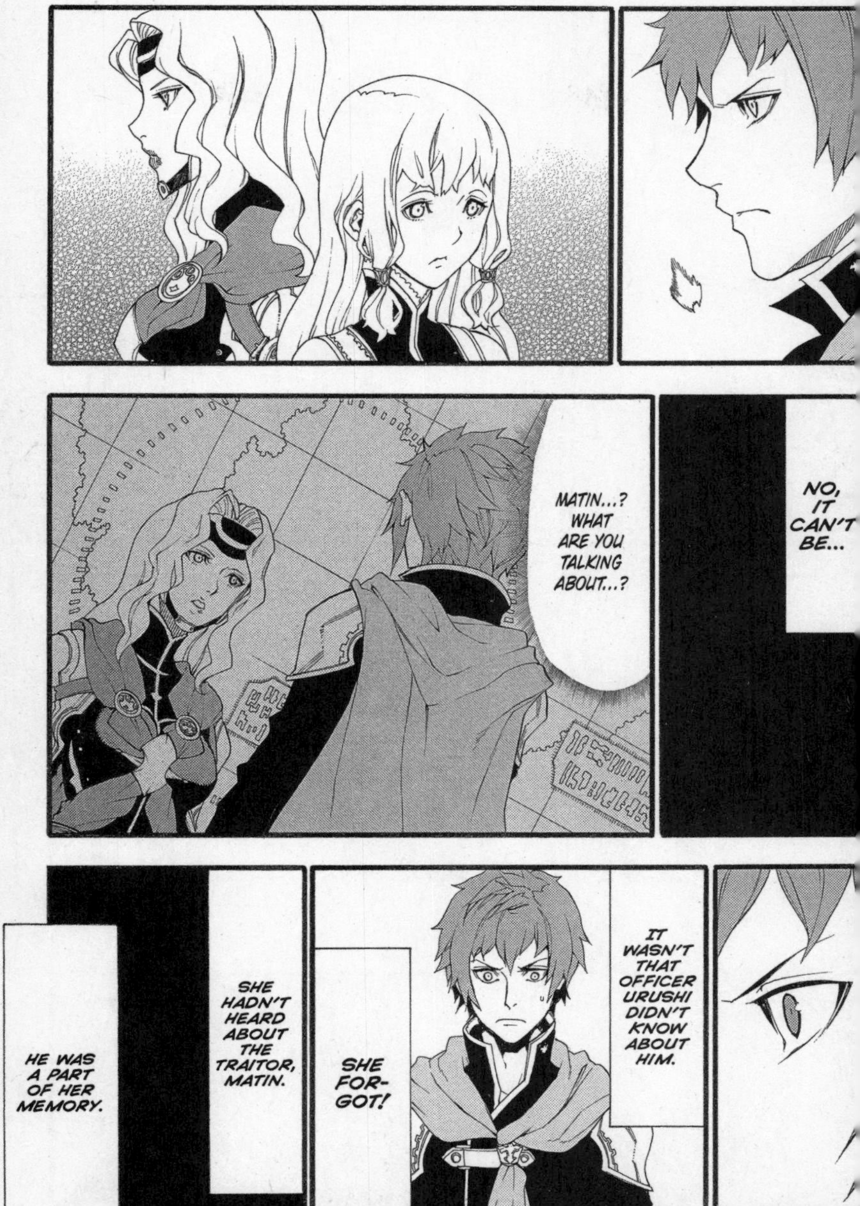
NO, IT CAN'T BE...
MATIN...? WHAT ARE YOU TALKING ABOUT...?
IT WASN'T THAT OFFICER URUSHI DIDN'T KNOW ABOUT HIM.
SHE FORGOT!
SHE HADN'T HEARD ABOUT THE TRAITOR, MATIN.
HE WAS A PART OF HER MEMORY.

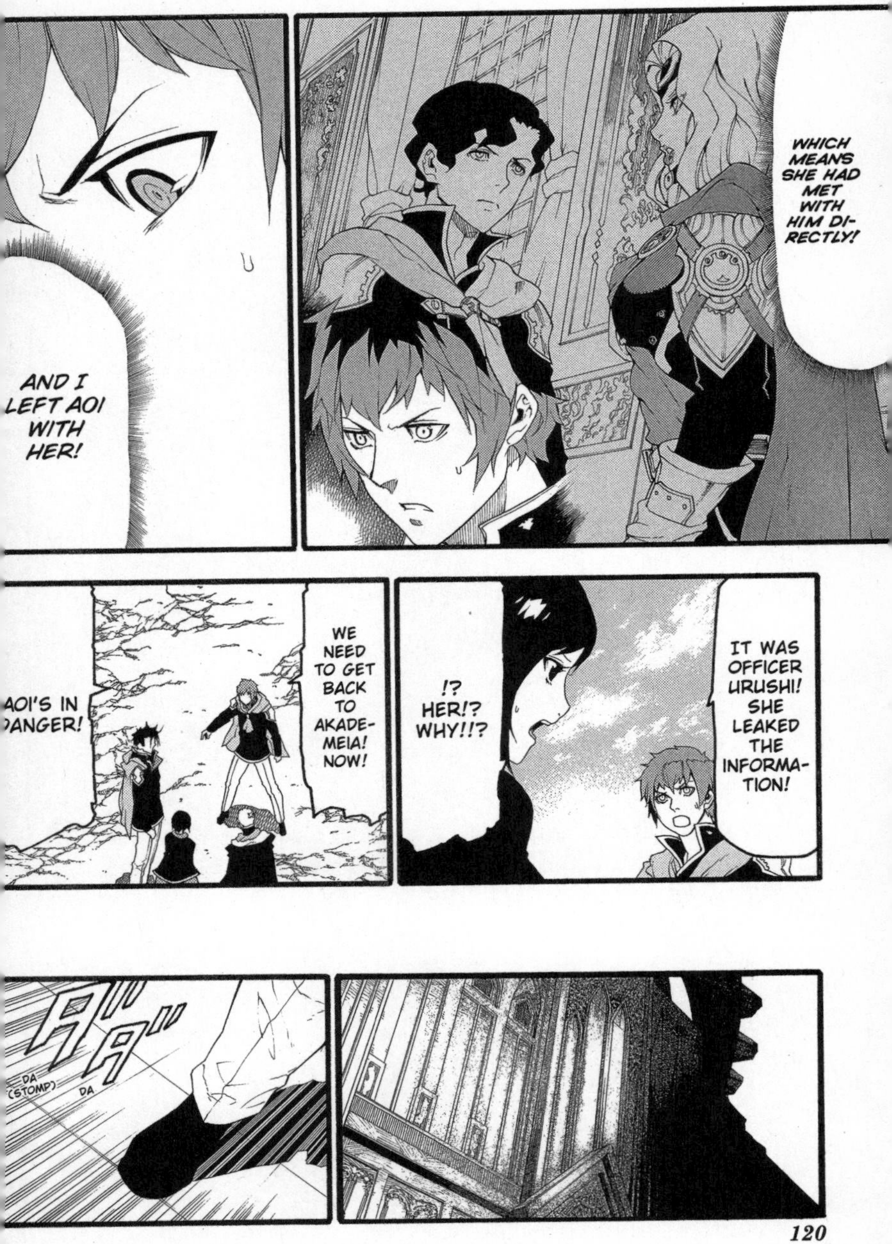
WHICH MEANS SHE HAD MET WITH HIM DIRECTLY!
AND I LEFT AOI WITH HER!
IT WAS OFFICER URUSHI! SHE LEAKED THE INFORMATION!
!? HER!? WHY!!?
WE NEED TO GET BACK TO AKADEMEIA! NOW!
AOI'S IN DANGER!
DA DA (STOMP)

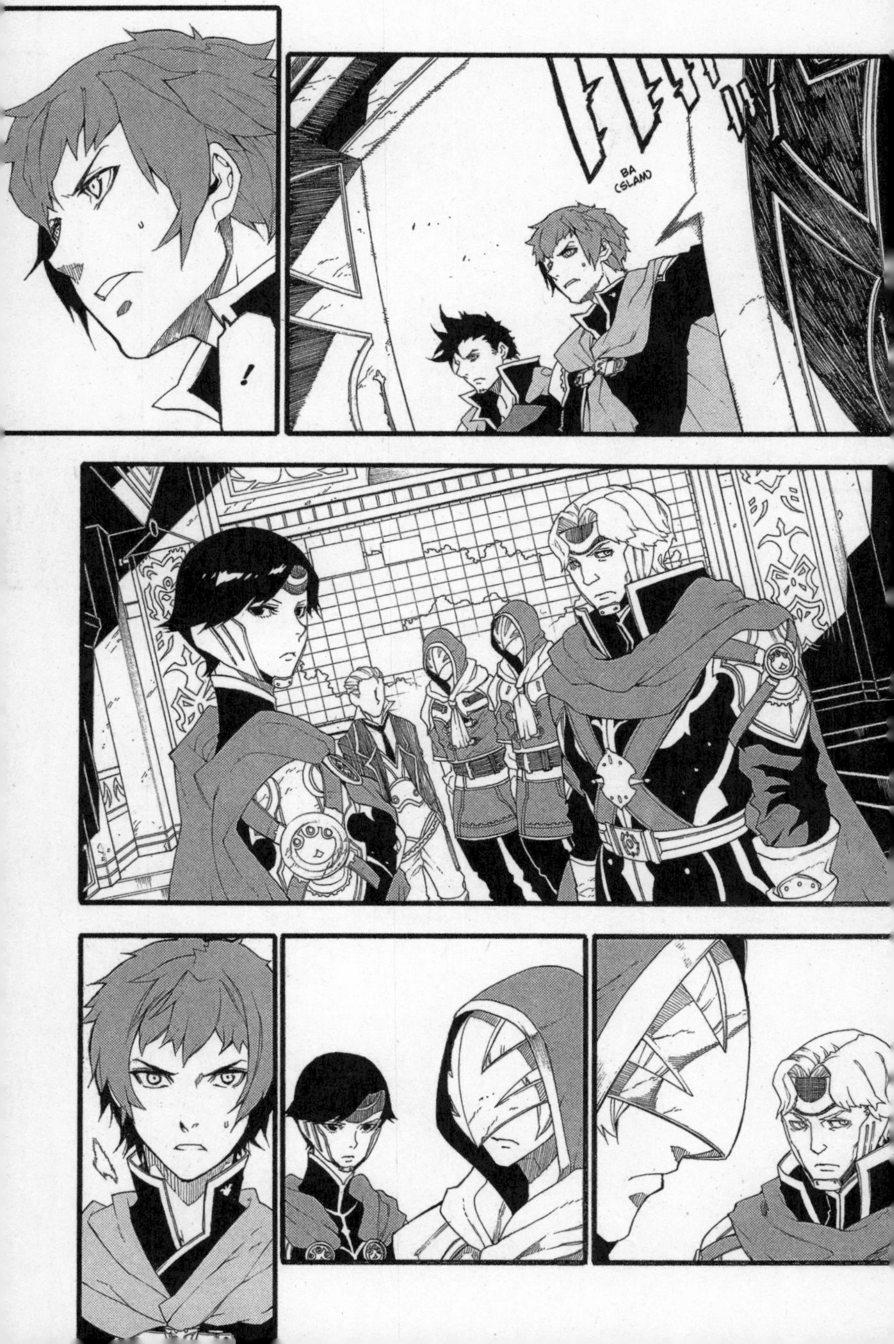
BA
(SLAM)
. . .
!

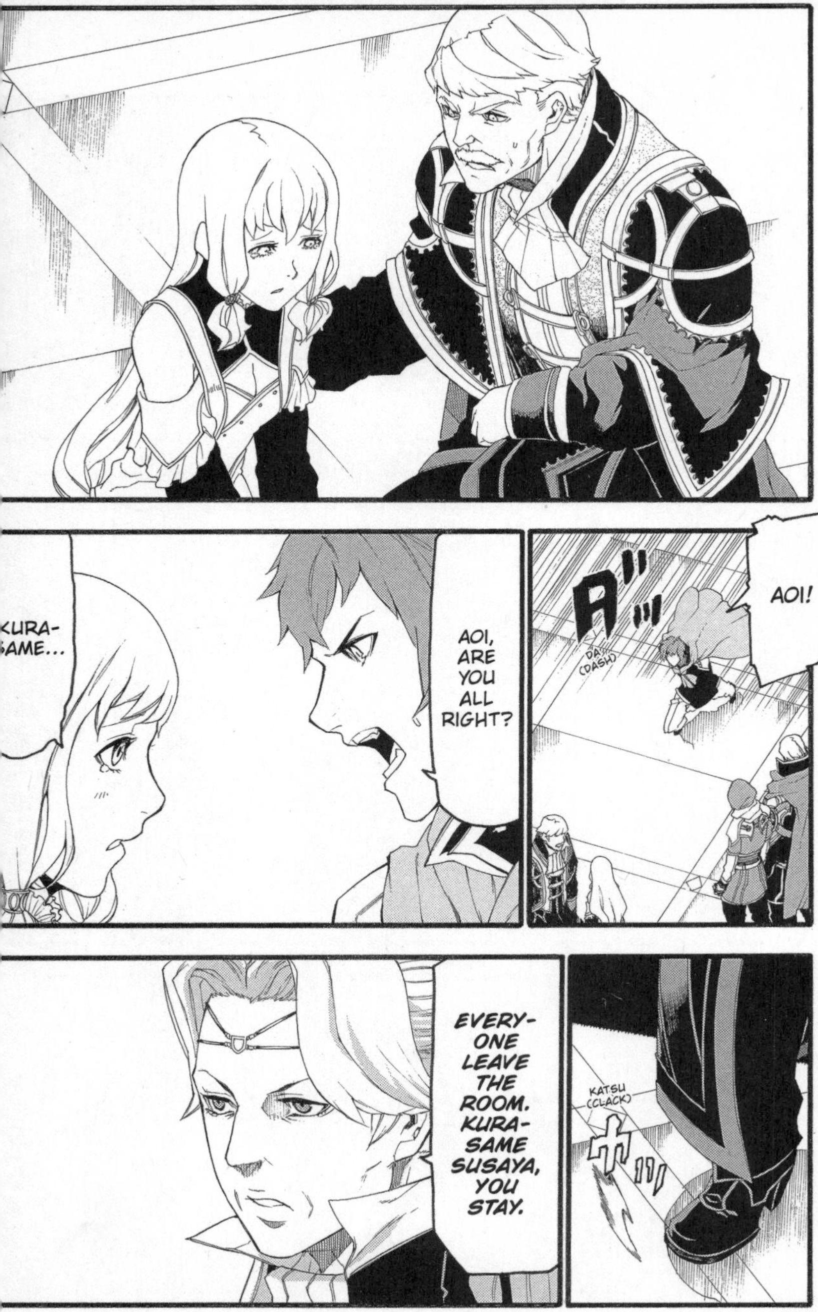
AOI!
DA (DASH)
AOI, ARE YOU ALL RIGHT?
KURA-SAME...
KATSU (CLACK)
EVERY-ONE LEAVE THE ROOM. KURA-SAME SUSAYA, YOU STAY.

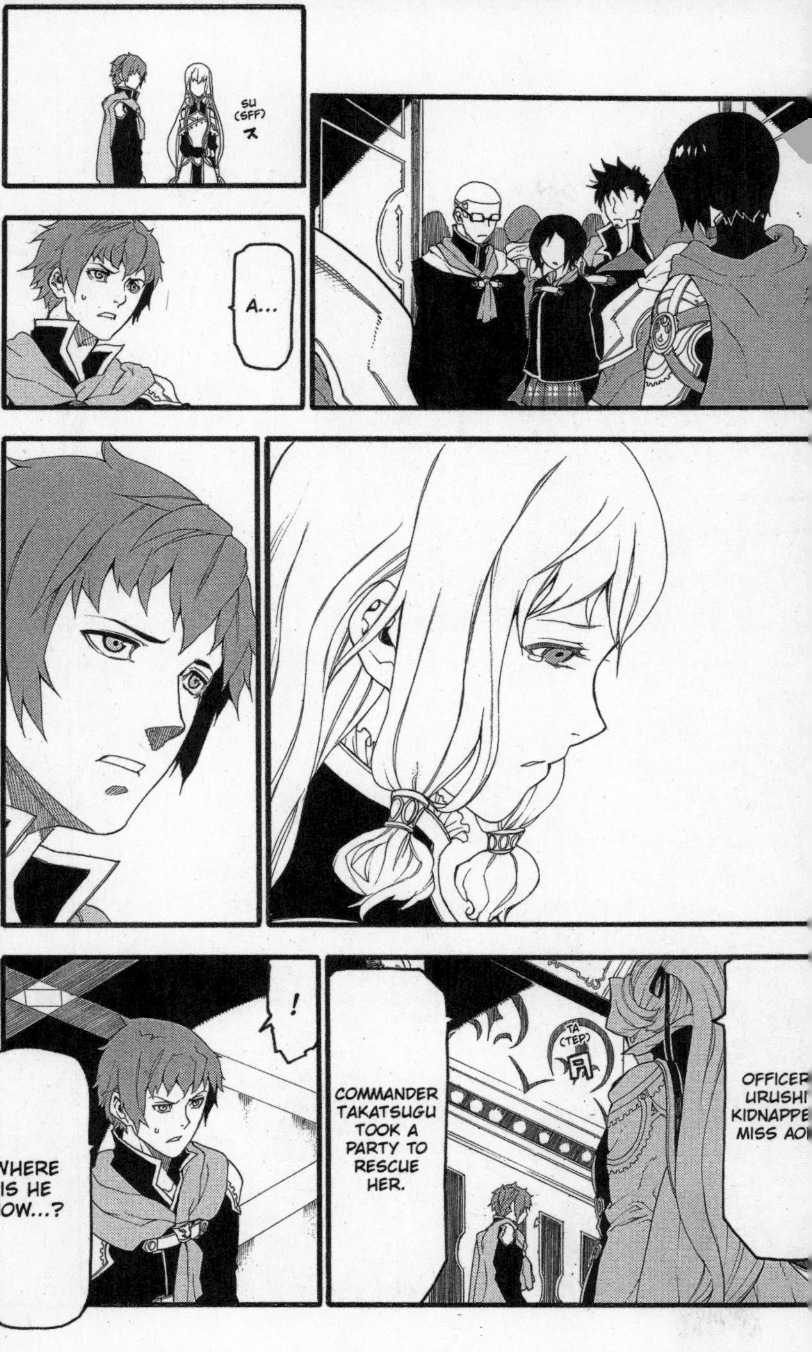
SU (SFF) ス
A...
OFFICER URUSHI KIDNAPPE MISS AO
TA (TEP) ⽉
COMMANDER TAKATSUGU TOOK A PARTY TO RESCUE HER.
!
WHERE IS HE NOW...?

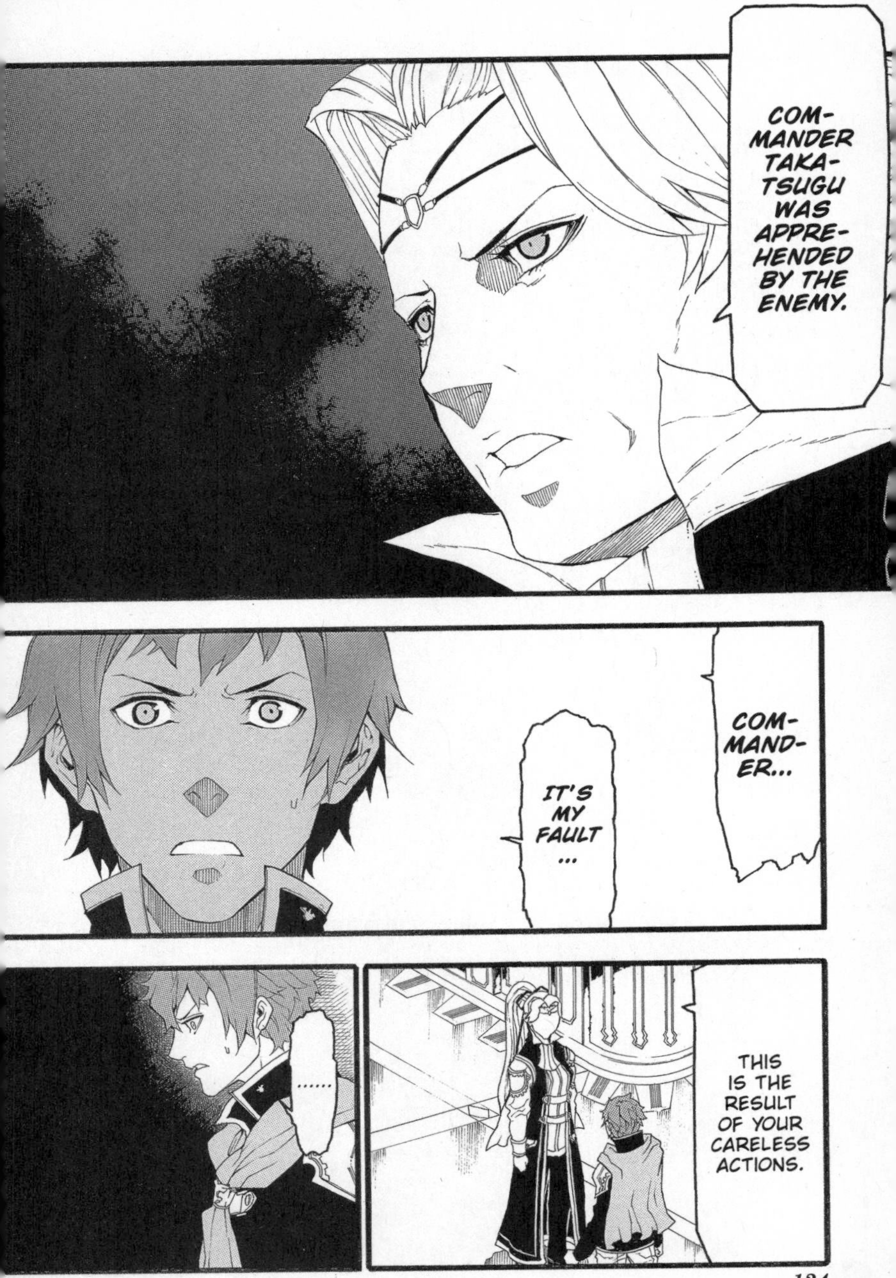
COM-MANDER TAKA-TSUGU WAS APPRE-HENDED BY THE ENEMY.
COM-MAND-ER...
IT'S MY FAULT...
THIS IS THE RESULT OF YOUR CARELESS ACTIONS.
......

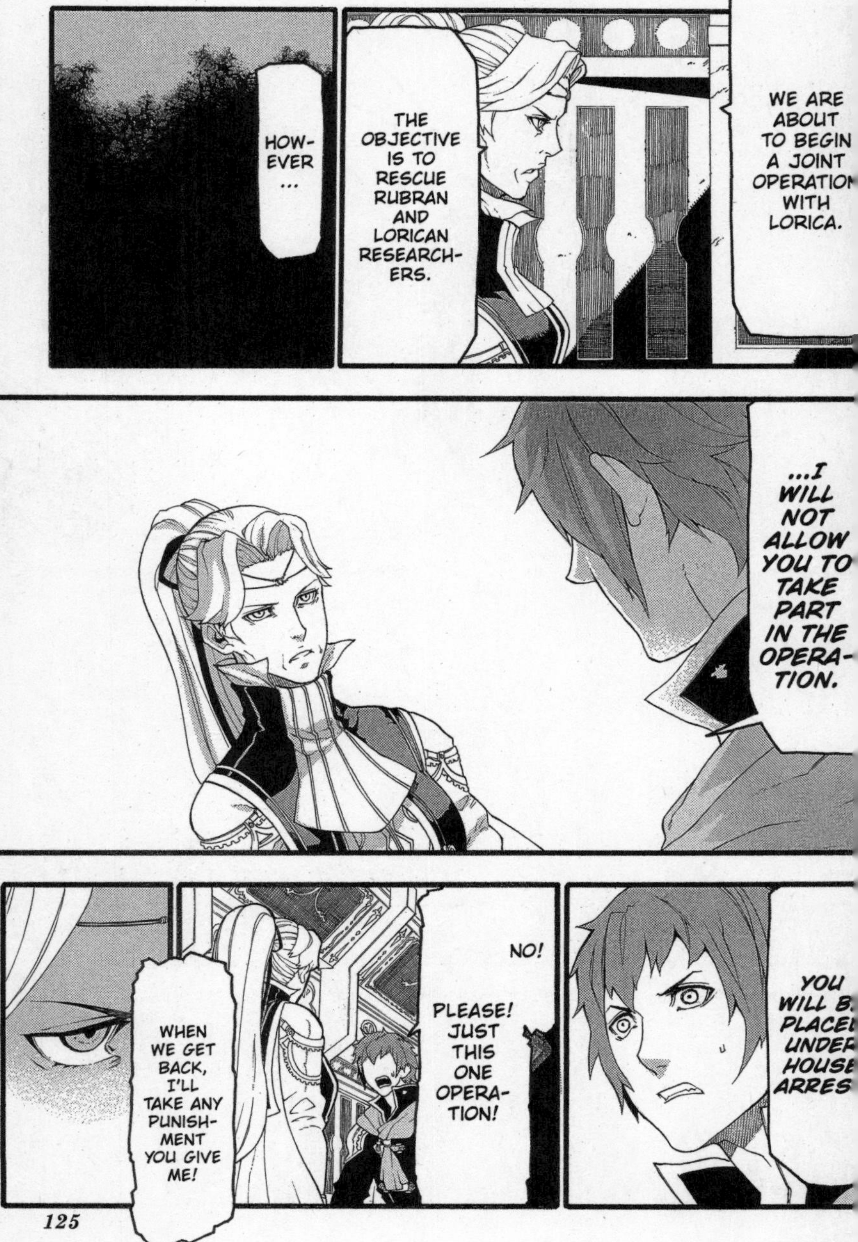
WE ARE ABOUT TO BEGIN A JOINT OPERATIO
WITH LORICA.
THE OBJECTIVE IS TO RESCUE RUBRAN AND LORICAN RESEARCH-ERS.
HOW-EVER ...
...I WILL NOT ALLOW YOU TO TAKE PART IN THE OPERA-TION.
YOU WILL B PLACE UNDE HOUSE ARRES
NO!
PLEASE! JUST THIS ONE OPERA-TION!
WHEN WE GET BACK, I'LL TAKE ANY PUNISH-MENT YOU GIVE ME!

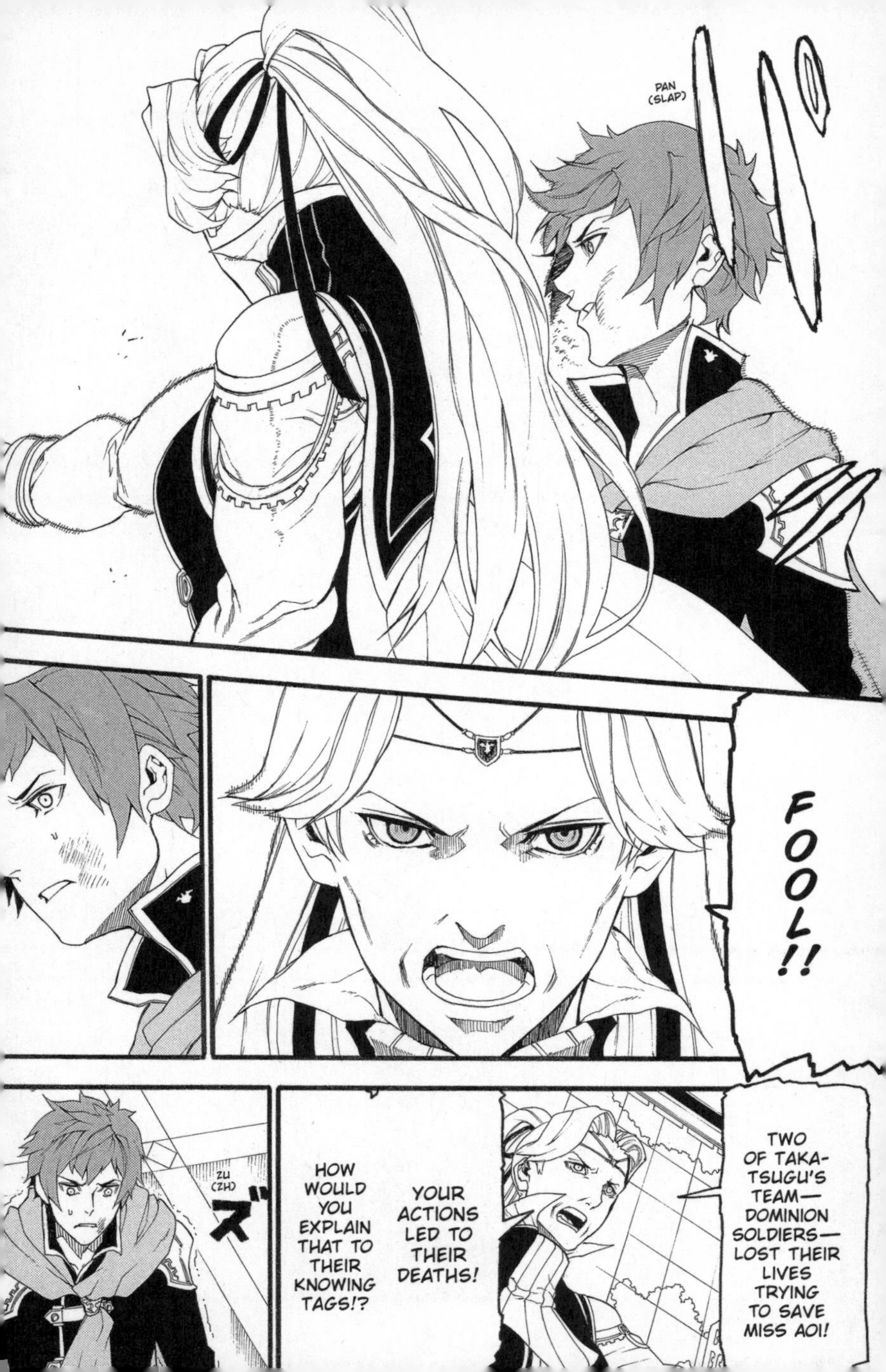
PAN (SLAP)
FOOL!!
TWO OF TAKA-TSUGU'S TEAM—DOMINION SOLDIERS—LOST THEIR LIVES TRYING TO SAVE MISS AOI!
YOUR ACTIONS LED TO THEIR DEATHS!
HOW WOULD YOU EXPLAIN THAT TO THEIR KNOWING TAGS!?
ZU (ZH)
ズ

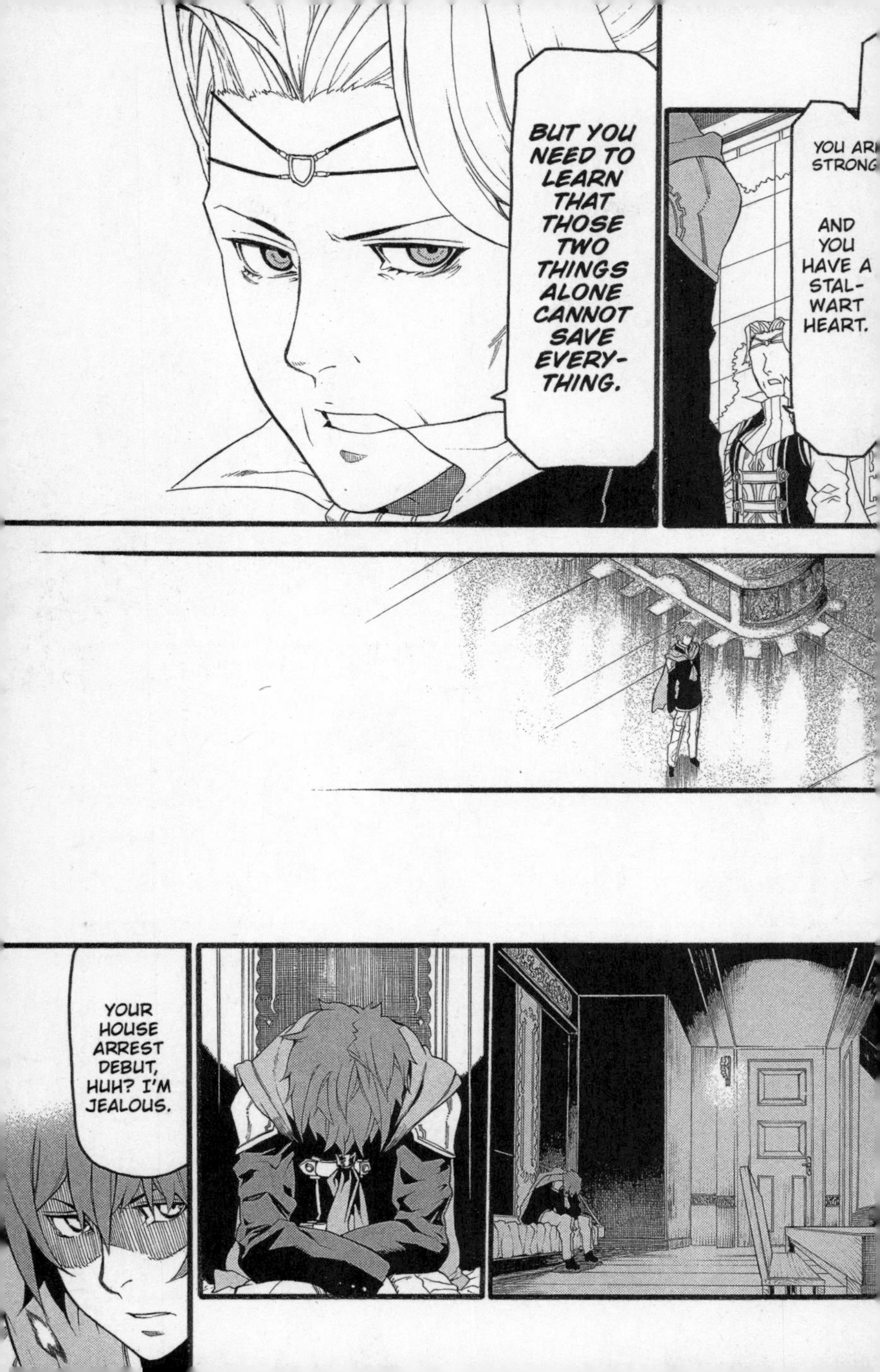
YOU AR STRONG
AND YOU HAVE A STAL-WART HEART.
BUT YOU NEED TO LEARN THAT THOSE TWO THINGS ALONE CANNOT SAVE EVERY-THING.
YOUR HOUSE ARREST DEBUT, HUH? I'M JEALOUS.

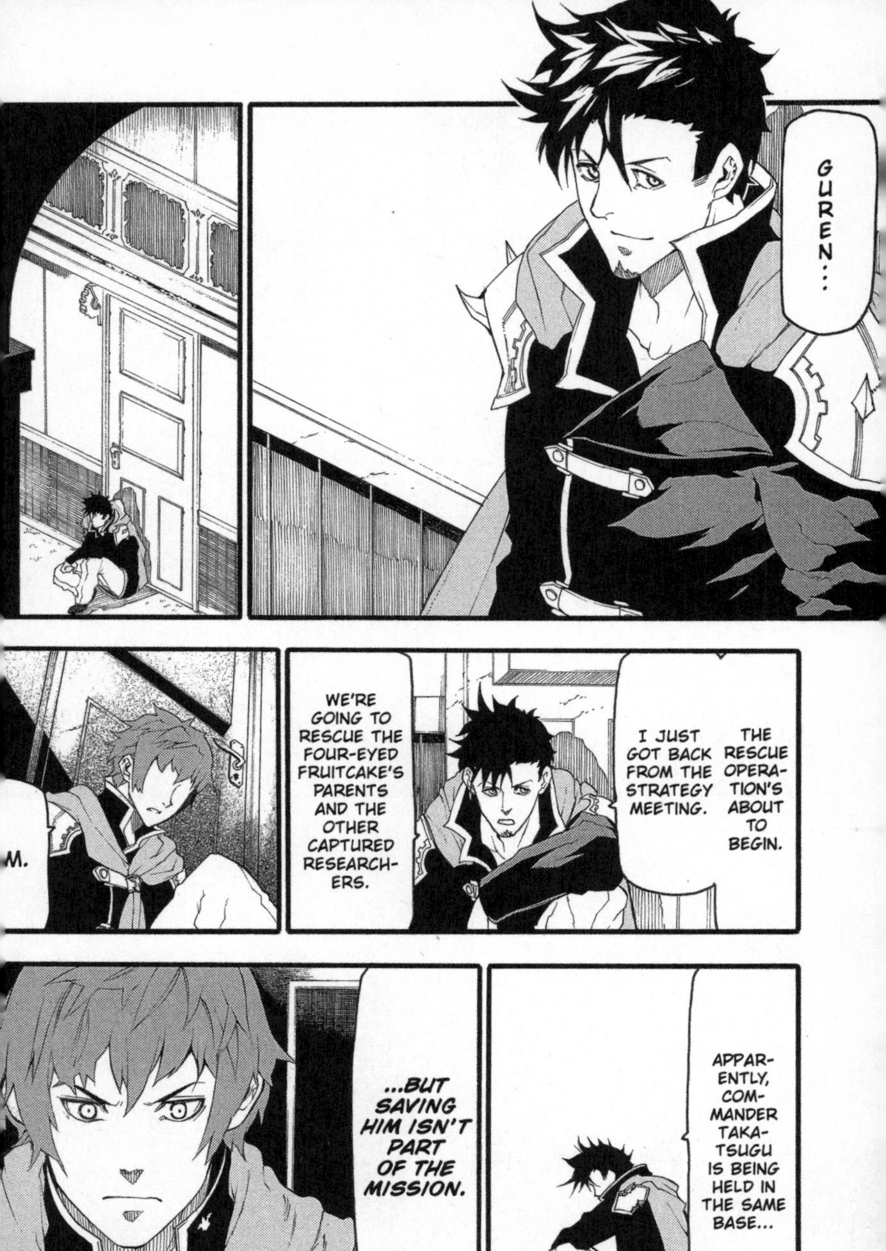
GUREN...
THE RESCUE OPERATION'S ABOUT TO BEGIN.
I JUST GOT BACK FROM THE STRATEGY MEETING.
WE'RE GOING TO RESCUE THE FOUR-EYED FRUITCAKE'S PARENTS AND THE OTHER CAPTURED RESEARCHERS.
APPARENTLY, COMMANDER TAKATSUGU IS BEING HELD IN THE SAME BASE...
...BUT SAVING HIM ISN'T PART OF THE MISSION.

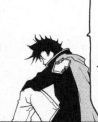

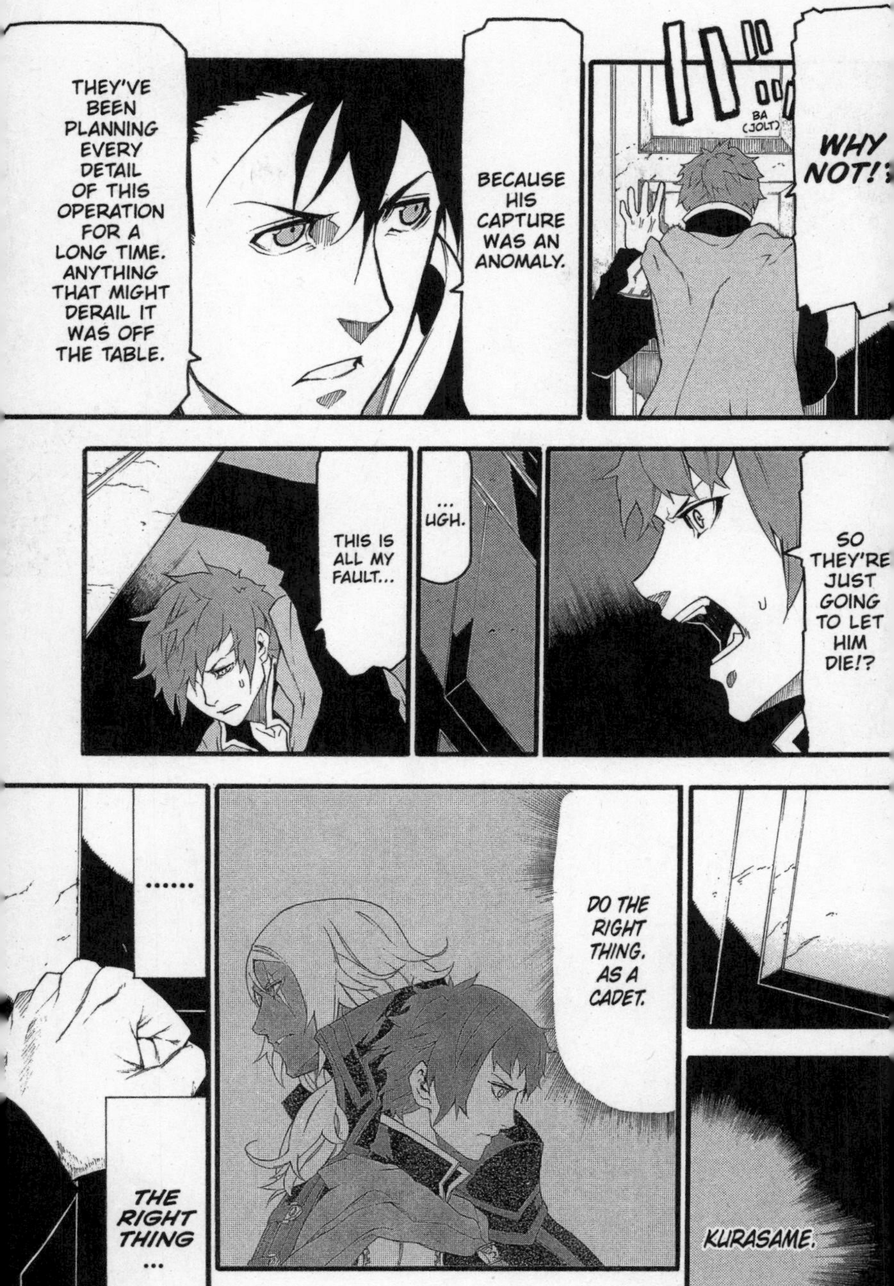
BA (JOLT)
WHY NOT!?
BECAUSE HIS CAPTURE WAS AN ANOMALY.
THEY'VE BEEN PLANNING EVERY DETAIL OF THIS OPERATION FOR A LONG TIME. ANYTHING THAT MIGHT DERAIL IT WAS OFF THE TABLE.
SO THEY'RE JUST GOING TO LET HIM DIE!?
... UGH.
THIS IS ALL MY FAULT...
KURASAME.
DO THE RIGHT THING. AS A CADET.
......
THE RIGHT THING ...

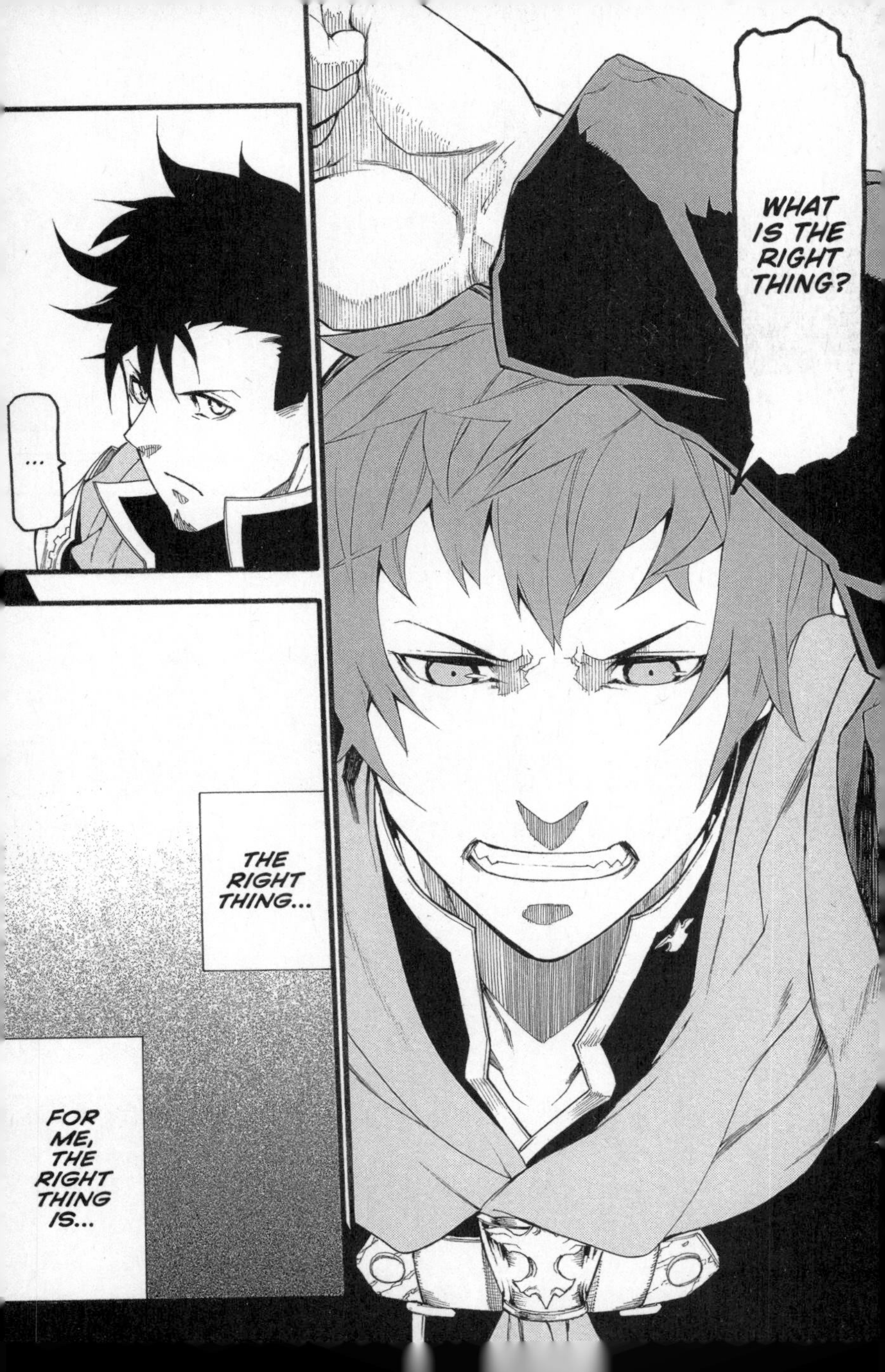
WHAT IS THE RIGHT THING?
...
THE RIGHT THING...
FOR ME, THE RIGHT THING IS...

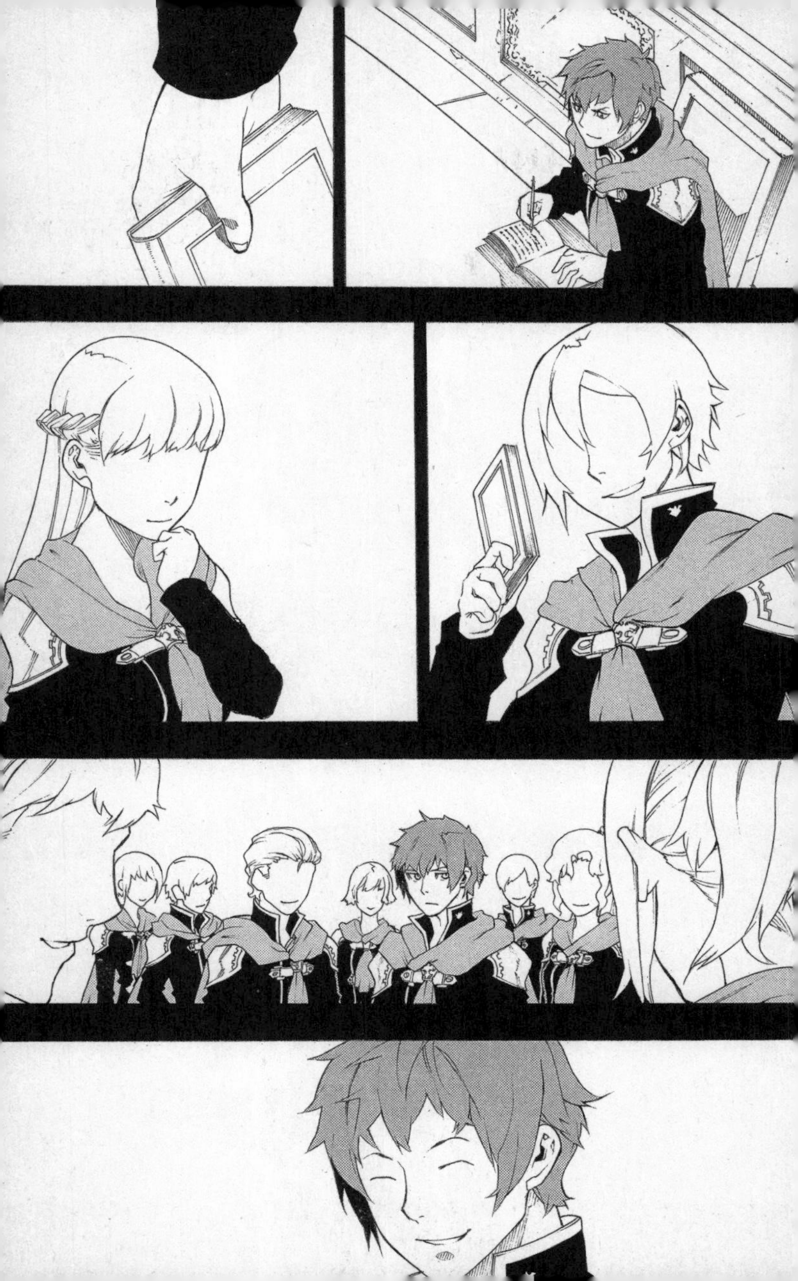

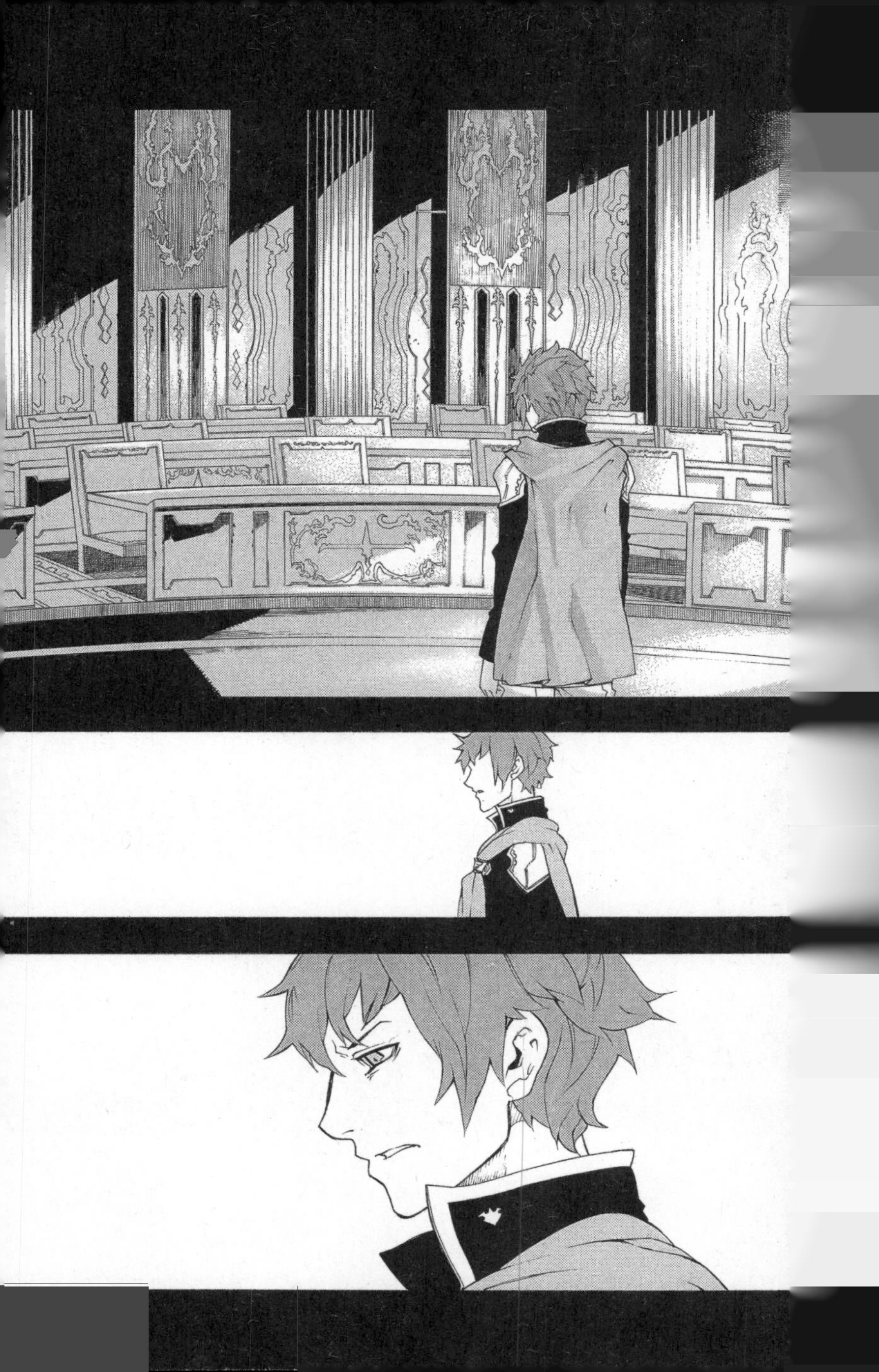

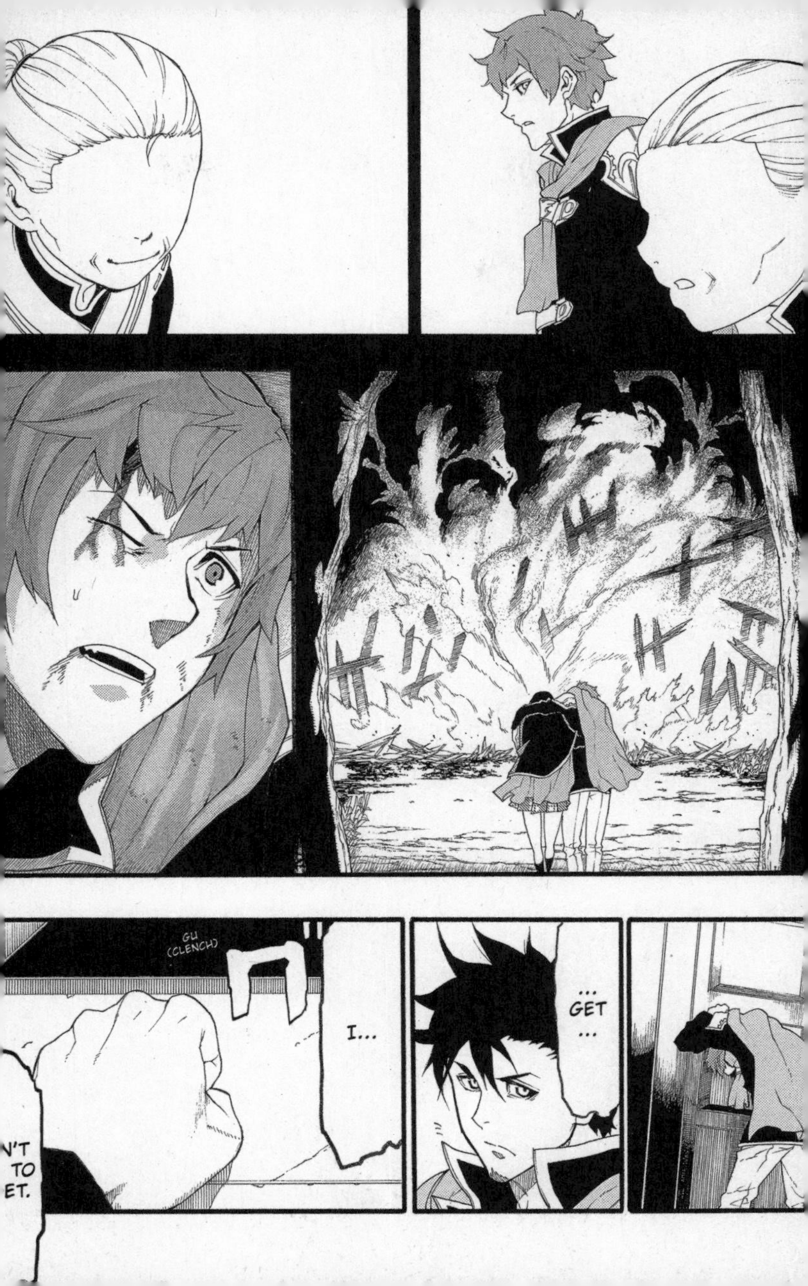
... GET ...
GU (CLENCH)
I...
N'T
TO
ET.

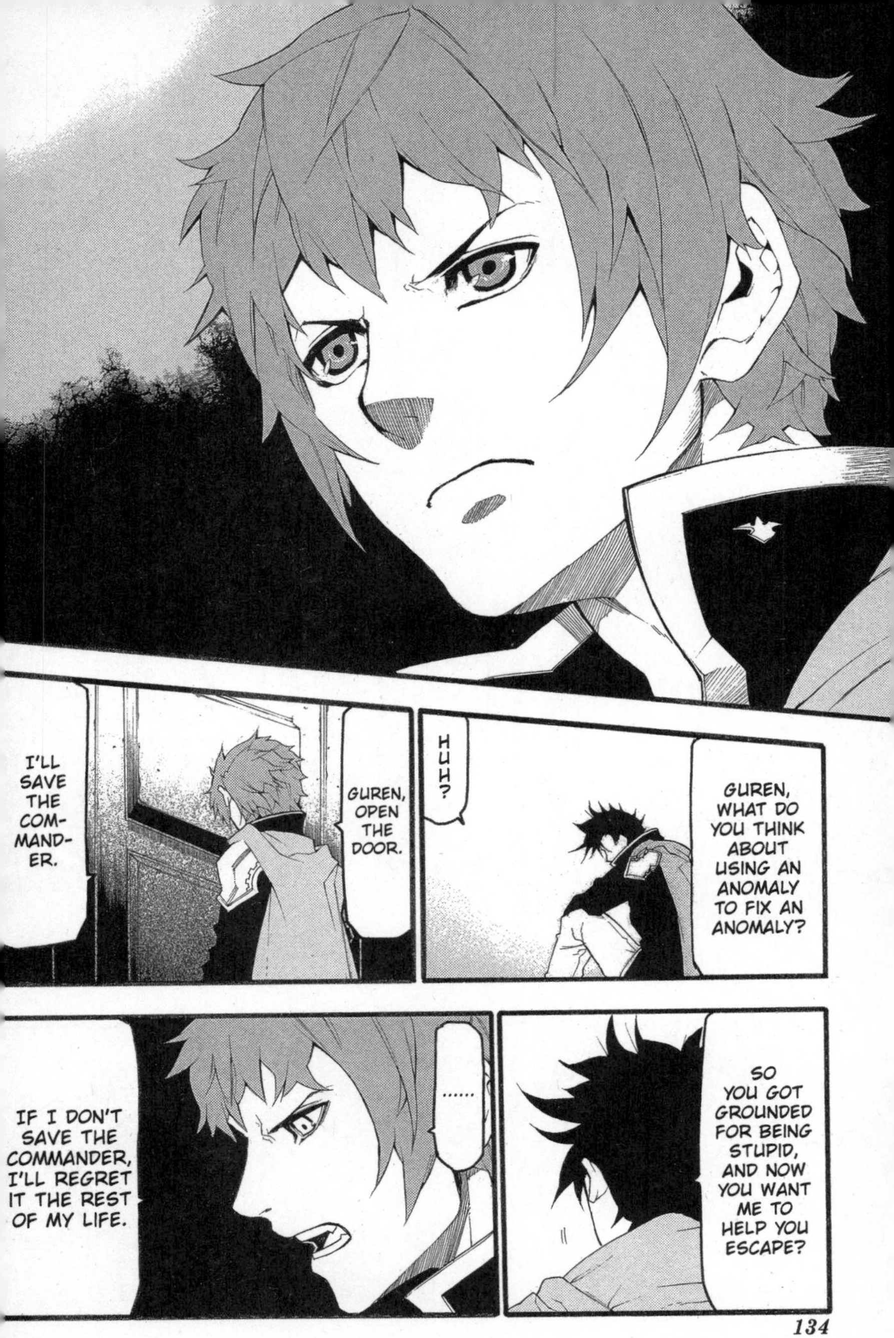
GUREN, WHAT DO YOU THINK ABOUT USING AN ANOMALY TO FIX AN ANOMALY?
HUH?
GUREN, OPEN THE DOOR.
I'LL SAVE THE COM-MANDER.
SO YOU GOT GROUNDED FOR BEING STUPID, AND NOW YOU WANT ME TO HELP YOU ESCAPE?
......
IF I DON'T SAVE THE COMMANDER, I'LL REGRET IT THE REST OF MY LIFE.

GIII
(CREEEAK)

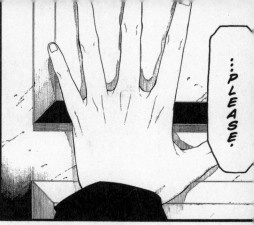

...PLEASE.

THANKS.

I KNEW THAT'S WHAT YOU'D SAY.

GACHA
(KACHAK)

!

KON
(KNOCK)

KON

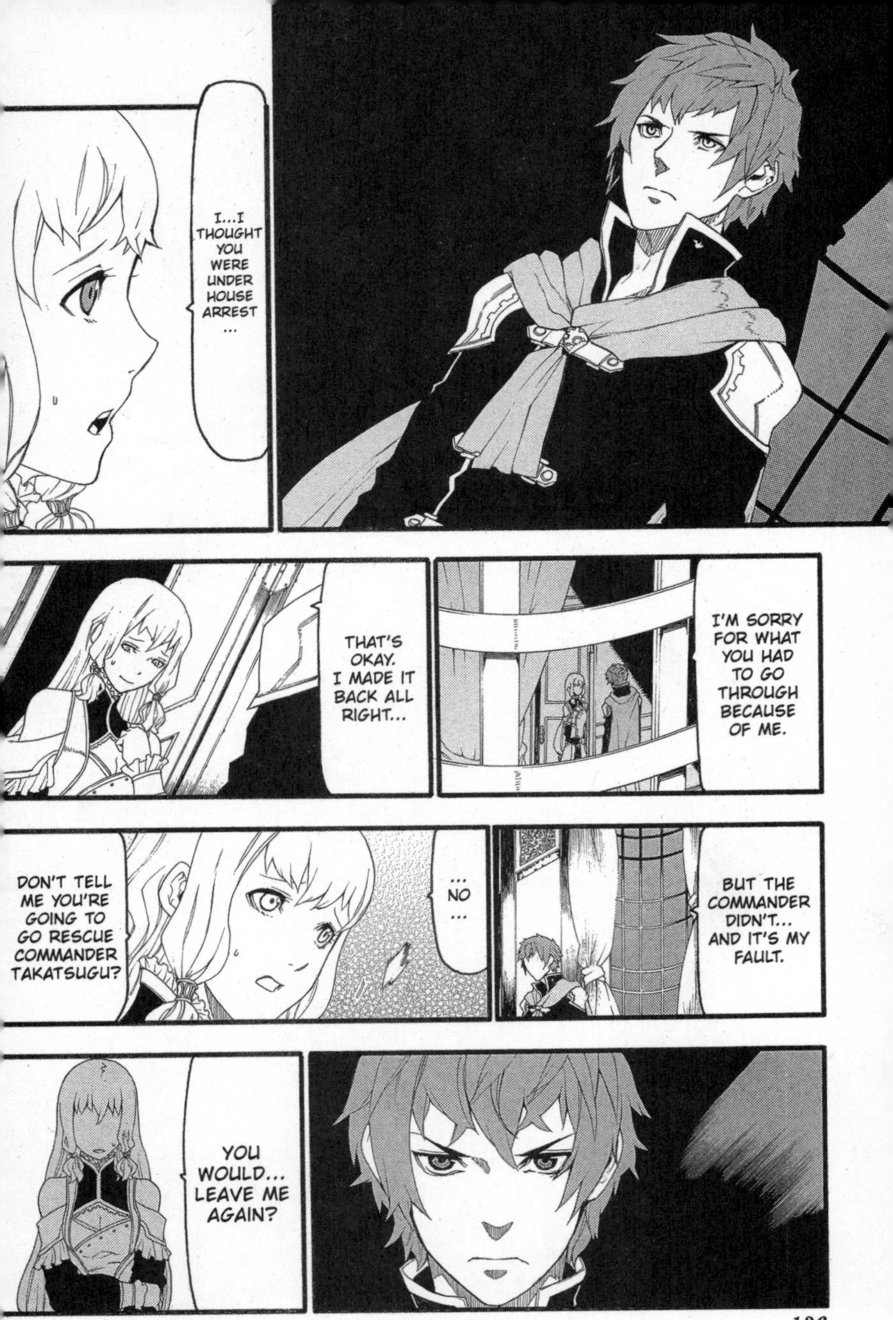
I...I THOUGHT YOU WERE UNDER HOUSE ARREST ...
I'M SORRY FOR WHAT YOU HAD TO GO THROUGH BECAUSE OF ME.
THAT'S OKAY. I MADE IT BACK ALL RIGHT...
BUT THE COMMANDER DIDN'T... AND IT'S MY FAULT.
... NO ...
DON'T TELL ME YOU'RE GOING TO GO RESCUE COMMANDER TAKATSUGU?
YOU WOULD... LEAVE ME AGAIN?

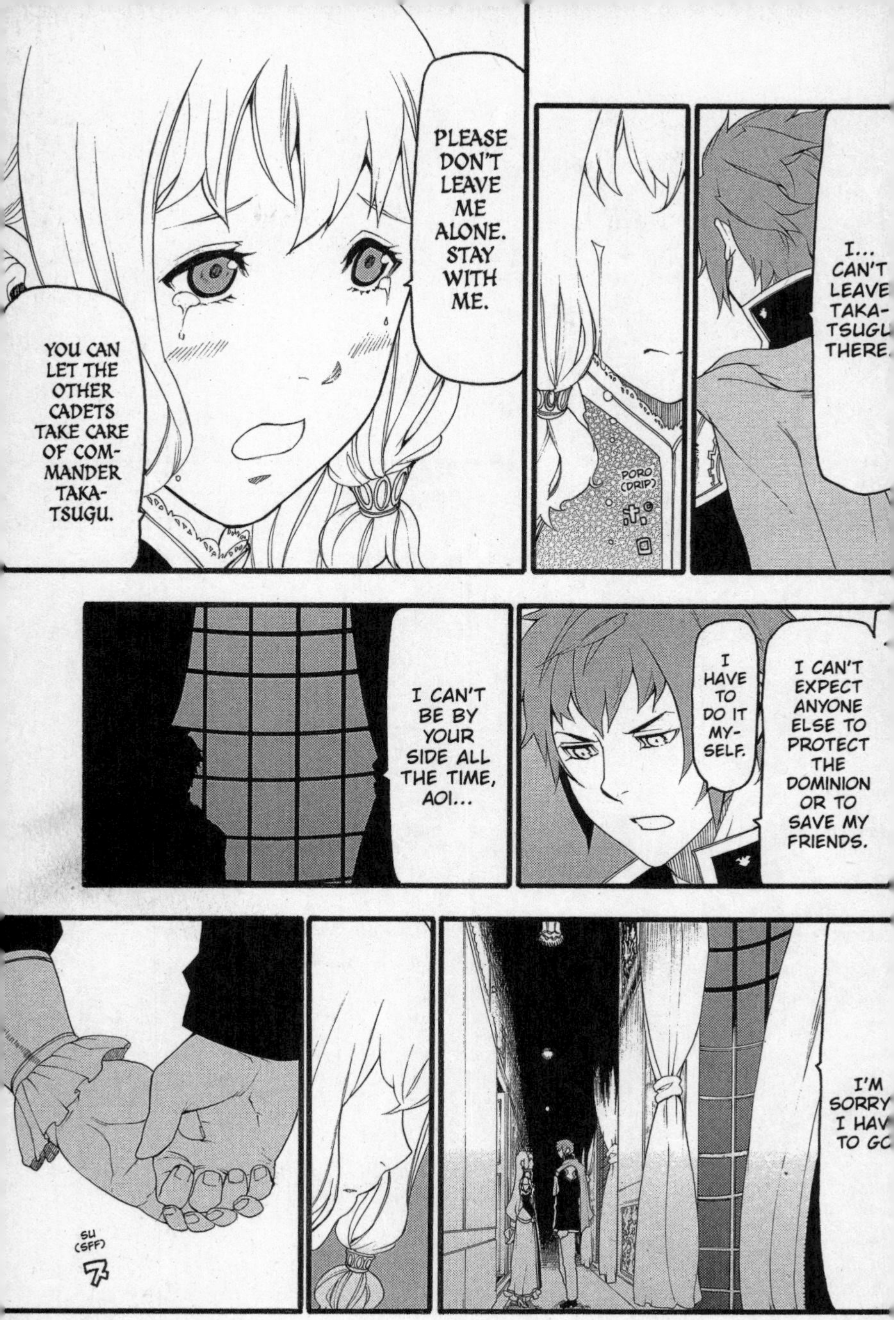
I... CAN'T LEAVE TAKA-TSUGU THERE.
PORO (DRIP)
PLEASE DON'T LEAVE ME ALONE. STAY WITH ME.
YOU CAN LET THE OTHER CADETS TAKE CARE OF COM-MANDER TAKA-TSUGU.
I CAN'T EXPECT ANYONE ELSE TO PROTECT THE DOMINION OR TO SAVE MY FRIENDS.
I HAVE TO DO IT MY-SELF.
I CAN'T BE BY YOUR SIDE ALL THE TIME, AOI...
I'M SORRY I HAV TO GO
SU (SFF)

KURA-SAME... DON'T GO.

I DON'T...

PLEASE UNDER-STAND...

THEY'RE GOOD CADETS—I'D TRUST THEM WITH MY LIFE. YOU WON'T HAVE TO WORRY THIS TIME.

I'LL TELL KAZUSA AND EMINA TO KEEP YOU SAFE.

...

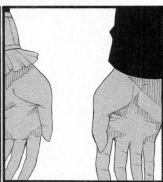

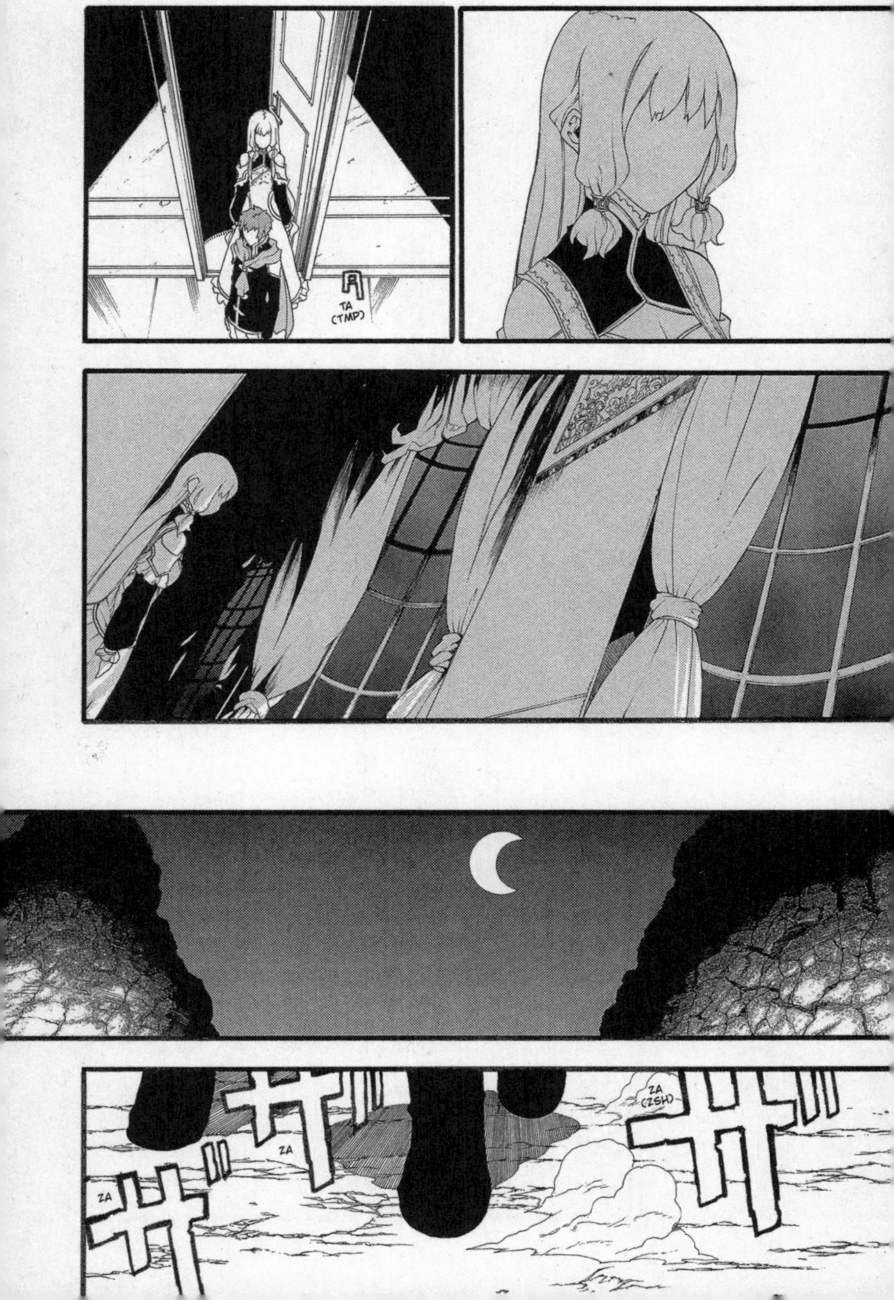
TA
(TMP)
ZA
(ZSH)
ZA
ZA

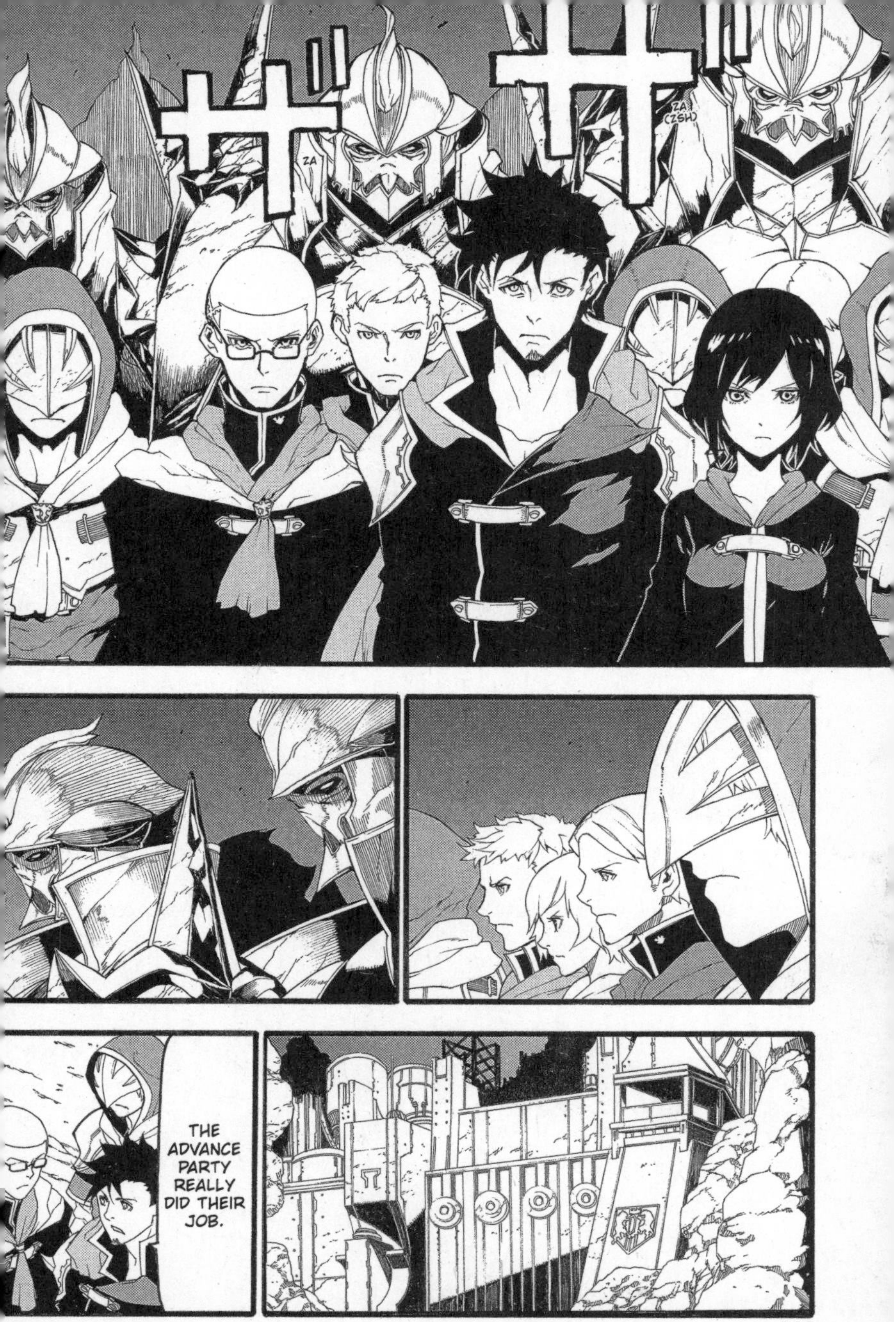
ZA (ZSH)
ZA
THE ADVANCE PARTY REALLY DID THEIR JOB.

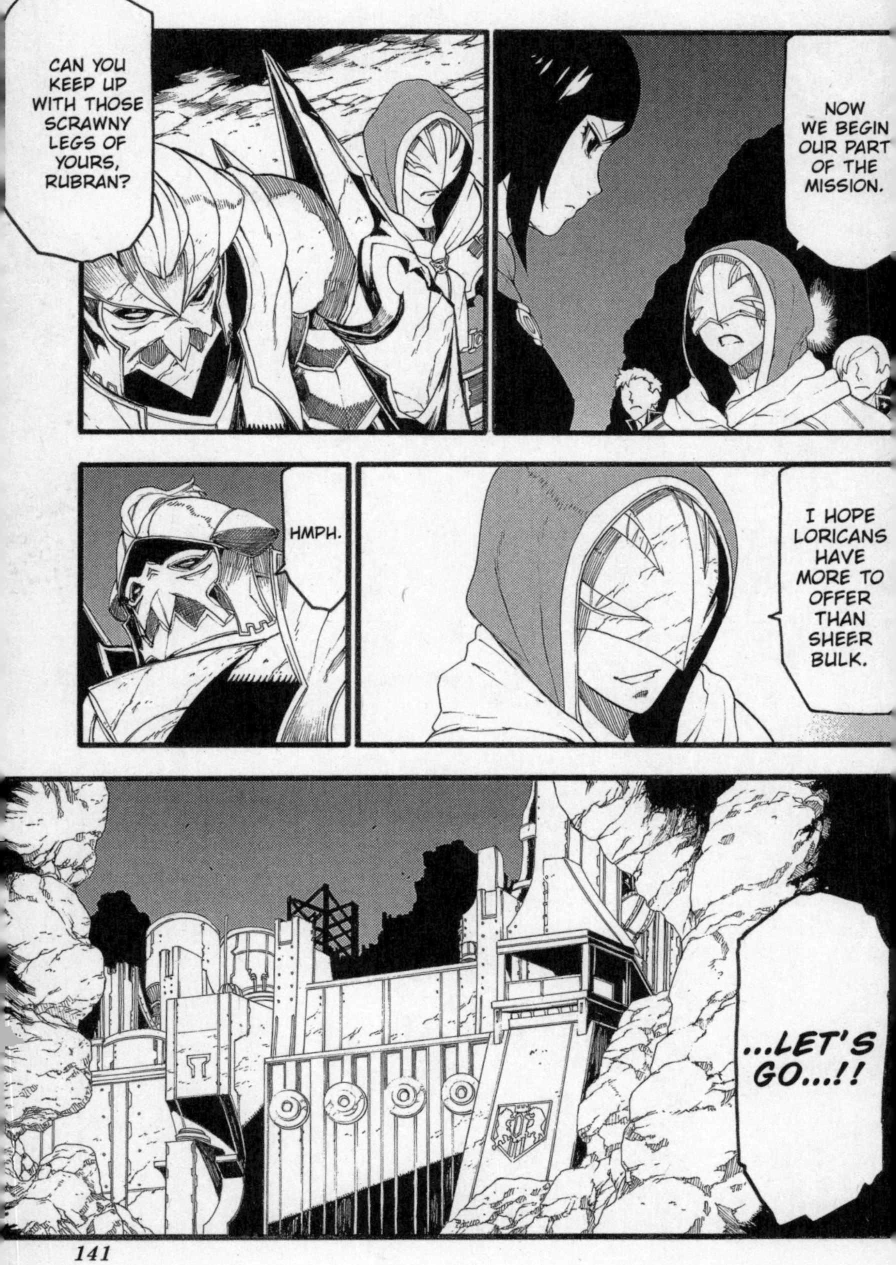
NOW WE BEGIN OUR PART OF THE MISSION.
CAN YOU KEEP UP WITH THOSE SCRAWNY LEGS OF YOURS, RUBRAN?
I HOPE LORICANS HAVE MORE TO OFFER THAN SHEER BULK.
HMPH.
...LET'S GO...!!

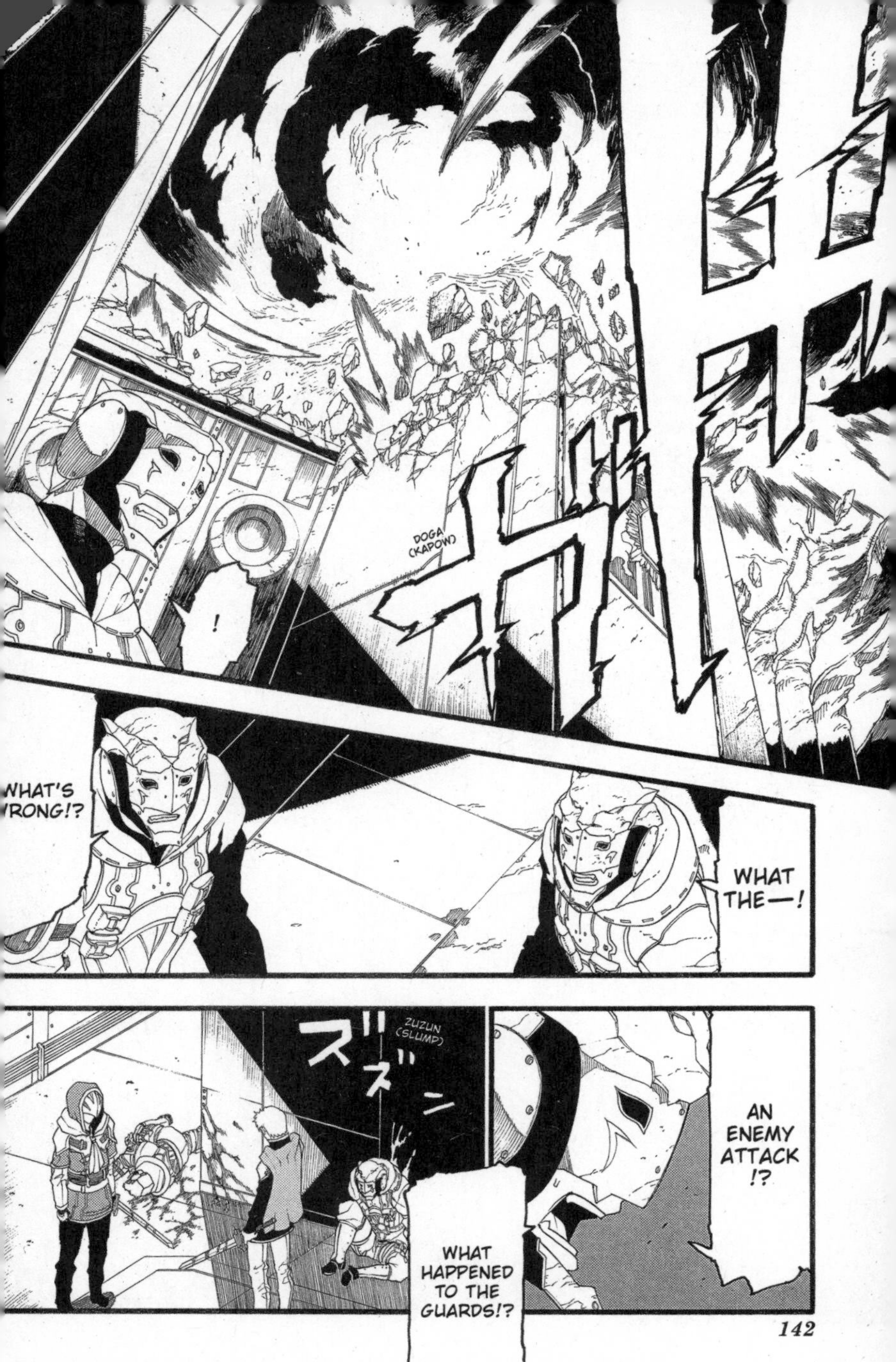
DOGA (KAPOW)
!
WHAT THE—!
WHAT'S WRONG!?
AN ENEMY ATTACK!?
ZUZUN (SLUMP)
WHAT HAPPENED TO THE GUARDS!?

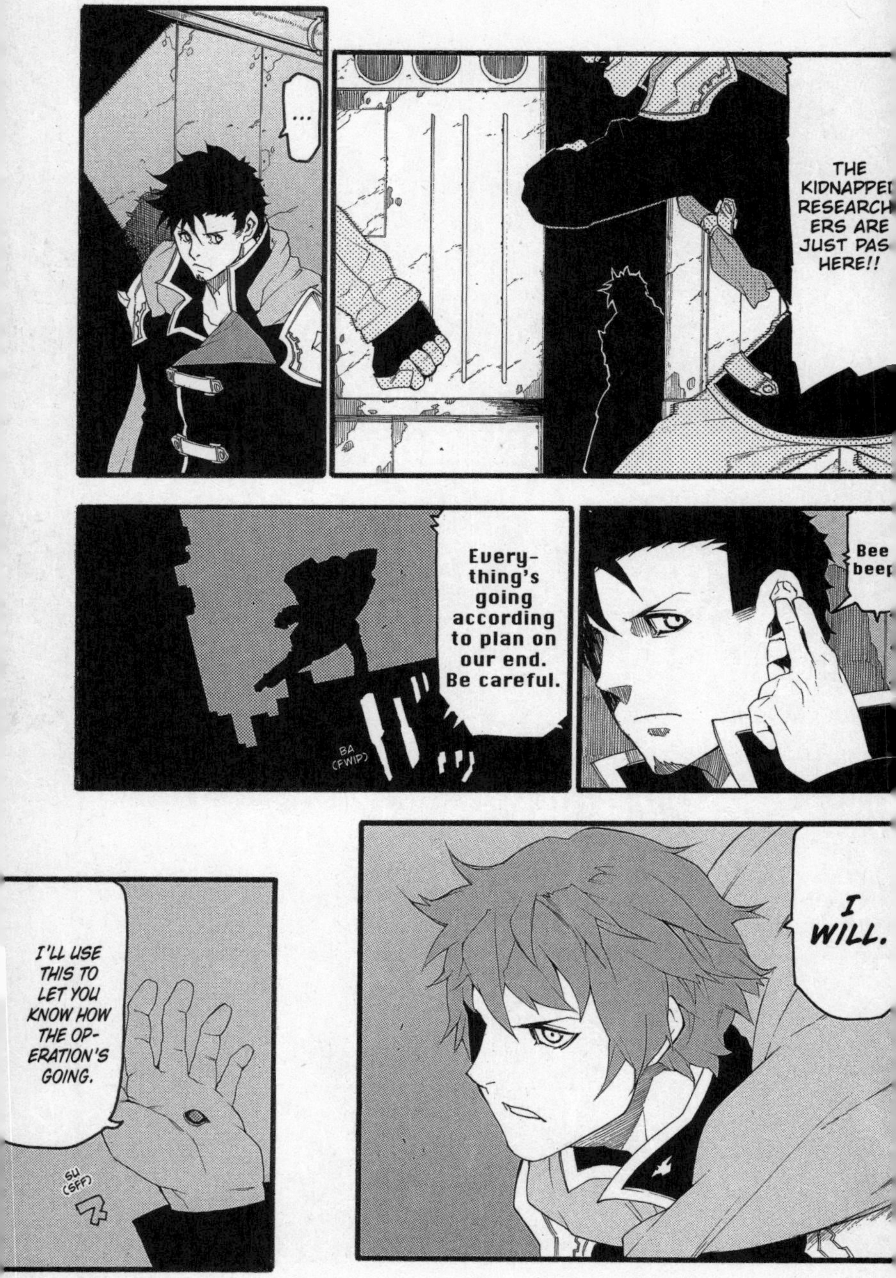
THE KIDNAPPE RESEARCH ERS ARE JUST PAS HERE!!
...
Bee beep
Every-thing's going according to plan on our end. Be careful.
BA (FWIP)
I WILL.
I'LL USE THIS TO LET YOU KNOW HOW THE OP-ERATION'S GOING.
SU (SFF)

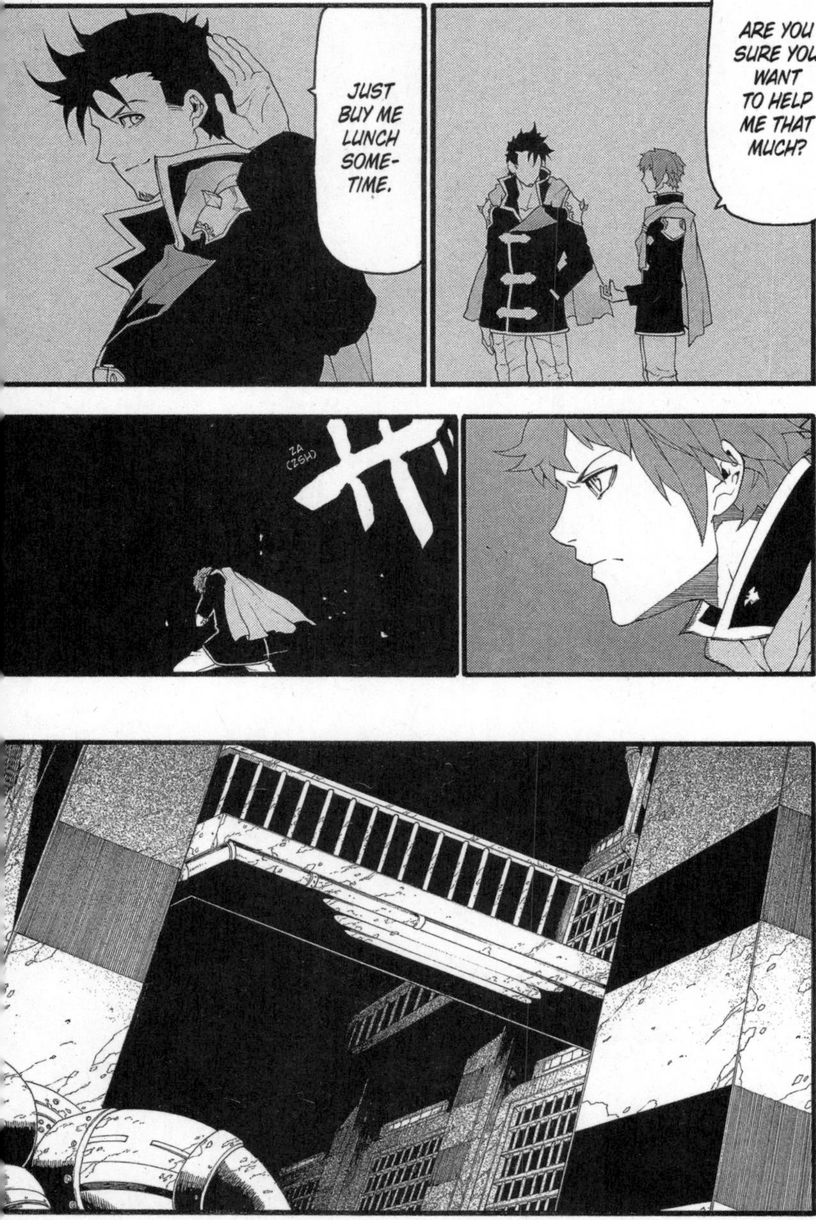
ARE YOU SURE YOU WANT TO HELP ME THAT MUCH?
JUST BUY ME LUNCH SOME-TIME.
ZA (ZSH)

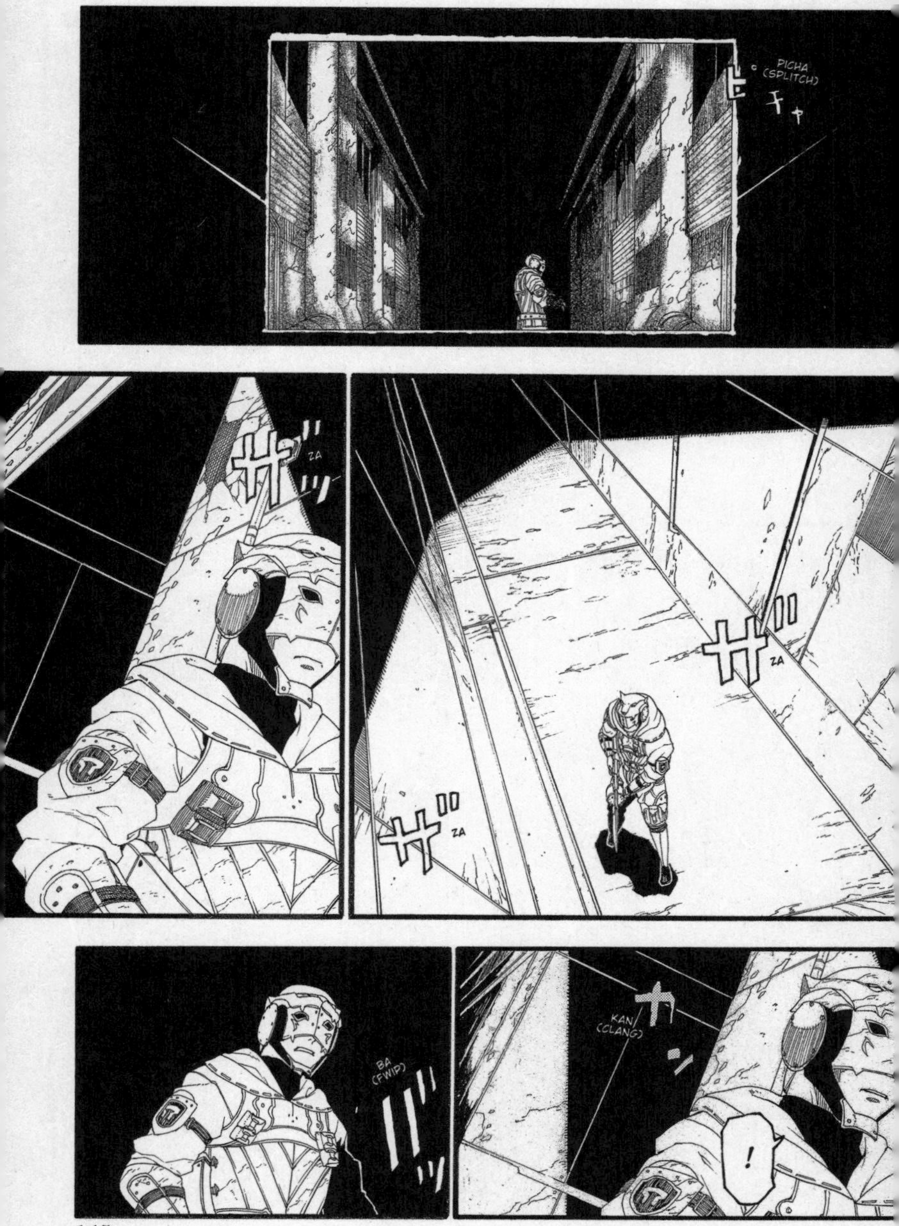
PICHA (SPLITCH)
ZA
ZA
ZA
KAN (CLANG)
!
BA (FWIP)

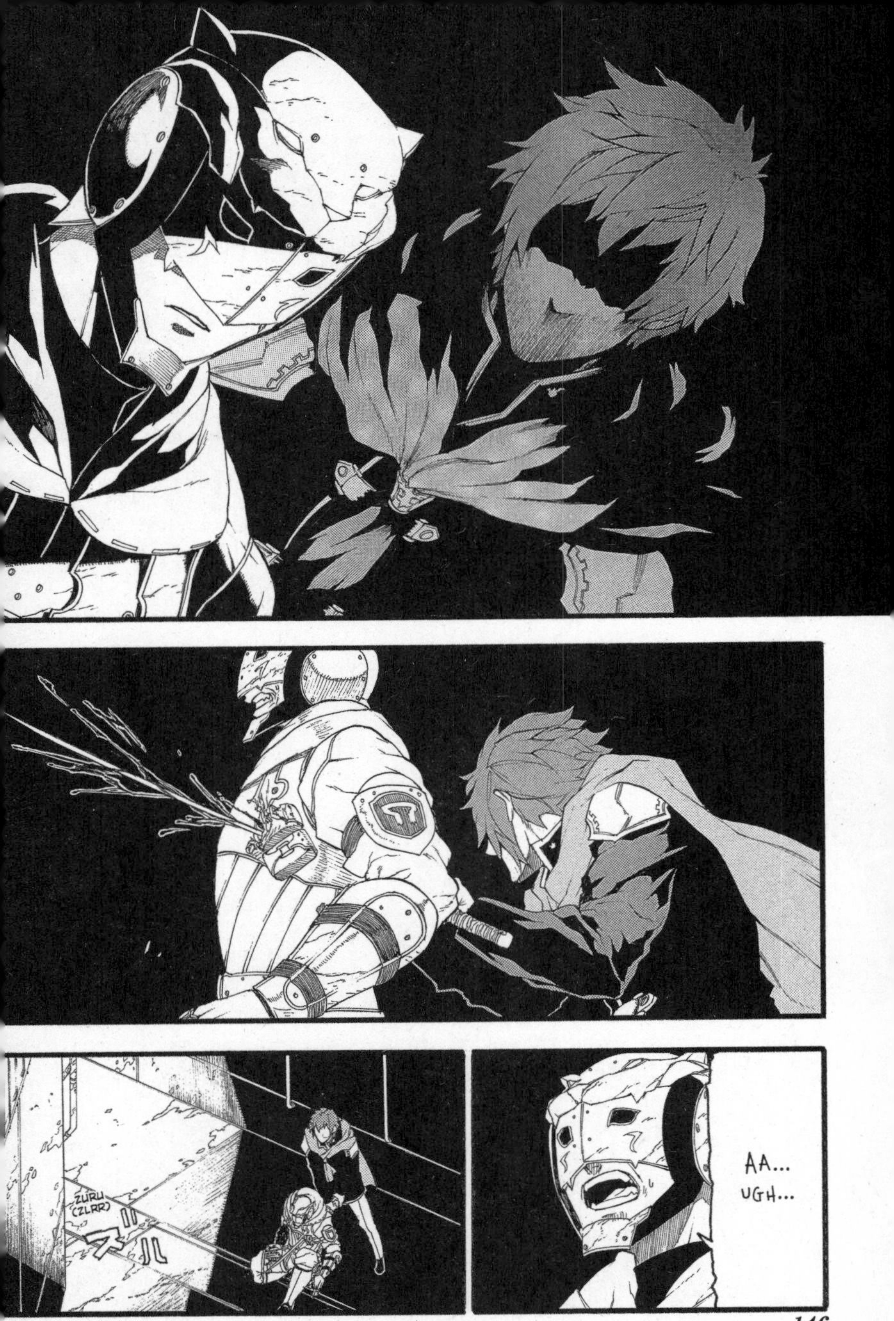
AA...
UGH...
ZURU
(ZLRR)

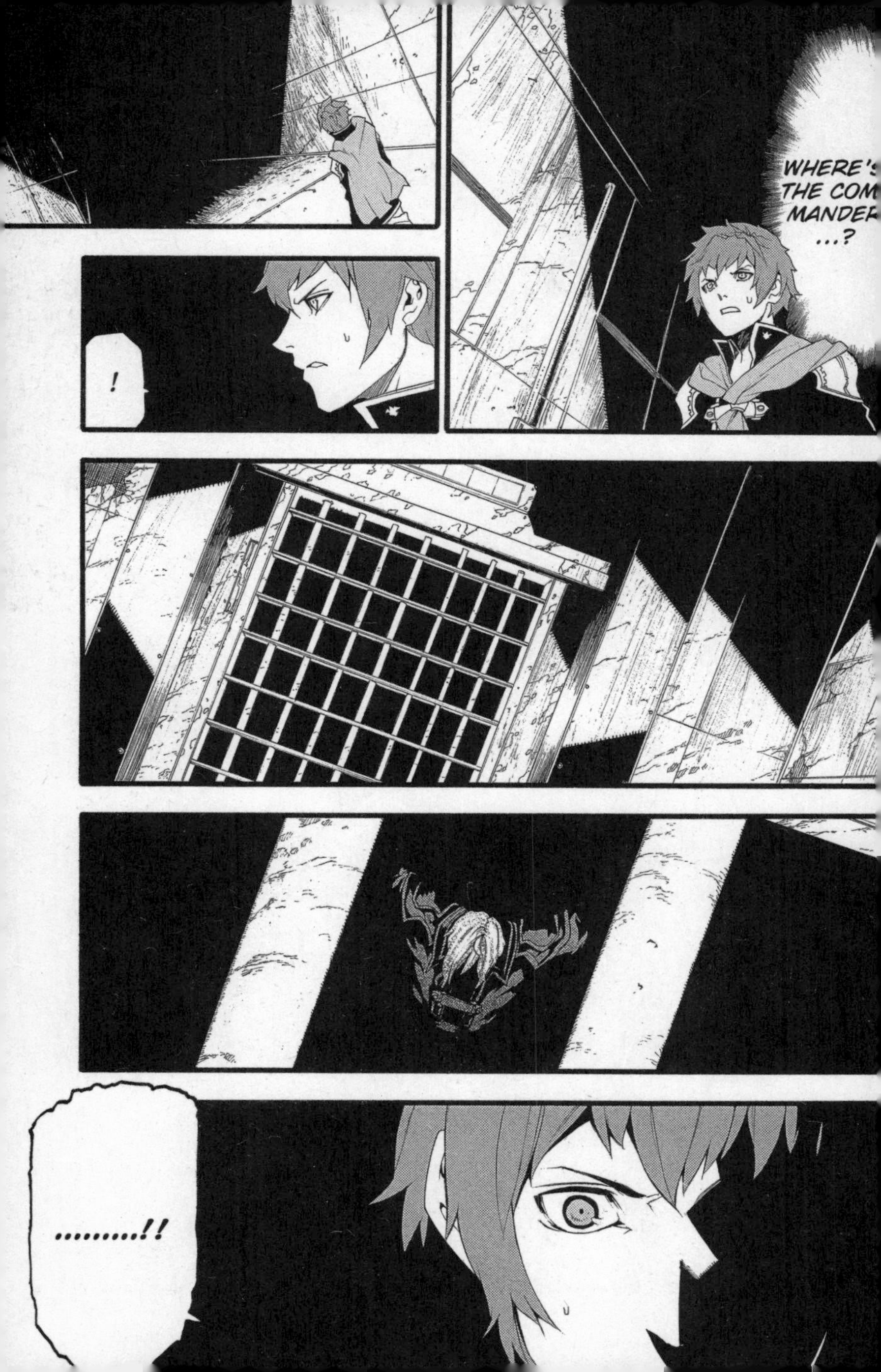
WHERE'S THE COMMANDER ...?
!
.........!!

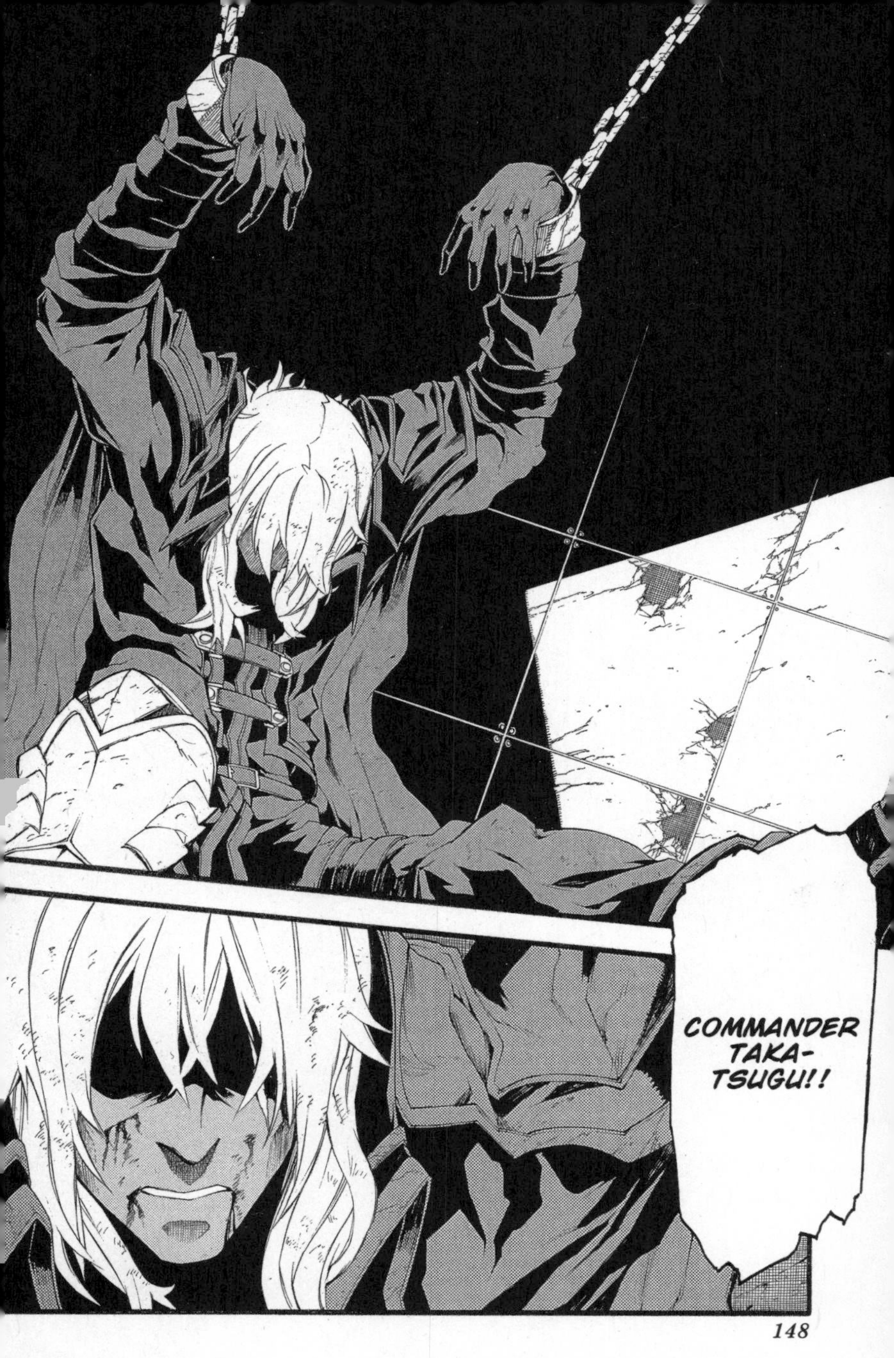
COMMANDER TAKA-TSUGU!!

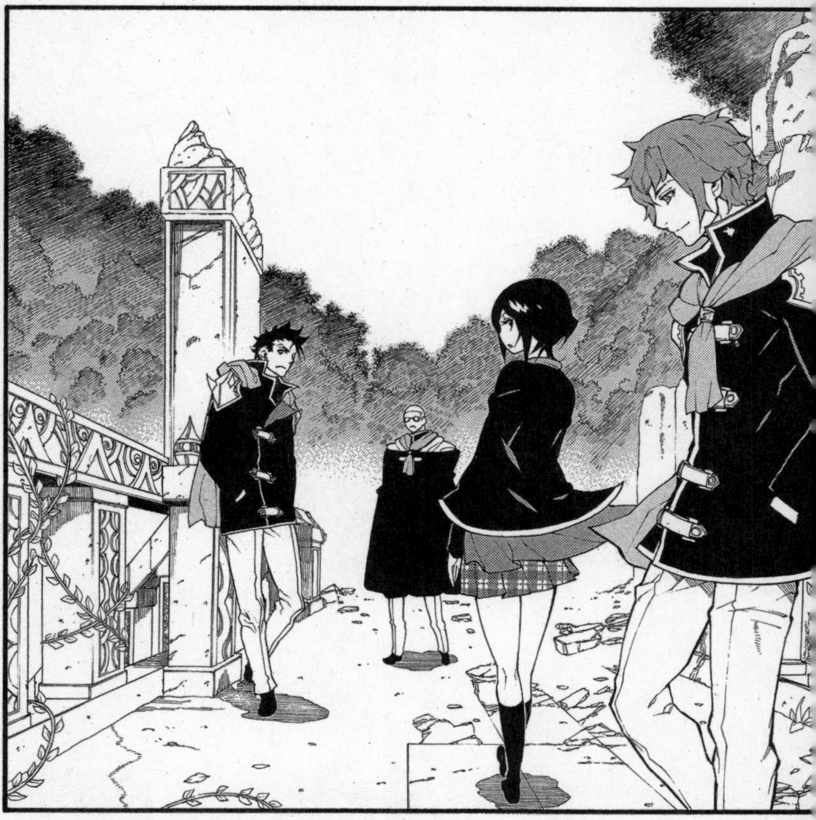

FINAL FANTASY 零式 TYPE-0™ SIDE STORY

The Ice Reaper

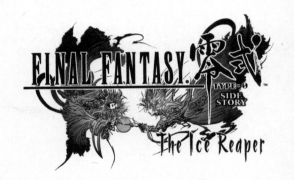

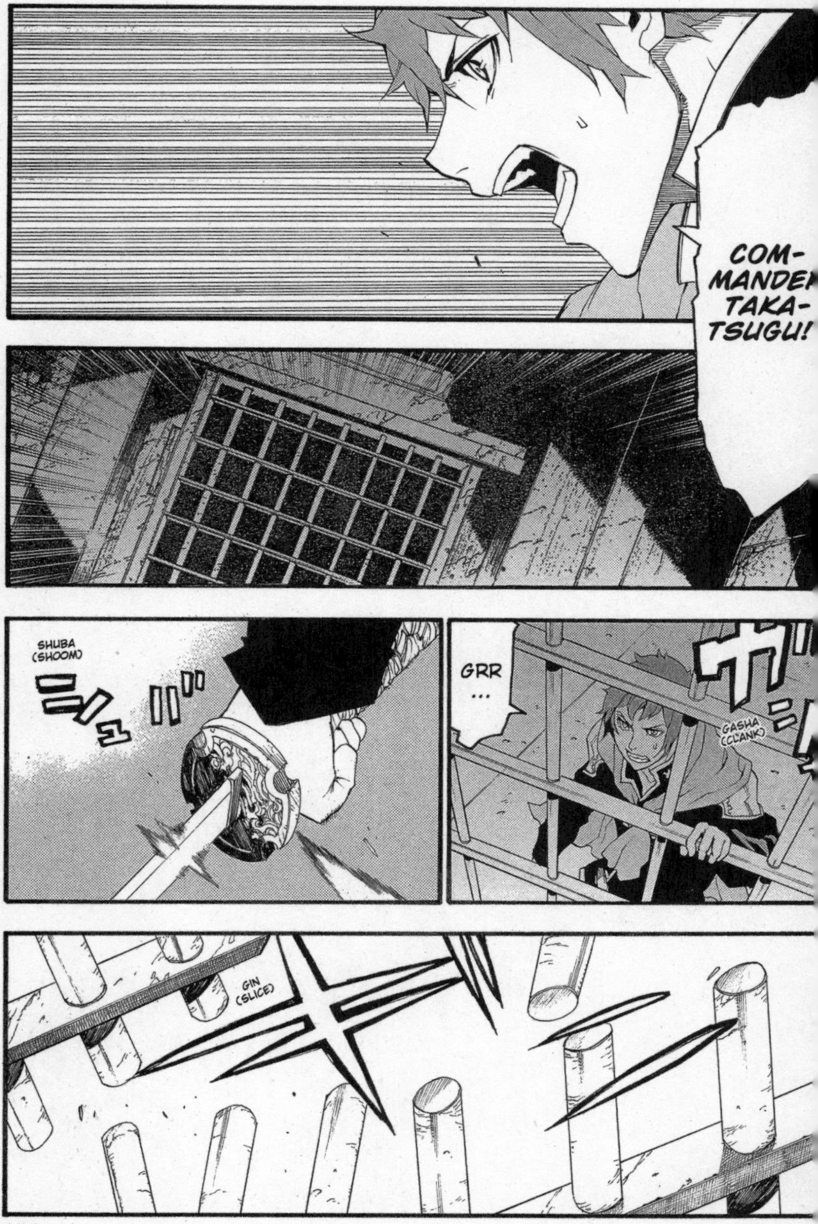
COM-
MANDE
TAKA-
TSUGU!
GASHA (CLANK)
GRR ...
SHUBA (SHOOM)
GIN (SLICE)

CHAPTER 13: THE ICE REAPER ①

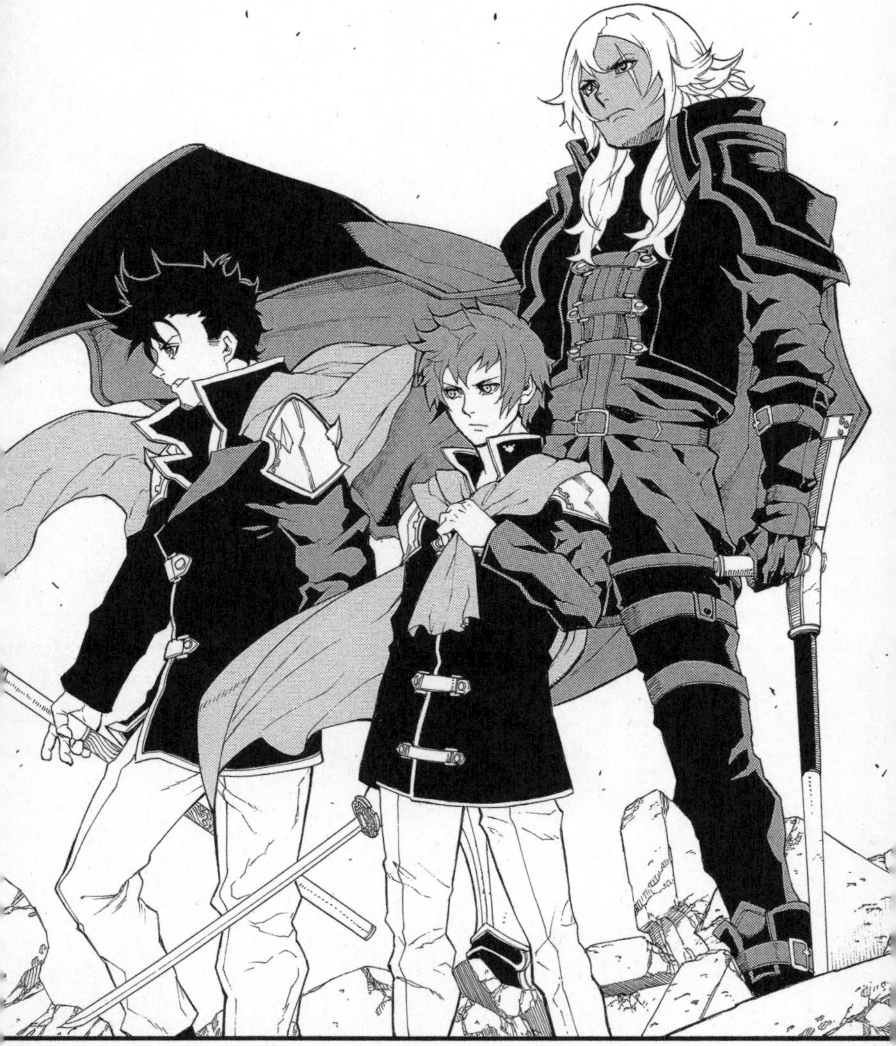

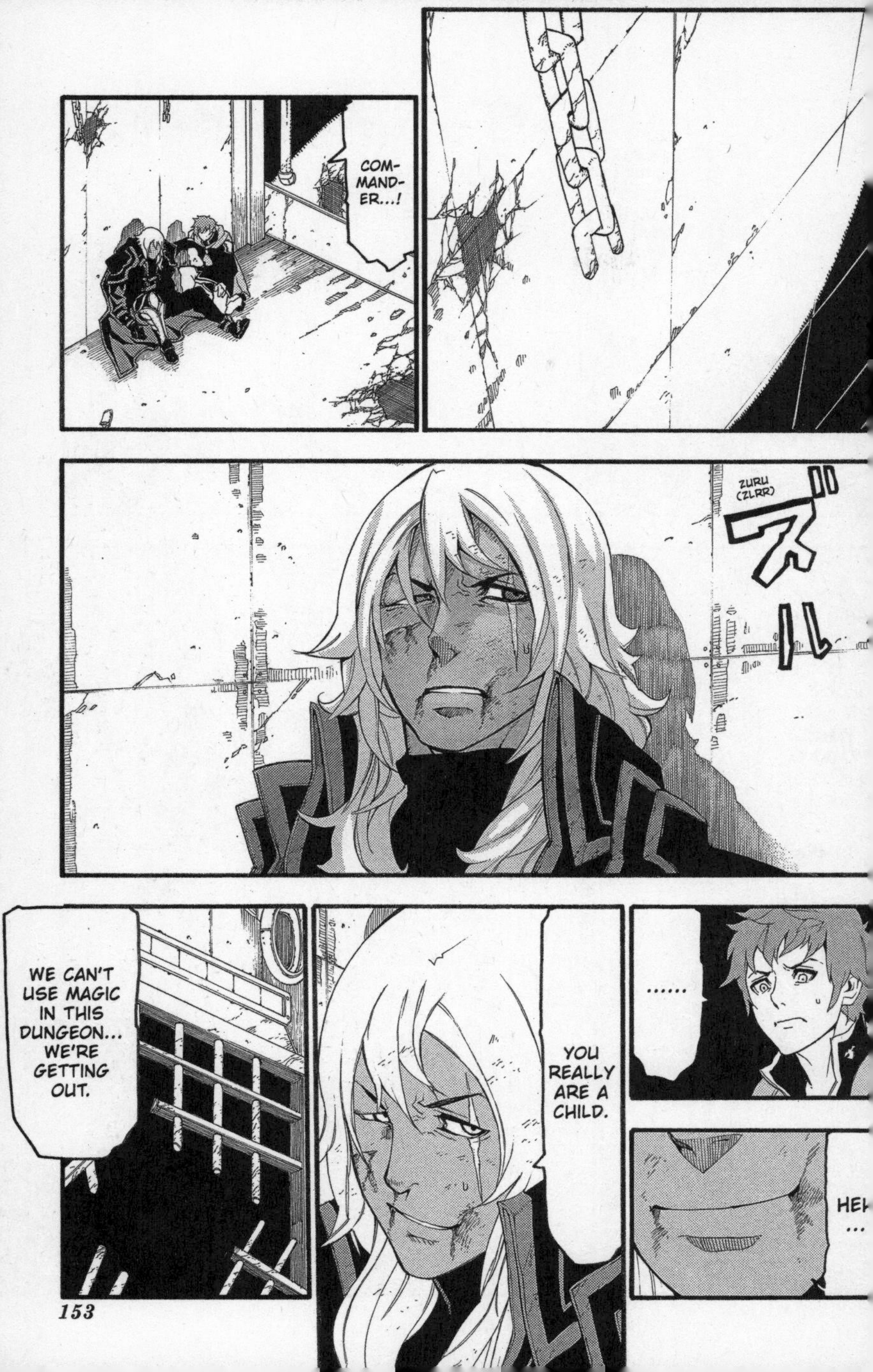
COM-MANDER...!
ZURU (ZLRR)
ズル
......
HEH ...
YOU REALLY ARE A CHILD.
WE CAN'T USE MAGIC IN THIS DUNGEON... WE'RE GETTING OUT.

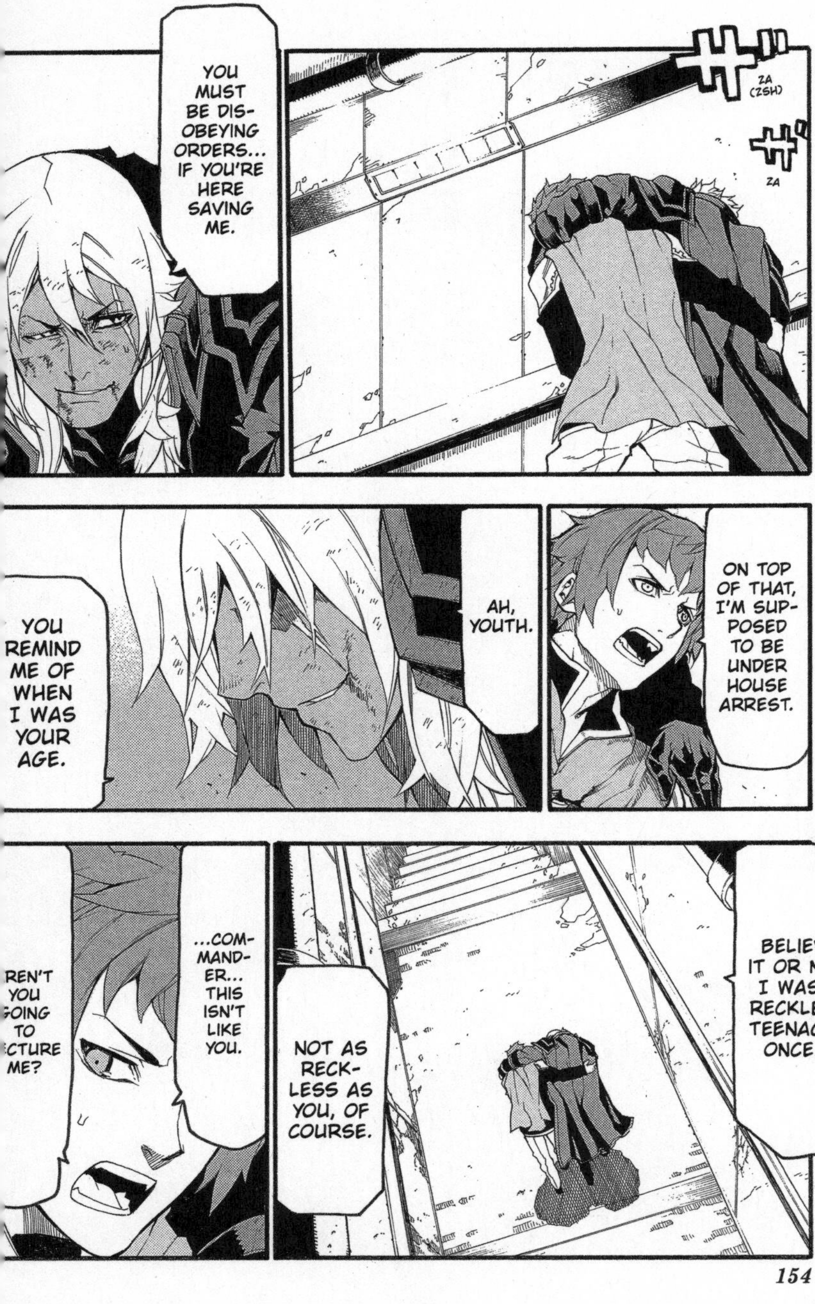

ZA (ZSH)
ZA
YOU MUST BE DISOBEYING ORDERS... IF YOU'RE HERE SAVING ME.
ON TOP OF THAT, I'M SUPPOSED TO BE UNDER HOUSE ARREST.
AH, YOUTH.
YOU REMIND ME OF WHEN I WAS YOUR AGE.
BELIEVE IT OR NOT, I WAS A RECKLESS TEENAGER ONCE...
NOT AS RECKLESS AS YOU, OF COURSE.
...COMMANDER... THIS ISN'T LIKE YOU.
RENT YOU GOING TO ECTURE ME?

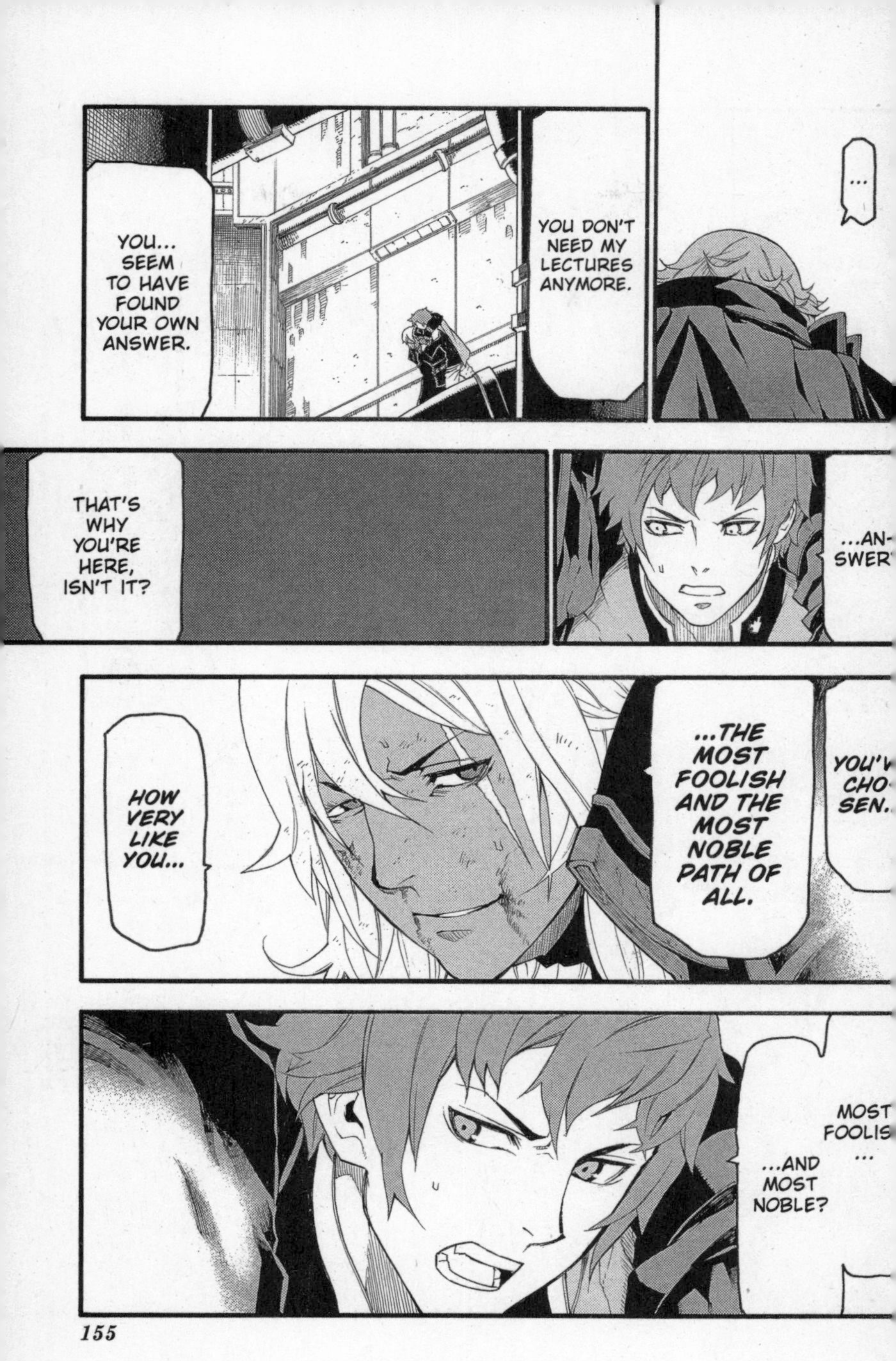
...
YOU DON'T NEED MY LECTURES ANYMORE.
YOU... SEEM TO HAVE FOUND YOUR OWN ANSWER.
...AN- SWER
THAT'S WHY YOU'RE HERE, ISN'T IT?
YOU'V CHO- SEN..
...THE MOST FOOLISH AND THE MOST NOBLE PATH OF ALL.
HOW VERY LIKE YOU...
MOST FOOLIS ...
...AND MOST NOBLE?

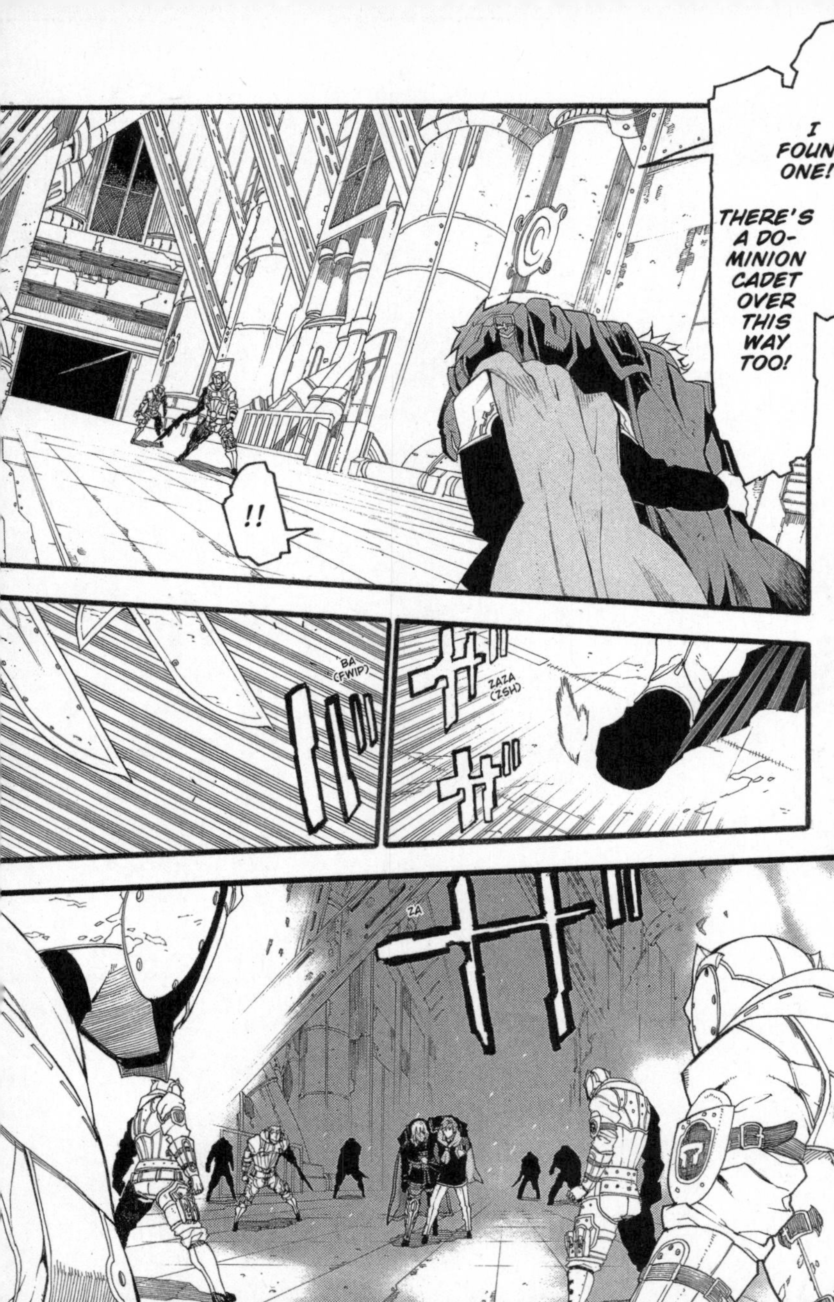
I FOUND ONE!!
THERE'S A DO-MINION CADET OVER THIS WAY TOO!
!!
ZAZA (ZSH)
BA (FWIP)
ZA

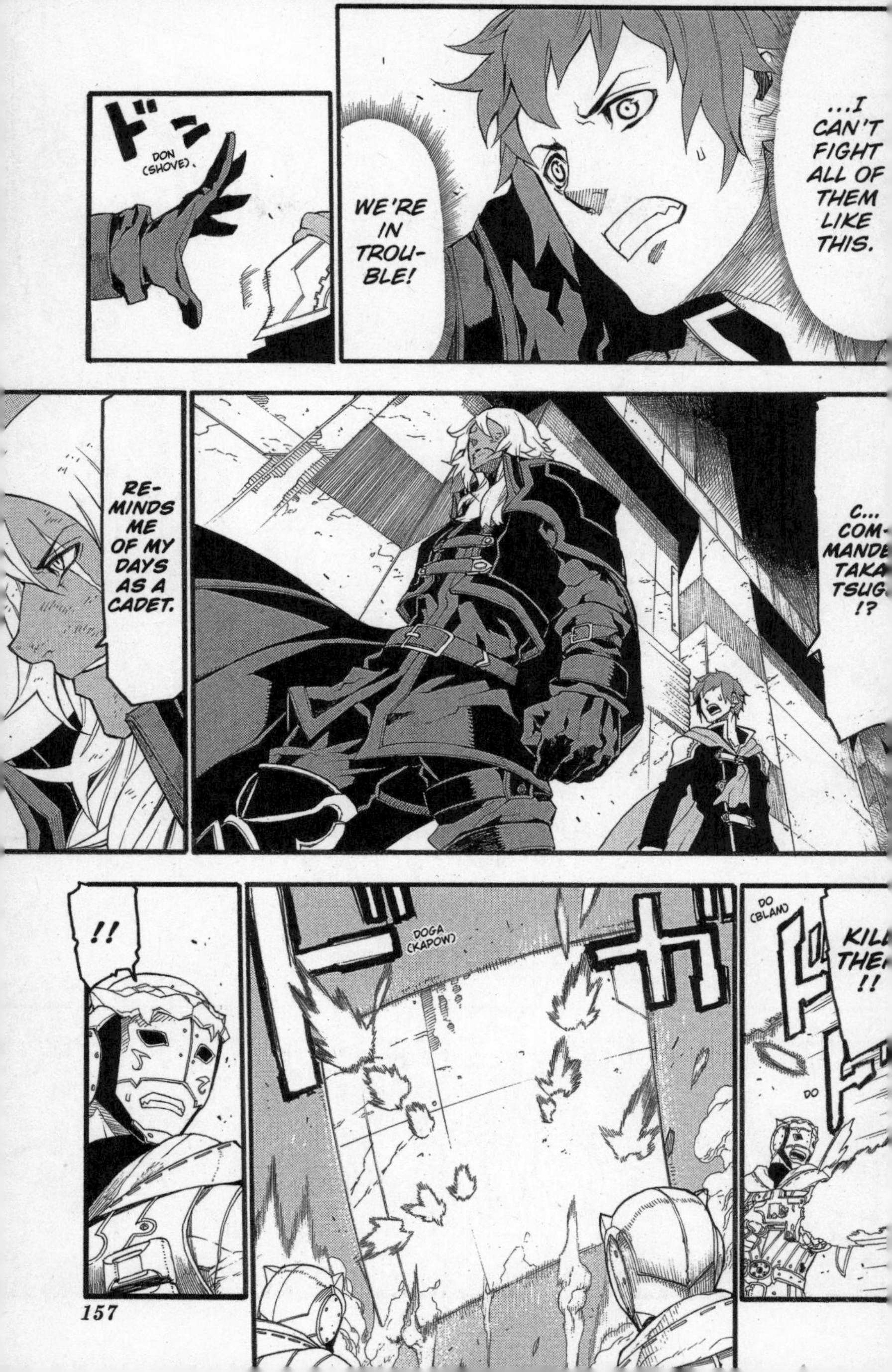
...I CAN'T FIGHT ALL OF THEM LIKE THIS.
WE'RE IN TROUBLE!
ドン
DON (SHOVE)
C... COMMANDE TAKA TSUG !?
REMINDS ME OF MY DAYS AS A CADET.
KIL THE !!
DO (BLAM)
DO
DOGA (KAPOW)
!!

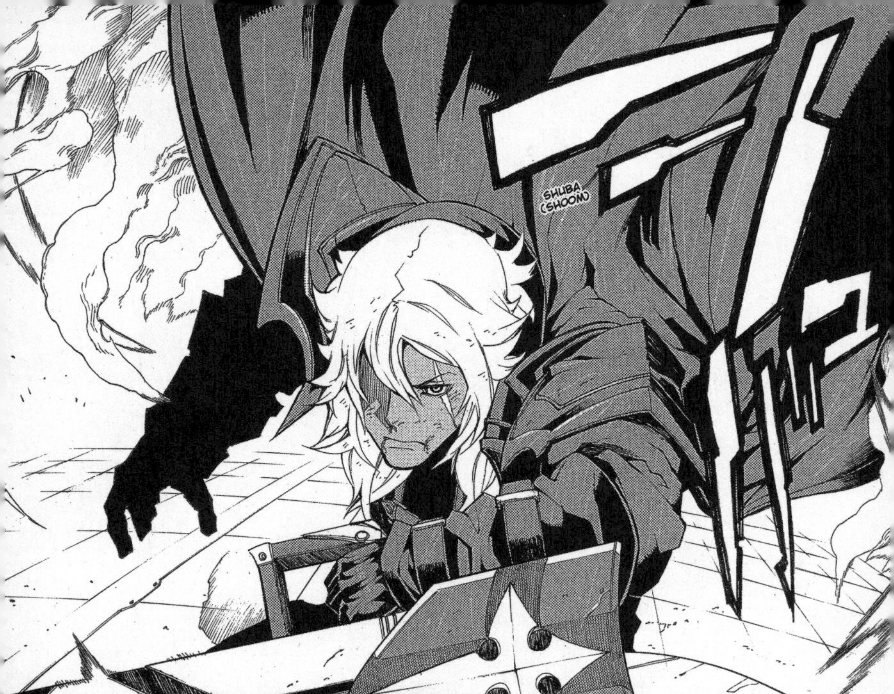
SHUBA
(SHOOM)

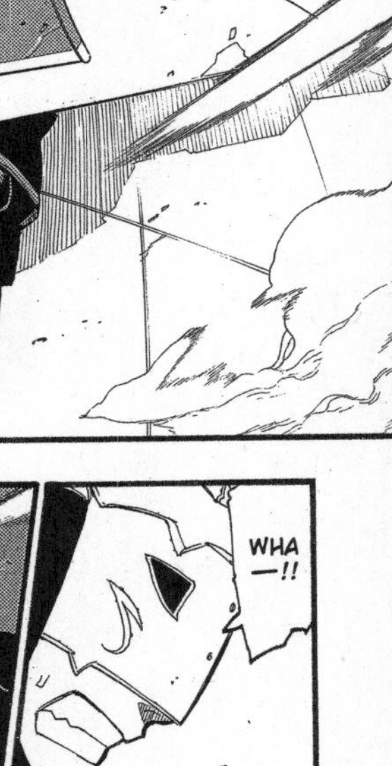
WHA—!!

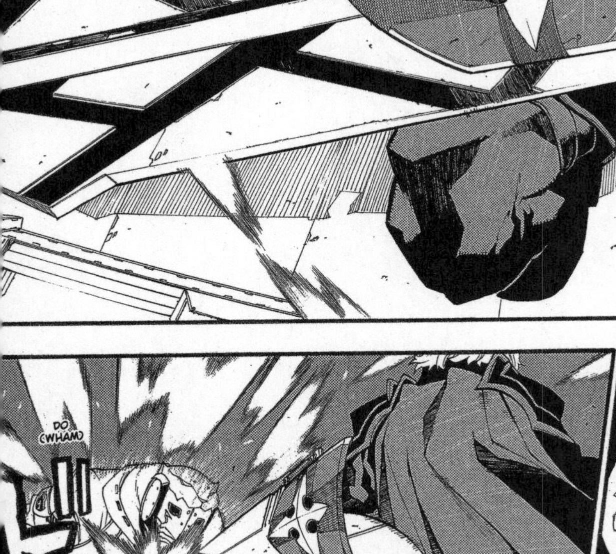
DO
(WHAM)

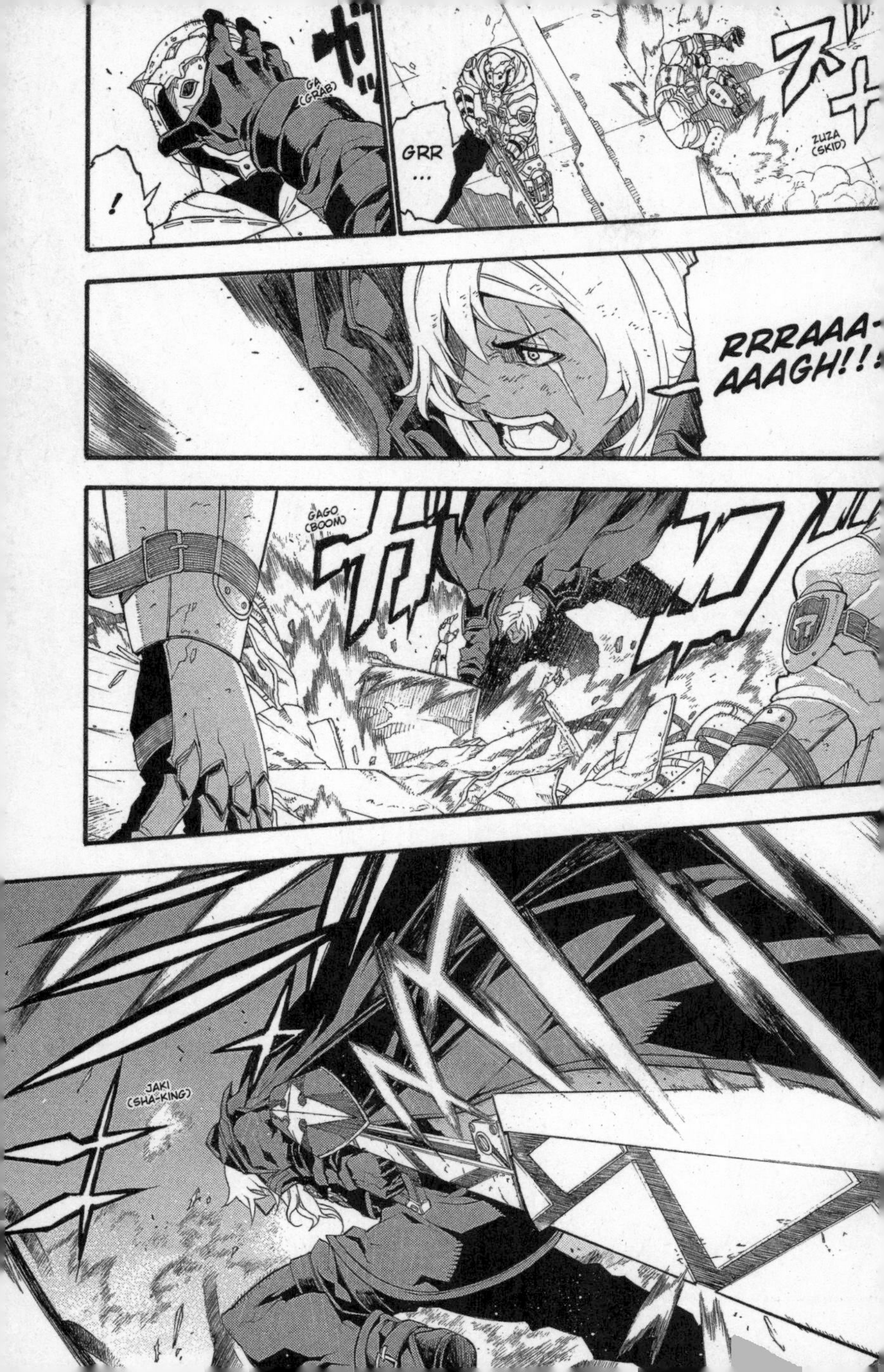
ZUZA (SKID)
GRR ...
GA (GRAB)
!
RRRAAA-AAAGH!!!
GAGO (BOOM)
JAKI (SHA-KING)

ZUBA
(SLICE)

SAH
...!

ズドド
ZUDO
(SLASH)

DON'T
LET 'EM
SCARE
YOU! WE
HAVE
THEM
OUT-
MANNED
!!

GRR
...!

*THERE ARE
TOO MANY—
I DON'T
HAVE TIME
TO INCANT
A SPELL!*

GRR
...

ザッ
ZA
(ZSH)

ザ
ZA

ザ
ZA

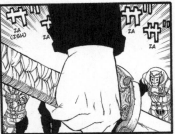

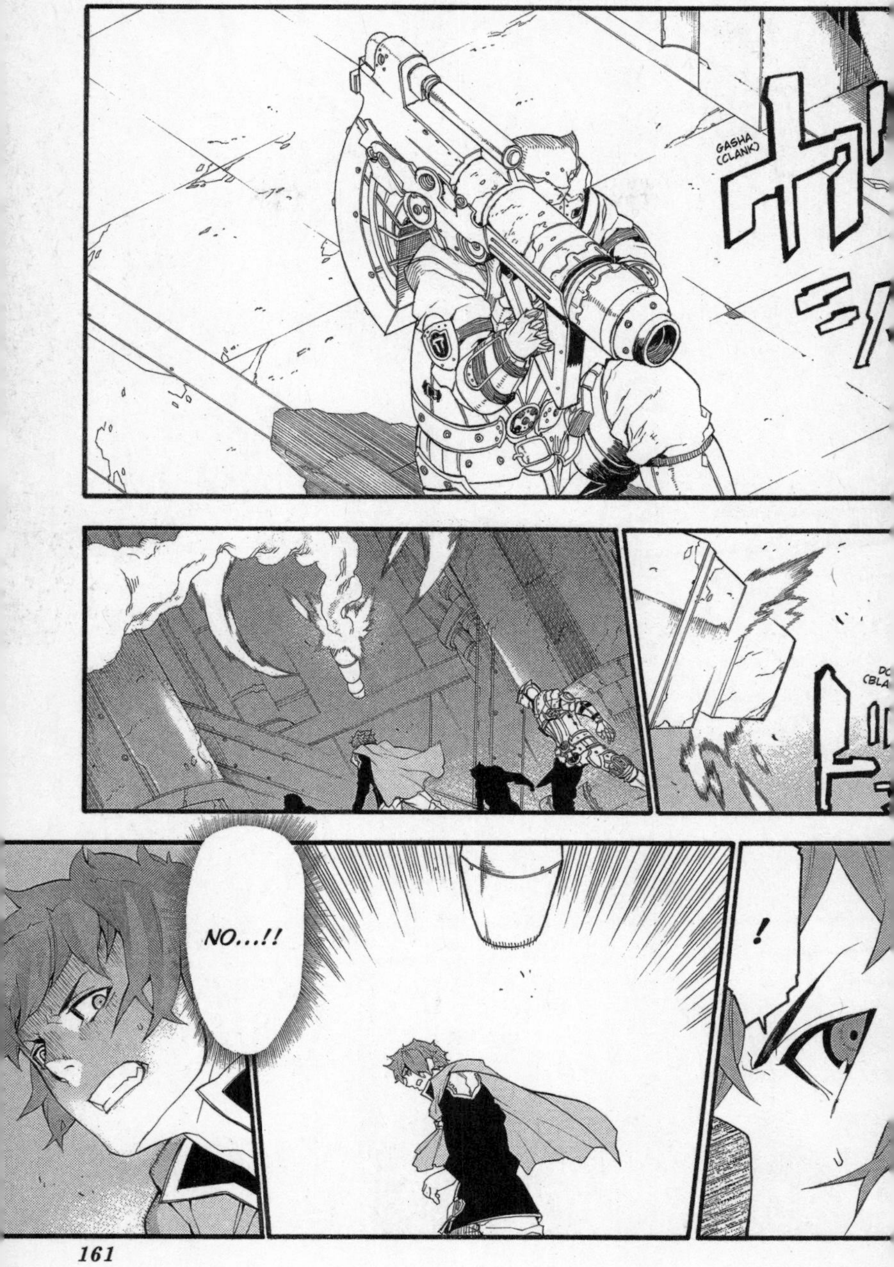
GASHA (CLANK)
!
NO...!!

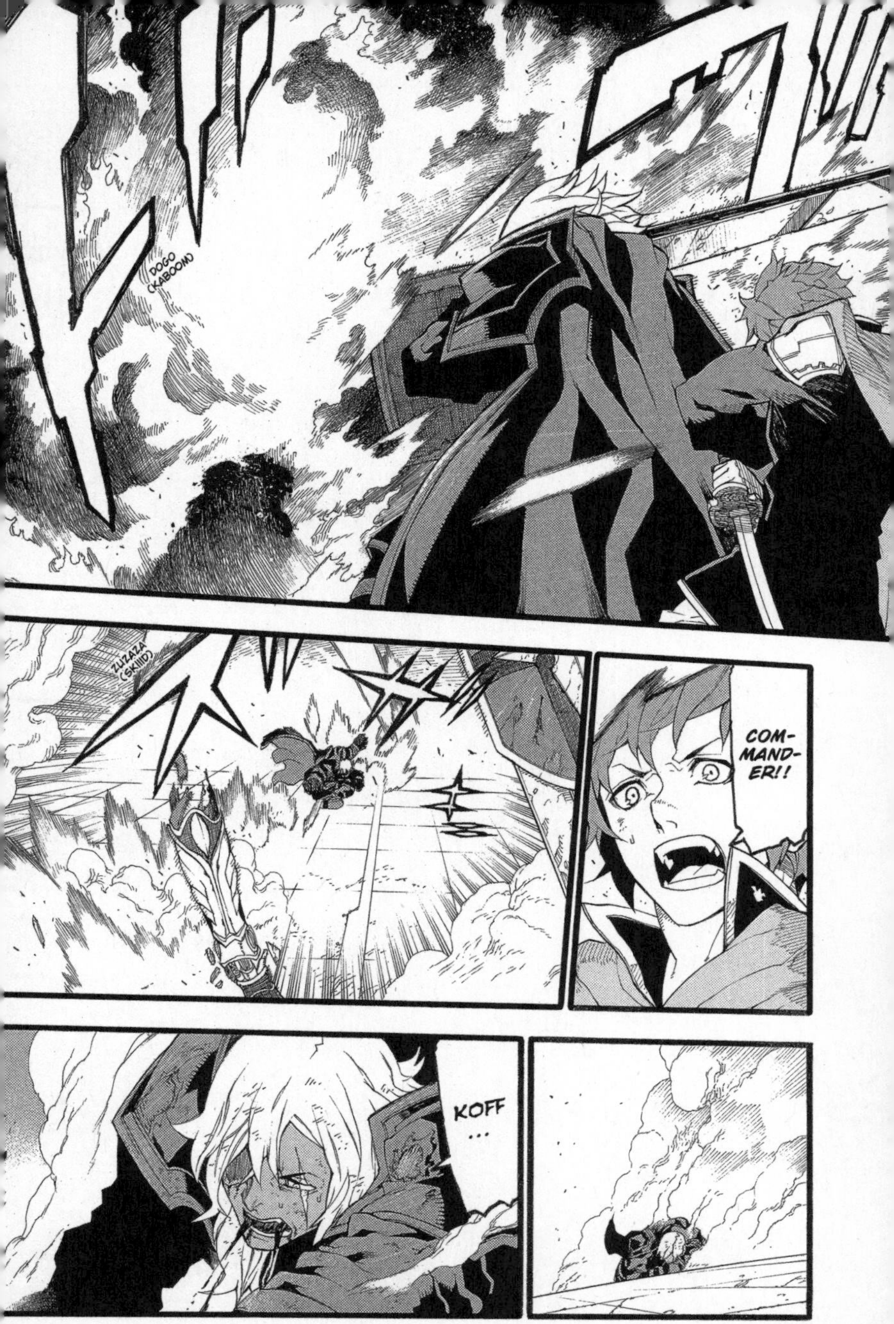
DOGO (KABOOM)
COMMANDER!!
ZUZAZA (SKIIID)
KOFF...

DOSU (SHOONK)

GAH...!

YOU SON OF A —!!

HYU (SWISH)

!?

...MY SWORD! IT'S NOT LISTENING TO ME!?

GUGU (STRAIN)

RE-TURN

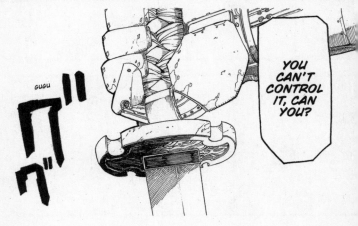

GUGU

YOU CAN'T CONTROL IT, CAN YOU?

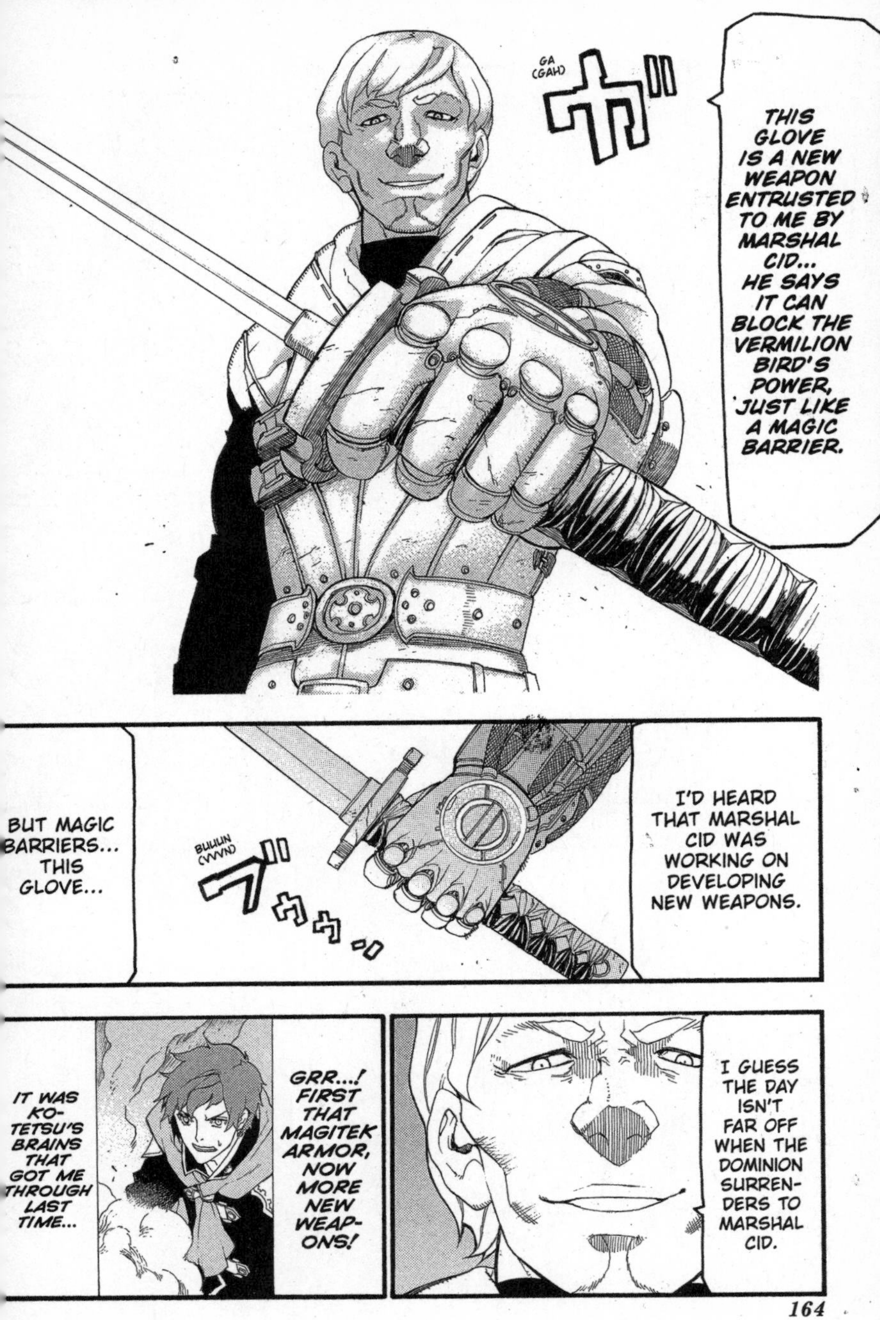
THIS GLOVE IS A NEW WEAPON ENTRUSTED TO ME BY MARSHAL CID... HE SAYS IT CAN BLOCK THE VERMILION BIRD'S POWER, JUST LIKE A MAGIC BARRIER.
GA (GAH)
I'D HEARD THAT MARSHAL CID WAS WORKING ON DEVELOPING NEW WEAPONS.
BUUUN (VVVN)
BUT MAGIC BARRIERS... THIS GLOVE...
I GUESS THE DAY ISN'T FAR OFF WHEN THE DOMINION SURREN-DERS TO MARSHAL CID.
GRR...! FIRST THAT MAGITEK ARMOR, NOW MORE NEW WEAP-ONS!
IT WAS KO-TETSU'S BRAINS THAT GOT ME THROUGH LAST TIME...

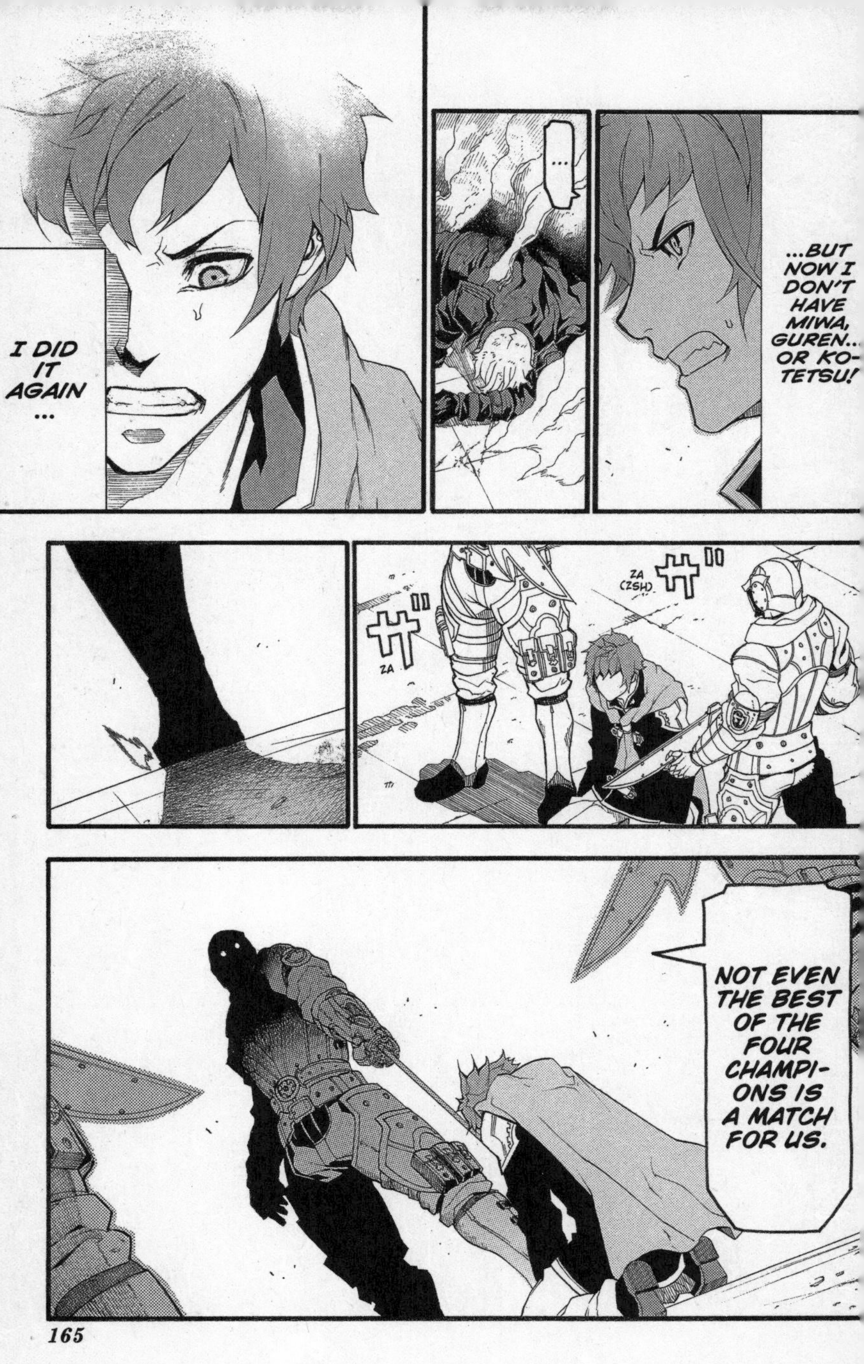
...BUT NOW I DON'T HAVE MIWA, GUREN... OR KOTETSU!
...
I DID IT AGAIN ...
ZA (ZSH)
ZA
NOT EVEN THE BEST OF THE FOUR CHAMPI-ONS IS A MATCH FOR US.

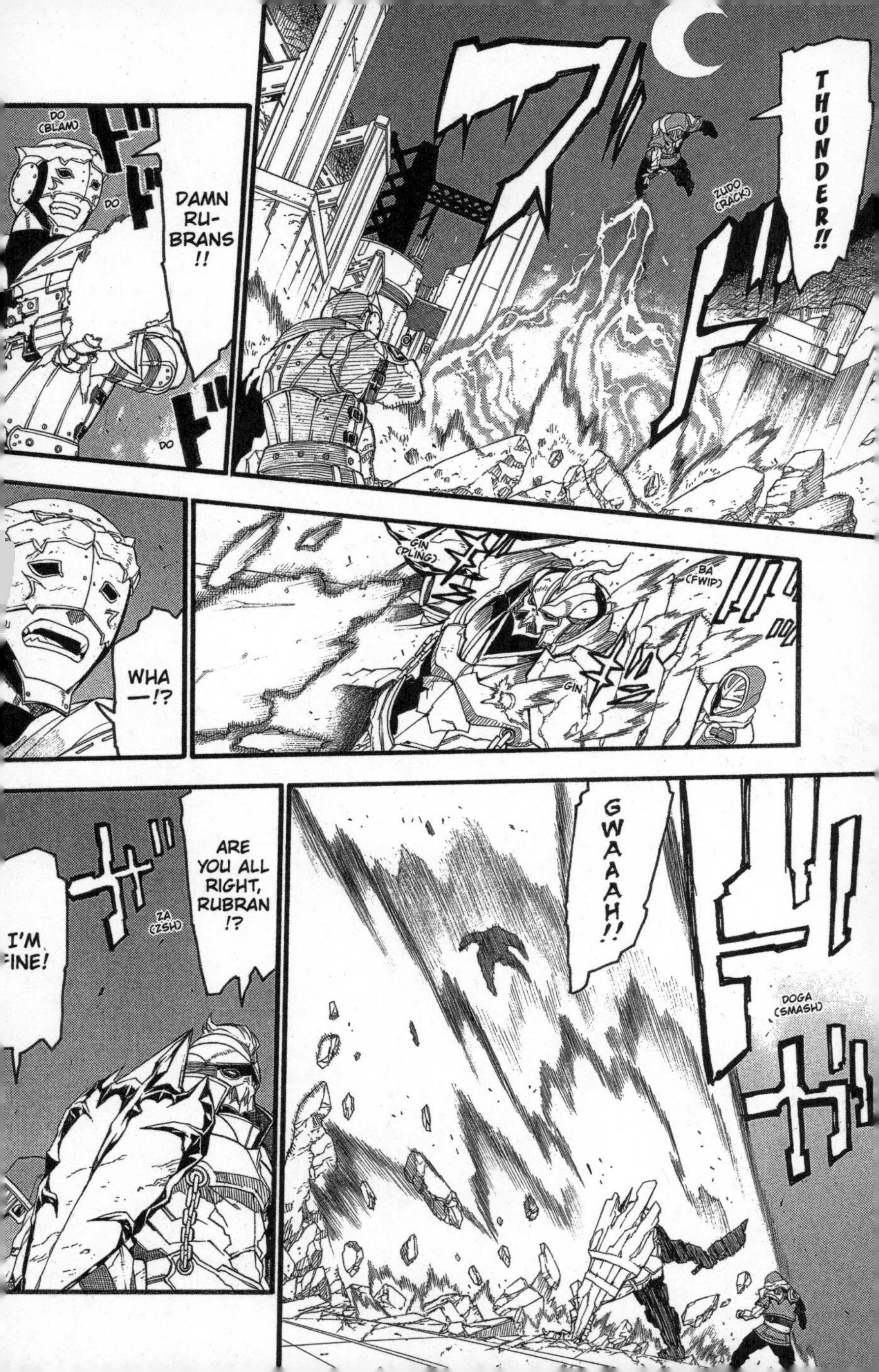
THUNDER!!
ZUDO (RACK)
DO (BLAM)
DO
DAMN RU-BRANS!!
DO
GIN (PLING)
BA (FWIP)
GIN
WHA—!?
GWAAAAH!!
DOGA (SMASH)
ARE YOU ALL RIGHT, RUBRAN!?
ZA (ZSH)
I'M FINE!

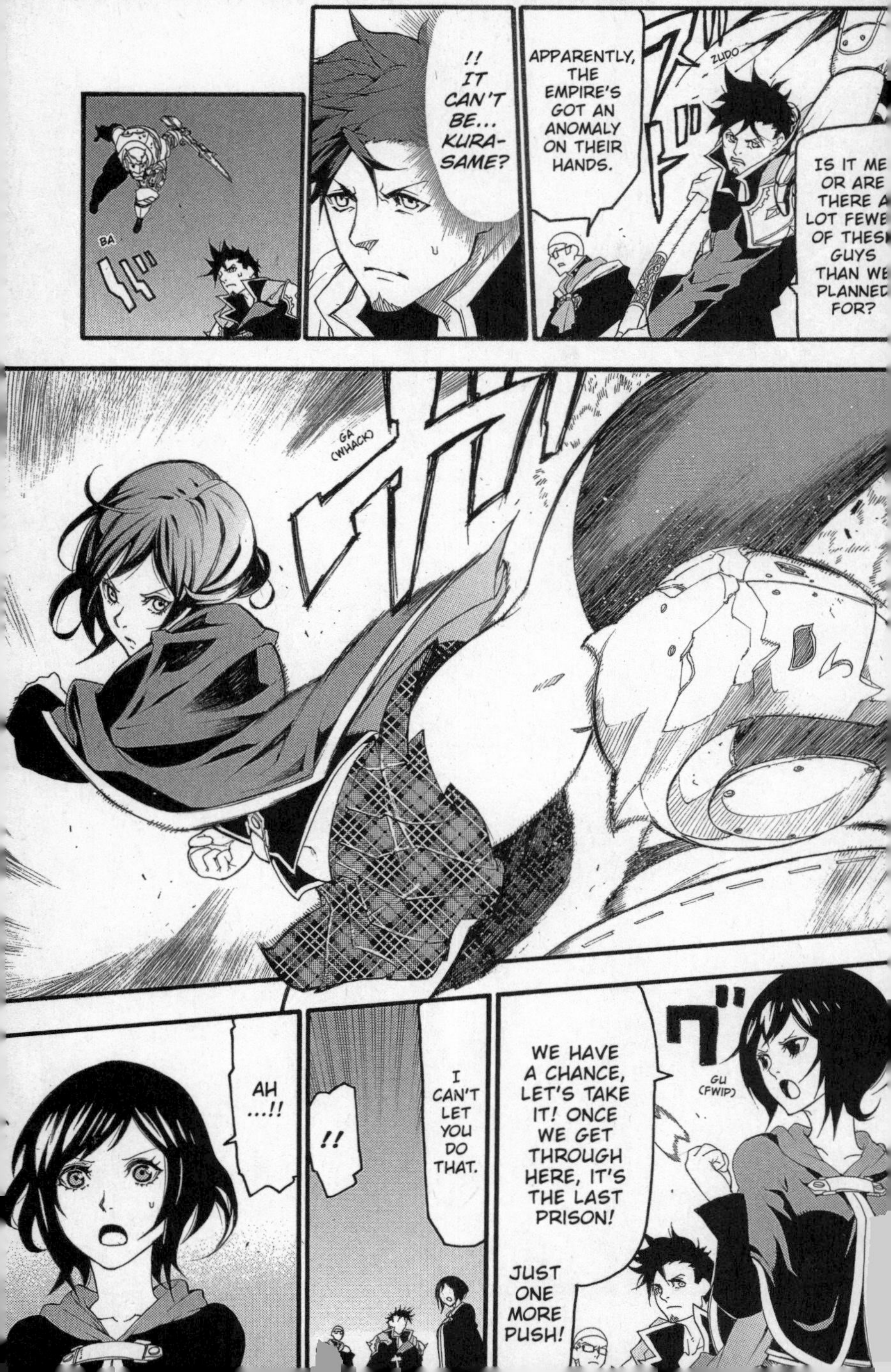
ZUDO
IS IT ME OR ARE THERE A LOT FEWE OF THES GUYS THAN WE PLANNED FOR?
APPARENTLY, THE EMPIRE'S GOT AN ANOMALY ON THEIR HANDS.
!! IT CAN'T BE... KURA-SAME?
BA
GA (WHACK)
GU (FWIP)
WE HAVE A CHANCE, LET'S TAKE IT! ONCE WE GET THROUGH HERE, IT'S THE LAST PRISON!
JUST ONE MORE PUSH!
I CAN'T LET YOU DO THAT.
!!
AH ...!!

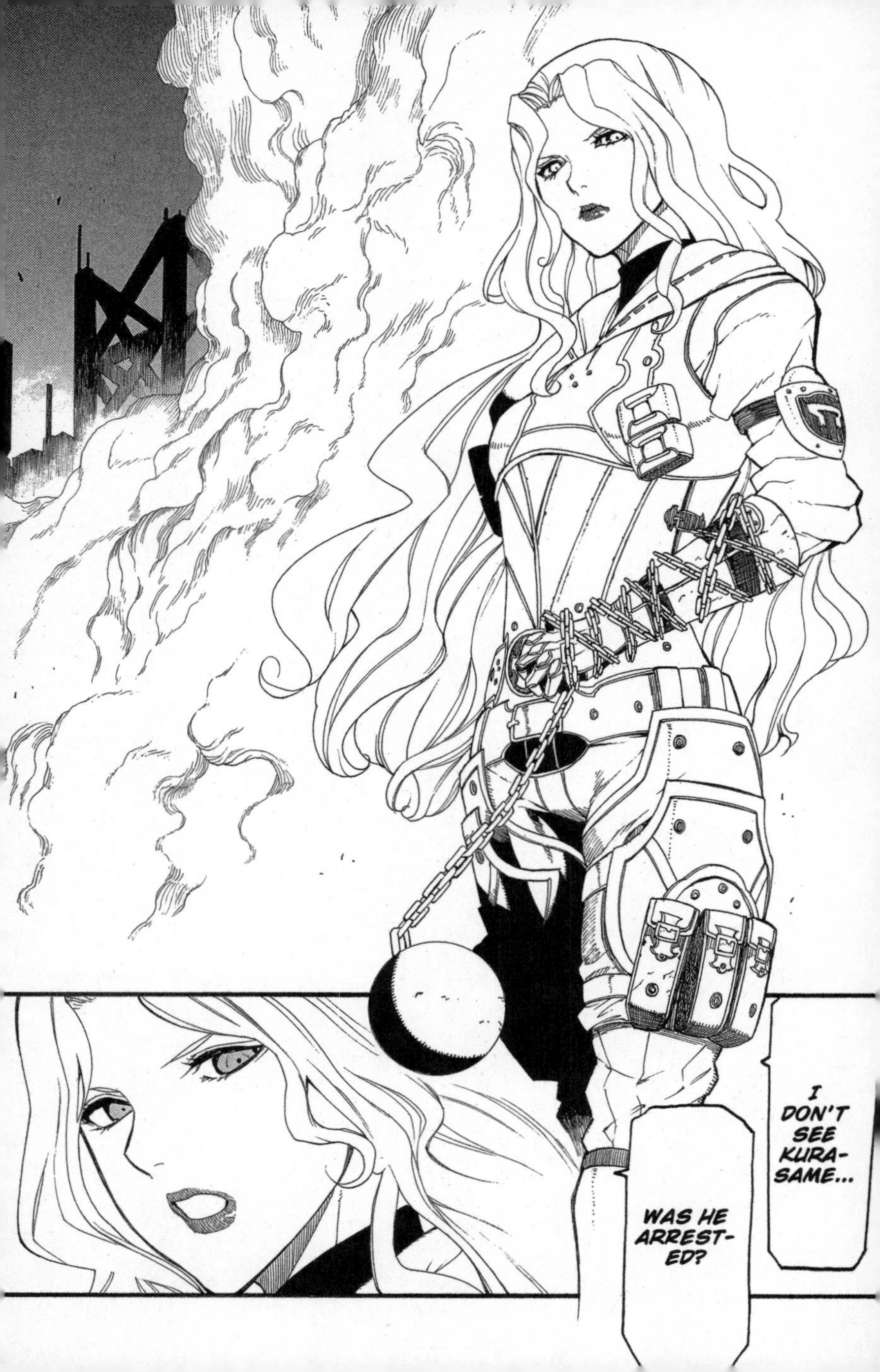
I DON'T SEE KURA-SAME...
WAS HE ARREST-ED?

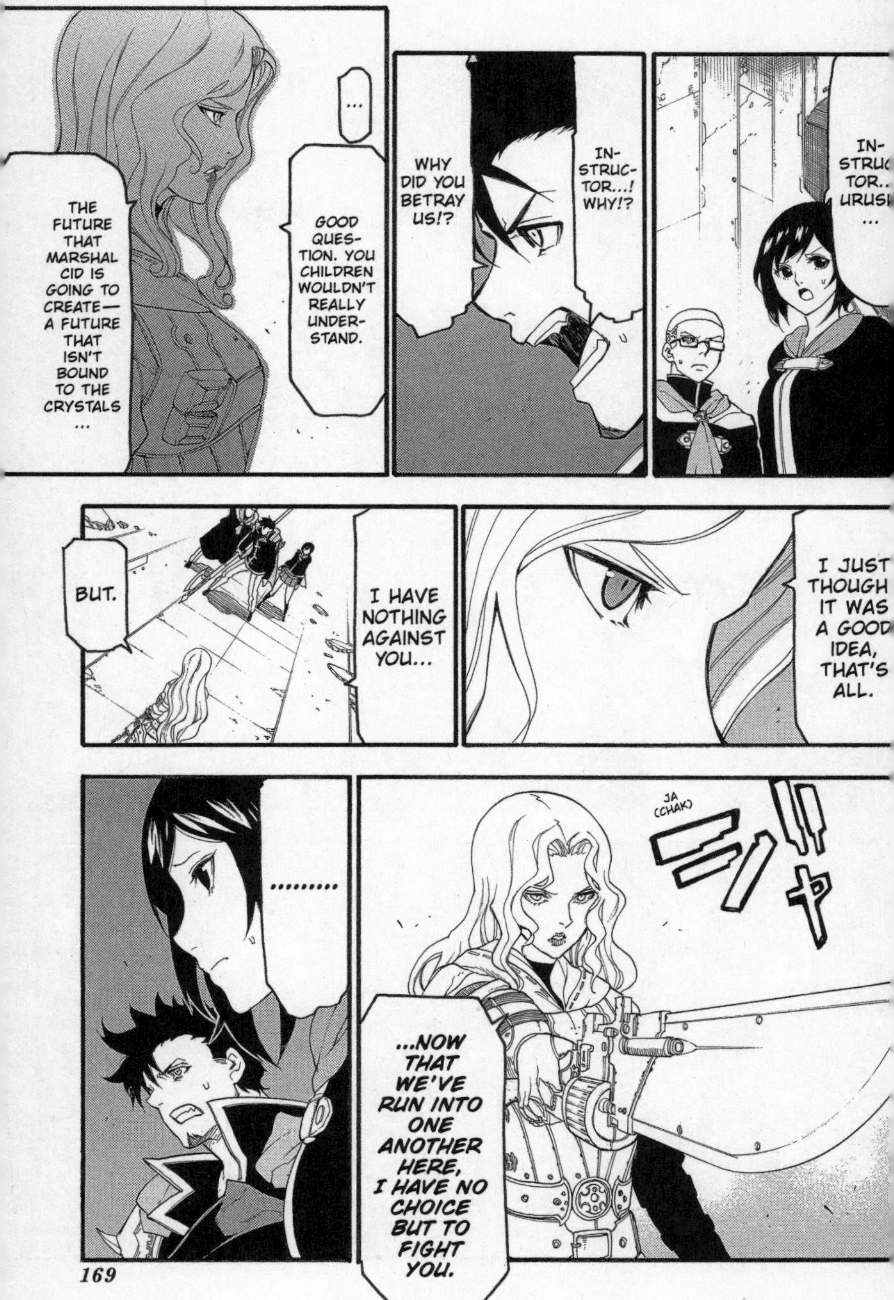

IN-STRUC TOR.. URUSI ...
IN-STRUC-TOR...! WHY!?
WHY DID YOU BETRAY US!?
...
GOOD QUES-TION. YOU CHILDREN WOULDN'T REALLY UNDER-STAND.
THE FUTURE THAT MARSHAL CID IS GOING TO CREATE—A FUTURE THAT ISN'T BOUND TO THE CRYSTALS...
I JUST THOUGH IT WAS A GOOD IDEA, THAT'S ALL.
I HAVE NOTHING AGAINST YOU...
BUT.
JA (CHAK)
...NOW THAT WE'VE RUN INTO ONE ANOTHER HERE, I HAVE NO CHOICE BUT TO FIGHT YOU.
....

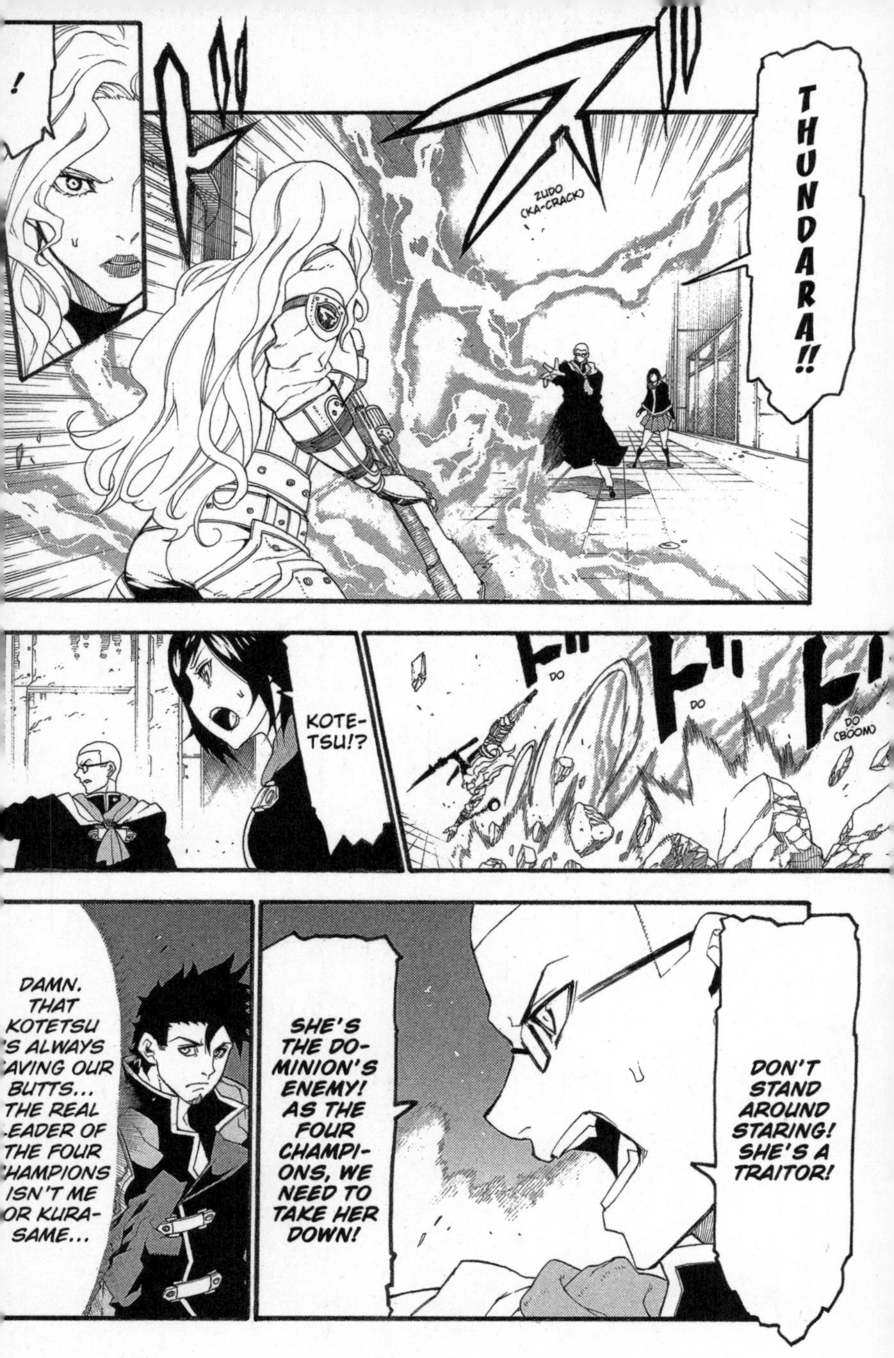
THUNDARA!!
ZUDO (KA-CRACK)
!
DO DO DO (BOOM)
KOTE-TSU!?
DON'T STAND AROUND STARING! SHE'S A TRAITOR!
SHE'S THE DO-MINION'S ENEMY! AS THE FOUR CHAMPI-ONS, WE NEED TO TAKE HER DOWN!
DAMN. THAT KOTETSU 'S ALWAYS AVING OUR BUTTS... THE REAL EADER OF THE FOUR HAMPIONS ISN'T ME OR KURA-SAME...

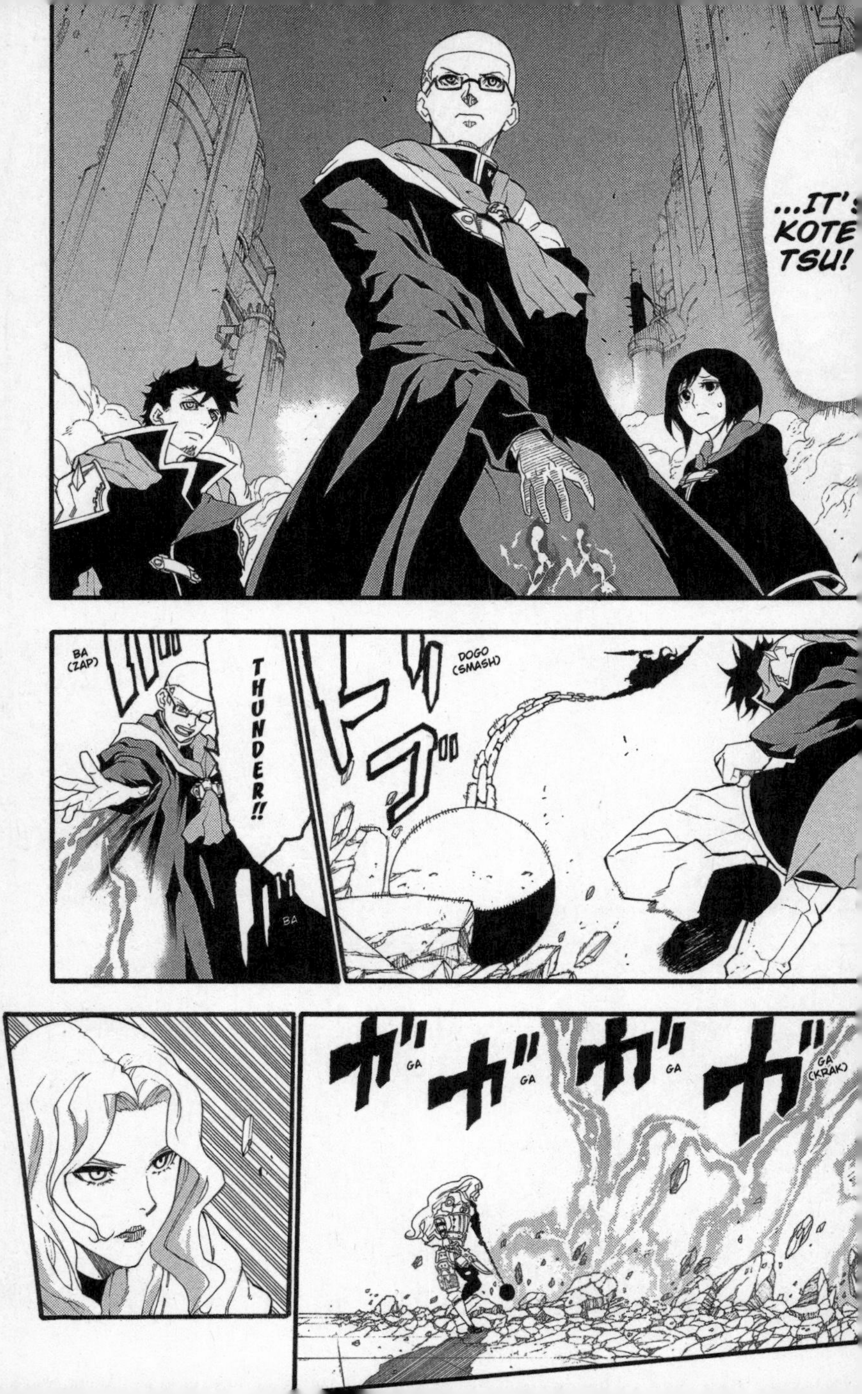
...IT'S KOTETSU!
DOGO (SMASH)
BA (ZAP)
THUNDER!!
BA
GA (KRAK)
GA
GA
GA

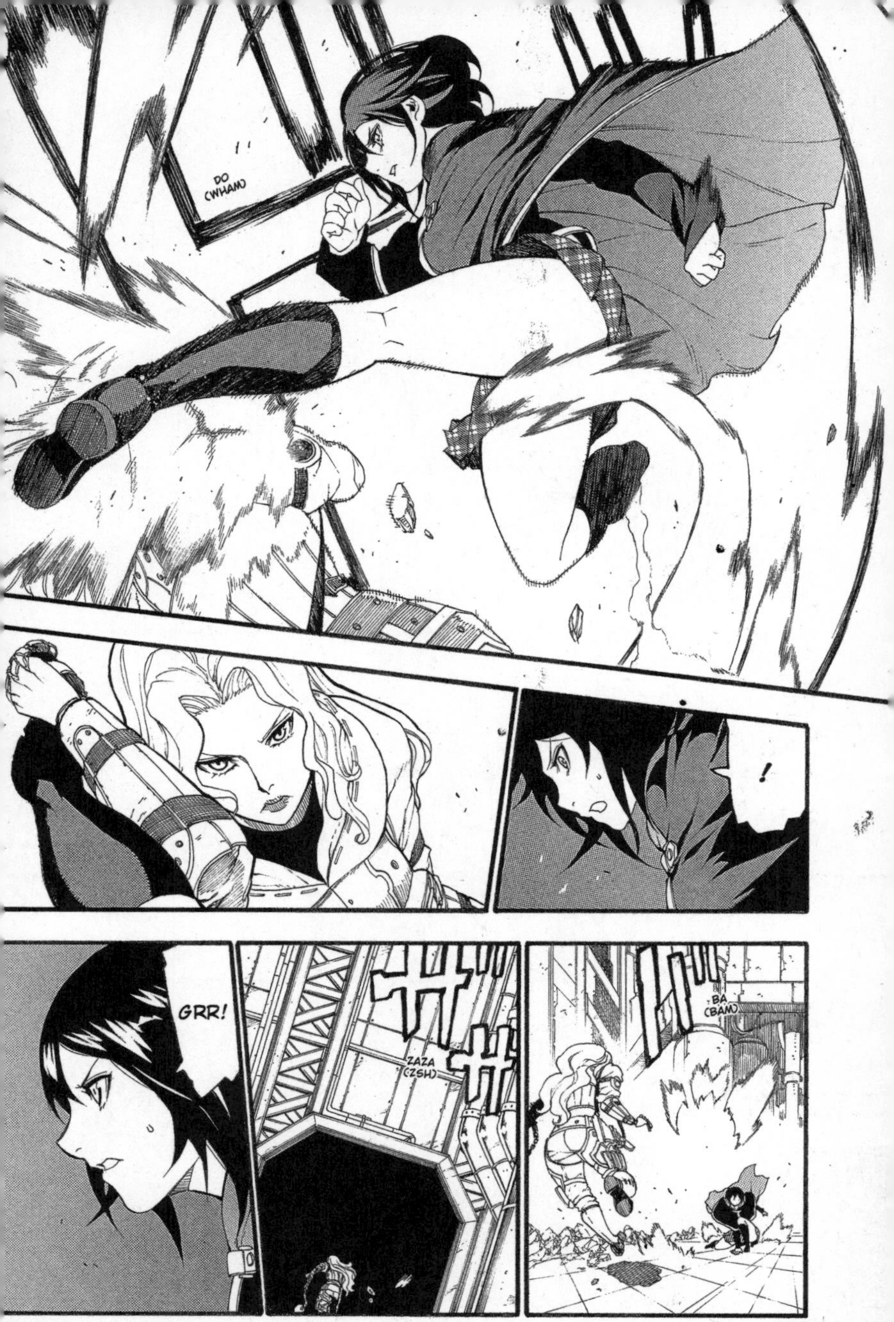
!!
DO
(WHAM)
!
BA
(BAM)
ZAZA
(ZSH)
GRR!

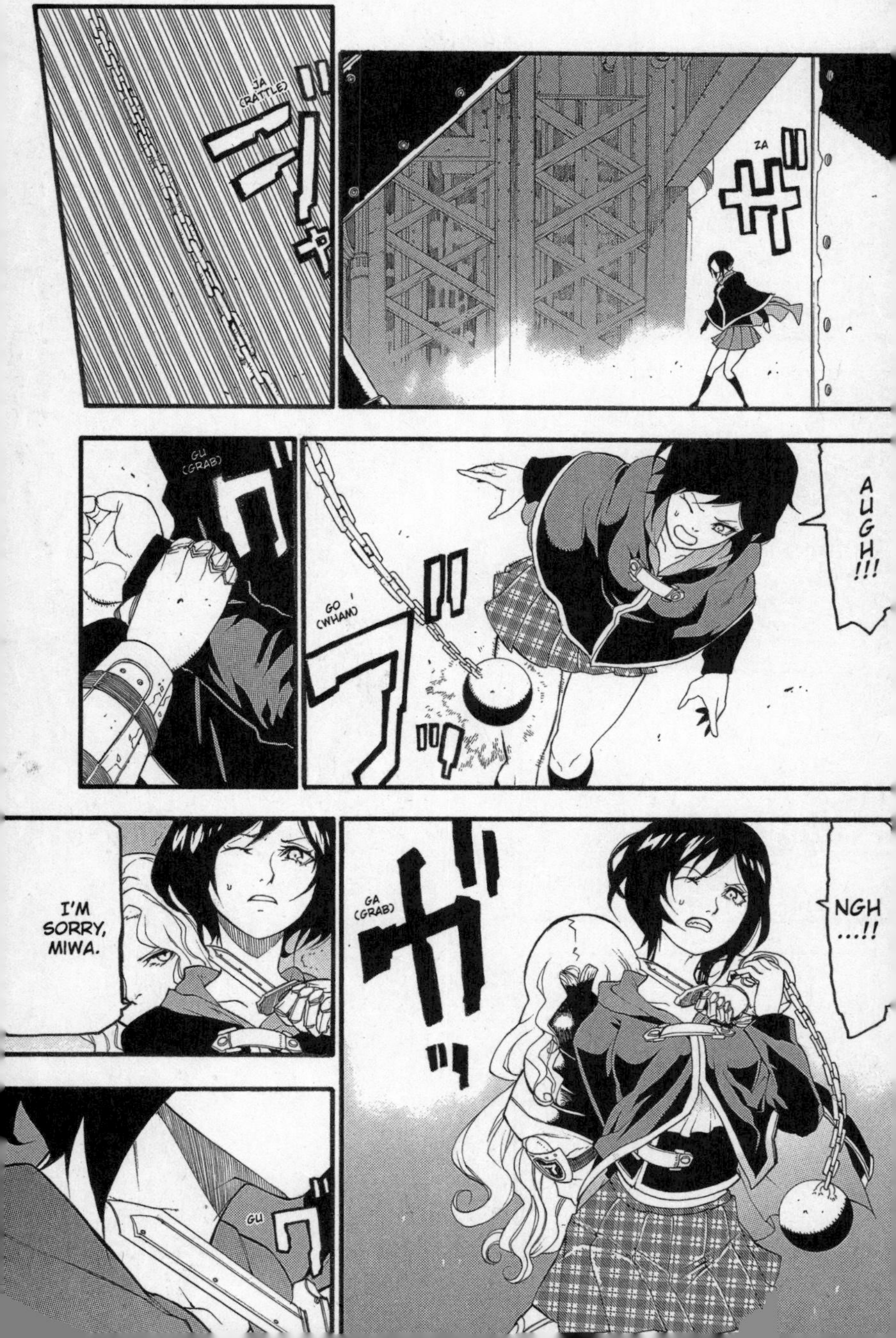
ZA
JA (RATTLE)
AUGH!!!
GO (WHAM)
GU (GRAB)
NGH ...!!
GA (GRAB)
I'M SORRY, MIWA.
GU

BUN
(SWOOSH)

MIWA, ARE YOU OKAY!?

ASHA
(LANK)

BUN
(SWOOSH)

DAM-MIT...!

THIS SPACE IS TOO NARROW FOR ME TO SWING MY AX!!

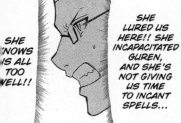

SHE KNOWS IS ALL TOO WELL!!

SHE LURED US HERE!! SHE INCAPACITATED GUREN, AND SHE'S NOT GIVING US TIME TO INCANT SPELLS...

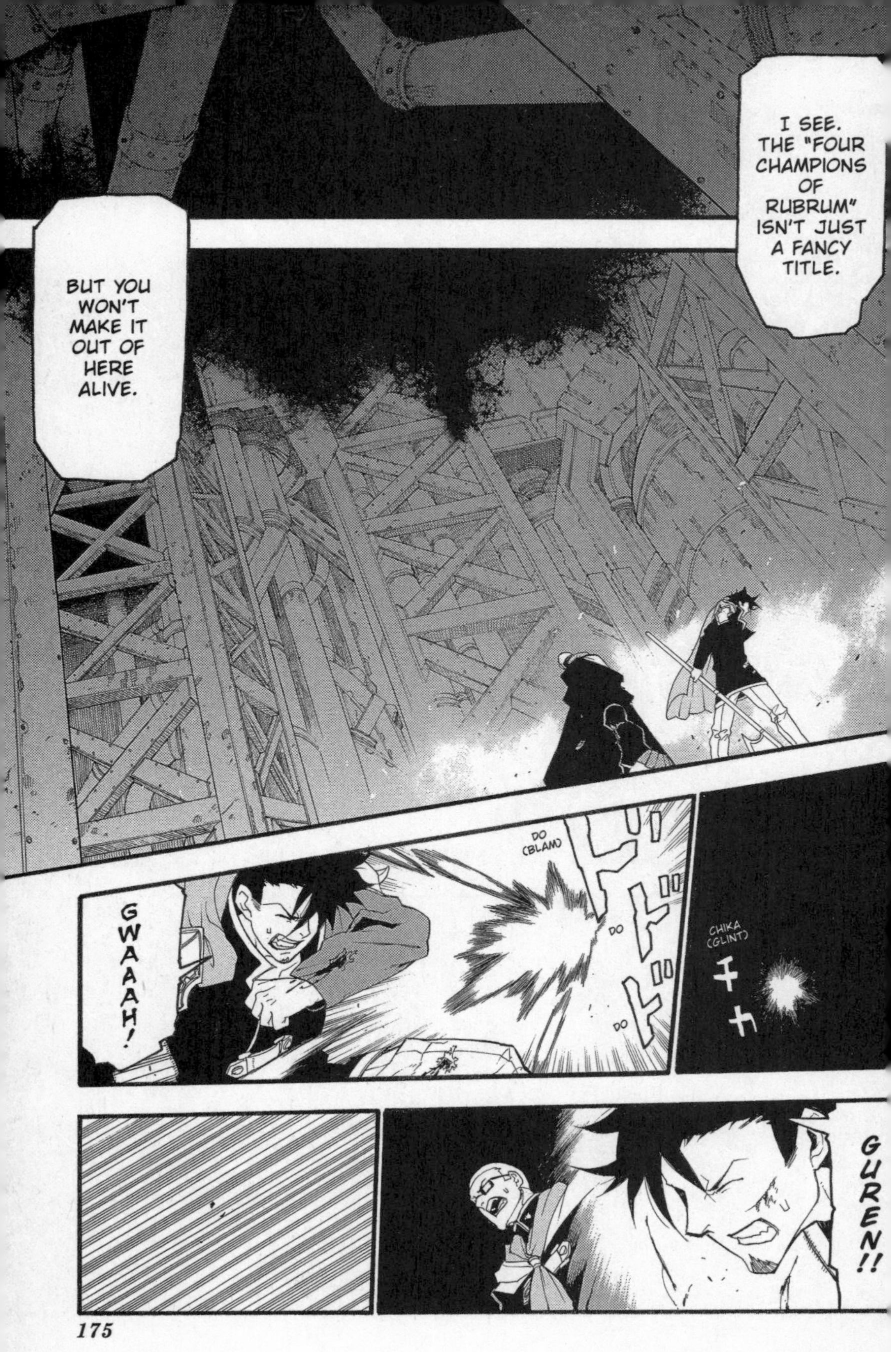
I SEE. THE "FOUR CHAMPIONS OF RUBRUM" ISN'T JUST A FANCY TITLE.
BUT YOU WON'T MAKE IT OUT OF HERE ALIVE.
CHIKA (GLINT)
チカ
DO (BLAM)
DO
DO
GWAAAAH!
GUREN!!

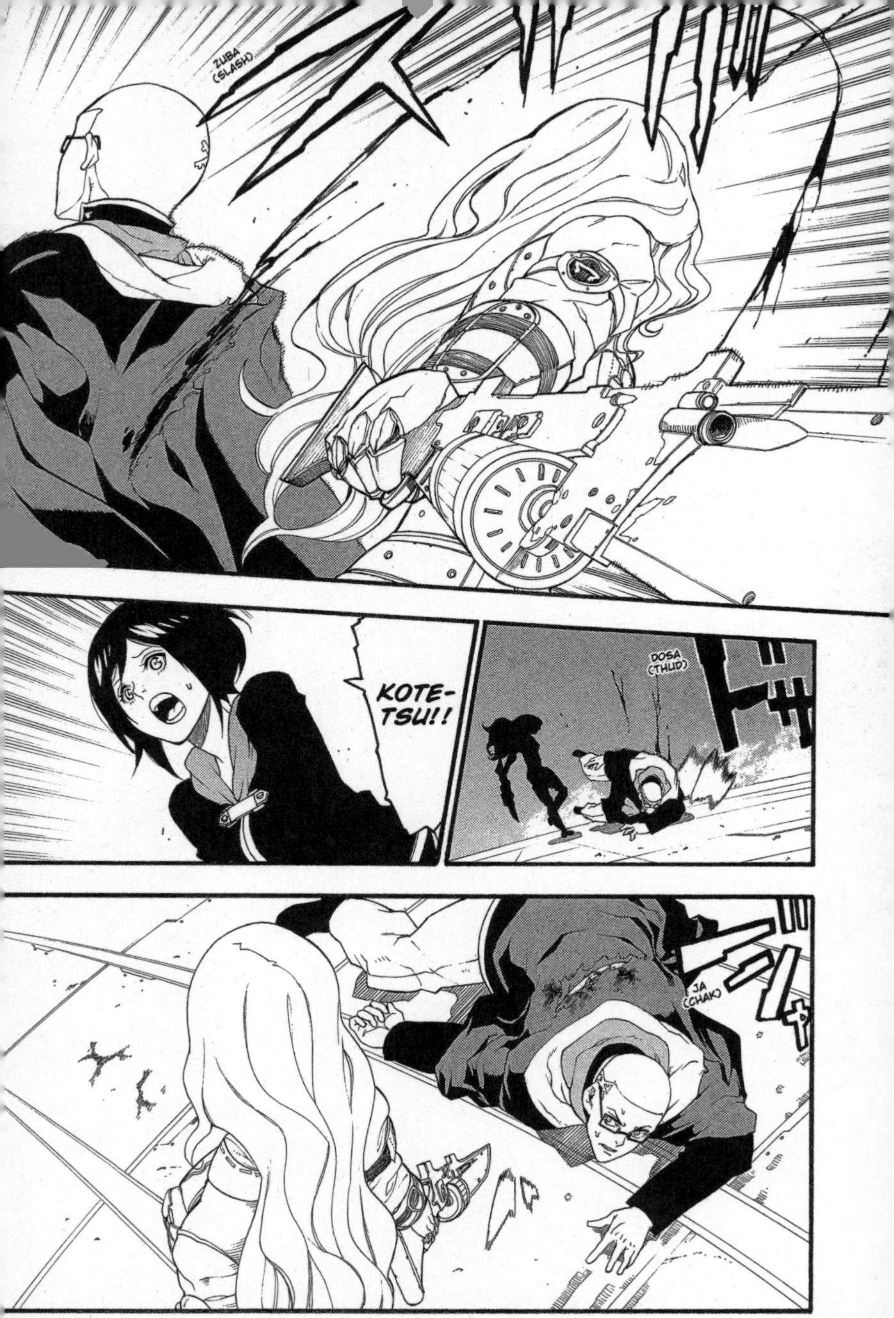
ZUBA (SLASH)
DOSA (THUD)
KOTETSU!!
JA (CHAK)

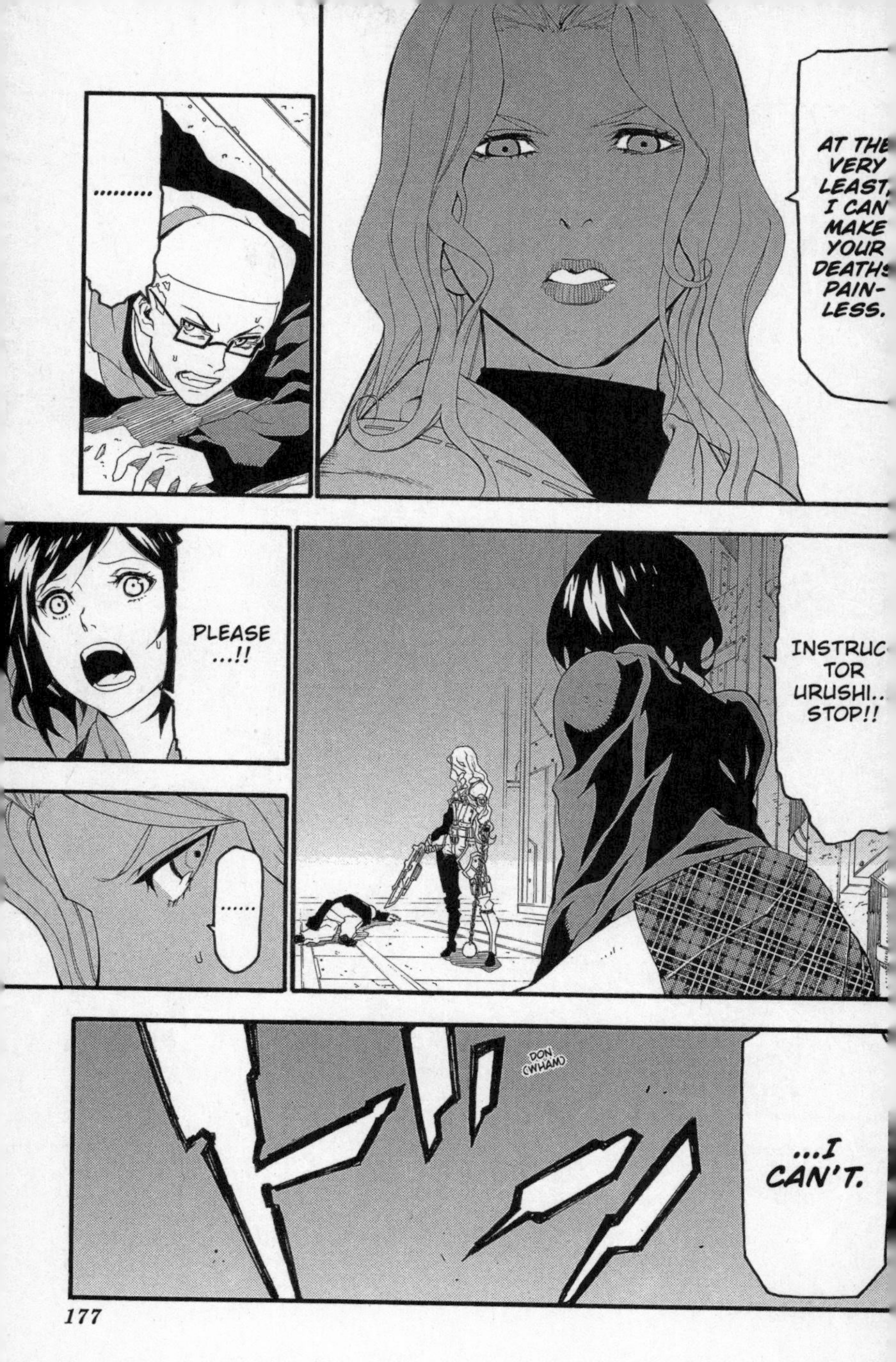
AT THE VERY LEAST, I CAN MAKE YOUR DEATHS PAINLESS.
....
INSTRUCTOR URUSHI.. STOP!!
PLEASE ...!!
......
...I CAN'T.
DON (WHAM)

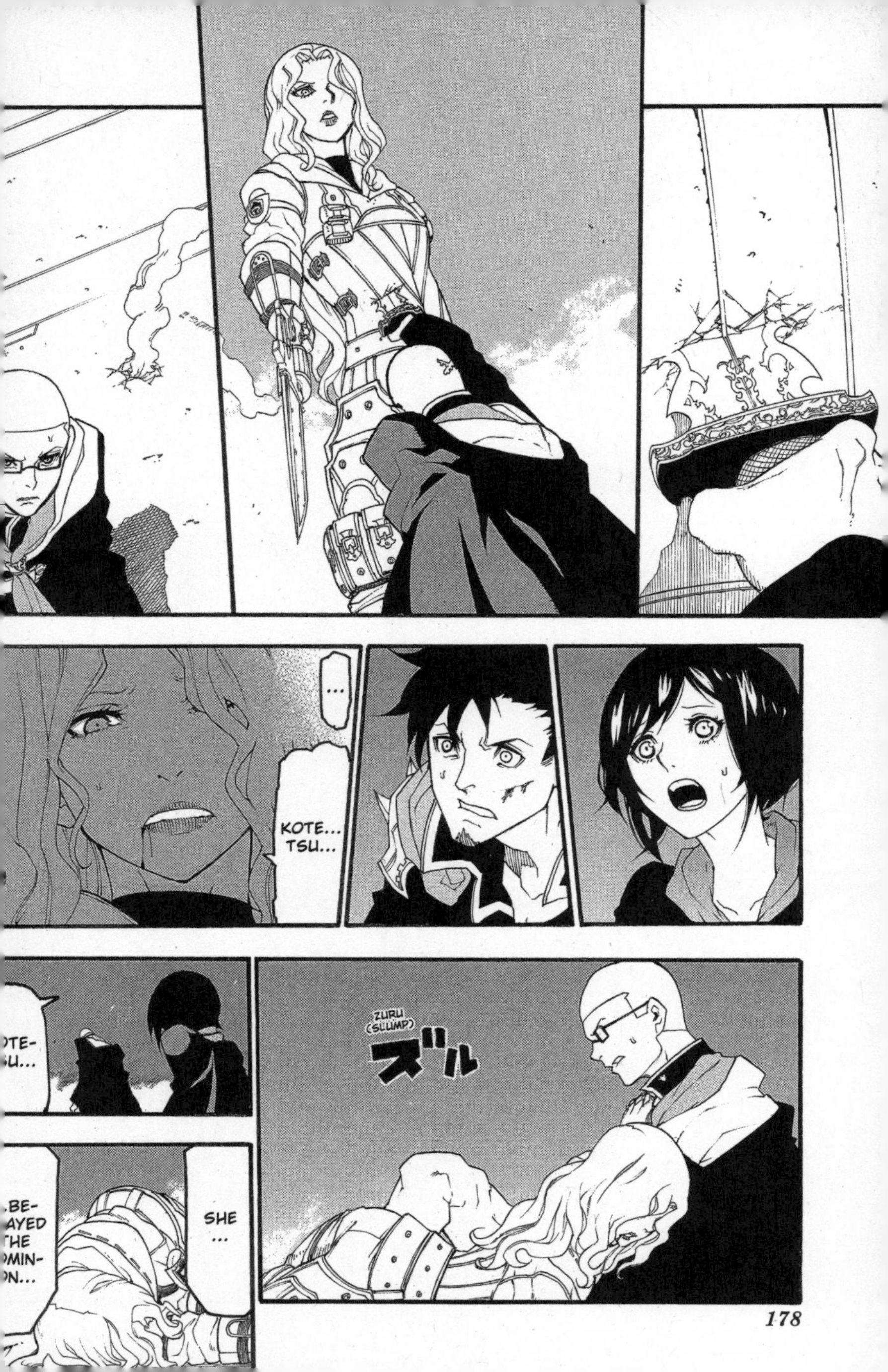
...
KOTE... TSU...
ZURU (SLUMP)
ズル
OTE- SU...
SHE ...
.BE- AYED THE OMIN- ON...

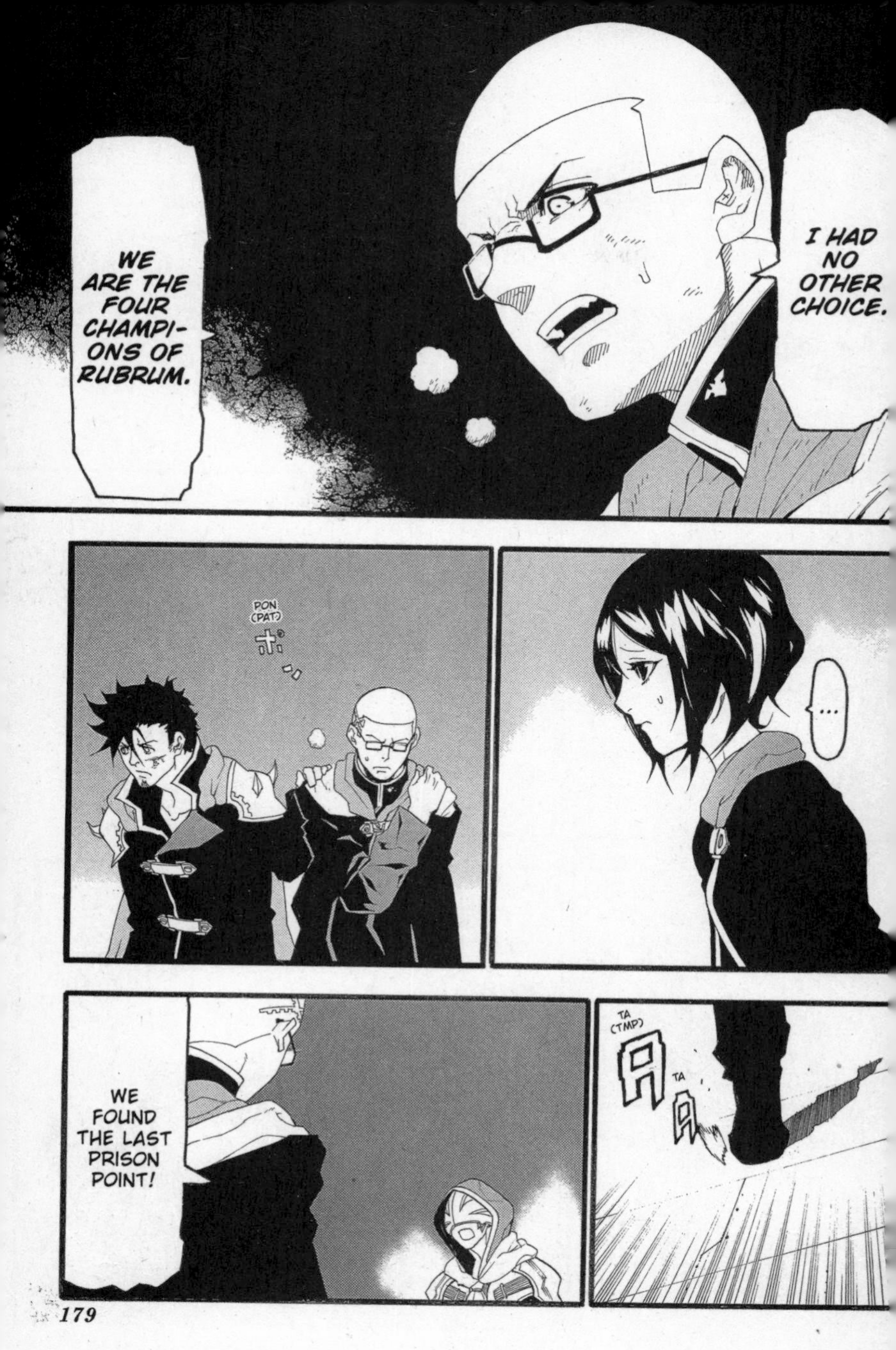
I HAD NO OTHER CHOICE.
WE ARE THE FOUR CHAMPIONS OF RUBRUM.
...
PON (PAT)
TA (TMP)
TA
WE FOUND THE LAST PRISON POINT!

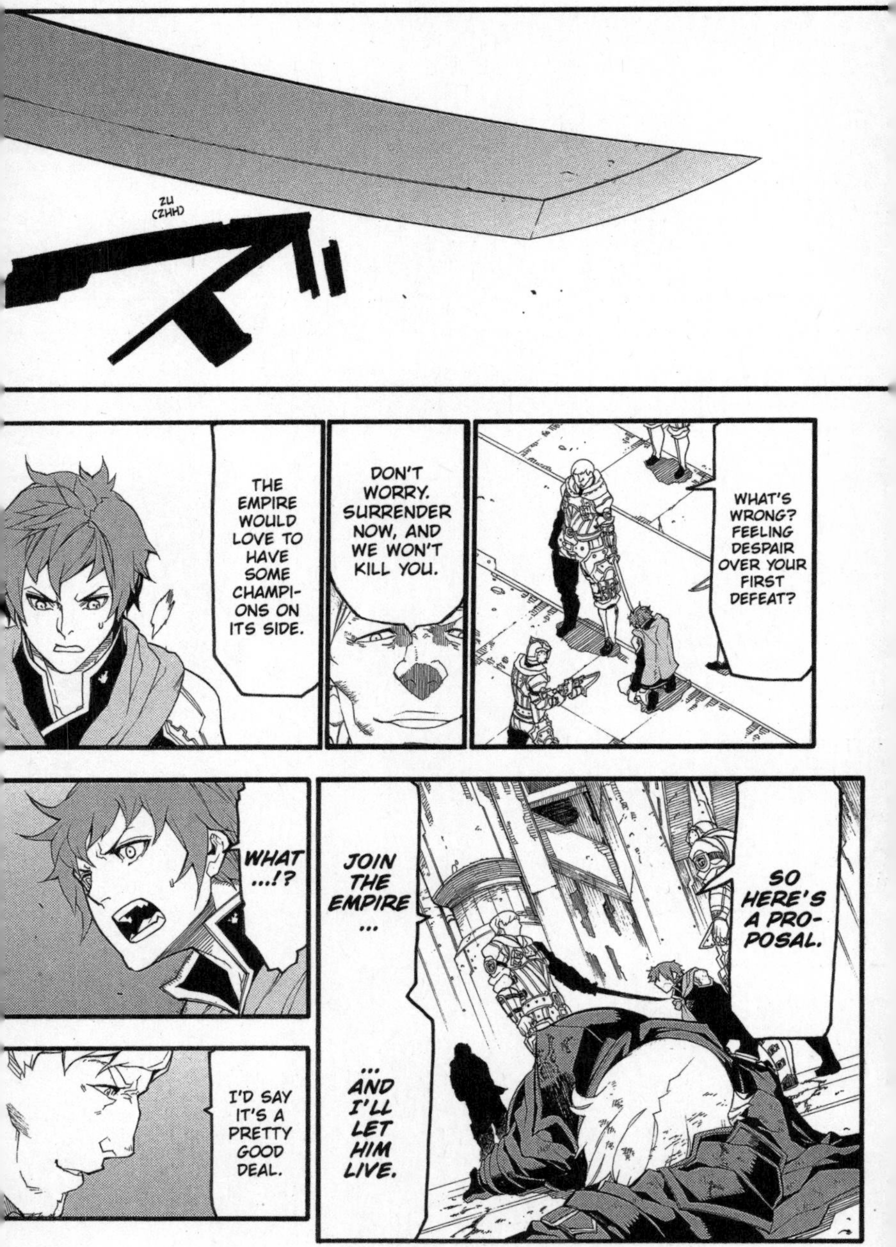
ZU (ZHH)
WHAT'S WRONG? FEELING DESPAIR OVER YOUR FIRST DEFEAT?
DON'T WORRY. SURRENDER NOW, AND WE WON'T KILL YOU.
THE EMPIRE WOULD LOVE TO HAVE SOME CHAMPIONS ON ITS SIDE.
SO HERE'S A PROPOSAL.
JOIN THE EMPIRE ...
... AND I'LL LET HIM LIVE.
WHAT ...!?
I'D SAY IT'S A PRETTY GOOD DEAL.

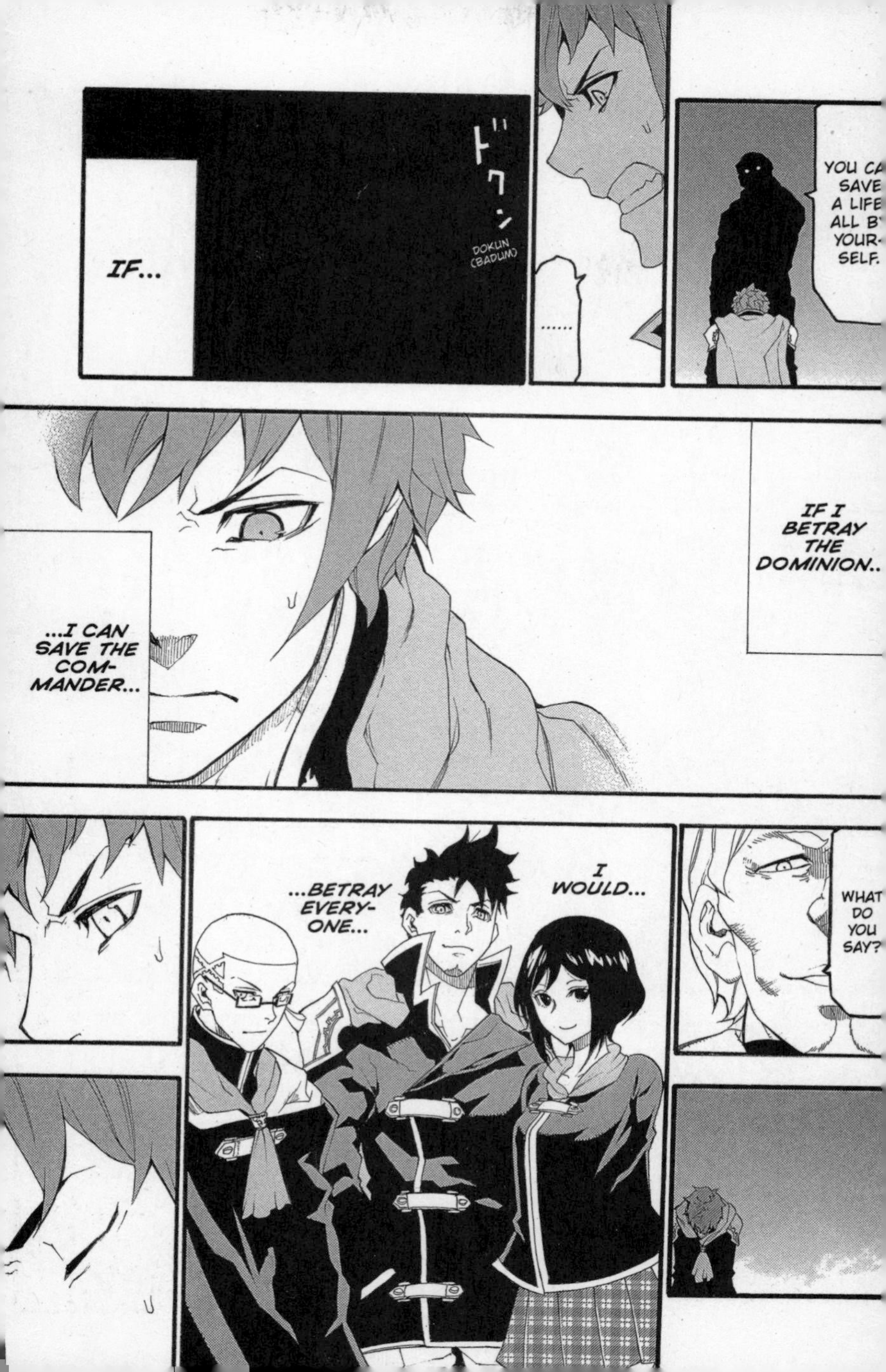
YOU CA SAVE A LIFE ALL B YOUR-SELF.
......
ドクン
DOKUN (BADUM)
IF...
IF I BETRAY THE DOMINION..
...I CAN SAVE THE COM-MANDER...
WHAT DO YOU SAY?
I WOULD...
...BETRAY EVERY-ONE...

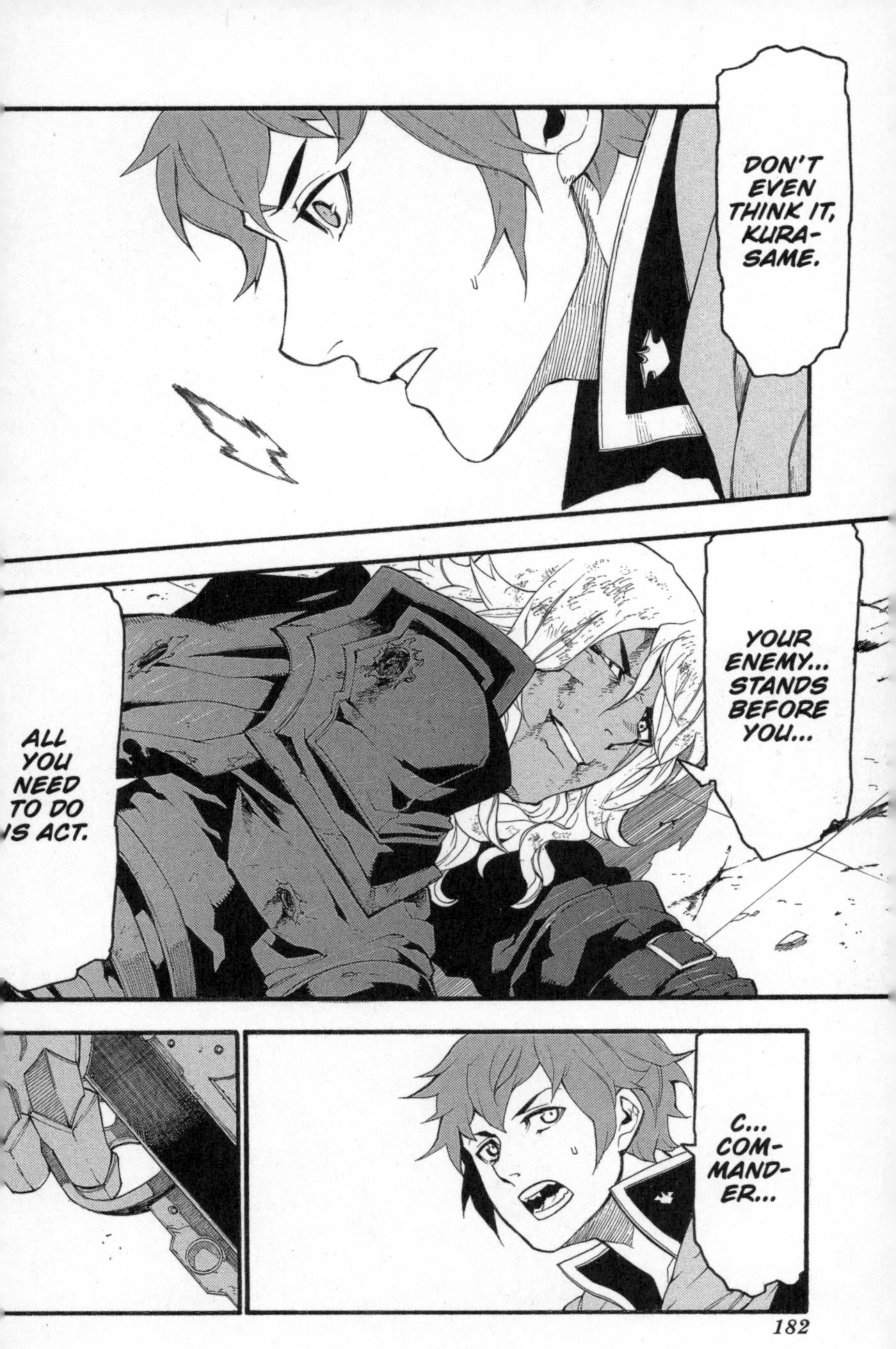
DON'T EVEN THINK IT, KURA-SAME.
YOUR ENEMY... STANDS BEFORE YOU...
ALL YOU NEED TO DO IS ACT.
C... COM-MAND-ER...

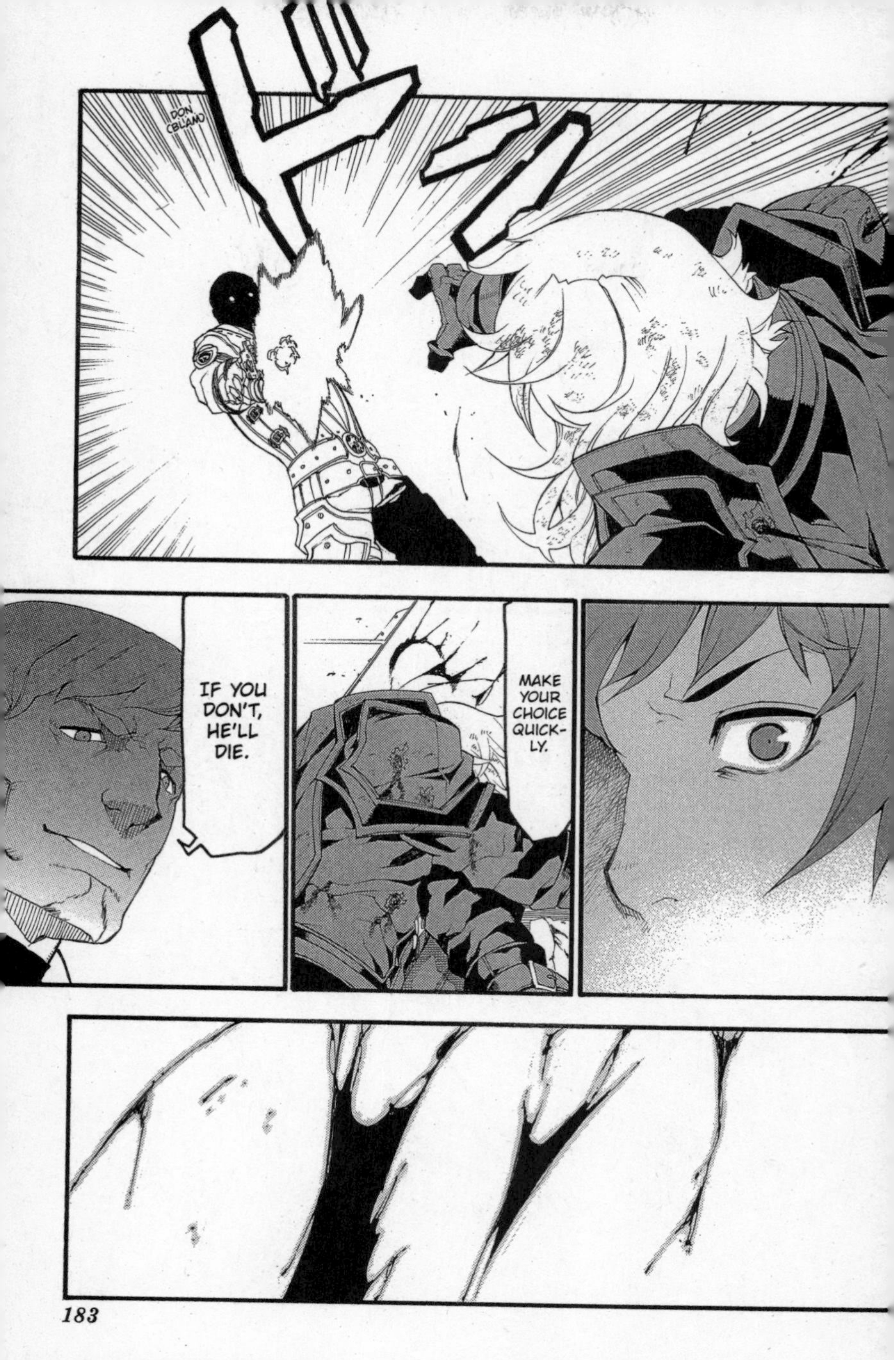
DON
(BLAM)
MAKE YOUR CHOICE QUICK-LY.
IF YOU DON'T, HE'LL DIE.

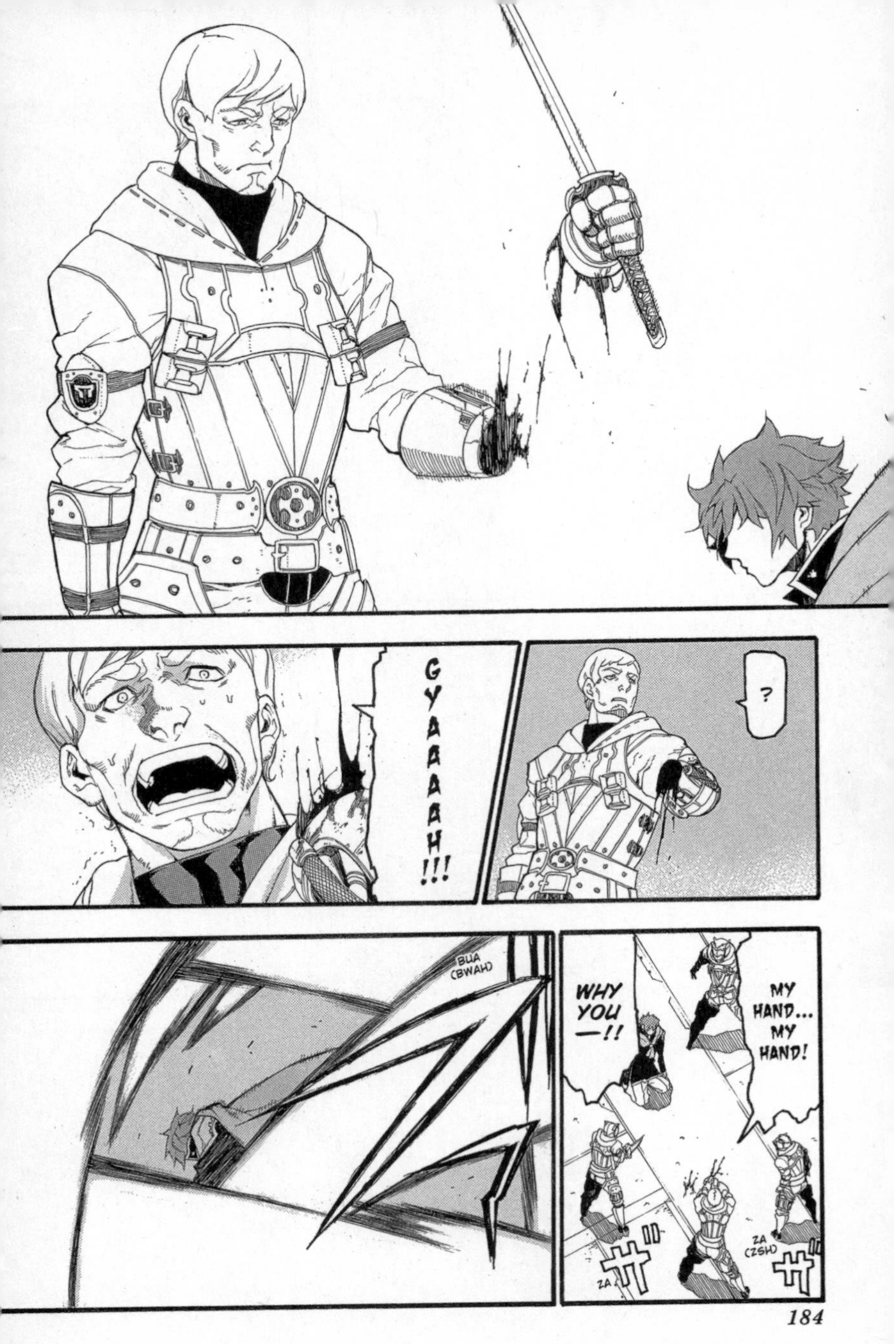
?
GYAAAAAH!!!
MY HAND... MY HAND!
WHY YOU—!!
ZA (ZSH)
ZA
BUA (BWAH)

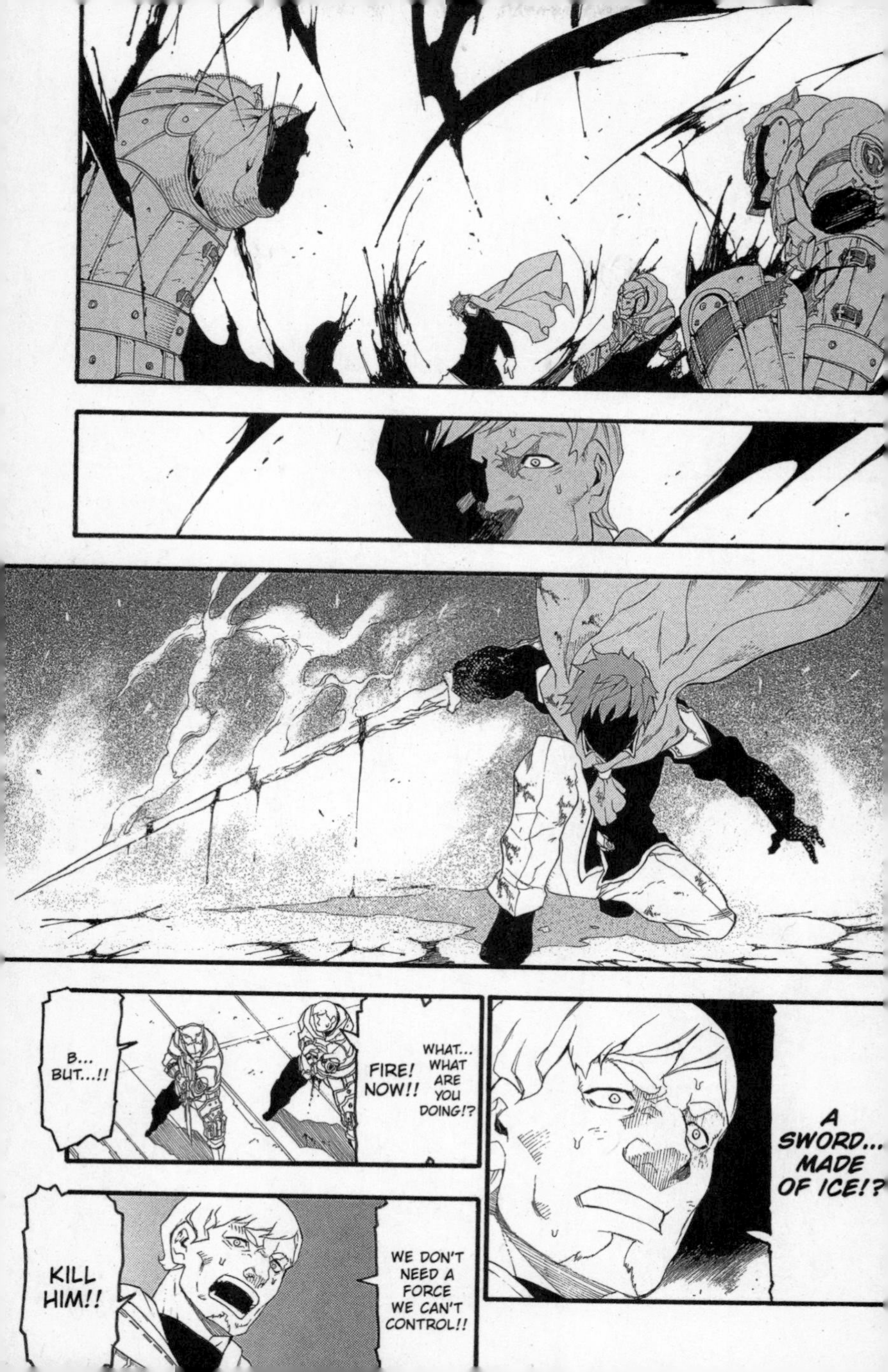
A SWORD... MADE OF ICE!?
WHAT... WHAT ARE YOU DOING!?
FIRE! NOW!!
B... BUT...!!
WE DON'T NEED A FORCE WE CAN'T CONTROL!!
KILL HIM!!

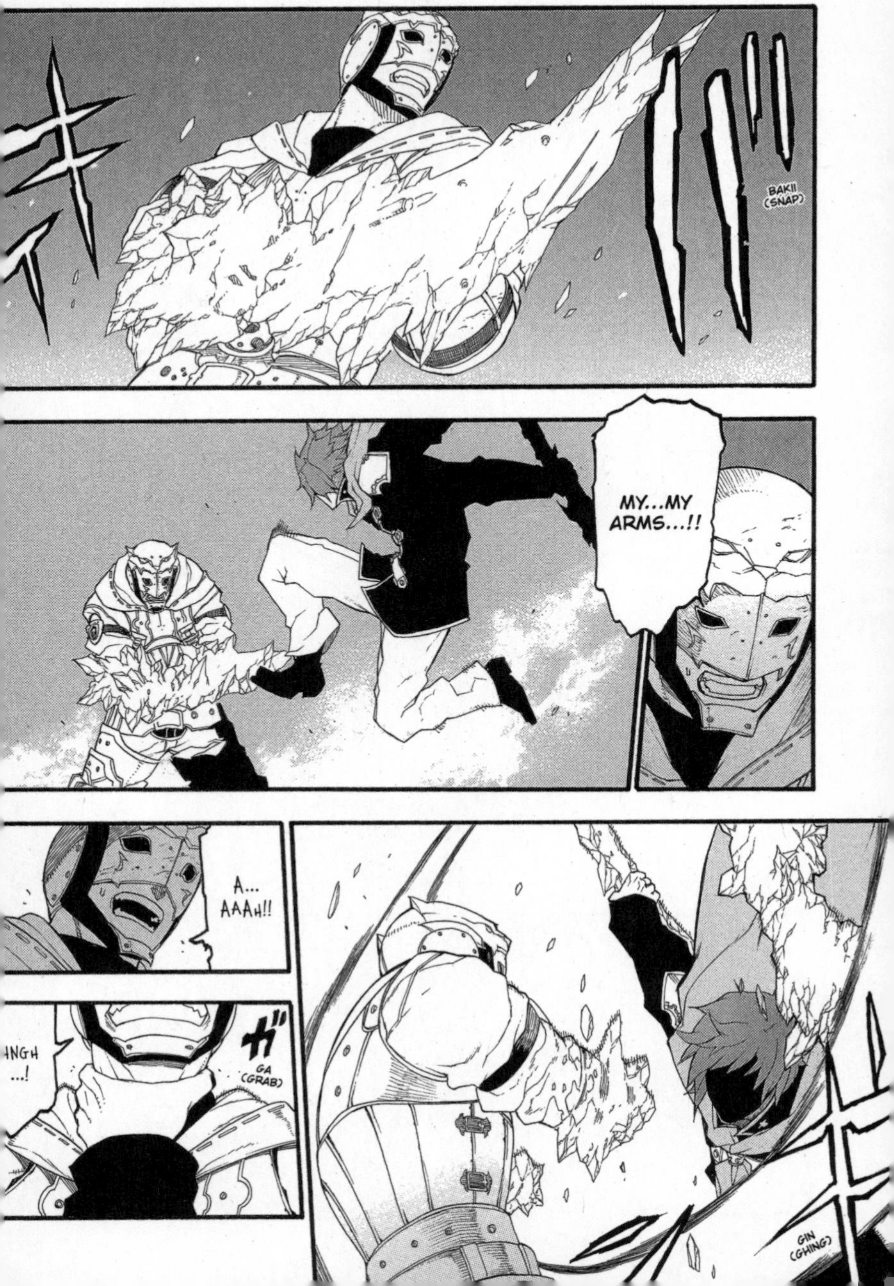
BAKII (SNAP)
MY...MY ARMS...!!
GIN (GHING)
A... AAAH!!
NGH ...!
GA (GRAB)

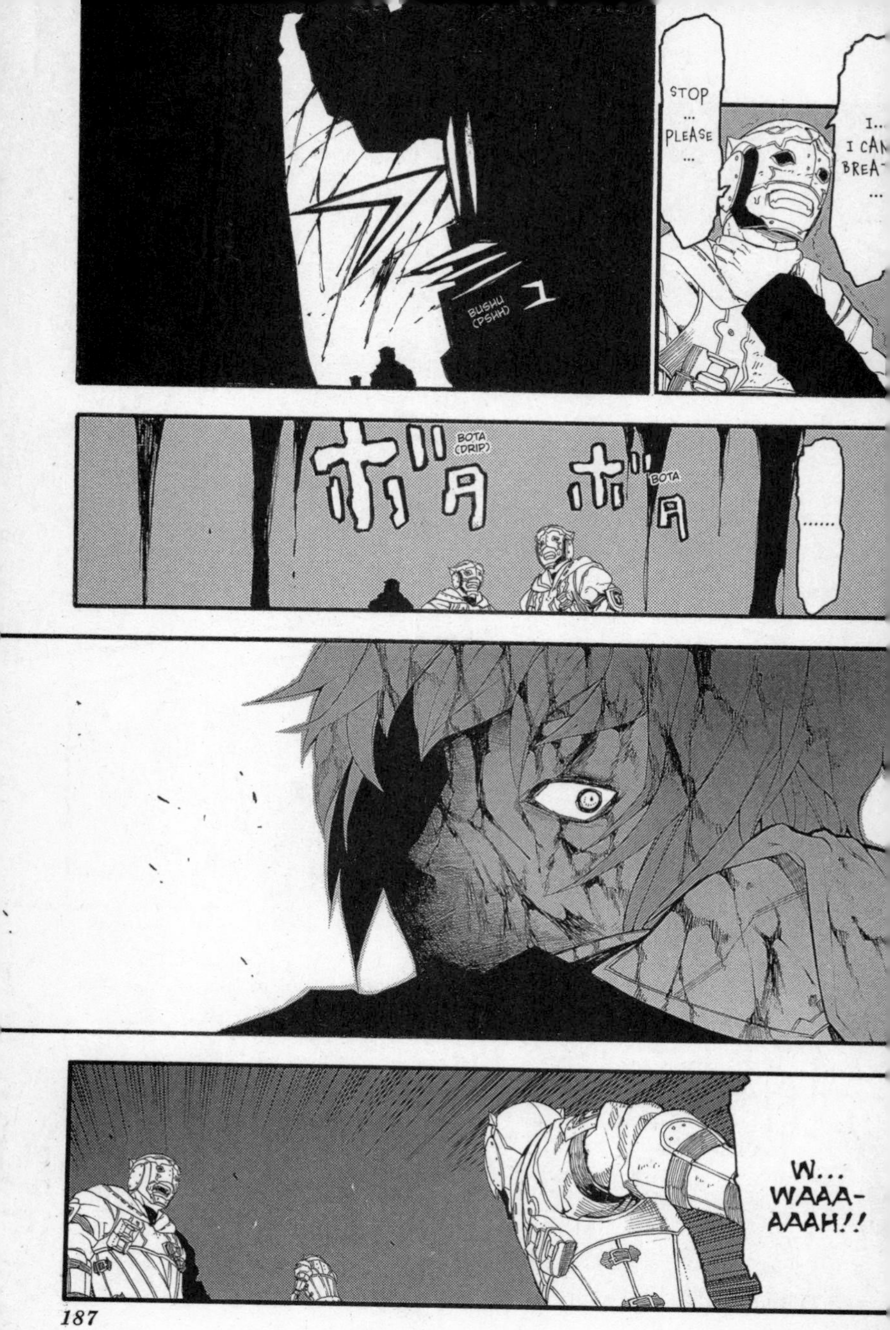
I... I CAN BREA- ...
STOP ... PLEASE ...
BUSHU (PSHH)
......
BOTA
BOTA (DRIP)
W... WAAA-AAAH!!

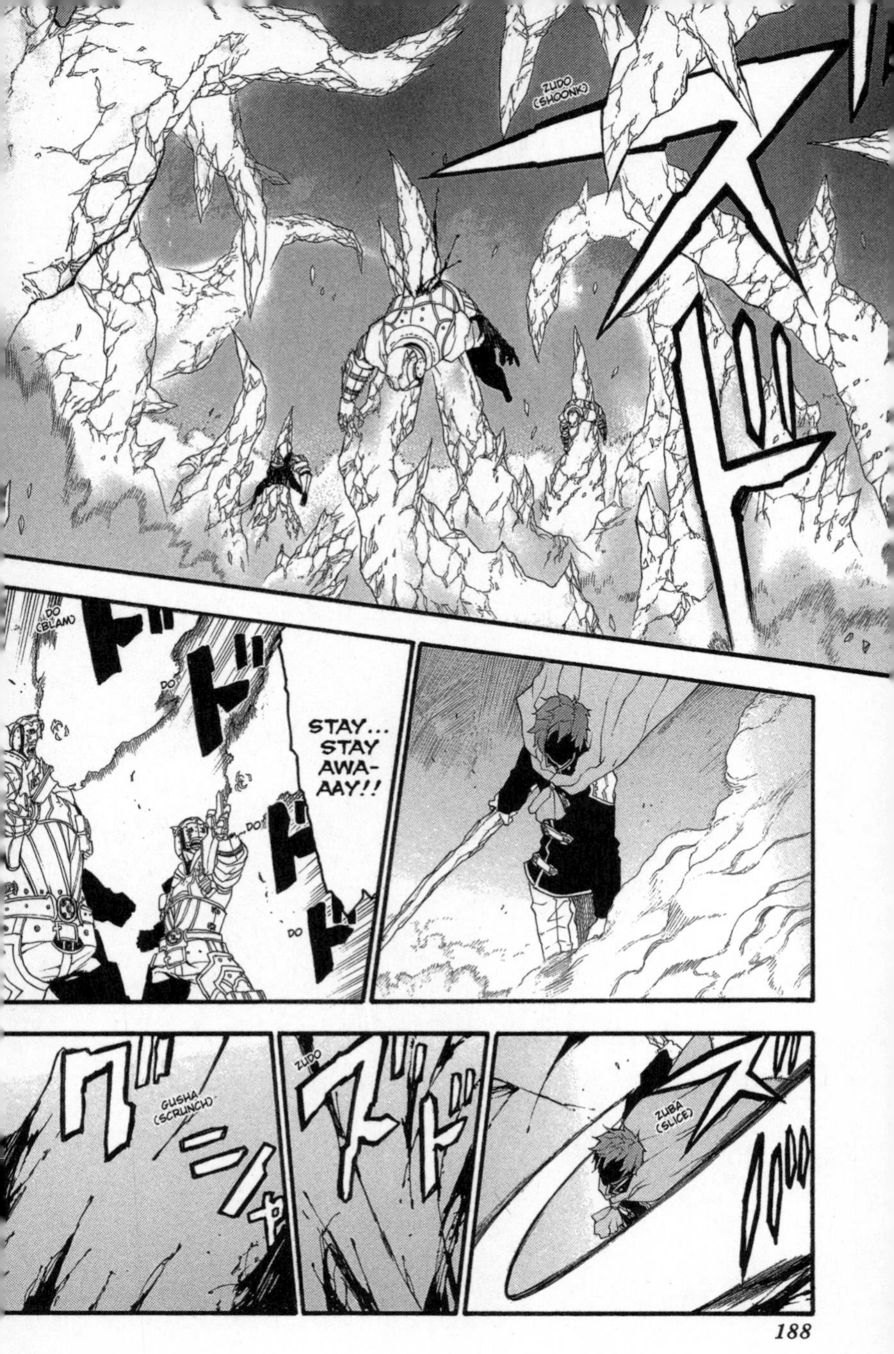
ZUDO (SHOONK)
DO (BLAM)
DO
STAY... STAY AWA-AAY!!
DO
DO
ZUBA (SLICE)
ZUDO
GUSHA (SCRUNCH)

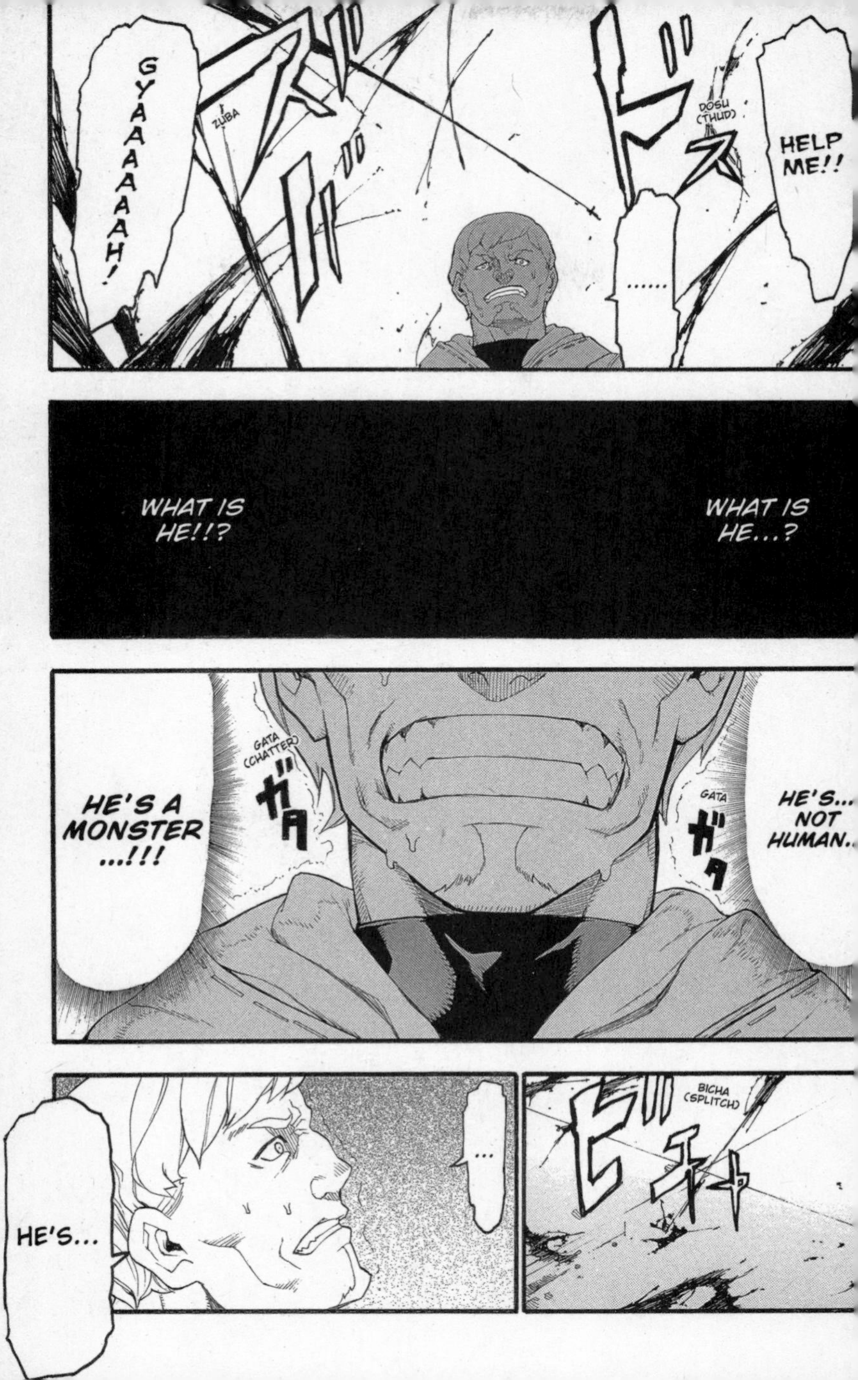
HELP ME!!
DOSU (THUD)
......
ZUBA
GYAAAAAAAH!
WHAT IS HE...?
WHAT IS HE!!?
HE'S... NOT HUMAN..
GATA
GATA (CHATTER)
HE'S A MONSTER ...!!!
BICHA (SPLITCH)
...
HE'S...

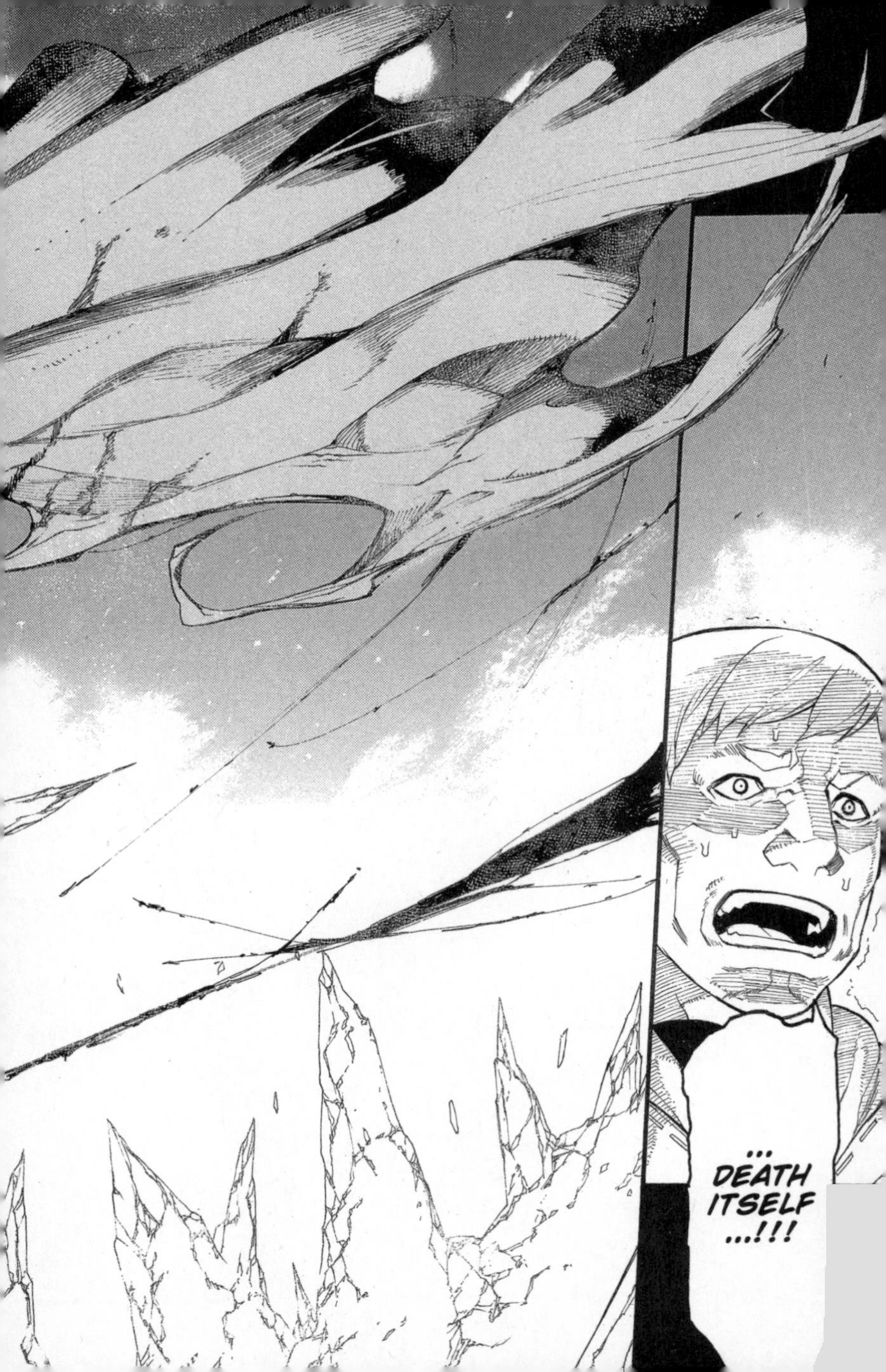
...DEATH ITSELF ...!!!

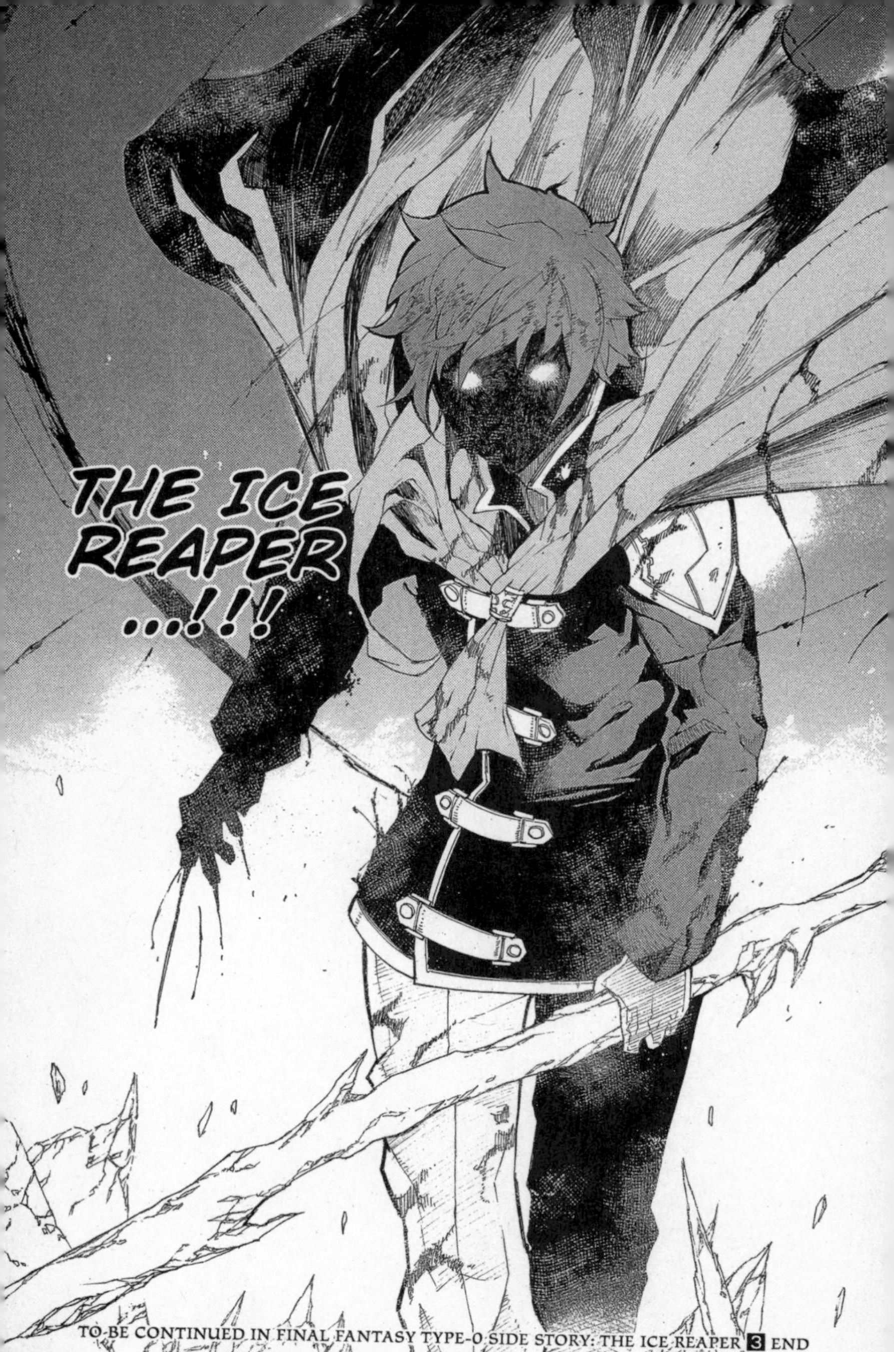
THE ICE REAPER ...!!!

TO BE CONTINUED IN FINAL FANTASY TYPE-0 SIDE STORY: THE ICE REAPER 3 END

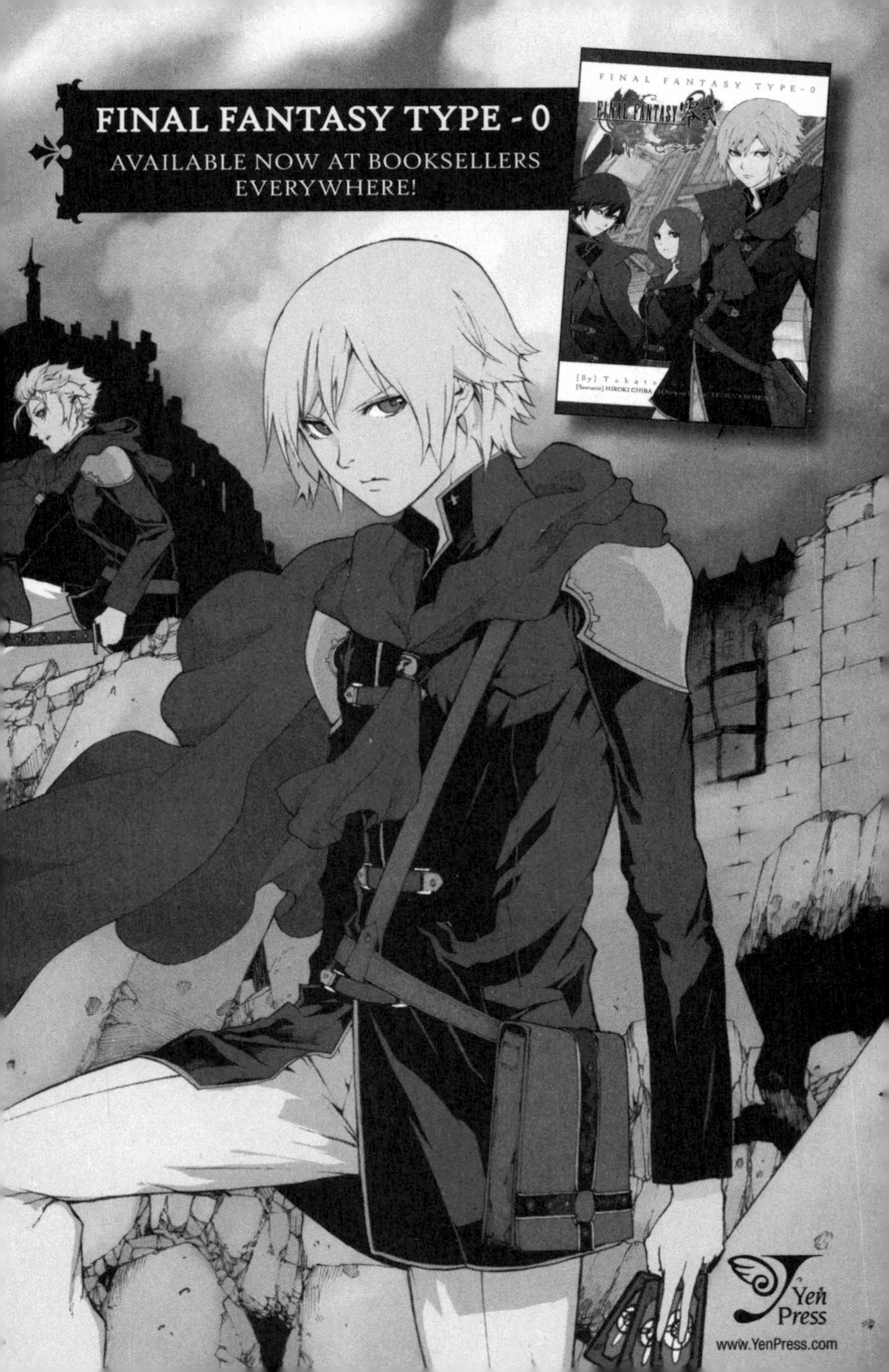
FINAL FANTASY TYPE - 0
AVAILABLE NOW AT BOOKSELLERS EVERYWHERE!
FINAL FANTASY TYPE-0
FINAL FANTASY
[Scenario] HIROKI CHIBA
Yen Press
www.YenPress.com

FINAL FANTASY 零式 TYPE-0™

Art: TAKATOSHI SHIOZAWA
Character Design: TETSUYA NOMURA
Scenario: HIROKI CHIBA

The cadets of Akademeia's Class Zero are legends, with strength and magic unrivaled, and crimson capes symbolizing the great Vermilion Bird of the Dominion. But will their elite training be enough to keep them alive when a war breaks out and the Class Zero cadets find themselves at the front and center of a bloody political battlefield?!

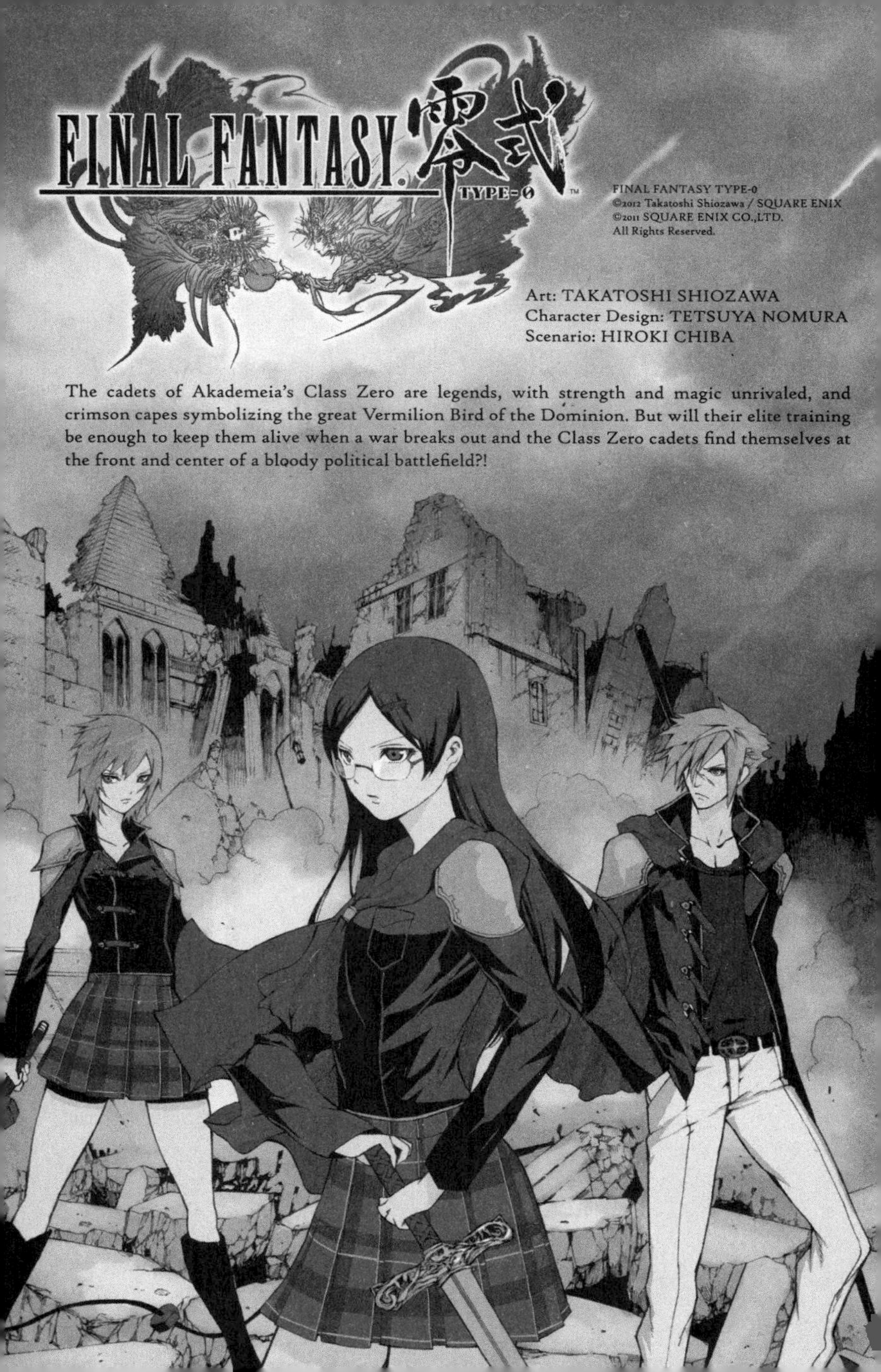

FINAL FANTASY TYPE-0
SIDE STORY:
THE ICE REAPER ❸

TAKATOSHI SHIOZAWA
CHARACTER DESIGN: TETSUYA NOMURA

Translation: Alethea and Athena Nibley

Lettering: Lys Blakeslee

FINAL FANTASY TYPE-0 GAIDEN HYOKEN NO SHINIGAMI Vol. 3
© 2013 Takatoshi Shiozawa / SQUARE ENIX CO., LTD.
© 2011 SQUARE ENIX CO., LTD. All rights reserved.
CHARACTER DESIGN: TETSUYA NOMURA
First published in Japan in 2013 by SQUARE ENIX CO., LTD. English translation rights arranged with SQUARE ENIX CO., LTD. and Hachette Book Group through Tuttle-Mori Agency, Inc., Tokyo.

Translation © 2016 by SQUARE ENIX CO., LTD.

Yen Press
Hachette Book Group
1290 Avenue of the Americas
New York, NY 10104

www.HachetteBookGroup.com
www.YenPress.com

Yen Press is an imprint of Hachette Book Group, Inc. The Yen Press name and logo are trademarks of Hachette Book Group, Inc.

The publisher is not responsible for websites (or their content) that are not owned by the publisher.

Library of Congress Control Number: 2015952580

First Yen Press Edition: January 2016

ISBN: 978-0-316-26891-2

10 9 8 7 6 5 4 3 2 1

BVG

Printed in the United States of America